Commentary on

THE CONSTITUTION OF INDIA

Commentary on

THE CONSTITUTION OF INDIA

Dr. P.K. Agrawal, IAS (Retd.)
ex-Joint Secretary, Deptt. of Justice,
Ministry of Law & Justice, Govt. of India

&

Dr. K.N. Chaturvedi
ex-Secretary, Legislative Deptt.,
Ministry of Law & Justice, Govt. of India

Published by
PRABHAT PRAKASHAN PVT. LTD.
4/19 Asaf Ali Road,
New Delhi-110 002 (INDIA)
e-mail: prabhatbooks@gmail.com

ISBN 978-93-86231-76-5
Commentary on
THE CONSTITUTION OF INDIA
by Dr. P.K. Agrawal, IAS (Retd.)
Dr. K.N. Chaturvedi

Edition
2025

Price
₹ 900.00 (Rupees Nine Hundred only)

Printed at
Shree Sai Printers, Sahibabad

INTRODUCTION

While drafting the Constitution, the founding father had long history of India in mind along with immediately preceding British colonial rule. India became slave whenever the Central powers had become weak in India and there were fissiparous tendencies. The Constitution is to be acceptable throughout the length and breadth of India with multiplicity of religions, races, languages and other diversities. Therefore, parliamentary system with some federal features was adopted. As there were no formal agreements by the States to join in a "federation of States", the Indian Union has been held as 'quasi federal'. In an ideal situation, it may be called 'co-operative federation'.

Dr. B.R. Ambedkar, Chairman of the Drafting Committee of the Constitution, justified to adopt this system because the parliamentary system makes executive more responsible to the representatives of people which is essential in a democracy. The parliamentary system has worked well during the last 66 years, as is evident from the change of Government at the Centre and in States. We must remember the words of Dr. Rajendra Prasad, the President of Constituent Assembly, who appealed that the system requires men of strong character, men of vision, men who will not sacrifice the interests of the country at large for the sake of smaller groups. This means that men behind the working of the Constitution are equally important.

The Constitution was adopted on 26th November, 1949. The Constitution was finally signed by members of the Constituent Assembly on 24 January, 1950, the last day of the Constituent Assembly. The Constitution of India came in operation on 26 January 1950, the Republic Day. The Constitution of India is one of the most voluminous constitutions of the world. The Constitution as originally adopted had 22 parts, 395 Articles and 8 schedules. Its text has been amended from time to time. During the last 66 years, there have been amendments. The number of schedules has gone up to 12 and total numbers of Articles as stand today are 448. The Constitution is the living organism of its institutions. Therefore, it is flexible. The Constitution reflects the thinking and aspirations of people of India. As the provisions have been well thought out, the bulk need not disturb the equanimity of our mind. But its basic features cannot be changed. This is born by many decisions of the Apex Court of the country and is sworn by all concerned including political executive on the Constitution Day, i.e. 26th November every year.

The Constitution is to be interpreted as it stands. Things like the spirit of the Constitution or the views of the Constitution makers expressed in the Constituent Assembly debates cannot be taken into consideration except that these debates may be treated as aids to understand the background and minds of the Constitution makers.

The Constitution of India is a great document which may be captioned as 'Guard of the Nation' as it provides Nation to face external aggression or armed rebellion, serious internal disturbances or financial debacle with all its united might through Emergency provisions by immediate action. If the country is not protected, the Constitution will also be in jeopardy. However, the Constitution has inherent mechanism against the vices of Emergency powers by few, firstly through regular voting and by making the implementation of Emergency provisions justiciable by the higher judiciary. Thus, independent judiciary created under the Constitution is there to safeguard against the misuse of the Constitution. The Constitution of India contains a chapter on Fundamental Rights, which are basic human rights of freedom, equality and livelihood and are bulwark of democracy. The Directive Principles are unique features of our Constitution. These are guidelines for governance of country and contain socio-economic rights of people. However, according to Dr. Ambedkar, political equality, i.e. one vote to one person will lose meaning unless it is followed by the economic equality. Only time will tell how the Constitution of India will shape the destiny of the people of India.

Many books have been written on the Constitution of India. This book has been prepared jointly by Dr. P.K. Agrawal and Dr. K.N. Chaturvedi. The major part of the book has been authored by Dr. P.K. Agrawal. Dr. K.N. Chaturvedi has authored chapters on the Interpretation of the Constitution, Legislature, Judiciary, Elections, Directive Principles and on the Constitution of Jammu and Kashmir and on the Sixth Schedule of the Constitution.

The book is arranged Article-wise and references have been given at the end of each chapter. As almost each Article of the Constitution has been judicially interpreted, the meaning determined by the judiciary has been explained along with the citation of the case. The bulk of the book has been kept moderate and essential information under each Article has been provided. To err is human and authors jointly own the responsibility for any error factual or otherwise.

—Dr. P.K. Agrawal
—Dr. K.N. Chaturvedi

CONTENTS

Chapter 1
PREAMBLE

WE, THE PEOPLE OF INDIA, having solemnly resolved to constitute India into a SOVEREIGN SOCIALIST SECULAR DEMOCRATIC REPUBLIC and to secure to all its citizens:

JUSTICE, social, economic and political;

LIBERTY of thought, expression, belief, faith and worship;

EQUALITY of status and of opportunity; and to promote among them all

FRATERNITY assuring the dignity of the individual and the unity and integrity of the Nation;

IN OUR CONSTITUENT ASSEMBLY this twenty-sixth day of November, 1949, do hereby adopt, enact and give to ourselves this Constitution.

COMMENTS

The Preamble declares that 'the People of India' are the source of the Constitution. The sovereignty in the Indian polity vests in the people and the Indian polity is of democratic form. It has elected head of State. It will ensure economic equality. The State will treat all religions alike and doesn't have its own religion. It doesn't seek to promote or interfere with religions. State will ensure, justice, liberty and equality of status and opportunities, harmony among the people, dignity of the individual, and unity and integrity of the country are assured.

The Preamble contains highest values and ideals for which India stands. Earlier the Preamble was not considered part of the Constitution. It was considered as key to open the Constitution.

However, in Kesavananda Bharati's [1] case, it has been held part of the Constitution and continues to be treated as an integrated part of the Constitution. It is the edifice of the Constitution and contains the grand and noble vision of the Indian polity. It is an aid to interpreting the Constitution. Following are the basic or intractable or indestructible features of the Constitution based on various judgements of the Supreme Court of India, which is the ultimate arbiter of the text or meaning of the provisions of the Constitution of India. In Kesavananda Bharati case, following features were laid down as basic structure:

1. Supremacy of the Constitution.
2. Republic and Democratic form of Government.
3. Secular character of the Constitution.
4. Separation of powers between the legislatures, the executive and the judiciary.
5. Federal character of the Constitution.

Later on, some more features were added by the Supreme Court from time to time as basic features such as-

1. Power of Review by the courts
2. Dignity of individual and Right to livelihood
3. Right to freedom of religion

However, the list may be longer but it may not be constricted. Thus, the Preamble read with other provisions of the Constitution lays down the basic norms of the Constitution of India. Sometimes, some basic features may overlap. For example, the concept of secularism is one facet of the right to equality woven as the Central golden thread in the fabric depicting the pattern of the scheme in our Constitution.[2] That is why, Constitution of a country is called 'ground norm' as all other laws, Acts or statutes, rules and regulations, etc. emanate from the constitution or should conform with it and should not be inconsistant with the Constitution. To that extent, if severable, will be void or invalid.

REFERENCES

1. Kesavananda Bharati vs. State of Kerala, (1973) 4 SCC 225.
2. Ayodya Case, AIR 1995 SC 605.

□

Chapter 2

INDIA AND ITS TERRITORIES

1. Name and territory of the Union: (1) India, that is Bharat, shall be a Union of States.

(2) The States and the Territories thereof shall be as specified in the First Schedule.

(3) The territory of India shall comprise:

(a) The Territories of the States;

(b) The Union Territories specified in the First Schedule; and

(c) Such other Territories as may be acquired.

(Part I, Article 1)

2. Admission or establishment of new States: Parliament may by law admit into the Union, or establish, new States on such terms and conditions as it thinks fit.

(Part I, Article 2)

2A. Sikkim is associated with the Union Repealed by the Constitution. (Thirty-sixth Amendment) Act, 1975, w.e.f. 26-4-1975.

(Part I, Article 2A)

3. Formation of new States and alternation of areas, boundaries or names of existing States: Parliament may by law:

(a) Form a new State by separation of territory from any State or by uniting two or more States or parts of States or by uniting any territory to a part of any State;

(b) Increase the area of any State;

(c) Diminish the area of any State;
(d) Alter the boundaries of any State;
(e) Alter the name of any State.

Provided that no Bill for the purpose shall be introduced in either House of Parliament except on the recommendation of the President and unless, where the proposal contained in the Bill effect the area, boundaries or name of any of the States the Bill has been referred by the President to the Legislature of that State for expressing its views thereon within such period as may be specified in the reference or within such further period as the President may allow and the period so specified or allowed has expired.

(Part I, Article 3)

4. Laws made under Articles 2 and 3 to provide for the amendment of the First and the Fourth Schedules and supplemental, incidental and consequential matters:

(1) Any law referred to in Article 2 or Article 3 shall contain such provisions for the amendment of the First Schedule and the Fourth Schedule as may be necessary to give effect to the provisions of the law and may also contain such supplemental, incidental and consequential provisions (including provisions as to representation in Parliament and in the Legislature or Legislatures of the State or States affected by such law) as Parliament may deem necessary.

(2) No such law as aforesaid shall be deemed to be an amendment of this Constitution for the purposes of Article 368.

(Part I, Article 4)

COMMENTS

The phrase 'India', that is Bharat, conveys the meaning that both the ancient name 'Bharat' and the modern name 'India' have been adopted. The Union represents that no State could secede from the Union nor could it suo motu vary its territory. However, Parliament has power to form new States and can also alter the boundaries or even the name of any State. While the Constitution has provided for acquisition of fresh territory, there is the provision for cession or transfer of Indian territory. One such transfer of territory was effected to Bangladesh by 100th Constitution Amendment Act.

During the last 66 years, the map of India has been redrawn due to reorganisation of States. Demands for further reorganisation of States are being raised now and then. But it is debatable whether smaller States have been successfully fulfilling the needs and aspirations of their people.

□

Chapter 3
CITIZENSHIP

5. Citizenship at the commencement of the Constitution: At the commencement of this Constitution, every person who has his domicile in the territory of India and:

(a) Who was born in the territory of India; or

(b) Either of whose parents was born in the territory of India; or

(c) Who has been ordinarily resident in the territory of India for not less than five years preceding such commencement, shall be a citizen of India.

6. Rights of citizenship of certain persons who have migrated to India from Pakistan: Notwithstanding anything in Article 5, person who has migrated to the territory of India from the territory now included in Pakistan shall be deemed to be a citizen of India at the commencement of this Constitution if:

(a) He or either of his parents or any of his grandparents was born in India as defined in the Government of India Act, 1935; and

(b) (i) in the case where such person has so migrated before the nineteenth day of July, 1948, he has been ordinary resident in the territory of India since the date of his migration, or

(ii) in the case where such person has so migrated on or after the nineteenth day of July, 1948, he has been registered as a citizen of India by an officer appointed in that behalf by the Government of the Dominion of India on an application made by him, therefore, to such officer before the commencement of this Constitution in the form and manner prescribed by that Government.

Provided that no person shall be so registered unless he has been resident in the territory of India for at least six months immediately preceding the date of his application.

7. Rights of citizenship of certain migrants to Pakistan: A person who has after the first day of March, 1947, migrated from the territory of India to the territory now included in Pakistan shall not be deemed to be a citizen of India:

Provided that nothing in this Article shall apply to a person who, after having so migrated to the territory now included in Pakistan, has returned to the territory of India under a permit for resettlement or permanent return issued by or under the authority of any law and every such person shall for the purposes of clause (b) of Article 6 be deemed to have migrated to the territory of India after the nineteenth day of July, 1948.

8. Rights of citizenship of certain persons of Indian origin residing outside India: Notwithstanding anything in Article 5, any person who or either of whose parents or any of whose grandparents was born in India as defined in the Government of India Act, 1935, and who is ordinarily residing in any country outside India as so defined shall be deemed to be a citizen of India if he has been registered as a citizen of India by the diplomatic or consular representative of India in the country where he is for the time being residing on an application made by him, therefore, to such diplomatic or consular representative, in the form and manner prescribed by the Government of India.

9. Persons voluntarily acquiring citizenship of a foreign State not to be citizens: No person shall be a citizen of India, if he has voluntarily acquired the citizenship of any foreign State.

10. Continuance of the rights of citizenship: Every person who is or is deemed to be a citizen of India under any of the foregoing provisions of this Part shall, subject to the provisions of any law that may be made by Parliament, continue to be such citizen.

11. Parliament to regulate the right of citizenship by law: Nothing in the foregoing provisions of this Part shall derogate from the power of Parliament to make any provision with respect to the acquisition and termination of citizenship and all other matters relating to citizenship.

(Part II, Articles 5-11)

COMMENTS

Citizenship is the legal relationship between the individual and the country under which the individual undertakes loyalty and to perform his duties to the country and the country offers its protection to the individual.

The Constitution avoids dual citizenship. There is one citizenship related to the domicile in the territory of whole of India and not a part of it. Domicile is an important criterion for citizenship of any country.

Domicile ordinarily connotes a person's residence where he intends to live on a permanent basis. The whole gamut of the citizenship is governed by the Citizenship Act, 1955 under the Constitution. Section 3 of the Act, 1955 provides that citizenship by birth could be acquired by a person only if either of his parents was a citizen of India at the time of birth. Besides, the Act made detailed provision for acquisition of Indian citizenship by birth, descent, registration, naturalization or through incorporation of territory. Likewise, the Act provides for termination of citizenship by way of renunciations, voluntary acquisition of citizenship of another country, or through compulsory deprivation by the Government of India on certain grounds.

The Act has been amended from time to time. Provision has been made for maintenance of a national register of the Indian citizens and for 'overseas citizenship of India'. A person of Indian origin, subject to certain conditions, may be registered as an overseas citizen of India (OCI) and extended some of the citizenship rights, like owning property, travelling to India without visa, making investment in business, etc.

This provision has been added to strengthen emotional ties with non-resident Indians living abroad, who are more than 30 million and remit or invest lot of foreign currency in India. The provision of double citizenship to overseas citizens of India has been extended so far only to Australia, France, Greece, Ireland, Israel, Italy, Netherlands, Canada, New Zealand, Portugal, Cyprus, Sweden, Switzerland, United Kingdom and United States of America. However, special protections for citizenship in Jammu and Kashmir and notified tribal areas are prescribed. □

Chapter 4
FUNDAMENTAL RIGHTS

Fundamental rights proclaim the fundamental values and constitute the fundamental principles of the Constitution. These are cornerstone of the democratic way of life. These are basic human rights and impose negative obligations on the State or its instrumentality not to encroach the individual liberty in its various dimensions.

The object is to provide protection for the freedoms and rights against arbitrary invasion by the State.

The Fundamental Rights are classified under six groups:

1. Right to equality
2. Right to freedom of speech, etc.
3. Right against exploitation
4. Rights to freedom of religion
5. Cultural and educational rights
6. Right to constitutional remedies

12. Definition of State: In this Part, unless the context otherwise requires, "the State" includes the Government and Parliament of India and the Government and the Legislature of each of the States and all local or other authorities within the territory of India or under the control of the Government of India.

(Part III, Article 12)

COMMENTS

Local authorities include Panchayats, Improvement Trust, etc. The definition is inclusive and includes other authority. The tests to determine 'other authority' as 'State' are substantial, financial and control by Government, performance of public functions and entrustment of governmental activities. All these are not essential and, in particular case, one or a combination of more than one of them may suffice.[1]

Nationalized banks like State Banks of India, Children Aid Society, Delhi Transport Corporation were held State.

However, Board of Control for Cricket in India (BCCI) is not financially, functionally or administratively dominated by Government nor it is under the control of Government. Therefore, it not a State.[2]

Mere dealing in a subject by the State, or the monopoly of the State in a particular field would not render an enterprise sovereign in nature and hence not a State.

13. Laws inconsistent with the fundamental rights: (1) All laws in force in the territory of India immediately before the commencement of this Constitution, insofar as they are inconsistent with the provisions of this Part, shall, to the extent of such inconsistency, be void.

(2) The State shall not make any law which takes away or abridges the rights conferred by this Part and any law made in contravention of this clause shall, to the extent of the contravention, be void.

(3) In this Article, unless the context otherwise requires:

(a) "law" includes any Ordinance, order, bye-law, rule, regulation, notification, custom or usage having in the territory of India the force of law;

(b) "laws in force" include laws passed or made by a Legislature or other competent authority in the territory of India before the commencement of this Constitution and not previously repealed, notwithstanding that any such law or any part thereof may not be then in operation either at all or in particular areas.

(4) Nothing in this Article shall apply to any amendment of this Constitution made under Article 368.

(Part III, Article 13)

COMMENTS

The existing laws which violate fundamental rights

conferred by Part III of the Constitution shall, to that extent, be void. "There has to be clear Constitutional violation and not merely because of its falling into disuse or because the perception of society has changed regarding legitimacy of purpose and need of the law in question"[3]

The 'doctrine of basic features' of the Constitution doesn't apply to ordinary legislation. It imposes limitation on power of Parliament to annul the Constitution.

Right to Equality

14. Equality before law: The State shall not deny to any person equality before the law or the equal protection of the laws within the territory of India.

(Part III, Article 14)

COMMENTS

The principle of equality is the essence of democracy, Equality before law implies the absence of any discrimination without rational basis.

Equal protection of laws would mean "that among equals, the law should be equal and equally administrated and that likes should be treated alike...."

It means the right to equal treatment in similar circumstances both in privileges conferred and in the liabilities imposed by the laws. It does not prohibit classification but it should not be arbitrary.

It should be reasonable and be based on qualities and characteristics that have relation to the object of legislation. The reasonable classification must be found on an intelligible differentia which distinguishes persons or things that are grouped together from those that are left out of the group. Even a law can be made for one single person. The reasonableness of a provision depends upon the circumstances obtaining at a particular time and the urgency of the evil sought to be controlled.

The guarantee of equal protection includes absences of any arbitrary discrimination by the laws themselves or in the matter of their administration. The decision-making process should be transparent, fair and open and non-arbitrary. "The principles of natural justice are to check the arbitrary exercise of power by the State or its functionaries"[4] Thus, inaction actions are also subjects to scrutiny by courts.

Thus, test to analyse permissible classification to be valid, must fulfil two conditions:

The classification must be founded on an intelligible differentia, and

The differentia must have a rational relation to the object sought to be achieved by the statute in question:

The classification based on geographical or special circumstances will be valid. If a classification is conducive to the functioning of modern society, it would be certainly reasonable and rational and not violation of Article 14. 'The creamy layer in Backward class is to be treated 'on par' with the forward classes and is not entitled to benefits of reservation."[5]

There has to be equal pay for equal work. Land ceiling is not violation of Article 14 but land allotment by Government on consideration of caste, community or religion, favouritism or nepotism or on political consideration to nurture the vote bank is impermissible. Natural resources constitute public property/national asset and while distributing them, the State is bound to act in consonance with the principles of equality and public trust, and ensure that no action is taken which may be detrimental to public interest. Thus, the grant of licenses for spectrum was held prima facie arbitrary, illegal and violative of Article 14 of the Constitution.[6]

"Similarly, method of allotment of Coal Blocks by the Government since 1993 to 2011 was held invalid as the allotments were made without application of mind, without assessment of comparative merit and without following guidelines."[7]

The Right to Equality embodies Rule of Law and is a basic feature of the Constitution.[8]

15. Prohibition of discrimination on grounds of religion, race, caste, sex or place of birth: (1) The State shall not discriminate against any citizen on grounds only of religion, race, caste, sex, place or birth or any of them.

(2) No citizen shall, on grounds only of religion, race, caste, sex, place of birth or any of them, be subject to any disability, liability, restriction or condition with regard to—

(a) access to shops, public restaurants, hotels and places of public entertainment; or

(b) the use of wells, tanks, bathing ghats, roads and places of public resort maintained wholly or partly out of State funds or dedicated to the use of the general public.

(3) Nothing in this Article shall prevent the State from making any special provision for women and children.

(4) Nothing in this Article or in clause (2) of Article 29 shall prevent the State from making any special provision for the advancement of any socially and educationally backward classes of citizens or for the Scheduled Castes and the Scheduled Tribes.

(5) Nothing in this Article or in sub-clause (g) of clause (1) of Article 19 shall prevent the State from making any special provision, by law, for the advancement of any socially and educationally backward classes of citizens or for the Scheduled Castes or the Scheduled Tribes insofar as such special provisions relate to their admission to educational institutions including private educational institutions, whether aided or unaided by the State, other than the minority educational institutions referred to in clause (1) of Article 30.

(Part III, Article 15)

COMMENTS

Clause (4) of Article 15 may appear to be a blanket provision, protecting any kind of beneficial discrimination for the benefit of the backward classes, the Scheduled castes and the Scheduled Tribes. But reservation of an excessively high percentage of seats in technical institutions for each classes would be void. Ordinarily, reservation in excess of 50 percent of available seats may not be upheld. This is justified because risk cannot be taken in highly technical fields like medical, space.

If reservation cannot be so excessive that the institution itself may lose relevance or place in the modern-day world of competition. More meritorious and competent institution from other countries will occupy the vacuum created by them specially in this age of globalisation and information technology.

The Article permits the State to make special provision for the following:

Socially and educationally backward classes of citizens.

Scheduled castes, and

Scheduled tribes

"Children born to intercaste marriage of which either father or mother belongs to SC-ST category can claim reservation benefits only on proof that he is subjected to some handicap and disadvantages having been born as member of SC-ST.[9]

'Reservation on the basis of domicile is not impermissible in terms of clause (i) of Article 15.'[10]

A person by reason of marriage alone cannot ipso facto become a member of scheduled caste or scheduled tribe.

Similarly, university-wise preference is valid if it is reasonable. Domicile-wise preference is valid, if it does not exceed reasonable limits. College-wise preference is bad.

Reservation of 50% of posts in favour of female candidates, not arbitrary."[11] In particular, provisions in the criminal law, in favour of women, or in the procedural law discriminatory in favour of women have been upheld.

Sexual harassment of working women amounts to violation of the rights guaranteed by Articles 14, 15 and 23 (equality and dignity). The Supreme Court issued detailed directions on the subject which are being followed in public as well as in private sectors.[12]

16. Equality of opportunity in matters of public employment: (1) There shall be equality of opportunity for all citizens in matters relating to employment or appointment to any office under the State.

(2) No citizen shall, on grounds only of religion, race, caste, sex, descent, place of birth, residence or any of them, be ineligible for, or discriminated against in respect of, any employment or office under the State.

(3) Nothing in this Article shall prevent Parliament from making any law prescribing, in regard to a class or classes of

employment or appointment to an office under the Government of, or any local or other authority within, a State or Union territory, any requirement as to residence within that State or Union territory prior to such employment or appointment.

(4) Nothing in this Article shall prevent the State from making any provision for the reservation of appointments or posts in favour of any backward class of citizens which, in the opinion of the Sate, is not adequately represented in the services under the State.

(4A) Nothing in this Article shall prevent the State from making any provision for reservation in matters of promotion of any class or classes of posts in the services under the State in favour of Scheduled Tribes which, in the opinion of State, are not adequately represented in the services under the State.

(5) Nothing in this Article shall affect the operation of any law which provides that the incumbent of an office in connection with the affairs of any religious or denominational institution or any member of the governing body thereof shall be a person professing a particular religion or belonging to a particular denomination.

(Part III, Article 16)

COMMENTS

The words 'employment or appointments' are wide enough to include tenure, duration, emoluments and duties and obligations, whether employment is temporary or permanent. These cover not merely the initial appointment, but also salary, increments, revision of pay, promotion, gratuity, leave, pension and age of superannuation.

"Appointment/recruitment of temporary, contractual, casual, daily-wage or adhoc employment dehors the Constitutional scheme cannot be regulated. Such opportunities cannot claim to be made permanent[13] and are not covered under Article 16.

The policy of the State regarding reservation should be consistent with the maintenance of efficiency of administration.[14]

The Mandal Commission had in its report recommended 27 percent reservation for backward classes in view of the limit of 50 percent imposed by the Supreme Court.

In its judgement in the Mandal case[15], the Supreme Court held that 27 per cent reservation for the socially and educationally backward classes was in order.

The Court laid down:

(i) In the Indian context, lower castes are treated as backwards. A caste may by itself constitute a class.

(ii) The backwardness contemplated by Artcile. 16(4) is mainly social. It need not be both social and educational.

(iii) Income or the extent of property can be taken as a measure of social advancement and on that basis, the 'creamy layer' of a given caste can be excluded.[16]

(iv) For getting reservation, class must be backward and should not be adequately represented in the services under the State.

(v) The reservation contemplated in Artcile. 16(4) should not exceed 50%.

(vi) The rule of 50% should be applied to each year. It cannot be related to the total strength of the class, service or cadre, etc.

(vii) Reservation of posts cannot extend in the matter of promotion.

(viii) Identification of backward classes is subject to judicial review.

The State has been empowered by 81st Constitutional Amendment that they can fill up unfilled vacancies as separate class to be filled up in any succeeding years keeping the overall administrative efficiency intact as required by Article 335.[16]

It may not be advisable to provide for reservations in certain areas, e.g. in technical posts, research and development organisations in specialty and superspecialty, in medicine, engineering and in higher posts like those of professors in education, pilots in airlines, scientists and technicians in nuclear and space applications, etc.

However, on the behest of Tamil Nadu Government, Parliament passed 76th Amendment to allow reservation upto 69 percent. This approach requires reconsideration. If the country cannot exist, no caste or community within it will be able to exist. Therefore, overall interest of the country should be kept in mind while considering the whole gamut of reservation in public services.

The words 'employment or appointment' are wide enough to include tenure, duration, emoluments, duties and obligations, whether the employment is temporary or permanent, or salary, increments, promotion, etc.

However, Government cannot totally dispense with minimum qualifying marks for post-graduate medial courses for scheduled castes, etc. However, relaxation in shape of lower standards of eligibility is permissible for scheduled caste candidates, etc.

Reservation to single post cadre is void as it creates 100 per cent reservation. When a company is sustaining continuous losses, and does not have the financial capacity to revise or enhance the pay scale, the petitioners cannot claim any legal right.

To deny a public employment solely on the basis of the police report regarding political affinity offends the fundamental rights. Similarly, requirement of being employed through proper channel could not be relaxed in an arbitrary and cavalier manner for the benefit of a few persons.[17].

Thus, the reservation in employment, though not discriminatory, cannot be unlimited or uncontrolled so as to deny efficiency to the state instrumentality.

17. Abolition of untouchability: "Untouchability" is abolished and its practice in any form is forbidden. The enforcement of any disability arising out of "Untouchability" shall be an offence punishable in accordance with law.

(Part III, Article 17)

COMMENTS

Parliament had enacted the Untouchability (Offences) Act, 1955, which has been amended and renamed (1976) as the Protection of Civil Rights Act, 1955 to declare and punish pernicious social practice of Untouchability in all its aspects.

The Supreme Court has held that the fundamental right against untouchability guaranteed in this Article is available against private individuals.[18]

The act 1955 provides punishment for the following offences relating to untouchability-

(a) Refusing admission to any person to public institutions, such as hospital, dispensary, educational institution;

(b) Preventing any person from worshipping or offering prayers in any place of public worship;

(c) Subjecting any person to any disability with regard to access to any shop, public restaurant, hotel or public entertainment or with regard to the use of any reservoir, tap or other sources of water, road, cremation grounds or any other place where services are rendered to the public;

(d) Insulting a member of a Scheduled caste on the ground of untouchability;

(e) Preaching untouchability;

(f) Justifying untouchability.

Further, the Scheduled Caste and the Scheduled Tribes (Prevention of Atrocities) Act, 1989 was promulgated in 1989 by Parliament. The Act prevents injustice against the Scheduled Castes and Scheduled Tribes even by the revenue and police officer under Section 3 of the Act to neglect his duties towards these poor classes of cultivators, pattadars against wrongful occupation of their land by others or against wrongful dispossession from their lands, even filing false malicious or vexatious suits or criminal or other legal proceedings against a member of a Scheduled castes or a Scheduled Tribe. An officer who wilfully neglect, his duties is punishable at least with six months imprisonment. This is a positive Act which has gone miles ahead of the Civil Rights Act, 1955.

18. Abolition of titles: (1) No title, not being a military or academic distinction, shall be conferred by the State.

(2) No citizen of India shall accept any title from any foreign State.

(3) No person who is not a citizen of India shall, while he holds any office of profit or trust under the State, accept without the consent of the President any title from any foreign State.

(4) No person holding any office of profit or trust under the State shall, without the consent of the President, accept any present, emolument, or office of any kind from or under any foreign State.

(Part III, Article 18)

COMMENTS

The Supreme Court held that Bharat Ratna, Padma Vibhushan, Padma Bhushan and Padma Shri are not titles of nobility and are not violative of Article 18 of the Constitution provided they are not used as titles or prefixes or suffixes to the name of awardee.

However, abolition of titles is also a step towards equality because erstwhile Rajas, Maharajas were branded somewhat superior to the common man.

Right to Freedom

19. Protection of certain rights regarding freedom of speech, etc.: (1) All citizens shall have the right.

(a) to freedom of speech and expression;
(b) to assemble peaceably and without arms;
(c) to form associations or unions;
(d) to move freely throughout the territory of India;
(e) to reside and settle in any part of the territory of India; and
(g) to practice any profession, or to carry on any occupation, trade or business.

(2) Exceptions to subclause (a) of clause (1) are reasonable restrictions on the exercise of the right conferred by the said sub-clause in the interests of the sovereignty and integrity of India, security of the State, friendly relation with foreign States, the public order, decency or morality or in relation to contempt of court, defamation or incitement to an offence.

(3) Exceptions to subclause (b) of the said clause are any law imposing, in the interests of the sovereignty and integrity

of India or public order, reasonable restrictions on the exercise of the right conferred by the said sub-clause.

(4) Exceptions to subclause (c) are in respect of any law imposing, in the interests of the sovereignty and integrity of India or public order or morality, reasonable restrictions on the exercise of the right conferred by the said sub-clause.

(5) Exceptions to subclause (d) and (e) are any law imposing reasonable restrictions on the exercise of any of the rights conferred by the said sub-clauses either in the interests of the rights conferred by the said sub-clauses either in the interests of the general public or for the protection of the interests of any Scheduled Tribe.

(6) Exception is any law imposing, in the interests of the general public, reasonable restrictions on the exercise of the right conferred by the said sub-clause, and, in particular, nothing in the said sub-clause shall affect the operation of any existing law insofar as it relates to, or prevent the State from making any law relating to:

- (i) the professional or technical qualification necessary for practising any profession or carrying on any occupation, trade or business, or
- (ii) the carrying on by the State, of any trade, business, industry or service, whether to the exclusion, complete or partial, of citizens or otherwise.

(Part III, Article 19)

Right to freedom is one of the basic insignia of democracy.

The right to the protection of the six freedoms against State action is available to all citizens. Article 19 does not confer an absolute or unlimited right. Social interest is absolute or unlimited. Individual liberty may well have to be subordinated to other greater social interest. Corporation is not a citizen. Therefore, this freedom is not available to it but is available to the shareholders as citizens.

COMMENTS

(a) Freedom of speech and expression: The freedom of expression includes freedom of press in India. The freedom of press is the bulwark of the democracy. Freedom of press and speech lay at the foundation of all democratic organisations, for without free political discussion, no public education, or discussion or dialogue, so essential for the proper functioning of the process of popular government, is possible. Elections and change of governments through general franchise are two pillars of democracy which are based on public opinion. Freedom of speech and expression and freedom of press are two major means to form or change public opinion. In the modern world of information technology, social media like facebook, whatsapp are also playing important role in the field of freedom of expression. However, sometimes, the unfiltered and uninhibited news or opinions form wrong public opinion which are harmful for the society or country in general. On the other hand, newspapers and electronic media like television have a system of self-control and regulation through one of their appointe as regulator apart from what regulations are in place by the government. The freedom of press cannot be unlimited. It is a fact that the freedom of press is not so free as it has to subserve the interest of its owner who are more propelled by commercial or financial interest than the interest of the freedom of press or the interest of the country. It is well known that many media houses have definite line of ideology and they twist news or presentations accordingly and thus they exploit the nascent mind of public. To increase popularity or TRP, many media, i.e. newspapers and television channels publish some breaking news without properly verifying their veracity or their impact on society. Truth is sacrosanct but its presentation should also result into truth unlike Yudhister who announced a truth obliquely during the Mahabharata war but, in fact, it amounted to an untruth. The media presents the truth in their own ways but it should not harm the society or individual. One wonders whether few newspapers or television channels are controlled by some invisible masters.

"If a newspaper publishes what is important, mischievously false or illegal and abuses its liberty, it must be punished by Court of Law. Some restrictions are, therefore, essential even for preservation of the freedom of the press itself."[18] It is a common knowledge that all press is not above suspicion. Sometimes, local press tries to blackmail some government officers or officials or individuals with a view to extract some favours or financial enrichment.

Thus, the people who advocate for freedom of press should ensure that press should be purveyor of truth and exposition of illegal activities. It has also to follow all commercial laws to regulate its commercial activities like purchase of newsprint papers, etc. and ensure freedom of speech and expression to its anchors, reporters or correspondents.

As far as individual right to freedom of speech and expression is concerned, it is held that "right to speech implies the right to silence. It implies freedom, not to listen, and not to be forced to listen." [19] "Right to information is an integral part of freedom of expression, particularly a voter's right to know the antecedents-assets of a candidate contesting election"[20]

'Telephone tapping unless it comes within grounds of restrictions under Article 19 (2) would infringe Article 19(1) (a) of the Constitution.

Article 19(1)(a) includes the right to know or to seek information. The Right to Information Act, 2005 specifically confers on all citizens the right to access information and makes it obligatory for all public authorities to disclose official information only subject to certain essential restrictions. The Act has promoted openness, transparency and accountability in administration. However, some of the officers especially in States dominated by feudal bureaucracy still create hurdles to pass on the information to the petitioners. On the other hand, some of the petitioners ask vague and lengthy information which may not serve any public purpose. Many RTI activists have been killed. It shows that the Act needs review for its better implementation. Courts have generally supported this right as a precious right to the citizen. Even the Supreme Court has gone out of way and allowed to fly the National Flag on private or commercial buildings under Article 19(1)(a) subject to certain restrictions in Union of India vs. Naveen Jindal & Anr. Appeal (Civil) 2920 of 1996 decided on 23/1/2004). It was held that ordinary or local breaches of public order were no grounds for imposing restrictions on freedom of speech and expression. Blatant restriction of entry of some publication in a State without right of representation is not valid. Pre-censorship generally violates the freedom of press but it may be valid with reasonable safeguards both from substantive and procedural standpoints. However, during Emergency, on the ground of internal disturbances valid and pre-censorship may be imposed.

As regards contempt of court as exception, Justice Iyer asserted in Mulgaonkar (AIR 1978 SC (72) matter that the keynote was to be 'justice' and not 'judge' and that activist efforts at judicial reforms should not be stalled under contempt action. Secondly, truth is also a defense against contempt charges. In a far-reaching judgement, the court held that 'Bandhs' do not fall within the fundamental right of speech. A 'Bandh' is a warning to a citizen that if he goes for work or opens his shop, he would be prevented. Even if Legislature does not prohibit them, courts should intervene to protect the right to work or right to study.[21]

(b) Freedom to Assemble: Meetings, processions and demonstrations are corrollaries of a democratic system. The people can be informed, educated or persuaded only through such exercises. The two inherent restrictions for any assembly under Article 19(1)(b) are of remaining peaceful and to be unarmed. However, if an assembly is declared unlawful, it can be validly banned and the members of the assembly can be ordered to be dispersed.

(c) Freedom of Association: The associations so formed would include political parties, societies, clubs, companies, organisations, partnership firms, trade unions and anybody of persons. There is full liberty to form associations for lawful purpose subject to reasonable restriction. The Supreme Court has held that even a liberal interpretation of Article 19(1)(c) cannot mean that the trade unions have a guaranteed right to strike. The right to strike can be controlled by appropriate industrial legislation.[22] This may not be accepted by the Marxists in India but this is the position. Similarly, the government cannot regulate the eligibility criteria for contesting the elections of the student unions.

However, an unincorporated association cannot claim these rights.

(d) Freedom of Movement and Residence: The Indian citizen has right to reside and settle in any part of India. However, such restrictions to purchase land and settle in tribal hilly areas have been held valid prostitutes under Article 19(5). Restrictions imposed to carry on the trade by prostitutes within specified area and to reside in or move for particular areas have been held to be valid. Similarly, a person suffering from AIDS can be restricted in his movements by law.

(e) Freedom of Profession and Trade: The State can carry on a business either as a monopoly, complete or partial, to the exclusion of all or some citizens only, or in competition with any citizen. But socialism cannot go to the extent of ignoring interests of shareholders or creditors of private sector which is a larger segment of the Indian economy.

There could be no fundamental right to carry on trade or business in noxious, hazardous or dangerous goods like intoxicating drugs or liquors, adulterated foods, etc. or to indulge in trafficking in women or children. Granting of licenses and permits for carrying trade should be based on relevant considerations. License once granted can be cancelled after giving the licensee an opportunity of hearing. Similarly, there can be conditions imposed in a tender by the government but the procedure cannot be arbitrary or biased. It has to be fair and reasonable. "Education can be an occupation under Article 19(1)(g) of the Constitution only when it is charitable in nature."[23]

Price fixation, being a legislative act, prior consultation is not required.

20. Protection in respect of conviction for offences: (1) No person shall be convicted of any offence except for violation of a law in force at the time of the commission of the Act charged as an offence, nor be subjected to a penalty greater than that which might have been inflicted under the law in force at the time of the commission of the offence.

(2) No person shall be prosecuted and punished for the same offence more than once.

(3) No person accused of any offence shall be compelled to be a witness against himself.

(Part III, Article 20)

COMMENTS

Article 20 guarantees protection in certain respects against conviction for offences, by prohibiting:

1. Retrospective criminal legislation, commonly known as ex-post-facto legislation.
2. Double jeopardy or punishment for the same offence more than once.
3. Compulsion to give self-incriminating evidence.

Retrospective laws are not good from jurisprudence point of view. Thus, this is a revolutionary Constitutional provision provided in the Constitution of India. Accordingly, substantive law imposing liability or penalty cannot be altered to the prejudice of the person supposed to be guilty with retrospective effect. There is no such vested right in procedure. However, the same provision is not applicable to civil and specially tax statutes.

Double Jeopardy: If a person has been prosecuted and punished in a previous proceeding of an offence, he cannot be prosecuted and punished for the same offence again in a subsequent proceeding. Where an appellant already convicted under Section 138 of the Negotiable Instruments Act, he cannot be punished again on the same facts under Section 420 or any other provision of the Indian Penal Code. However, a subsequent trial and punishment are not barred if the ingredients of two offences are distinct.

The rule of double jeopardy would not apply where the accused was punished under Section 364 of the Penal Code and wife of the deceased asked for compensation.[24]

The offences for which accused was tried and convicted in foreign country and for which he is tried in India are distinct and separate.[25]

The departmental or disciplinary proceedings, even if punitive in amplitude, would not be outlawed by Article 20(2) of the Constitution.[26]

Protection against Self-incrimination: The accused person is protected against incriminating himself under compulsion, e.g. "making a Statement which makes the case against the accused person at least probable considered by itself."

Compulsion in this context would mean duress. Relevant replies which furnish a real and clear link in the chain of evidence indeed to bind down the accused with the crime become incriminatory and offend Article 20(3) if elicited by pressure from the mouth of the accused."[27]

It amounts to right of silence of the accused person. It widened the scope of compulsion and held that 'compelled testimony' is evidently procured not merely by physical threats or violence but also by psychic torture, atmospheric pressure, environmental coercion, tiring interrogative proximity, overbearing and intimidating methods and the like. The court also laid down some guidelines, for the police authorities for due observance, e.g. the accused must be informed of the grounds of arrest against him and he has a right to call a lawyer before answering to any of their questions. The arrestee subjected to inhuman treatment during police custody should be paid compensation by the State.[28]

The immunity granted to the accused does not extend to compulsory production of material objects or compulsion to give specimen writing, specimen signature, finger impression or compulsory exhibition of the body or giving of blood specimens or voice samples. However, compulsion for production of documents is prohibited only if the documents convey the personal knowledge of the accused relating to the charge. Similarly, macro analysis technique amounts to "testimonial compulsion" and is hit by Artcile 20(3) of the Constitution.

21. Protection of life and personal liberty: No person shall be deprived of his life or personal liberty except according to procedure established by law.

(Part III, Article 21)

COMMENTS

This right is available to the citizens as well as non-citizens. In the famous Gopalan case, 'personal liberty' was held to mean liberty relating to or concerning the person or body of the individual. It also covers protection against arbitrary executive action. It has been extended to right to livelihood. Right to live includes the right to live with human dignity. In the case popularly known as the Pavement Dwellers case, the word 'life' in Article included the right to livelihood.[29]

Imprisonment of a poor person for non-payment of debts amounted to deprivation of his personal liberty.[30]

Provisions of guarantee of 100 or 150 day employment to every household on demand in a year under the Mahatma Gandhi National Rural Employment Guarantee Act, 2005 is also a part of right to livelihood provided a person asking for the work and is desirous to work on the scheme. This is a revolutionary step. Naturally none should expect to eat without working. Similarly, the National Food Security Act, 2013 is a guarantee to the poor in India against starvation. However, implementation of these schemes is also subject to judicial review because a law without implementation is just a dry piece of paper which serves no purpose. Earlier, the Supreme Court had held that non-payment of minimum wages to the workers amounted to denial of their right to live with basic human dignity and violated Article 21. Similarly, under the Bonded Labour System (Abolition) Act, 1976, it is not enough merely to identify and release bonded labourers but it is more important that they should be suitably rehabilitated to meet the plainest requirement of Article 21.[31] In Maneka Gandhi[32] case, the Supreme Court held that the right to life under Article 21 means more than survival or animal existence and would include the right to live with human dignity.

21A. Right to Education: The State shall provide free and compulsory education to all children of the age six to fourteen years in such manner as the State may, by law, determine.

(Part III, Article 21A)

COMMENTS

The new Article provides for free and compulsory education for all children between the age of 6 to 14 years. This will ensure consciousness among public when these children grow up. The compulsory education at primary education is considered panacea for the country. But its implementation should be done sincerely. The Supreme Court has commented that 'the total indifference of the Government authorities is leading to the violation of the fundamental rights of the children."[34] However, one has to wait for some time for its proper implementation. It took more than sixty years which is basic foundation for the progress of the nation. 'The right of a child should be extended to have quality education without discrimination on the ground of child's economic, social and cultural backgrounds."[35] It is heartening to know that even private English medium schools are allowing children from economically weaker sections of society to be admitted for primary education.

The Right of Children to Free and Compulsory Education Act, 2009 entitles child to free and education in neighbourhood unaided school to admit 25% students from weaker sections.

On the other hand, the guardians who do not send their wards to schools for education in the age group of 6 to 14 should also be accountable by law to be made by Parliament or State Legislatures.

22. Protection against arrest and detention in certain cases: (1) No person who is arrested shall be detained in custody without being informed, as soon as may be, of the grounds for such arrest nor shall he be denied the right to consult, and to be defended by, a legal practitioner of his choice.

(2) Every person who is arrested and detained in custody shall be produced before the nearest magistrate within a period of twenty-four hours of such arrest, excluding the time necessary for the journey from the place of arrest to the court of

the magistrate and no such person shall be detained in custody beyond the said period without the authority of a magistrate.

(3) Nothing in clauses (1) and (2) shall apply—(a) to any person who for the time being is an enemy alien; or (b) to any person who is arrested or detained under any law providing for preventive detention.

"(4) No law providing for preventive detention shall authorise the detention of a person for a longer period than three months unless an Advisory Board constituted in accordance with the recommendations of the Chief Justice of the appropriate High Court has reported before the expiration of the said period of two months that there is in its opinion sufficient cause for such detention: Provided that an Advisory Board shall consist of a Chairman and not less than two other members, and the Chairman shall be a serving Judge of the appropriate High Court and the other members shall be serving or retired Judges of any High Court: Provided further that nothing in this clause shall authorise the detention of any person beyond the maximum period prescribed by any law made by Parliament under subclause (b) of clause (7).

(5) When any person is detained in pursuance of an order made under any law providing for preventive detention, the authority making the order shall, as soon as may be, communicate to such person the grounds on which the order has been made and shall afford him the earliest opportunity of making a representation against the order.

(6) Nothing in clause (5) shall require the authority making any such order as is referred to in that clause to disclose facts which such authority considers to be against the public interest to disclose.

(7) Parliament may by law prescribe—

(a) the circumstances under which, and the class or classes of cases in which, a person may be detained for a period longer than three months under any law providing for preventive detention without obtaining the opinion of an Advisory Board in accordance with the provisions of sub-clause (a) of clause (4);

(b) the maximum period for which any person may in any class or classes of cases be detained under any law providing for preventive detention; and

(c) the procedure to be followed by an Advisory Board in an inquiry under sub-clause (a) of clause (4).

(Part III, Article 22)

COMMENTS

Article 22 consists of two parts. Clauses (1) and (2) apply to persons arrested or detained under a law otherwise than a preventive detention law. Clauses (4) to (7) apply to persons arrested or detained under a preventive detention law.

The Supreme Court has held that the communication of the grounds of arrest to the detenu allowing consultation with and defence by a counsel and production before the nearest magistrate within 24 hours are mandatory requirements.

The right not to be arrested except for heinous offences and to have someone informed of the arrest and to consult privately with lawyers is inherent in Articles 21 and 22(1) of the Constitution and required to be recognised and scrupulously protected.

Preventive Detention is provided in the Constitution to preserve peace and order for the general public. Sometimes, the dangerous criminals and organised gangs are more resourceful and organised than the archaic police administration in India. The police administration, through control of executive magistrates, therefore, should be entrusted with power of Preventive Detention in exceptional cases and for a temporary period provided as per the Constitutional provisions, with certain safeguards. Preventive Detention is designed to prevent the abuse of freedom by antisocial and subversive elements which might imperial the national welfare and subvert or disrupt the basis of an established order. In case of preventive detention, documents which are vital should be supplied and also documents which are considered by the detaining authority.

The following Acts were enforced:

(1) The Preventive Detention Act, 1950.

(2) The Maintenance of Internal Security Act, 1971 known as MISA.

(3) The Conservation of Foreign Exchange and Prevention of Smuggling Activities Act, 1974 referred to as the COFEPOSA.

(4) The National Security Act, 1980 (NASA repealed MISA)

(5) The Prevention of Black Marketing and Maintenance of Supplies of Essential Commodities Act, 1980.

(6) The Terrorist and Disruptive Activities (Prevention) Act, 1985 (commonly called TADA) has since been repealed. Some States, i.e. Jammu and Kashmir, Madhya Pradesh, Uttar Pradesh, Maharashtra, Andhra Pradesh, and Rajasthan have enacted States laws, authorising preventive detention, which recall the old Preventive Detention Act of 1950. Thus, the power of preventive detention is divided between the Union and the States. The Supreme Court held that the State Government may, if satisfied with respect to any bootlegger or drug offender (or forest offender) or goonda or immoral traffic offender or slum grabber that with a view to prevent him from acting in any manner prejudicial to the maintenance of public order, it is necessary to do so, make an order directing such person be detained[36] (without opportunity of hearing). But this power of trial by the executive should be sparingly used in exceptional circumstances to prevent larger damage to the public interest.

Right Against Exploitation

23. Prohibition of traffic in human being and forced labour: (1) Traffic in human being and begar, and other similar forms of forced labour are prohibited and any contravention of this provision shall be an offence punishable in accordance with law.

(2) Nothing in this Article shall prevent the State from imposing compulsory service for public purposes, and in imposing compulsory service for public purposes, and in imposing such service, the State shall not make any discrimination on grounds only of religion, race, caste or class or any of them.

24. Prohibition of employment of children in factories, etc.: No child below the age of fourteen years shall be employed to work in any factory or mine or engaged in any other hazardous employment.

(Part III, Articles 23 & 24)

COMMENTS

Under the old Zamindari system, the sharecroppers have sometimes been forced to render free service to their landlords. This was called 'begar'. Courts have held that even if some remuneration is paid, the labour may be a forced one.[37]

Article 24 specifically prohibited the employment of children below the age of 14 in factories or mines or in any other hazardous jobs. This is in keeping with the human rights concepts and the United Nations norms.

The employers of children below 14 years must comply with the provisions of the Child Labour (Prohibition and Regulation) Act providing for compensation, employment of their parents-guardians and their education.

Right to Freedom of Religion

25. Freedom of conscience and free profession, practice and propagation of religion: (1) Subject to public order, morality and health and to the other provisions of Part. All persons are equally entitled to freedom of conscience and the right freely to profess, practise and propagate religion.

(2) Nothing in this Article shall affect the operation of any existing law or prevent the State from making any law:

(a) Regulating or restricting any economic, financial, political or other secular activity, which may be associated with religious practice;

(b) Providing for social welfare and reform or the throwing open of Hindu religious institutions of a public character to all classes and sections of Hindus.

Explanation I: The wearing and carrying of Kirpans shall be deemed to be included in the profession of the Sikh religion.

Explanation II: In sub-clause (b) of clauses (2), the reference to Hindus shall be construed as including a reference to persons professing the Sikh, Jain or Buddhist religion, and the reference to Hindu religious institutions shall be construed accordingly.

(Part III, Article 25)

COMMENTS

Religion is a matter of faith but belief in God is not essential to constitute religion. Doctrines of each religion constitute its essential part. The practice means religious worship, rituals and observations. The Court is competent to examine it. The State cannot allow people to fight in the name of religion. A secular State is founded on the idea that State is concerned with the relation between man and man and not with relation between man and God, which is a matter of the individual concerned. The emphasis is that an individual is free to practise his religion within forewalls of a premise privately, Cow slaughter on 'Bakrid' was held not to be an essential practice of Islam and could, therefore, be prohibited by law in the interest of public order.[38]

Propagation is concerned with right to communicate beliefs to another person or to expound the tenets of one's religion, but does not include a right to forcible conversions. Article 18(2) of the International Convenant on Civil and Political Rights, 1966 also provides, "No one shall be subject to coercion which would impair his freedom to have or to adopt a religion or belief of his choice. Similarly, the honour killings, for whatever reason come within the category of the rarest of rare cases deserving death penalty.[39]

Secularism in India does not mean that the State should be hostile to religion but that it should be neutral as between different religions or give equal patronage to all religions.

"The neutrality of the State would be violated if religion is used for political prospects and advocated by political parties for their political ends. An appeal to the electorate on grounds of religion offends secular democracy. Politics and religion cannot be mixed."[40]

26. Freedom to manage religious affairs: Subject to public order, morality and health, every religious denomination or any section thereof shall have the right:

(a) To establish and maintain institutions for religious and charitable purposes;

(b) To manage its own affairs in matters of religion;

(c) To own and acquire movable and immovable property; and

(d) To administer such property in accordance with law.

(Article 26 Part III)

Under Article 26, it is the fundamental right of a religious denomination, trust or its representatives to administer properties. But law or State can regulate activities like management of properties subject to reasonable regulatory restrictions to prevent maladministration. Placing the administration of a religious denomination under an administrator without sufficient justification for such an appointment would violate Article 26(d).

Religious denomination must satisfy three conditions common faith, common organisation and designation by distinctive name.

Sir Aurobindo Society is not a denomination whereas Ramkrishna Mission is.

27. Freedom as to payment of taxes for promotion of any particular religion: No person shall be compelled to pay any taxes, the proceeds of which are specifically appropriated in payment of expenses for the promotion or maintenance of any particular religion or religious denomination.

(Article 27, Part III)

COMMENTS

According to Article 27, no person shall be compelled to pay any taxes for expenses on promotion or maintenance of any particular religion. However, there could be no objection if the taxes were used for promotion of all religions.

"On challenge to subsidy given to Haj Pilgrims under the Haj Committee Act, 2002, the Court held the prohibition of Article 27 applies both to tax or appropriation from general exchequer. But if the amount appropriated is small or insignificant, Artcile. 27 is not violated."[41]

The decision is justified in view of general trend prevailing in the country, where many fairs or mass gathering like in 'Kumbh' or 'Ardh Kumbh' are managed by administration by spending lot of public fund to avoid law and order problem or stampede. Without help and direct intervention by government, such mass gatherings will be converted into mass graves.

28. Freedom as to attendance at religious instruction or religious worship in certain educational institutions: (1) No religious instruction shall be provided in any educational institution wholly maintained out of State funds.

(2) Nothing in clause (1) shall apply to an educational institution, which is administered by the Sate but has been established under any endowment or trust which requires that religious instruction shall be imparted in such institution.

(3) No person attending any educational institution recognised by the State or receiving aid out of State funds shall be required to take part in any religious instruction that may be imparted in such institution or to attend any premises attached thereof unless such person or, if such person is a minor, his guardian has given his consent thereof.

(Article 28, Part III)

Article 28 forbids totally any religious instruction being imparted in educational institutions wholly maintained by State funds. In case of other institutions recognised and aided by the State, there will be freedom for every person not to participate in religious instructions or worship. Religious instructions prohibited in Article 28 must be distinguished from study of religions.

"There is no prohibition for having study of religious philosophy and culture, particularly for having value-based social life in a society which is degenerating for power, post or property."[42]

However, the court saw no violation of Article 28 in the National Curriculum Framework for School Education approved by the National Council of Educational and Research and Training which required education for value development, such as birth, righteous conduct, peace, love and non-violence.

In educational institutions receiving aid from the State fund, the admission cannot be denied on ground of race, religion, language or caste.

Thus, Christian Missionary schools and other schools, like Madrasas cannot deny admission to other castes or communities if they receive funds from the State.

Cultural and Educational Rights

29. Protection of interests of minorities: (1) Any section of the citizens residing in the territory of India or any part thereof having a distinct language, script or culture of its own shall have the right to conserve the same.

(2) No citizens shall be denied admission into any educational institution maintained by the State funds on grounds only of religion, race, caste, language or any of them.

(Part III, Article 29)

COMMENTS

The Article though titled for minorities, it extends in clause (1) to all communities. But residents of a State having different script, language or culture may also object to illegal migration from a neighbouring country resulting in adverse impact on the language, script or culture of that State.[43] Thus, State has to perform its duty to prevent illegal migration.

The right to conserve one's script is that citizens have the right to agitate for the protection of their language. Not holding an entrance examination (pre-medical test), in any particular language, viz. Hindi or any regional language, does not violate Article 29(2).[44] Clause (2) is more specific and relates to admission into educational institutions which are maintained or aided by State funds.

In St. Stephen's College Vs. University of Delhi,[45] the Supreme Court held that minority community may reserve upto 50 per cent seats for the members of its own community. Later, it has been relaxed by the Court that the minority educational institutions should permit admission of citizens belonging to the non-minority class to a reasonable extent based upon merit though the institution admits students of the minority group of its own choice for whom the institution was meant.[46]

The Constitution's 93rd Amendment further enlarged scope for non-minority students by asking minority educational institutions to admit 25 per cent students from the economically weaker sections of the society in the age group of 6 to 14 under the Right of Children to Free and Compulsory Education Act, 2009.[47]

30. Right of minorities to establish and administer educational institutions: (1) All minorities, whether based on religion or language, shall have the right to establish and administer educational institutions of their choice.

(1A) In making any law providing for the compulsory acquisition of any property of an educational institution established and administered by minority, the state shall ensure that the amount fixed by or determined under such law for the acquisition of such property is such as would not restrict or abrogate the right guaranteed under that clause.

(2) The State shall not, in granting aid to educational institutions, discriminate against any educational institution on the ground that it is under the management of a minority, whether based on religion or language.

(Part III, Article 30)

COMMENTS

An institution retains its minority character as long as it continues to achieve two objectives, viz.:

(i) to enable such minority to conserve its religion and language, and

(ii) to give a thorough, good, general education to children belonging to such minority.[48]

The right to establish and administer would include the right to have choice of medium of instruction. The Supreme Court has laid down general principles relating to establishment and administration of educational institutions by minorities.

(a) to choose its governing body;

(b) to appoint teaching staff and heads; and non- teaching staff and to take action for their dereliction of duty;

(c) to admit eligible students of their choice and to set up a reasonable fee structure;

(d) to use its properties and assets for the benefit of the institution.

However, they cannot discriminate against majority students.

Further, these institutions are subject to regulatory measures by the State for ensuring educational character and standards and maintaining academic excellence. Subject to the eligibility conditions/qualifications prescribed by the State being met, the unaided minority educational institutors will have the freedom to appoint teachers/lecturers by adopting any rational procedure of selection. "However, the Government, the University and the Court could go behind the claim of a minority institution. Where the claim was a mere cloak or pretension and the real motive was business adventure, the protection of Article 30(1) would not be available.[49]

However, autonomy of a minority institution cannot be completely taken away.

31A. Saving of laws providing for acquisition of estates, etc.: Notwithstanding anything contained in Article 13, no law providing for—

(a) The acquisition by the State of any estate or of any rights therein or the extinguishment or modification of any such rights, or

(b) The taking over of the management of any property by the State for a limited period either in the public interest or in order to secure the proper management of the property, or

(c) The amalgamation of two or more corporations either in the public interest or in order to secure the proper management of any of the corporations, or

(d) The extinguishment or modification of any rights of managing agents, secretaries and treasurers, managing directors, directors or managers of corporations, or of any voting rights of shareholders thereof, or

(e) The extinguishment or modification of any rights accruing by virtue of any agreement, lease or license for the purpose of searching for, or winning, any mineral or mineral oil, or the premature termination or cancellation of any such agreement, lease or license, shall be deemed to be void on the ground that it is inconsistent with, or takes away or abridges any of the rights conferred by Article 14 or Article 19:

Provided that where such law is a law made by the Legislature of a State, the provisions of this Article shall not apply thereto unless such law, having been reserved for the consideration of the President, has received his assent:

Provided further that where any law makes any provision for the acquisition by the State of any estate and where any land comprised therein is held by a person under this personal cultivation, it shall not be lawful for the State to acquire any portion of such land as is within the ceiling limit applicable to him under any law for the time being in force or any building or structure standing thereon or appurtenant thereto, unless the law relating to the acquisition of such land, buildings or structure provides for payment of compensation at a rate which shall not be less than the market value thereof.

(2) In this Article—

(a) The expression "estate" shall, in relation to any local area, have the same meaning as that expression or its local equivalent has in the existing law relating to land tenures in force in that area and shall also include—

(i) any jagir, inam or muafi or other similar grant and in the States of Tamil Nadu and Kerala, any janmam right;

(ii) Any land held under ryotwari settlement;

(iii) Any land held or let for purposes of agriculture or for purposes ancillary thereto, including waste land, forest land, land for pasture or sites of buildings and other structures occupied by cultivators of land, agricultural labourers and village artisans;

(iv) The expression "rights", in relation to an estate, shall include any rights vesting in a proprietor, sub-proprietor, under-proprietor, tenure-holder, raiyat, under-raiyat or other intermediary and any rights or privileges in respect of land revenue.

31B. Validation of certain Acts and Regulations: Without prejudice to the generality of the provisions contained in Article 31A, none of the Acts and Regulations specified in the Ninth Schedule nor any of the provisions thereof shall be deemed to be void, or ever to have become void, on the ground that such Act, Regulation or provision is inconsistent with, or takes away or abridges any of the rights conferred by any provisions of this Part and notwithstanding any judgement, decree or order of any court or tribunal to the contrary, each of the said Acts and Regulations shall, subject to the power of any competent Legislature to repeal or amend it, continue in force.

31C. Saving of laws giving effect to certain directive principles: Now law shall be deemed to be void on the ground that it is inconsistent with Part IV, or takes away or abridges any of the rights conferred by Article 14 or Article 19.

Provided that where such law is made by the Legislature of a State, the provisions of this Article shall not apply thereto unless such law, having been reserved for the consideration of the President, has received his assent.

(Part III, Articles 31A, 31B and 31C)

COMMENTS

Article 31A was a part of Article 31 (Right to property) before Article 31 was repealed by the Constitution Forty Fourth Amendment, 1978 and was made a Constitutional right in new Article 300A. The fundamental right to property conferred by Article 31, had been modified six times since the commencement of the Constitution. The 1st Amendment added two explanatory Articles.

Articles 31A and 31B to the Constitution, the 4th Amendment amended Clause (2) of Article, added Clause

(2-A), inserted new provisions in Article 31A, 17th Amendment further enlarged the definition of "estate" in clause (2) of Article 31A(a), and the 25th Amendment amended Article 31 (2), added clause (2B) and added a new Article 31C.

The 1st Amendment through two explanatory Articles-Articles 31A and 31B fully secured the constitutional validity of Zamindari abolition and other agrarian reforms or land reform legislations.

The 4th Amendment established State's power of eminent domain subject to certain restrictions. The power of eminent domain is an essential attribute of sovereignty which means that king can do no wrong. This power connotes the legal capacity of the State to take private property of individuals for public purposes. This power is subject to three limitations-

(1) There must be a law authorising the taking of property,
(2) The property must be taken for some public use,
(3) Just compensation should be paid.

The above principles guide the implementation under Article 31A in the present form and in Jammu and Kashmir, Article 31 still holds the field. In the case of Shri Mata Vaishno Devi Shrine Act, 1988, the Supreme Court has held that the vesting management, administration and governance of the Shrine and Shrine Fund in Shri Mata Vaishno Devi Shrine Board and extinguishment of right of Baridars does not amount to acquisition of property under Article 31(2). It fell within the ambit of Article 31(2A). Therefore, the Baridars were not entitled to any compensation.[51]

However, it was felt necessary that land reform legislations cannot achieve their purpose unless they are immune from invasion of counter -rights under any of Articles, under Part III and they are given protection for assessment of compensation. Otherwise, no purpose will be served to bring these welfare legislations in use. Thirdly, they have to be protected by umbrella of Schedule of the Constitution of India under Article 31B. By 17th Constitution Amendment, the definition of estate was elaborated so that land reform legislations may not be struck down on technical grounds.

Similarly, to overcome the ruling of market value of compensation in Bela Banerjee case,[52] 25th Constitution Amendment was passed by Parliament as State governments were unable to pay market value of compensation for ceiling surplus land and was rightly so because the erstwhile landlords or by landowners possessed these lands as the system was functioning in their favour and concentration of properties or wealth less the landed properties cannot be allowed to be in few hands. Lands belong to the earth and are held in trust of the society. Secondly, in Golak Nath case,[53] the Supreme Court reversing its earlier decisions in Shankari Prasad[54] and Sajjan Singh's[55] cases held that Parliament had no power to abridge or abrogate the fundamental rights.

This reversed position was again reconsidered by the Supreme Court in Kesavananda Bharti case,[56] which finally decided in full judges' bench by 7:6 majority that (a) the power of amendment is limited. It does not enable Parliament to alter the basic structure or framework of the Constitution; and (b) the substantive provision of Article 31C which abrogates the fundamental rights is valid on the ground that it does not alter the basic structure or framework of the Constitution and (c). But the latter part of Article 31C, which ousts the jurisdiction of the Court is invalid.

Thus, judicial review was held as the one of the basic features of the Constitution. It was further held that the Directive Principles of social justice are placed above individual rights and whenever or wherever it is considered necessary, individual rights can be subordinated or cut down to give effect to the principles of social justice as enshrined in the Directive Principles of the State policy.

To set the controversy at rest and allow government to undertake social welfare measures for social justice, the right to property from the chapter on fundamental rights was taken away and was made a constitutional right under Article 300 A by deleting Article 19(1)(f) and Article 31.

Now, we can discuss the present position of Article 31A.

Status of Article 31A

Laws providing for acquisition of estates, takeover of corporation, etc. have been saved by Article 31A against challenge on the ground of alleged infringement of Article 14 or Article 19.

By Article 31B, acts and regulations specified in the Ninth Schedule have been saved against challenge on the ground of inconsistency with taking away or abridging any fundamental right. However, after the decision in Keshavananda's case, inclusion in the Ninth Schedule of any law is open to challenge on the ground of damage to the basic structure of the Constitution. Thus, the court can still consider whether a particular law purporting to implement any directive principle is valid if it finds that the nexus between that law and the Directive Principle relied on is illusory or colourable or whether it be direct and reasonable nexus with the directive principle in Article 39(b) or Article 39(c).

The agrarian reform legislation is generally considered synonymous with ceiling legislation. But "a law providing for agrarian reform need not provide for land ceiling.[57]" It includes host of other measures.

It includes land tenure systems in the areas under Permanent Settlement and under Ryotwari settlement in South India. Excess land includes waste land, forest land, land for pasture or sites of buildings occupied by cultivators of land.

Article 31A(2)(b) also provides constitutional protection to tenure holders, i.e., Bataidars or Bargadars or sharecroppers. Thus, Article 31A covers most of the tenure holdings including right in all types of land, viz. waste land, forest land, land for pasture, sites of buildings occupied by cultivators, agricultural labourers and even village artisans.

The above rights have found place in the new Land Acquisition Act titled 'The Right to Fair Compensation and Transparency in Land Acquisition, Rehabilitation and Resettlement Act, 2013. The compensation is now about four times the market value for rural areas and twice the market value in urban areas. It shows that Parliament has tried to undo injustice so far done to the farmers or landowners in the name of land acquisition for public purpose.

In Shantilal Mangaldas cases,[58] the Supreme Court held that adequacy of compensation fixed by the Legislature or awarded according to the principles specified by the Legislature for determination of compensation was not justiciable. However, it should not be illusory. In Banks' Nationalisation case[59], the Supreme Court adopted earlier line and held that the bank nationalisation law was liable to be struck down as it failed to provide to the expropriated banks compensation determined according to the relevant principles. The principle specified by law for determining compensation was beyond the pale of challenge only if it was relevant for the determination of compensation. Time will only tell what stand will be taken by the Apex Court whereas under the new Land Acquisition Act, 2013, the amount of compensation to be determined and paid is two to four times of the market value of the land or property to be acquired for the public purpose along with resettlement and rehabilitation in cases of land acquisition for schemes involving 100 acres or more lands. Calcutta High Court also thwarted the attempt by the group of land owners to stall the land reform implementation by the Left Front Government by holding that the State can give retrospective effect to such legislations[60] to give effect to Articles 39(b) and (c).

However, executive orders are not sufficient to deprive of a person of his/her property. It has been held that a law which aims at elevating the statutes of tenants, (sharecroppers) by conferring on them 'bhoomidhari' rights (full ownership rights) cannot be said to be wanting in public purpose.[61] Similarly, there is a public purpose where the property is taken over to keep labour going on and contended and to maintain the supply of essential commodities. Such was the commitment of the Supreme Court towards ceiling laws or land reform legislations. Due to patronage of the Supreme Court, the laws kept in the Ninth Schedule enjoyed immunity and the executive had free hand to undertake implementation of land reform measures like distribution of surplus vested land among the landless and marginal farmers in India and recording of sharecroppers

(Bargadars in West Bengal) who are poorest among the poor in India and require maximum attention or patronage from the State. They also constitute the majority of persons below poverty line. Democracy and republic are meaningless to them unless they can have two meals a day. They can fight hunger if they are provided land to work on it. Otherwise, they will remain unemployed. Even 100 or 150 day work to them under the Mahatma Gandhi National Rural Employment Guarantee Act, 2005 will not be effective to them for the rest of the year. Secondly, in a corrupt system like ours, the unvocal or silent majority of landless poor or land poor cannot secure their due rights under MNREGA or the Food Security Act. The only protection to them against hunger is to equip them with land or right of cultivation as sharecropper, which can only be implemented if arable land is vested in government or acquired by government through ceiling or other land reform legislations. The Supreme Court was well appreciating their predicament but after the Keshavananda Bharati case, the Supreme Court has started scrutinising the laws being put under the Ninth Schedule of the Constitution whether these laws are just and reasonable and fulfill the object or purpose of the legislation.[62] In Ratnagiri Engineering Pvt. Ltd.[63] the Supreme Court has gone to the extent of declaring the order of Government of West Bengal in said for not allowing the conversion of land from the industrial classification to the real estate purpose. The justification was that the lands were held for a very long time with the petitioner and were lying unutilised. If this is allowed unfettered, the employment through industries will not be generated, which is the mainstay to provide livelihood to the urban poor. I am sure that the Supreme Court will reconsider its decisions and will reconsider its earlier stand specially when the State Government has passed the law invalidating the judgement of the Supreme Court. In the present era of globalisation, the poorest of the poor in India are left with only ray of hope in the Supreme Court. The Supreme Court cannot appreciate that its small leeway to the landed rich or capitalists is implemented in a big way by the pro-rich executive and its bureaucratic instrumentality and police, whereas its most favourable orders in the interest of the land poor or urban poor are treated with indifference by the executing agency of the state. The Supreme Court, being the part of the State, has onerous responsibility and a sacrosanct duty to protect the interest of the poor, who form the backbone of the Republic of India. Their interest is to be guarded against the flurry of pleadings by great legal experts and battery of very important advocates, who can only be hired to argue before the Supreme Court by the haves or rich clients. It is high time that the brief of poor men has to be kept by the higher courts themselves, when they are elevated to the seat of justice by the State.

Justice Krishna Iyer has summarised the line of demarcation between the private right vis-à-vis social welfare[64] as below:

"If legislation does go that far, it shakes the democratic foundation and must suffer the death penalty. But to permit the Kesvananda Bharati's ghost to haunt the corridors of the court brandishing fatal writs for every feature of inequality is judicial paralysation of Parliamentary function."

Right to Constitutional Remedies

32. Remedies for enforcement of rights conferred by this Part: (1) The right to move the Supreme Court by appropriate proceedings for the enforcement of the rights conferred by this Part is guaranteed.

(2) The Supreme Court shall have power to issue directions or orders or writs, including writs in the nature of habeas corpus, mandamus, prohibition, quo warrant and certiorari, whichever may be appropriate, for the enforcement of any of the rights conferred by this Part.

(3) Without prejudice to the powers conferred on the Supreme Court by clauses (1) and (2), Parliament may be law empower any other court to exercise within the local limits of its jurisdiction all or any of the powers exercisable by the Supreme Court under clause (2).

(4) The right guaranteed by this Article shall not be suspended except as otherwise provided for by this Constitution.

(Part III, Article 32)

COMMENTS

Unlike other rights, it is remedial and not substantive in nature. Right without remedy is meaningless. Dr. Ambedkar called it the heart and soul of the Constitution. The fundamental rights to move the court can, therefore, be appropriately described as the cornerstone of the democratic edifice, raised by the Constitution. In discharging the duties assigned to it, the court is to play the role of sentinel of the justice. However, it is an urgent remedy and is not available where alternative remedy is available. But the right to move the Supreme Court is through appropriate proceedings.

The word "appropriate" does not refer to any form but to the purpose of the proceeding and so long as the purpose of the proceedings is enforcement of a fundamental rights of poor, disabled or ignored by a public spirited person. Even a letter addressed by him to the court can legitimately be regarded as an appropriate proceeding.[65] Accordingly, letters in any form, including postcard and telegram addressed to any judge, have been entertained as appropriate proceedings.[66]

Even if the petitioner has not asked for the proper writ applicable to his case, the Supreme Court must grant him the proper writ to suit the exigencies of the case. This remedy is immune from being overridden by legislation by law. Any law which renders nugatory or illusory the Supreme Court's power except in exceptional circumstances like declaration of Emergency to grant this remedy, shall be void. Following writs can be issued by the Supreme Court in different circumstances:

I. Habeas Corpus: The object of the writ is to secure the release of a person found to be detained illegally. It asks first 'let the person or body of person be produced before the court'. This writ is also issued to remove a person confined in one place for trial to another place. The writ is issued if the arrest or detention is under an invalid law, invalid order, is malafide or on irrelevant or extraneous consideration. If an authority passes an order of preventive detention for reasons not connected with the grounds mentioned in P.D. (Preventive Detention) law, the court can always declare the detention illegal and release the detainee but it is not possible for the Supreme Court to function if there is prohibition against disclosing the grounds, which have been served upon him.

II. Mandamus: Mandamus literally means a command. The mandamus will issue if the applicant has a legal right to the performance of a legal duty of a public nature and the party against whom the writ is sought is bound to perform the duty 'against the officers and the government'. Apart from the enforcement of fundamental rights, mandamus is also available to compel a court or judicial tribunal to exercise its jurisdiction where it has refused to exercise it. The mandamus cannot be issued against the President or the Governor of a State (Article-361). No mandamus can be issued to the rulemaking authority to make the rules either within a specific time or in a particular manner.[67] It is not for courts to determine whether a particular policy or a decision taken in fulfillment of policy is fair.[68] However, directions can be issued to control pollution.[69]

III. Prohibition: 'Prohibition' is issued against courts or tribunals exercising judicial or quasi-judicial powers to prohibit the tribunal from making the ultra-vires order or decision. The writ of prohibition is available during the tendency of the proceeding before the lower authorities. Thus, while prohibition commands inactivity, mandamus commands activity. Defect of jurisdiction attracts prohibition.

IV. Certiorari: Certiorari is available if the courts or tribunals or officers have acted without jurisdiction or in excess of the legal authority vested in such quasi-judicial authority, or in contravention of the rules of natural justice or there is an 'error apparent on the face of its record'. Even purely administrative actions are also now subject to issuance of writ of certiorari, provided the decision is against natural justice, malafide, perverse or based on non-applicability of ground. The writ will be available if the court or tribunal is not properly constituted or the subject matter is beyond the scope of the jurisdiction of tribunal or the tribunal has assumed the jurisdiction or the decision has been obtained by fraud, collusion or corruption.

V. Quo Warranto: In writ of quo warranto, the court enquires into the legality of the claim which a party asserts to a public office, and to oust him from its enjoyment if the claim is not well founded. A writ of quo warranto lies against the person who is not entitled to hold an office of public nature and is only an usurper of the office. Such a person is required to show by what authority he is entitled to hold that office. The challenge can be made on the grounds such as he does not fulfill the required qualifications or suffers from any disqualification debarring him to hold such office.[70] A writ of quo warranto lies only when the appointment is contrary to a statutory provision.

Public Interest Litigation: Public interest litigation is an unique jurisdiction assumed by the Supreme Court in India as compared to other jurisdiction in other countries in the world. For social or public interest actions, any person may move to the court. This is called expansion of the 'right to be heard'. It is an exception to locus standi rule where the public in general are interested in the vindication of some right or the enforcement of some public duty. But this right is also not unfettered. The petitioner has to prove real public cause and not the frivolous or illusory one only based on presumptions and hypothesis. "A PIL would not be maintainable where it is filed at the behest of some powerful business houses."[71] The jurisdiction of Supreme Court in PIL cannot be pressed into service where the matters have been completely and effectively adjudicated upon in the individual petitions and also in the writ petitions raising larger questions.[72]

However, PIL is being misused by some advocates who want to come in limelight to brighten their legal practice by making non-issues even as public interest issues.

This results into wastage of precious court's time, whereas many bonafide litigants are constantly waiting for years for disposal of their long pending cases. There is no doubt that the invocation of jurisdiction by the Supreme Court has done more benefit to the public and the country than the loss because the executive had become non-responsive and exercises unbridled and unfettered power. It has made the executive more accountable and lot of benefit has percolatd down to the people. A confidence has been created in the country to stand against misuse of authority by persons in power.

However, now the PIL has reached the subordinate courts and some magistrates or judges are assuming the jurisdiction on application by some lawyers to come in public glare or media which is against the professional ethics of the judicial officers. It is high time that proper checks and balance are to be put in place, otherwise the institution by PIL will divert the judiciary into a field which is not its field of expertise. The elected representatives in democracy are there to understand the people's problems and the remedies thereof. They are also accountable to public for their actions or inaction after every five years or earlier. Petitioners by some lawyers on the basis of newspaper reports or some research may cause irreparable damage to the judiciary which is already overburdened with cases.

It is happily noted that the Supreme Court has fined many PIL litigants but that is not enough. Regular PIL petitioner and advocate ML Sharma got penalized for the hazards of pushing the already stretched limits of public interest litigation in the recent case dated 2nd September, 2014 as the Supreme Court imposed ₹ 50,000/- cost on him for seeking a direction to the Centre to find the whereabouts of Netaji Subhash Chandra Bose. A bench of Chief Justice. R.M. Lodha and Justices Kurian Joseph and R.F. Nariman allowed Sharma, dressed in lawyer's uniform with forked band neatly tied to his white shirt collar, to go the full distance in arguing the PIL and explaining why he filed the habeas corpus (produce the body) petition. At the end of his argument, Sharma got an unexpected order. "We find the petition hopeless and frivolous. Such petitions should not only be dismissed but exemplary cost should be awarded for wasting the court's time, "the bench said and quantified the cost at ₹ 1 lakh. Immediately, there was a torrent of apology from Sharma, who was also pulled up by the bench for violating rules by choosing to appear in lawyer's uniform despite arguing as 'petitioner in person'. But Sharma kept apologising, expressing inability to pay the hefty sum. He had been recently asked to pay cost of ₹ 25,000 for another PIL.

This was one of the most required and benchmark step taken by the Supreme Court for curtailing the misuse of provision of PIL, which is vested for the public motive. Since now-a-days, it has become, practice for the vested interest, it is required to be discouraged. The PILs are also now multiplying by heaps and bounds and in future, the main- course litigation will be grossly overlooked. This is not what is expected of the PIL. A decision, judgement or order remaining unimplemented is just a piece of paper.

An analysis of orders in PILs will show that the governments do not have the funds, resources or infrastructures to implement all PILs for the next ten years as per the rough estimate. The Apex Court is, therefore, urged to come hard on PIL and keep the power only with it and no further.

The Supreme Court held that the government policy cannot be enforced by writ under Article 32. A directive principle cannot be enforced by writ under Article 32.[73] But the Supreme Court is veering around to attach more sanctity to the directive principles vis-à-vis fundamental rights. However, the judicial review in matters of appointment of High Court judges would be permissible only on the ground, i.e. lack of eligibility and lack of effective consultation.[74] A writ petition cannot be filed to circumvent an earlier decision in the Supreme Court. But for deprivation of right to life and personal liberty, compensation may be awarded. In a false encounter, rupees 20 lacs was awarded due to loss of his son.[75]

33. Power of Parliament to modify the rights conferred by this Part in their application to Forces, etc.: Parliament may, by law, determine to what extent any of the rights conferred by this Part shall, in their application to,

(a) the members of the Armed Forces; or
(b) the members of the Forces charged with the maintenance of public order; or
(c) persons employed in any bureau or other organisation established by the State for purposes of intelligence or counter-intelligence; or
(d) person employed in, or in connection with, the telecommunication systems set up for the purposes of any Force, bureau or organisation referred to in clauses

(a) to (c), be restricted or abrogated so as to ensure the proper discharge of their duties and the maintenance of discipline among them.

(Part III, Article 33)

COMMENTS

The Article empowers Parliament to restrict or abrogate the application of fundamental rights in relation to armed forces, paramilitary forces, the police, etc. Parliament may empower Government to impose restrictions.[76] Such legislation may restrict the operation of fundamental rights, such as equality, free expression, freedom of association, personal liberty under Articles 20 and 21. Unless the substantive fundamental right itself has been excluded by a law made under Article 33, the right of services and consequently the remedy of writ also survives like in quasi judicial proceedings in relation to court martial. The Supreme Court may interfere if the sentence imposed by the court martial is disproportionate to the crime.[77] Or there are breaches of natural justice or there is error of jurisdiction on law on the face of record. However, the Supreme Court will not enter into question of fact or irregularities caused. Similarly, the Air Force Act, 1950 and the Rules made under it were not found violative of Article 21 insofar as they did not provide for a counsel at State expenses in the court martial proceedings. They were protected by Article 33.[78]

So long as the restriction is in respect of the forces covered by Article 33 and for the purpose specified in that Article, i.e. proper discharge of their duties by such forces and the maintenance of discipline among them, the court cannot examine the propriety or suitability of the restrictions.[79]

34. Restriction on rights conferred by this Part while martial law is in force in any area: Notwithstanding anything in the foregoing provisions of this Part. Parliament may by law indemnify any person in the service of the Union or of a State or any other person in respect of any act done by him in connection with the maintenance or restoration of order in any area within the territory of India where martial law was in force or validate any sentence passed, punishment inflicted, forfeiture ordered or other act done under martial law in such area.

(Part III, Article 34)

COMMENTS

In Martial Law, the right of trial by the ordinary court is suspended. The Constitution does not have a provision authorising proclamation of martial law. However, Parliament may by law indemnify any person for anything done in contravention of fundamental rights for maintenance of order during the operation of martial law.

35. Legislation to give effect to the provisions of this Part: Notwithstanding anything in this Constitution—

(a) Parliament shall have, and the Legislature of a State shall not have, power to make laws—

(i) with respect to any of the matters which under clause (3) of Article 16, clause (3) of Article 32, Article 33 and Article 34 may be provided for by law made by Parliament; and

(ii) for prescribing punishment for those acts which are declared to be offences under this Part; and Parliament shall, as soon as may be after the commencement of this Constitution, make laws for prescribing punishment for the acts referred to in sub-clause (ii); (b) any law in force immediately before the commencement of this Constitution in the territory of India with respect to any of the matters referred to in sub-clause (i) of clause (a) or providing for punishment for any act referred to in sub-clause (ii) of that clause shall, subject to the terms thereof and to any adaptations and modifications that may be made therein under Article 372, continue in force until altered or repealed or amended by the Parliament.

Explanation—In this Article, the expression "law in force" has the same meaning as in Article 372.

(Part III, Article 35)

COMMENTS

Article 35 lays down that the power to make laws to give effect to certain specified fundamental rights shall vest only in Parliament and not in State Legislatures. Section 8 of Jammu and Kashmir Preventive Detention Act is not in excess of or inconsistent with the provisions of clause (C) added to Article 35 of the Constitution by the Constitution (Application to J&K) Order, 1954.[80]

REFERENCES

1. Ajay Hasia V Khalid Mujib (1981) SCC 722.
2. Zee Tele films Ltd. Vs. Union of India, (2005) 4 SCC 649.
3. Suresh Kumar Kanshal Vs. Naz Foundation, (2014) SCC I.
4. Kesar Enterprises Ltd. Vs. State of Utter Pradesh, AIR 2011 SC 2709 (2714).
5. India Sawhney vs. Union of India, (2000) 1 SCC 168
6. Centre for Public Interest litigation vs. Union of India, (2012) 3 SCC 1.
7. Manohar Lal Sharma vs. Union of India (2014), 9 SCC 614.
8. M. Nagraj vs. Union of India, AIR 2007 SC7.
9. M. C. Valsala vs. State of Kerala, AIR 2006 Kerala, AIR 2006, Ker1.
10. Saurabh Chandra vs. Union of India, (2003) 11 SCC 146.
11. Rajesh Kumar Gupta vs. State of Uttar Pradesh, (2005) 5 SCC 172.
12. Vishakha vs. State of Rajasthan, (1997) 6 SCC 24, AIR 1997 SC 3011.
13. Secretary, State of Karnataka vs. Umadevi (3), AIR 2006 SC 1806.
14. Amita vs. Union of India, (2005) 13 SCC 721.
15. Indra Sawhney vs. Union of India (1992) Supp (3) SCC 217.
16. Ashok. Kumar Thakur (8) vs. Union of India (2007), 4 SCC 361.
17. Pondicherry Khadi & Village Industries Board V K.A. Radja (2013) SCC 780 (790).
18. People's Union for Democratic Rights vs. Union of India, AIR 1982 SC 1473.
19. In re. Harijai Singh, In re. Vijay Kumar, AIR 1997 SC 73.
20. Noise Pollution (V), In re, AIR 2005 SC 3136.
21. People's Union for Civil Liberties vs. Union of India, AIR 2004 SC 1442.
22. Communist Party of India (M) vs. Bharat Kumar, (1998) 1 SCC 201.

23. Delhi Police Sangh vs. Union of India, AIR (1987) SC 379.
24. Indian Medical Association vs. Union of India, (2011) 7 SCC 179.
25. Suba Singh vs. Davinder Kaur, AIR 2011 SC 3163.
26. Jitendra Panchal vs. Intelligence Officer, NCB, AIR 2009 SC 1938.
27. Union of India vs. Purushottam, AIR 2015 SC 961.
28. Nandini Sathpathy vs. P.L. Dani AIR,1978 SC 1025.
29. D.K. Basu vs. State of West Bengal, AIR,1997 SC 610.
30. Olga Tellis vs. Bombay Municipal Corporation, AIR 1986 SC 180.
31. Jolly George Verghese vs. Bank of Cochin, AIR 1980 SC 470.
32. Neerja Chaudhari vs. State of M.P., AIR 1984 SC, 1099.
33. Maneka vs. Union of India, AIR 1978 SC 597.
34. Inserted by the Constitution (Eighty Sixth Amendment) Act, 2002 w.e.f. 01.04.2010.
35. Environment and Consumer Protection Foundation vs. Delhi Administration (2011) 7 SCC 57.
36. State of Tamilnadu V.K. Shyam Sunder, (2011) 8 SCC 737 (756).
37. T. Devaki vs. Government of Tamil Nadu, AIR 1990 SC 1086.
38. Mohd. Hanif Quareshi vs. State of Bihar, AIR 1958 SC 731.
39. People's Union vs. Union of India, AIR 1982 SC 1473.
40. Bhagwan Das vs. State of NCT Delhi (2011) 6 SCC 396 (404).
41. Bommai vs. Union of India, AIR 1994 SC 1918, a 9 Judges Bench decision.
42. Prafull Gordia vs. Union of India, (2011) 2 SCC 568.
43. Aruna Roy vs. Union of India (2002) 7 SCC 368.
44. Sarbananda Sanowal vs. Union of India (2005) 5 SCC 719.
45. Hindi Hitrakhak Samiti vs. Union of India, (1990 2 SCC, 352) (1992) SCC1 558.
46. T.M.A Pai Foundation vs. State of Karnataka (2002) 8 SCC 481.
47. Society for Unaided Private Schools of Rajasthan vs. Union Of India, (2012) 6 SC.
48. P.A. Inamdar vs. State of Maharashtra, AIR 2005 SC 3226.
49. A.P. Christians Medical Education Society vs. Government of A.P., AIR 1986 S.C. 1490.
50. St. Stephen's College vs. University of Delhi, (1992) 1 SCC 558.
51. Bhuri Nath vs. State of J & K, (1997) 2 SCC 745.
52. State of West Bengal vs. Bela Banerjee, AIR 1954 SC 170.
53. Golak Nath vs. State of Punjab AIR, 1967 SC 1643.
54. Shankari Prasad Singh Deo vs. Union of India, AIR 1951 SC 458.
55. Sajjan Singh vs. State of Rajasthan, AIR 1965 SC 845.
56. Kesavananda Bharti vs. State of Kerala, AIR 1973 SC 1461.
57. Union Territory of Goa, Daman & Diu vs. Lakshmibai Narayan Patil, (1990) 4 SCC 102.

58. State of Gujarat vs. Shanti Lal Mangaldas, (1969) 1 SCC 509.
59. R.C. Cooper vs. Union of India, (1970) 1 SCC 248.
60. Paschim Banga Bhumijibi Sangh vs. State of West Bengal, (1996) CHN 212: (1996) 2 Cal LJ 285.
61. Sasanka Sekhar Maity vs. Union of India, (1980) 4 SCC 716.
62. Waman Rao vs. Union of India, (1981) 2 SCC 362, Minerva Mills Ltd. vs. Union of India, (1980) 3 SCC.
63. State of West Bengal vs. Ratnagiri Engg. (P) Ltd., (2009) 4 SCC 453.
64. Bhim Singh Ji vs. Union of India, (1981) 1 SCC 166.
65. Bandhua Mukti Morcha vs. Union of India, (1984) 3 SCC 161.
66. Mohanlal Sharma vs. State of U.P., (1989) 2 SCC 600.
67. Union of India vs. Namit Sharma, AIR (2014) SC 122 (140).
68. G. Sundarrajan vs. Union of India, (2013) 6 SCC 620 (646).
69. Subhash Kumar vs. State of Bihar, (1991) 1 SCC 598.
70. Centre for PIL vs. Union of India, (2011) 4 SCC 1.
71. Arun Kumar Agrawal vs. Union of India, (2014) 2 SCC 609.
72. Joy deep Mukherjee vs. State of West Bengal, (2011) 2 SCC 706.
73. B. Krishna Bhat vs. Union of India, (1990) 3 SCC 65.
74. M. Manohar Reddy vs. Union of India, (2013) 3 SCC 99.
75. Rohtash Kumar vs. State of Haryana, (2013) 14 SCC 290.
76. Viswan vs. Union of India, (1983) 3 SCC 401.
77. Ranjit Thakur vs. Union of India, (1987) 4 SCC 611.
78. Union of India vs. G.S. Bajwa (Ex. Flt. Ltd.), (2003), 9 SCC 630.
79. Ibid 79.
80. P.L. Lakhanpal vs. State of Jammu and Kashmir, AIR 1956, SC 197.

□

Chapter 5
DIRECTIVE PRINCIPLES OF STATE POLICY

The Indian Constitution is first and foremost a social document. It is the Directive Principles which nourish the roots of a democracy, provide strength and vigour to it and attempt to make it a real participatory democracy which does not remain merely a political democracy but also becomes a social and economic democracy with Fundamental Rights available to all irrespective of their power, position or wealth. The dynamic provisions of the Directive Principles fertilise the static provisions of the Fundamental Rights. The object of the Fundamental Rights is to protect individual liberty, but individual liberty cannot be considered in isolation from the socio-economic structure in which it is to operate. There is a real connection between individual liberty and the shape and form of the social and economic structure of the society. There cannot be any individual liberty at all for the large mass of people who are suffering from want and privation of their individual rights by the exploitative economic system. Their individual liberty would come in conflict with the liberty of the socially and economically more powerful class and in the process gets mutilated or destroyed. The real controversy in the present-day society is not between power and freedom but between one form of liberty and another. Under the present socio-economic system, it is the liberty of the few which is in conflict with the liberty of the many. The Directive Principles, therefore, impose an obligation on the State to take positive action for creating socio-economic conditions in which there will be an egalitarian social order with social and economic justice to all so that individual liberty will become a cherished value and the dignity of the individual a living reality, not only for a few privileged persons but for the entire people of the country. Thus, the Directive Principles enjoy a very high place in the constitutional scheme and it is only in the framework of the socio-economic structure envisaged in the Directive Principles that the Fundamental Rights are intended to operate, for it is only then they can become meaningful and significant for the millions of our poor and deprived people, who do not have even the bare necessities of life and who are living below the poverty level.[1]

36. Definition: In this Part, unless the context otherwise requires, "the State" has the same meaning as in Part III.

(Part IV, Article 36)

COMMENTS

The definition of the term "State" is given under Article 12 of the Constitution. The term "the State" includes the Government and Parliament of India and the Government and the Legislature of each of the States and all local or other authorities within the territory of India or under the control of the Government of India. It is wide definition and besides legislature and executive, all government-owned entities, whether a company, a society registered under the Societies Registration Act, 1860 are included within the term "the State."

37. Application of the principles contained in this Part: The provisions contained in this Part shall not be enforceable by any court, but the principles therein laid down are nevertheless fundamental in the governance of the country and it shall be the duty of the State to apply these principles in making laws.

(Part IV, Article 37)

COMMENTS

Part IV Articles 37-51 contain what may be described as the positive obligations of the State and shall secure a social order in which social economic and political justice shall conform to all the institutions of the national life. Wealth and its source of production shall not be concentrated in the hands of the few but shall be distributed so as to subserve the common good.

Characteristics:

1. They are not enforceable in any court and therefore, if a directive principle is infringed, no remedy is available to the aggrieved party in judicial proceedings.
2. They are fundamental in the governance of the country and it shall be the duty of the state to apply these principles in making laws.

It was also quoted by Dr. Ambedkar that "The Constitution also wished to lay down the ideal before those who would be forming the government. That ideal is economic democracy whereby, as far as I am concerned, I understand to mean, one man one vote."

We have left enough room for people with different ways of thinking, with regard to reaching of the ideal of economic democracy to strive in their own way. Without economic democracy, political democracy is meaningless. Directive principles ensure economic democracy.

Article 37 says that the Directive Principles shall not be enforceable by any court, makes the Directive Principles fundamental in the governance of the country and enacts that it shall be the duty of the State to apply the Directive Principles in making laws. However, the courts are giving special importance to the directive principles vis-à-vis fundamental rights as regards their enforceability.[2] The Court can even order the State to enforce the law, particularly when non-enforcement of law leads to denial of a fundamental right. [3] Neither fundamental right is superior to the directive principle nor one supersedes the other. The golden rule is that the fundamental rights and directive principles are to be harmoniously interpreted.

38. State to secure a social order for the promotion of welfare of the people: (1) The State shall strive to promote the welfare of the people by securing and protecting as effectively as it may a social order in which justice, social, economic and political, shall inform all the institutions of the national life.

(2) The State shall, in particular, strive to minimise the inequalities in income, and endeavor to eliminate inequalities in status, facilities and opportunities, not only amongst individuals but also amongst groups of people residing in different areas or engaged in different vocations.

(Part IV, Article 38)

COMMENTS

This provision recognised the need to eliminate and minimise the inequalities in income, which applied not only to individuals but also to groups in different geographical areas or different fields of work.

39. Certain principles of policy to be followed by the State: The State shall, in particular, direct its policy towards securing—

(a) that the citizens, men and women equally, have the right to an adequate means of livelihood;

(b) that the ownership and control of the material resources of the community are so distributed as best to subserve the common good;

(c) that the operation of the economic system does not result in the concentration of wealth and means of production to the common detriment;

(d) that there is equal pay for equal work for both men and women;

(e) that the health and strength of workers, men and women, and the tender age of children are not abused and that citizens are not forced by economic necessity to enter avocations unsuited to their age or strength;

(f) that children are given opportunities and facilities to develop in a healthy manner and in conditions of freedom and dignity and that childhood and youth are protected against exploitation and against moral and material abandonment.

(Part IV, Article 39)

COMMENTS

This Article specially requires the State to ensure for its people the adequate means of livelihood, fair distribution of wealth, equal pay for equal work and protection of child and labour.

Also in the case of Kameshwar Singh[4], it was stated that a law required at doing away with the concentration of big blocks of lands in the hands of few individuals, would subserve the doctrines contained in the sub. (b) and (c) of Article 39. The Monopolies and Restrictive Trade Practices Act, 1969 owes its existence to the provision provided under Article 39(c). After the enactment of the Competition Act, 2002, the Monopolies and Restrictive Trade Practices Act, 1969 stands repealed. Under the Competition Act, 2002, inter alia, the abuse of dominance is a restricted activity, which is to control concentration of wealth in few hands.

Article 39(d) is enforced through the Equal Remuneration Act, 1976. This statute commands against discrimination between men and women who perform similar works.

In Randhir Singh vs. Union of India[5], the Supreme Court has held that although the principle of 'equal pay for equal work' is not expressly declared by our Constitution to be a fundamental right, but it is certainly a constitutional goal under Articles 14, 16 and 39(d) of the Constitution.

In the landmark case, i.e. Kesavananda Bharati,[6] the Supreme Court held that the substantive provision of Article 31C which abrogates the fundamental rights in the interest of land reforms is valid but the latter part of Article 31C which ousts the jurisdiction of the court is invalid. Article 39(b) and (c) contain the elaborate mechanism of socialist and egalitarian society. Thus, even a socialist government can come in power and implement its wide-ranging socialist measures.

39A. Equal justice and free legal aid: The State shall secure that the operation of the legal system promotes justice, on a basis of equal opportunity, and shall, in particular, provide free legal aid, by suitable legislation or schemes or in any other way, to ensure that opportunities for securing justice are not denied to any citizen by reason of economic or other disabilities.

(Part IV, Article 39A)

COMMENTS

In pursuance of this provision, Parliament has passed the Legal Services Authorities Act, 1987 and free legal aid is available from the District court to the highest court.

40. Organisation of Village Panchayats: The State shall take steps to organise village panchayats and endow them with such powers and authority as may be necessary to enable them to function as units of self-government.

(Part IV, Article 40)

COMMENTS

In the Constitutional Assembly, members wanted to keep Panchayat Raj as one of the fundamental rights.[7] Mahatma Gandhi also advocated for Panchayats. But the new Legislators after assuming power overlooked Panchayats to wield unbridled powers themselves, which ultimately bred corruption. In the year 1992 by 73rd Constitution Amendment Act, Part IX was added to the Constitution creating Panchayats at three tiers, i.e. village, block and district. Now the ideal of the Constitution Makers is being realised making Panchayats as constitutional units of self-government.

41. Right to work, to education and to public assistance in certain cases: The State shall, within the limits of its economic capacity and development, make effective provision for securing the right to work, to education and to public assistance in cases of unemployment, old age, sickness and disablement, and in other cases of undeserved want.

(Part IV, Article 41)

COMMENTS

Article 41 directs the State to make effective provision for securing the right to work, to education and to public assistance in cases of unemployment, old age, sickness and disablement, and in other cases of undeserved want. This is social security in its widest sense. Even the State has to pay compensation to workers whose continuous employment has suffered due to short supply of electricity.[8] Poverty eradication continues to be a major challenge for social and economic policies. MNREGA is a major legislative initiative as well as executive action to reach to the poorest of the poor in the country.

42. Provision for just and humane conditions of work and maternity relief: The State shall make provision for securing just and humane conditions of work and for maternity relief.

(Part IV, Article 42)

COMMENTS

Article 42 also enumerates the State's obligation to make provision for Maternity Relief. The Maternity Benefit Act, 1961 and the Employee's State Insurance Act, 1948 for factories are important legislation. The Court even allowed the maternity benefit to the non-regulated female workers in view of this Directive.[9]

43. Living wage, etc., for workers: The State shall endeavor to secure, by suitable legislation or economic organisation or in any other way, to all workers, agricultural, industrial or otherwise, work, a living wage, conditions of work ensuring a decent standard of life and full enjoyment of leisure and social and cultural opportunities and, in particular, the State shall endeavor to promote cottage industries on an individual or co-operative basis in rural areas.

(Part IV, Article 43)

COMMENTS

The concept of living wage has been discussed by Supreme Court in the case of Express Newspaper vs. Union of India.[10] The idea is that every workman shall have a wage which will maintain him in the highest state of industrial efficiency, which will enable him to provide his family with all the material things which are needed for their health and physical well-being enough to enable him to qualify to discharge his duties as a citizen. The amount of living wage in money terms will vary as between trade and trade. However, the Minimum Wages Act is one statute which is beneficial law from the factory worker to the farm labourer, but remains largely unimplemented. The last part of the directive in the Article has now been incorporated as full- fledged chapter IX B on the Co-operative Societies in the Constitution by the Amendment in the year 2012 and in Article 43B itself.

43A. Participation of workers in management of industries: The State shall take steps, by suitable legislation or in any other way, to secure the participation of workers in the management of undertakings, establishments or other organisations engaged in any industry.

(Part IV, Article 43A)

COMMENTS

Article 43A which was introduced by the 42nd Amendment in 1976 provides that the State shall take steps by suitable legislation or any other means to secure the participation of workers in the management of industrial establishments. An appropriate law in general is required to implement Article 43A. However, the Banking Companies (Acquisition and Transfer of Undertakings) Act, 1970 provides to include representatives of the employees on the Board of Directors, so also in cases of some Central Public Sector Undertakings. This has helped to improve production, quality of product and work life.

43B. Promotion of co-operative societies: The State shall endeavour to promote voluntary formation, autonomous functioning, democratic control and professional management of co-operative societies.

(Part IV, Article 43B)

44. Uniform civil code for the citizens: The State shall endeavour to secure for the citizens a uniform civil code throughout the territory of India.

(Part IV, Article 44)

COMMENTS

When one has to consolidate a community, one has to take into consideration the benefit which may flow to the whole community and not to the customs or part of it. It is very necessary that our personal lives, subject to restrictions of secular aspects, must be unified in such a way that as early as possible, we may be able to say that we are a strong and a consolidated nation even by the way we live by our personal laws. The Supreme Court was earlier not in favour to impose a uniform civil code in the country and did not interfere in the Muslim Personal Law. Bu due to impact of globalisation and modernisation of India, even the Apex Court is veering around in favour of a uniform civil code.

45. Provision for early childhood care and education to children below the age of six years: The State shall endeavour to provide early childhood care and education for all children until they complete the age of six years.

(Part IV, Article 45)

COMMENTS

Earlier the Article contained for free and compulsory uptc the age of 14 years. This is the way to develop India. After the observation of the Supreme Court[11] that educated citizens are foundation of stability of democracy, social integration and to eliminate social evils, the original Article was incorporated in Article 21A as a fundamental right by Amendment in 2002.

46. Promotion of educational and economic interests of Scheduled Castes, Scheduled Tribes and other weaker sections: The State shall promote with special care the educational and economic interests of the weaker sections of the people, and, in particular, of the Scheduled Castes and the Scheduled Tribes, and shall protect them from social injustice and all forms of exploitation.

(Part IV, Article 46)

COMMENTS

The Supreme Court has also read the right to development in this Article read with Articles 21, 38 and 39.[12]

47. Duty of the State to raise the level of nutrition and the standard of living and to improve public health: The State shall regard the raising of the level of nutrition and the standard of living of its people and the improvement of public health as among its primary duties and, in particular, the State shall endeavor to bring about prohibition of the consumption except for medicinal purposes of intoxicating drinks and of drugs which are injurious to health.

(Part IV, Article 47)

COMMENTS

In the case of State of Bombay vs. F.M. Balsara:[13] The directive that the State shall endeavour to bring about prohibition of the consumption of the intoxicating drinks and drugs was taken into consideration. It was held that the restriction imposed by the Bombay Prohibition Act in respect of possession, sale, use or consumption of liquor were not unreasonable restrictions on the exercise of right guaranteed under Act 19 (1) to prevent misuse of intoxicating drinks or drugs in the name of medicinal purpose.

48. Organisation of agriculture and animal husbandry: The State shall endeavour to organise agriculture and animal husbandry on modern and scientific lines and shall, in particular, take steps for preserving and improving the breeds, and prohibiting the slaughter of cows and calves and other milch and draught cattle.

(Part IV, Article 48)

COMMENTS

The directive for taking steps for preventing the slaughter of animals is quite explicit and positive and contemplates a ban on the slaughter of the several categories of animals specified therein. There are only 7 States or Union Territories in India (out of a total of 29 States and 7 UTs), namely Arunachal Pradesh, Kerala, Meghalaya, Mizoram, Nagaland, Tripura and Lakshadweep, which have no law banning cow slaughter in one form or another. All other remaining States and UTs (Twenty-Nine) have enacted laws to prevent the slaughter of cow and its progeny in one form or another. However, the ban did not extend to cattle which ceased to be milch or draught.[14]

48A. Protection and improvement of environment and safeguarding of forests and wildlife: The State shall endeavour to protect and improve the environment and to safeguard the forests and wildlife of the country.

(Part IV, Article 48A)

COMMENTS

The Environment (Protection) Act, 1986, the Air (Prevention & Control of Pollution) Act, 1981, The Water (Prevention and Control of Pollution) Act 1974, etc. have been enforced for the protection of environment, forests, wildlife and even to control water, air and land pollution. Several principles of environmental law have been developed like 'polluter to pay', etc. under this Article in conjunction with Articles 21 and 51 (g).[15] The Supreme Court is even monitoring Ganga Cleaning Project against claims by the Union Government to make the Ganga free of pollution by the year 2017.

49. Protection of monuments and places and objects of national importance: It shall be the obligation of the State to protect every monument or place or object of artistic or historic interest, declared by or under law made by Parliament to be of national importance, from spoliation, disfigurement, destruction, removal, disposal or export, as the case may be.

(Part IV, Article 49)

COMMENTS

Article 49 of the Directive Principles requires the State to protect monuments and places and objects of national importance. For the purpose of protecting culture in all its facets and in developing it, the State has to set apart the necessary resources. Displaying notices under the Ancient Monuments Preservation Act, 1904 without due enforcement and preservation will be futile.

50. Separation of judiciary from executive: The State shall take steps to separate the judiciary from the executive in the public services of the State.

(Part IV, Article 50)

COMMENTS

Our Constitution contemplates that one organ of the government will not encroach upon the functions that essentially belong to another.[16] The idea was to take away judicial functions from the executive officers. But it does not mean that in the name of independence, judiciary is not accountable. It is very much a service to the people of India. And, therefore, there should be Judicial Impact Assessment[17] to undertake quantitative assessment of cases and statutes.

51. Promotion of international peace and security: The State shall endeavour to—

(a) Promote international peace and security;
(b) Maintain just and honourable relations between nations;
(c) Foster respect for international law and treaty obligations in the dealings of organised people with one another; and
(d) Encourage settlement of international disputes by arbitration.

51A. Fundamental Duties: It shall be the duty of every citizen of India—

(a) to abide by the Constitution and respect its ideals and institutions, the National Flag and the National Anthem;

(b) to cherish and follow the noble ideals which inspired our national struggle for freedom;
(c) to uphold and protect the sovereignty, unity and integrity of India;
(d) to defend the country and render national service when called upon to do so;
(e) to promote harmony and the spirit of common brotherhood amongst all the people of India transcending religious, linguistic and regional or sectional diversities; to renounce practices derogatory to the dignity of women;
(f) to value and preserve the rich heritage of our composite culture;
(g) to protect and improve the natural environment, including forests, lakes, rivers and wildlife, and to have compassion for-living creatures;
(h) to develop the scientific temper, humanism and the spirit of inquiry and reform;
(i) to safeguard public property and to abjure violence;
(j) to strive towards excellence in all spheres of individual and collective activity so that the nation constantly rises to higher levels of endeavour and achievement;
(k) who is a parent or guardian to provide opportunities for education to his child or, as the case may be, ward between the age of six and fourteen years.

(Part IVA, Article 51A)

COMMENTS

Rights and duties are two sides of a coin. According to Gandhiji, "The source of right is duty. If we all discharge our duties, rights will not be far to seek. If leaving duties unperformed we run after rights, they will escape us."

The Constitution of India has provided fundamental rights to all citizens-persons in India, i.e. right to equality, right to freedom including free speech and expression, right against exploitation, right to freedom of religion, cultural and educational rights, right to constitutional remedies. The Supreme Court has added few more rights through interpretation in various judgements like right to life, right to fair and speedy trial, right to health, right to livelihood right to work and even right to development. Other rights can make the life more meaningful and worth living, like prisoner's right to have necessities of life, right to women to be treated with decency and dignity, right of privacy, right to go abroad, right against custodial violence, right to health and medical aid of workers, right to reputation, right to freedom from noise pollution, right of hearing, etc. However, there are corresponding eleven fundamental duties in the new Article 51(A). The first and foremost duty assigned to every citizen of India is to abide by the Constitution and respect its ideals and institutions, the National Flag and the National Anthem. We are all governed and guided by this Constitution irrespective of caste, religion, race, sex, etc. Each citizen must, therefore, not only refrain from any such activity but also do his best to prevent any miscreant trying to show disrespect to our national symbols. Every nation is proud of its citizens because of their dedication, sincerity and patriotism. We, the citizens of India, have to be equally proud of our nation, our Constitution, our Flag and our Anthem.

We must put the nation above our narrow personal interests, and then only we will be able to protect our hard-earned freedom and sovereignty. Secondly, the citizens of India must cherish and follow the noble ideals, which inspired the national struggle for freedom. Thirdly, we should protect the sovereignty, unity and integrity of India is a pre-eminent national obligation of all citizens of India. In a democratic system of governance, sovereignty lies with the people. To defend our sovereignty is our own responsibility.

Fourthly, citizens at large play the most vital role in a variety of ways. Civilians may be required also to take up arms in defence of the country, if the situation warrants it. By fighting to defend the country, the citizens are fighting only to defend their own liberty and that of their posterity. The citizens will have to come forward if required by the State. Fifthly, the citizens should promote harmony and the spirit of common brotherhood amongst all the people of India transcending religious, linguistic and regional or sectional diversities; to renounce practices derogatory to the dignity of women. Thus, the Constitution advises not to indulge in conflicts based on religion, caste and to abhor fissiparous tendencies.

Spirit of brotherhood should come very normally among the citizens of a country like India where the norm has been to consider the entire world as one family. The Constitution also casts upon us the fundamental duty of ensuring that all practices derogatory to the dignity of women are renounced. Sixthly, we should preserve the rich heritage of our composite culture and preserve communal harmony as our fundamental duty. It becomes the ardent duty of every citizen to ensure that our rich monuments and pieces of art are not in any way damaged, disfigured, scratched or subjected to vandalism or greed of unscrupulous traders and smugglers.

In the face of menace of the increasing pollution and environmental degradation, it is the duty of every citizen to protect and improve natural environment, including forests, lakes, rivers and wildlife and to have noise pollution and large-scale denudation of forests under check which is causing immense harm to all human life on earth. The mindless and wanton deforestation in the name of the needs of development is causing havoc in the form of natural calamities and imbalances. By protecting our forest cover, planting new trees, cleaning rivers, conserving water resources, reforesting wastelands, hills and mountains and controlling pollution in cities, villages and industrial units, we can help save the future of our fellow citizens and of planet earth itself. What is needed is a concerted effort through voluntary citizen initiatives. One of our great founding fathers, Jawaharlal Nehru always laid great emphasis on the need for Indian citizens developing a scientific temper and a spirit of inquiry – an inquisitiveness for learning from developments around the world. It is the bounden duty of every citizen to preserve and promote a scientific temper and a spirit of inquiry to keep pace with the fast- changing world. Also, science and technology should be mixed with a sense of humanism because ultimately the end of all progress is the human being and the quality of life and relationships that is developed. It is most unfortunate that in a country which preaches non-violence to the rest of the world, we see from time to time spectacles of senseless violence and destruction of public property indulged in by a few of its citizens. This is why it became necessary to prescribe the responsibility "to safeguard public property and abjure violence" as a fundamental citizenship duty.

The tenth duty is the drive for excellence in all spheres of individual and collective activity. It is the demand of times and a basic requirement in a highly competitive world. Nothing but the best would have survival potential in tomorrow's world.

This would include respect for professional obligations and excellence. Whatever work we take up either as individual citizens or as groups, our effort should be directed to achieving the goal of excellence. Also, special emphasis is called for in the area of collective activity. Right to education is declared as a fundamental right. The eleventh duty is of the parents who do not send their wards to schools. They are not responsible citizens. Every parent or guardian is to help to provide opportunities for education to his child or ward between the age of 6 and 14 years. This has been included as the Eleventh duty in the Constitution in the year 2002.

Kesavananda Bharati case (1973), the Supreme Court held that each religion made its contribution to enrich the composite Indian culture as a happy blend or synthesis. Our religious tolerance received reflection in our Constitutional creed.

The Supreme Court suggested that since the duties are obligatory on citizens, the state should also observe them. In Vishaka Case (1997), the Supreme Court held that in appropriate cases, if non-observance of duty by one citizen can be established as violation of the right of another, appropriate remedy may be provided by courts inspite the fundamental duties are not enforceable generally in courts.

The purpose of incorporating the fundamental duties in the Constitution is to make the citizens aware of their social and economic obligations and to warn them to do and not to do certain things in the interest of their country, their fellow citizens and themselves. Even duty to vote should be included as a fundamental duty. This will make our government truly representative. A man who does not think it worthwhile to exercise this is strangely ignorant of the real basis of all prosperity that he has or hopes for and the real duty which rests upon him as a man of elementary morals.

A man who will not take the trouble to vote is a poor spirited fellow willing to live on the labours of others and to shirk an honourable obligation, to do his share in return. The 'Swachh Bharat' movement launched by Prime Minister Narendra Modi is to remind all citizens their duty to preserve and keep the environment clean around them. However, a country specially of size of India cannot be progress only by governmental efforts. A country progresses by the due awareness and performance of duties by its citizens.

REFERENCES

1. Minerva Mills vs. Union of India, (1980) 2 SCC 591.
2. Uni Krishnan, J.P. vs. State of A.P. (1993) 1 SCC 645.
3. Bandhua Mukti Morcha Vs. Union of India, (1984) 3 SCC 161.
4. State of Bihar vs. Kameshwar Singh, AIR (1952) SC 252.
5. AIR 1982 SC 879.
6. Kesavananda Bharati vs. State of Kerala and another, (1973) 4 SCC 225.
7. Constituent Assembly debate 3 Vol. IX P-1191-92.
8. Radha Krishna Mills Ltd. vs. Industrial Tribunal, AIR 1954 Mad. 686.
9. MCD vs. Female Workers (Muster Roll), (2000) 3 SCC 224.
10. AIR 1958 SC 578.
11. Bandhua Mukti Morcha vs. Union of India & Ors. (1997) 10 SCC 549.
12. Samatha vs. State of A.P. (1997) 8 SCC 191.
13. AIR 1951 SC 318, 327.
14. Mohd. Hanif Quareshi vs. State of Bihar, AIR 1958 SC 731.
15. M.C. Mehta vs. Union of India, (2002) 4 SCC 356.
16. Ram Jawaya Kapur vs. State of Punjab, AIR 1951 SC 549.
17. Salem Advocates Bar Association (II) vs. Union of India, (2005) 6 SCC 344.

□

Chapter 6
THE EXECUTIVE

A-Union Executive

52. The President of India: There shall be a President of India.

(Part V, Article 52)

COMMENTS

India has an elected President at the head of the Republic like the United States. India doesn't have a monarchy. But India has a unique position of being a Parliamentary democracy and a federal polity with permanent President.

53. Executive Power of the Union: (1) The executive power of the Union shall be vested in the President and shall be exercised by him either directly or through officers subordinate to him in accordance with this Constitution.

(2) Without prejudice to the generality of the foregoing provision, the supreme command of the Defence Forces of the Union shall be vested in the President and the exercise thereof shall be regulated by law.

(3) Nothing in this Article shall—(a) be deemed to transfer to the President any functions conferred by any existing law on the Government of any State or other authority; or (b) prevent Parliament from conferring by law functions on authorities other than the President.

(Part V, Article 53)

COMMENTS

The executive function comprises both the determination of the policy as well as carrying it into execution, the maintenance of order, the promotion of social and economic welfare, the direction of foreign policy, the carrying on or supervision of the general administration of the State executive functions etc. The executive power connotes the residue of governmental functions that remain after legislative and judicial functions are taken away. The executive power so long as it does not violate the Constitution or the law, may be exercised without prior legislative support. The President in India is also the supreme commander of armed forces. He has legislative power of the summoning, prorogation, dissolution, etc. of the Legislatures, initiation and assent to legislation and the like. President also has judicial power, i.e. granting of pardons, reprieves, etc. to persons convicted of crime.

The administrative power includes the power to appoint and remove the high dignitaries of the State like the Prime Minister of India, Chairman, UPSC. The Judges of the Supreme Court and High Courts, Attorney General for India, the Governors, etc.

A question was raised whether a person who was not a member of either House of Parliament could be appointed Prime Minister. It was held that under Article 75(5), such a person could be a Minister for six months and since the Prime Minister was also a Minister, he could be appointed from among non-members if he had the confidence of the House.[1]

In some such situations, the role of the President may become most crucial and decisive. This happened, for instance, when Charan Singh, Rajiv Gandhi and Chandra Shekhar came to be appointed to the office of Prime Minister.

54. Election of President: The President shall be elected by the Members of an electoral college consisting of:

(a) the elected members of both the Houses of Parliament; and

(b) the elected members of the Legislative Assemblies of the States.

Explanation: In this Article and in Article 55, "State"

includes the National Capital Territory of Delhi and the Union Territory of Pondicherry.

(Part V, Article 54)

55. Manner of Election of President: (1) As far as practicable, there shall be uniformity in the scale of representation of the different States at the election of the President.

(2) For the purpose of securing such uniformity among the States inter se as well as parity between the States as a whole and the Union, the number of votes which each elected member of Parliament and of the Legislative Assembly of each State is entitled to cast at such election shall be determined in the following manner: (a) every elected member of the Legislative Assembly of a State shall have as many votes as there are multiples of one thousand in the quotient obtained by dividing the population of the State by the total number of the elected members of the Assembly; (b) if, after taking the said multiples of one thousand, the remainder is not less than five hundred, then the vote of each member referred to in sub-clause (a) shall be further increased by one; (c) each elected member of either House of Parliament shall have such number of votes as may be obtained by dividing the total number of votes assigned to the members of the Legislative Assemblies of the States under sub-clauses (a) and (b) by the total number of the elected members of both the Houses of Parliament, fractions exceeding one-half being counted as one and other fractions being disregarded.

(3) The election of the President shall be held in accordance with the system of proportional representation by means of the single transferable vote and the voting at such election shall be by secret ballot.

Explanation: In this Article, the expression "population" means the population as ascertained at the last preceding census of which the relevant figures have been published: Provided that the reference in this Explanation to the last preceding census of which the relevant figures have been published shall, until the relevant figures for the first census taken after the year 2026 have been published, be construed as a reference to the 1971 census.

(Part V, Article 55)

COMMENTS

It is provided that the purpose of securing uniformity among the States inter se as well as parity between the States as a whole and the Union, the number of votes which each elected member of Parliament and of the Legislative Assembly of each State is entitled to cast at such election shall be determined in the following manner.

Every elected member of the Legislative Assembly of a State shall have as many votes as there are multiples of one thousand in the quotient obtained by dividing the population of the State by the total number of elected members of the Assembly.

If, after taking the said multiples of one thousand, the remainder is not less than five hundred, then the vote of each member referred to in (a) above shall be further increased by one.

Illustration

Total population of a State	43,502,708
Total no. of elected members in the Assembly	294
No. of votes for each value of each vote	43,502,708
	Divided by 1000 × 294
	147.96 or 148

(c) Each elected member of either House of Parliament shall have such number of votes as may be obtained by dividing the total number of votes assigned to the members of the Legislative Assemblies of the States under (a) and (b) above by the total number of elected members of both the Houses of Parliament, fractions exceeding one half being counted as one and other fractions being disregarded.

The total number of members in the electoral college for a Presidential election, for example, was 4,848 as detailed below:

Rajya Sabha	233
Lok Sabha	543
State assemblies	4,072
Total	4,848

The method of providing parity between the States as a whole on the one hand and the Union on the other meant that the whole process tilted towards justifying the federal polity of India. The States got double representation – first as members of the Council of States and secondly as members of the State Assemblies. The idea was to provide scale of representation of different States, inter se on the basis of population and to respect the 'one man one vote' principle.

56. Term of Office of President: (1) the President shall hold office for a term of five years from the date on which he enters upon his office:

Provided that:

(a) The President may, by writing under his hand addressed to the Vice President, resign his office;

(b) The President may, for violation of the Constitution, be removed from office by impeachment in the manner provided in Article 61;

(c) The President shall, notwithstanding the expiration of his term, continue to hold office until his successor enters upon his office.

(2) Any resignation addressed to the Vice President under clause (a) of the proviso to clause (1) shall forthwith be communicated by him to the Speaker of the House of the People.

(Part V, Article 56)

57. Eligibility for re-election: A person who holds, or who has held, office as President shall, subject to the other provisions of this Constitution, be eligible for re-election to that office.

(Part V, Article 57)

COMMENTS

Unlike American President, one person can be elected President a number of times.

58. Qualification for Election as President: (1) No person shall be eligible for election as President unless he—(a) is a citizen of India, (b) has completed the age of thirty-five years, and (c) is qualified for election as a member of the House of the People. (2) A person shall not be eligible for election as President if he holds any office of profit under the Government of India or the Government of any State or under any local or other authority subject to the control of any of the said Governments.

Explanation: For the purposes of this Article, a person shall not be deemed to hold any office of profit by reason only that he is the President or Vice-President of the Union or the Governor of any State or is a Minister either for the Union or for any State.

(Part V, Article 58)

COMMENTS

In order to be an office of profit, the office must carry various pecuniary benefits such as providing official accomodation or a chaffeur-driven car.[2]

However, persons holding employment under the State shall not be entitled to seek election to the President's office.

59. Conditions of President's Office: (1) The President shall not be a member of either House of Parliament or of a House of the Legislature of any State, and if a member of either House of Parliament or of a House of the legislature of any State be elected President, he shall be deemed to have vacated his seat in that House on the date on which he enters upon his office as President.

(2) The President shall not hold any other office of Profit.

(3) The President shall be entitled without payment of rent to the use of his official residences and shall also be entitled to such emoluments, allowances and privileges as may be determined by Parliament by law and, until provision in that behalf is so made, such emoluments, allowances and privileges as are specified in the Second Schedule.

(4) The emoluments and allowances of the President shall not be diminished during his term of office.

(Part V, Article 59)

60. Oath or affirmation by the President: Every President and every person acting as President or discharging the functions of the President shall, before entering upon his office, make and subscribe in the presence of the Chief Justice of India or, in his absence, the senior most Judge of the Supreme Court available, an oath or affirmation in the following form, that is to say—

"I, A.B., do swear in the name of God solemnly affirm that I will faithfully execute the office of President (or discharge the functions of the President) of India and will to the best of my ability preserve, protect and defend the Constitution and the law and that I will devote myself to the service and well-being of the people of India."

61. Procedure for impeachment of the President: (1) When a President is to be impeached for violation of the Constitution, the charge shall be preferred by either House of Parliament.

(2) No such charge shall be preferred unless—

(a) the proposal to prefer such charge is contained in a resolution which has been moved after at least fourteen days' notice in writing signed by not less than one-fourth of the total number of members of the House has been given of their intention to move the resolution, and

(b) such resolution has been passed by a majority of not less than two-thirds of the total membership of the House.

(3) When a charge has been so preferred by either House of Parliament, the other House shall investigate the charge or cause the charge to be investigated and the President shall have the right to appear and to be represented at such investigation.

(4) If as a result of the investigation a resolution is passed by a majority of not less than two-thirds of the total membership of the House by which the charge was investigated or caused to be investigated, declaring that the charge preferred against the President has been sustained, such resolution shall have the effect of removing the President from his office as from the date on which the resolution is so passed.

62. Time of holding election to fill vacancy in the office of President and the term of office of person elected to fill casual vacancy: (1) An election to fill a vacancy caused by the expiration of the term of office of President shall be completed before the expiration of the term.

(2) An election to fill a vacancy in the office of President occurring by reason of his death, resignation or removal, or otherwise shall be held as soon as possible after, and in no case later than six months from, the date of occurrence of the vacancy; and the person elected to fill the vacancy shall, subject to the provisions of Article 56, be entitled to hold office for the full term of five years from the date on which he enters upon his office.

63. The Vice-President of India: There shall be a Vice-President of India.

64. The Vice-President to be *ex officio* Chairman of the Council of States: The Vice-President shall be ex officio Chairman of the Council of States and shall not hold any other office of profit:

Provided that during any period when the Vice-President acts as President or discharges the functions of the President under Article 65, he shall not perform the duties of the office of Chairman of the Council of States and shall not be entitled to any salary or allowance payable to the Chairman of the Council of States under Article 97.

65. The Vice-President to act as President or to discharge his functions during casual vacancies in the office, or during the absence, of President: (1) In the event of the occurrence of any vacancy in the office of the President by reason of his death, resignation or removal, or otherwise, the Vice-President shall act as President until the date on which a new President elected in accordance with the provisions of this Chapter to fill such vacancy enters upon his office.

(2) When the President is unable to discharge his functions owing to absence, illness or any other cause, the Vice-President

shall discharge his functions until the date on which the President resumes his duties.

(3) The Vice-President shall, during, and in respect of, the period while he is so acting as, or discharging the functions of, President, have all the powers and immunities of the President and be entitled to such emoluments, allowances and privileges as may be determined by Parliament by law and, until provision in that behalf is so made, such emoluments, allowances and privileges as are specified in the Second Schedule.

66. Election of Vice-President: (1) The Vice-President shall be elected by the members of an electoral college consisting of the members of both the Houses of Parliament in accordance with the system of proportional representation by means of the single transferable vote and the voting at such election shall be by secret ballot.

(2) The Vice-President shall not be a member of either House of Parliament or of a House of the Legislature of any State, and if a member of either House of Parliament or of a House of the Legislature of any State be elected Vice-President, he shall be deemed to have vacated his seat in that House on the date on which he enters upon his office as Vice-President.

(3) No person shall be eligible for election as Vice-President unless he—

(a) is a citizen of India;

(b) has completed the age of thirty-five years; and

(c) is qualified for election as a member of the Council of States.

(4) A person shall not be eligible for election as Vice-President if he holds any office of profit under the Government of India or the Government of any State or under any local or other authority subject to the control of any of the said Governments.

Explanation: For the purposes of this Article, a person shall not be deemed to hold any office of profit by reason only that he is the President or Vice-President of the Union or the Governor of any State or is a Minister either for the Union or for any State.

67. Term of office of Vice-President: The Vice-President shall hold office for a term of five years from the date on which he enters upon his office:

Provided that—

(a) a Vice-President may, by writing under his hand addressed to the President, resign his office;

(b) a Vice-President may be removed from his office by a resolution of the Council of States passed by a majority of all the then members of the Council and agreed to by the House of the People; but no resolution for the purpose of this clause shall be moved unless at least fourteen days' notice has been given of the intention to move the resolution;

(c) a Vice-President shall, notwithstanding the expiration of his term, continue to hold office until his successor enters upon his office.

68. Time of holding election to fill vacancy in the office of Vice-President and the term of office of person elected to fill casual vacancy: (1) An election to fill a vacancy caused by the expiration of the term of office of Vice-President shall be completed before the expiration of the term.

(2) An election to fill a vacancy in the office of Vice-President occurring by reason of his death, resignation or removal, or otherwise shall be held as soon as possible after the occurrence of the vacancy, and the person elected to fill the vacancy shall, subject to the provisions of Article 67, be entitled to hold office for the full term of five years from the date on which he enters upon his office.

69. Oath or affirmation by the Vice-President: Every Vice-President shall, before entering upon his office, make and subscribe before the President, or some person appointed in that behalf by him, an oath or affirmation in the following form, that is to say—

"I, A.B., do swear in the name of God that I will bear true solemnly affirm faith and allegiance to the Constitution of India as by law established and that I will faithfully discharge the duty upon which I am about to enter."

(Part V, Article 59-69)

70. Discharge of President's function in other contingencies: Parliament may make such provisions as it thinks fit for the discharge of the functions of the President in any contingency not provided for in this chapter.

(Part V, Article 70)

71. Matters relating to, or connected with the election of a President or Vice-President: (1) All doubts and disputes arising out of or in connection with the election of a President or Vice-President shall be inquired into and decided by the Supreme Court whose decision shall be final.

(2) If the election of a person as President or Vice- President is declared void by the Supreme Court, acts done by him in the exercise and performance of the powers and duties of the office of President or Vice-President, as the case may be, on or before the date of the decision of the Supreme Court shall not be invalidated by reason of that declaration.

(3) Subject to the provisions of this Constitution, Parliament may by law regulate any matter relating to or connected with the elections of a President or Vice President.

(4) The election of a person as President or Vice President shall not be called in question on the ground of the existence of any vacancy for whatever reason among the members of the electoral college electing him.

(Part V, Article 71)

COMMENTS

The Supreme Court has been given the exclusive authority to decide all doubts and disputes connected with the election of the President or the Vice President. The election of N.S. Reddy was challenged which was held on 19th July, 1977. The Supreme Court held that the Petitioner had no locus standi as per law to maintain the petition. The petitioner was not duly nominated nor was one who could claim to be so nominated and that this nomination paper was rightly rejected by the returning officer as required under the Presidential and Vice Presidential Elections Act, 1952.[3]

In Indira Nehru Gandhi vs. Raj Narain case[4], the Supreme Court struck down Article 329-A Clause (4) of the Constitution on the ground that it violated the basic structure of the Constitution as Parliament could not exercise, judicial power for decisions of election disputes pending before the Supreme Court. The Supreme Court made the institution of President permanent and held that the Presidential Election cannot be stayed till all vacancies in Parliament and State Legislatures are filled.[5] Even if there is no elected member of the State Legislative Assembly who qualifies, the election of the President will be held.

72. Power of President to grant pardons, etc. and to suspend, remit or commute sentences in certain cases: (1) The President shall have the power to grant pardons, reprieves, respites or remissions of punishment or to suspend, remit or commute the sentence of any person convicted of any offence:

(a) in all cases where the punishment or sentence is by a Court Martial;

(b) in all cases where the punishment or sentence is for an offence against any law relating to a matter to which the executive power of the Union extends.

(c) in all cases where the sentence is a sentence of death.

(2) Nothing in sub clause (a) of clause (1) shall affect the power conferred by law on any office of the Armed Forces of the Union to suspend, remit or commute a sentence passed by a Court Martial.

(3) Nothing in sub-clause (c) of clause (1) shall affect the power to suspend, remit or commute a sentence of death exercisable by the Governor of a State under any law for the time being in force.

(Part V, Article 72)

COMMENTS

A pardon is an act of grace. It cannot be demanded as a matter of right. A pardon may be absolute or conditional. This power acts as safety valve against rigour of law which is very rigid and human action is very flexible. None can foresee all facets of human action or omission. No human system also of judicial administration can be free from imperfections.

Therefore, power of pardon can be exercised only by the head of executive. The pardoning power may be exercised at any time after commission of an offence either before legal proceedings are taken or during their pendency or either before or after conviction.

The President has wide power of clemency under the following categories:

1. Reprieve, i.e. a temporary suspension of punishment fixed by law;
2. Respite, i.e. postponement to the future of the execution of sentence.
3. Commutation, i.e. changing a punishment to one of a different sort than that originally proposed; and
4. Remission, i.e. reduction of the amount of punishment without changing the character of punishment.

In Kehar Singh's case,[6] the Supreme Court held that the President's power under Article 72 is of executive character and the petitioner (condemned person to death) has no right to insist on oral hearing before the President. But the Court reiterated that the scope of Article 72 is judicially determinable and the President was not right in rejecting, Kehar Singh's petition on the ground that he could not go into the merits of his conviction by the courts. However, this power of the President is not open to judicial review, except to the limited extent as in Mani Ram's case.[6] It should be exercised when the Presidential decision is irrational, arbitrary, discriminatory or mala fide. The power of clemency is to be exercised cautiously.

Following guidelines have been laid down for judicial review under Articles 72 and 161.[7]

1. That the order has been passed without application of mind.
2. That the order is mala fide;
3. That the order has been passed on extraneous or wholly irrelevant consideration;

4. That the relevant materials have been kept out of consideration;
5. That the order suffers from arbitrariness.

However, the delay in deciding the mercy petition under Article 72/161 has come under criticism by the Supreme Court. And the Supreme Court commuted the death sentence into life imprisonment because the condemned person has already suffered a lot under apprehension of death.[8]

However, while considering delay, the Court has overlooked the delay caused by the courts in disposal of cases and the misuse of clemency procedure by prisoners by way of multiple petitions before various authorities and courts.

(Part V, Article 73)

73. Extent of executive power of the Union: (1) Subject to the provisions of this Constitution, the executive power of the Union shall extend:

(a) to the matters with respect to which Parliament has power to make laws; and
(b) to the exercise of such rights, authority and jurisdiction as are exercisable by the Government of India by virtue of any treaty or agreement.

Provided that the executive power referred to in sub-clause (a) shall not, save as expressly provided in this Constitution or in any law made by the Parliament, extend in any State to matters with respect to which the Legislature of the State has also power to make laws.

(2) Until otherwise provided by the Parliament, a State and any officer or authority of a State may, notwithstanding anything in this Article, continue to exercise in matters with respect to which the Parliament has power to make laws for that State such executive power or functions as the State or officer or authority thereof could exercise immediately before the commencement of this Constitution.

(Part V, Article 73)

COMMENTS

The executive power headed by the President of the

Centre extends to matters with respect to which the Parliament can make laws. The executive power is co-extensive with the legislative competence of the Union. In respect of matters in Concurrent List under Seventh Schedule of the Constitution, the primary power lies with States and exceptionally in Union.

However, the Parliament can decide to take over the executive power in relation to such matters. The treaty making power, however, squarely falls within Article 73.[10] The Union executive can exercise such rights, authority and jurisdiction as are exercisable by India by virtue of any treaty or agreement. An adjustment of a boundary which international law regards as valid, between two nations should be recognised by the courts and the executive can always implement it unless it involves cession of territory in which case Parliamentary intervention should be had.

Council of Ministers

74. Council of Ministers to aid and advise President: (1) There shall be a Council of Ministers with the Prime Minister at the head to aid and advise the President who shall, in the exercise of his functions, act in accordance with such advice:

Provided that the President may require the Council of Ministers to reconsider such advice, either generally or otherwise, and the President shall Act in accordance with the advice tendered after such reconsideration.

(2) The question whether any, and if so what, advice was tendered by Ministers to the President shall not be inquired into in any court.

(Part V, Article 74)

COMMENTS

Though the executive power of the Union is vested in the President, he exercises his power with the aid and advice of the Council of Ministers. The Prime Minister is head of the Council of Ministers. The President has discretion to appoint the Prime Minister but he has to see that the Prime Minister enjoys the confidence of the Houses or commands the majority in the House. The Prime Minister functions as the link or the buckle between the President and the Council of Ministers. Article 75(3) contains that the Council of Ministers shall be collectively responsible to the House of People. This principle of 'collective responsibility' is the basis of the Parliamentary democracy which has been adopted in India. Accordingly, the Council of Ministers is answerable to the Parliament for the acts of the Government and not the President. It was made binding by Article 74(1) in 1976 by the 44th Amendment that the President shall, in exercise of his functions, act in accordance with the advice tendered by the Council of Ministers. However, he may send any advice by the Prime Minister for reconsideration by the Council of Ministers. But if the same advice is again tendered, the President shall be bound to okay that. If the President doesn't agree with the advice of the Council of Ministers, the Council of Ministers may resign and then the President will not be able to find another Prime Minister who can secure the support of the House of the People. "The President is bound in every case to act on the advice of the Cabinet." He is only the Constitutional or figure -head, though in some important appointments, he has lot of freedom and discretion.

The communication between the President and his Council of Ministers is confidential.[12] However, the courts are justified in looking into the basis of the advice and sometimes the advice tendered by the Council of Ministers.

75. Other provisions as to Ministers: (1) The Prime Minister shall be appointed by the President and the other Ministers shall be appointed by the President on the advice of the Prime Minister.

(2) The Ministers shall hold office during the pleasure of the President.

(3) The Council of Ministers shall be collectively responsible to the House of the people.

(4) Before a Minister enters upon his office, the President shall administer to him the oaths of office and Secretary according to the forms set out for the purpose in the Third Schedule.

(5) A Minister, who for any period of six consecutive months is not a member of either House of Parliament, shall at the expiration of that period cease to be a Minister.

(6) The salaries and allowances of Ministers shall be such as the Parliament may from time to time by law determine and, until the Parliament so determines, shall be as specified in the Second Schedule.

(Part V, Article 75)

COMMENTS

It is an accepted convention that the President cannot appoint anyone not recommended by the Prime Minister and will hold office at the satisfaction of the Prime Minister. Thus, the Prime Minister is the Chief Executive Officer of the Republic of India. The Prime Minister should not be appointed arbitrarily. In case of lack of majority of any single party, the golden rule in such an eventuality is to call the leader of the single largest party or alliance first having majority or seek to be satisfied in advance about a leader having the support of more than half of the members of the Lok Sabha. The Constitution provides only for collective responsibility of the Cabinet led by the Prime Minister. It means that there can be no confidence in a single Minister. The entire Council of Ministers is jointly responsible to the Lok Sabha for all the acts of the Government. Therefore, it stands or falls together. If it loses the confidence of the House, the entire Council of Ministers must resign. Also, collective responsibility would mean that the Minister must not speak in public in different voices. If any Minister disagrees with a decision taken or a policy adopted by the Cabinet, he must either resign or own equal or joint responsibility.

He is in a boat which either floats or sinks with all the members on board. However, in case of dissolution or loss of majority, the President cannot function alone at the Centre. He has to have with him a caretaker Prime Minister along with the Cabinet of his choice till the fresh elections are over and the relative strength of the parties in the newly elected House of people is known. It operates in all important Parliamentary governments, i.e. U.K., Australia, Canada, Ireland, France,

New Zealand and the Union of South Africa. The principle of collective responsibility is both the cause and effect of the Cabinet's solidarity.

(Part V Article 76)

The Attorney-General for India

76. Attorney-General for India: (1) The President shall appoint a person who is qualified to be appointed a Judge of the Supreme Court to be Attorney-General for India.

(2) It shall be the duty of the Attorney-General to give advice to the Government of India upon such legal matters, and to perform such other duties of a legal character, as may from time to time be referred or assigned to him by the President, and to discharge the functions conferred on him by or under this Constitution or any other law for the time being in force.

(3) In the performance of his duties the Attorney-General shall have the right of audience in all, courts in the territory of India.

(4) The Attorney-General shall hold office during the pleasure of the President, and shall receive such remuneration as the President may determine.

(Part V, Article 76)

COMMENTS

The Attorney-General is the Chief Law Officer of the Government. He has the first right of audience in all courts in India. He shall give legal advice to the Government of India on such matters as may be referred to him by the President. However, the Attorney General shall not advise or hold a brief against the Government of India. He is not barred from private practice except that he cannot advise or hold brief against the Government of India.

77. Conduct of Business of the Government of India: (1) All executive action of the Government of India shall be expressed to be taken in the name of the President.

(2) Orders and other instruments made and executed in the name of the President shall be authenticated in such manner

as may be specified in rules to be made by the President, and the validity of an order or instrument which is so authenticated shall not be called in question on the ground that it is not an order or instrument made or executed by the President.

(3) The President shall make rules for the more convenient transaction of the business of the Government of India, and for the allocation among Ministers of the said business.

(Part V, Article 77)

COMMENTS

Whenever executive action is to be taken by way of an order or instrument, it shall be expressed to be taken in the name of the President in whom the executive power of the Union is vested. However, immunity available to the President under Article 361 of the Constitution cannot be extended to the orders passed in the name of the President under Article 77 of the Constitution. Accordingly, an action against a Minister in the court for his illegal act could not be denied on the basis of Article 77(1). Thus, it does not prevent courts from inquiring into the correctness of recitals contained in an order or instrument. Nor does it prevent a person from challenging orders of Government as being bad or invalid or ultra-vires.

78. Duties of Prime Minister to inform President, etc.: It shall be the duty of the Prime Minister:

(a) to communicate to the President all decisions of the Council of Ministers relating to the administration of the affairs of the Union and proposals for legislation;

(b) to furnish such information relating to the administration of the affairs of the Union and proposals for legislation as the President may call for;

(c) if the President so requires, to submit for the consideration of the Council of Ministers any matter on which a decision has been taken by a Minister but which has not been considered by the Council.

(Part V, Article 78)

COMMENTS

The President is constitutionally entitled to criticise the conduct of the executive. Therefore, the Prime Minister is required to meet him from time to time and inform him about the Cabinet decisions, policy decisions and administrative functions. The President may also send back the decision taken by a single Minister to the Cabinet for reconsideration. The President may call for any other information relating to administration or legislation which will be furnished to him.

Position and Powers of the President of India

The President of India like the King or Queen is called the figure head or titular or ceremonial head. But it is better to call him the Constitutional head as per debate in the Constituent Assembly. The position of the President in the scheme of our Constitution is one of the highest honours, dignity and representation. He is the Head of the State. The Supreme Court has rightly summarised his position.

"The President has been made a formal or Constitutional head of the executive and the real executive powers are vested in the Ministers or the Cabinet headed by the Prime Minister. In the Indian Constitution, we have the same system of Parliamentary executive as in England and the Council of Ministers consisting, as it does, of the members of the Legislature is like the British Cabinet a hyphen which joins, a buckle which fastens, the legislative part of the State to the executive part."[15]

Indira Government put the question beyond political controversy, by amending the Constitution itself through Constitution 42nd Amendment Act, 1976. Later on, by 44th Amendment, a proviso was added that the President can refer any matter to the Council of Ministers back for reconsideration. But if the Council of Ministers reaffirms their previous advice, the President shall be bound to act according to that advice. The President has great power to exercise his discretion in the matter of choosing new Prime Minister specially in cases if no single party has the majority in the House of People and no Council of Ministers exists, on the sudden death of the Prime Minister. He can dismiss the Prime Minister or the Council of

Ministers when he is defeated in no Confidence Vote on the floor of the Parliament.

He has wide powers to appoint protem Speaker of Lok Sabha and an acting Chairman of Rajya Sabha. He can at times withhold his assent. When during the Ninth Lok Sabha an amendment proposing pension to Members of Parliament after only a year's tenure was allowed to be introduced and passed without President's recommendation, President Venkataraman did not give his assent to the Bill.

The President can withhold his assent to promulgate ordinances when the Parliament is not in session or delay it indefinitely, putting the Council of Ministers in an awkward situation. In his power to grant pardons, some of the Presidents have effectively exercised their powers. Similarly, in few matters of appointment of Supreme Court judges of doubtful integrity, one President never cleared the proposal and the proposal did not see the light of the day. None can question, time taken by the President to take a decision. Twice during his tenure, President Narayanan returned two proposals of imposition of President's rule in U.P. and Bihar. His 'satisfaction' stipulated under Article 356 is one exclusive prerogative. It is debatable whether in view of Article 74(2), what transpires between the President and his Ministers should become matters of public debate and controversy in the media.

There is a gradual change of perception among the public to have more confidence in the highest post of the President as successive Prime Minister had become more the leader of their political parties rather than statesman for the country. The occasions are being noticed less and lesser when the Prime Minister places the nation first over the interest of his party. Secondly, most of the countries do not realise that the Prime Minister has the primacy in India and, therefore, the President of India has to discharge many of his protocol duties with his counterpart in other countries. In fact, the President is now visiting many countries to witness signing of bilateral and international treaties along with top executives of the Union Government as the effective head. Thirdly, he is the real head for proclamation of Emergency and declaration of the President's rule in the States.

The President of India is not a hereditary head of State like his counterpart in England, Japan, Netherlands and many other countries. In fact, he is more directly elected by the people of India than the Prime Minister. There is a debate that India should have the Presidential form of government in view of delay in decision-making through Parliamentary procedure, non-acceptance of the primacy of the post of Prime Minister by the States having government by the opposition parties and thirdly instability at the Union level because of various constituents of coalition governments blackmailing the Prime minister to stay in the majority. As a result, corruption and unhealthy decision-making are resulting at the Centre. The Republic cannot afford to have a weak and unstable head of Central Government. The Parliament has become a forum to fight political battle rather than making consensus on issues of national development.

If the Prime Minister has majority in the House of People, he may not have the majority in the Council of States. As a result, he cannot implement his far-reaching reforms without the concurrence of both the Houses of the Parliament. The Constitution Commission (NCRWC) felt that instability of the elected governments was in part attributable to unprincipled opportunities, political realignments from time to time and defections and re-defections.

However, healthy convention has been developing in India, whereas the President dares advice publicly his Government on many issues recently on intolerance or communal discord surfaced during the year 2015. The Secretary of the President or his Secretariat is being associated more day by day before the seal of final decision is put by the President so that the decision may not only appear to be the decision of the President. It may be with application of his mind at least in very important decisions of national importance which are to be kept beyond the pale of political interest and bickering. The better co-ordination between the Prime Minister and the President can remove misgivings in the minds of people and they will then devote more sincerely and will give their hundred per cent to the nation which India requires at the moment to preserve its integrity and place herself in the comity of the developed nations at the international level. Thus, the debate for the presidential system of the Government loses its place in India and the existing Constitutional scheme will be implemented with new vigour and will be supported by all and sundry in India in letter and spirit.

However, India cannot afford the Presidential system as such because in that case, the Parliamentary democracy will lose its brand and there is every likelihood that the President may be more totalitarian than what the country experienced with Mrs. Indira Gandhi as Prime Minister during Emergency.

148. Comptroller and Auditor-General of India: (1) There shall be a Comptroller and Auditor-General of India who shall be appointed by the President by warrant under his hand and seal and shall only be removed from office in like manner and on the like grounds as a Judge of the Supreme Court.

(2) Every person appointed to be the Comptroller and Auditor-General of India shall, before he enters upon his office, make and subscribe before the President, or some person appointed in that behalf by him, an oath or affirmation according to the form set out for the purpose in the Third Schedule.

(3) The salary and other conditions of service of the Comptroller and Auditor-General shall be such as may be determined by the Parliament by law and, until they are so determined, shall be as specified in the Second Schedule:

(4) The Comptroller and Auditor-General shall not be eligible for further office either under the Government of India or under the Government of any State after he has ceased to hold his office.

(5) Subject to the provisions of this Constitution and of any law made by the Parliament, the conditions of service of persons serving in the Indian Audit and Accounts Department and the administrative powers of the Comptroller and Auditor-General shall be such as may be prescribed by rules made by the President after consultation with the Comptroller and Auditor-General.

(6) The Administrative expenses of the office of the Comptroller and Auditor-General, including all salaries, allowances and pensions payable to or in respect of persons serving in that office, shall be charged upon the Consolidated Fund of India.

(Part V, Article 148)

COMMENTS

A pivotal office in the Government of India is that of Comptroller and Auditor General of India who controls the entire financial system of the government at the Centre as well as at State levels. CAG is the guardian of the public purse. It is his duty to see that no amount is spent out of the Consolidated Fund of India or Contingency Fund of a State without the authority of the appropriate Legislature. He shall be the impartial head of the audit and accounts system of India.

In order to discharge this duty properly and effectively, it is highly essential that this office should be independent of any control of the Executive. The Legislature cannot discharge its function properly unless Legislature is aided by an agency, fully independent of the Executive, who would scrutinize the financial transactions of the Government and bring the results of such scrutiny before the Legislature.

149. Duties and powers of the Comptroller and Auditor-General: The Comptroller and Auditor-General shall perform such duties and exercise such powers in relation to the accounts of the Union and of the States and of any other authority or body as may be prescribed by or under any law made by the Parliament and, until provision in that behalf is so made, shall perform such duties and exercise such powers in relation to the accounts of the Union and of the States as were conferred on or exercisable by the Auditor-General of India immediately before the commencement of this Constitution in relation to the accounts of the Dominion of India and of the provinces respectively.

(Part V, Article 149)

COMMENTS

The CAG report is always subject to scrutiny by the Parliament through the Parliamentary Sub-committees. One of them, the most important, is known as Public Accounts Committee. The Government is allowed to offer its views on the report of the CAG. Then, the views of the Parliamentary Public Accounts Committee or other Sub-committees are placed for consideration by the Parliament.[16]

It is learnt that CAG is now authorised to do performance audit also, i.e. the CAG can now question the administrative decisions. Already the CAG is to audit and report on the receipts and expenditures of Government companies and other bodies which are substantially financed from the Union or State revenues. CAG has exposed some of the very important corruption scams like 2G spectrum and coal mines allocations by the Government of India.

150. Form of accounts of the Union and of the States: The accounts of the Union and of the States shall be kept in such form as the President may, on the advice of the Comptroller and Auditor-General of India, prescribe.

(Part V, Article 150)

151. Audit reports: (1) The reports of the Comptroller and Auditor General of India relating to the accounts of the Union shall be submitted to the President, who shall cause them to be laid before each House of Parliament.

(2) The reports of the Comptroller and Auditor-General of India relating to the accounts of a State shall be submitted to the Governor of the State, who shall cause them to be laid before the Legislature of the State.

(Part V, Article 151)

COMMENTS

The audit reports submitted by CAG are subject to scrutiny by the Parliament or the Legislature of the State as the case may be.[1]

(B) The State Executive

152. Definition: In this Part, unless the context otherwise requires, the expression "State" does not include the State of Jammu and Kashmir.

(Part VI, Article 152)

153. Governors of States: There shall be a Governor for each State:

Provided that nothing in this Article shall prevent the appointment of the same person as Governor for two or more States.

(Part VI, Article 153)

COMMENTS

Broadly speaking, the pattern of the Government in the States is the same as that for the Union except in matters in respect of which the Governor of a State is empowered by the Constitution to act in his discretion. The executive power of the State is vested in the Governor and all executive action of the State has to be taken in the name of the Governor.

154. Executive Power of State: (1) The executive power of the State shall be vested in the Governor and shall be exercised by him either directly or through officers subordinate to him in accordance with the Constitution.

(2) Nothing in this Article shall:

(a) be deemed to transfer to the Governor any functions conferred by any existing law on any other authority; or

(b) prevent the Parliament or the Legislature of the State from conferring by law functions on any authority subordinate to the Governor.

(Part VI, Article 154)

155. Appointment of Governor: The Governor of a State shall be appointed by the President by warrant under his hand and seal.

(Part VI, Article 155)

156. Term of office of Governor: (1) The Governor shall hold office during the pleasure of the President.

(2) The Governor may, by writing under his hand addressed to the President, resign his office.

(3) Subject to the foregoing provisions of this Article, a Governor shall hold office for a term of five years from the date on which he enters upon his office: Provided that a Governor shall, notwithstanding the expiration of his term, continue to hold office until his successor enters upon his office.

(Part VI, Article 156)

COMMENTS

Through the procedure of appointment of Governor by the President, the Union Government would be able to maintain its remote control over the States. He will act in contingencies as required by the President. Thus, he is eye and ear of the President in turn of the Union Government. He can be removed by the President sparingly in cases of gross delinquency, such as bribery, corruption, treason and the like or violation of the Constitution. But removal of Governors by change of government at the Centre cannot be rated as a good practice. The Constituent Assembly[18] desired that the Governor should be a more detached figure acceptable to the province.

It would be desirable to have people from outside, eminent in something like education, literature, science, public administration, social work or anti-insurgency job who would naturally co-operate fully with the Government in carrying out the policy of the Government and yet represent before the public something above politics.

He should not be seen by people of the State as an agent of the party in power or a stooge of the person in power who is being awarded by the party in power for party loyalty or leader's loyalty or to accommodate disgruntled persons in the party-in-power or the retired veterans of political party. The people in States look for the Governor as the person hearing the voice of the dissent and the politically oppressed people in the province. He is the ray of hope and justice amidst political turmoil or vendetta in a province.

157. Qualifications for appointment as Governor: No person shall be eligible for appointment as Governor unless he is a citizen of India and has completed the age of thirty-five years.

(Part VI, Article 157)

158. Conditions of Governor's Office: (1) The Governor shall not be a member of either House of Parliament or of a House of the Legislature of any State specified in the First Schedule, and if a member of either House of Parliament or of a House of the Legislature of any such State be appointed Governor, he shall be deemed to have vacated his seat in that House on the date on which he enters upon his office as Governor.

(2) The Governor shall not hold any other office of profit.

(3)The Governor shall be entitled without payment of rent to the use of his official residences and shall be also entitled to such emoluments, allowances and privileges as may be determined by the Parliament by law and, until provision in that behalf is so made, such emoluments, allowances and privileges as are specified in the Second Schedule.

(3A) Where the same person is appointed as Governor of two or more States, the emoluments and allowances payable to the Governor shall be allocated among the States in such proportion as the President may by order determine.

(4) The emoluments and allowances of the Governor shall not be diminished during his term of office.

(Part VI, Article 158)

159. Oath or affirmation by the Governor: Every Governor and every person discharging the functions of the Governor shall, before entering upon his office, make and subscribe in the presence of the Chief Justice of the High Court exercising jurisdiction in relation to the State, or, in his absence, the seniormost Judge of that Court available, an oath or affirmation in the following form, that is to say:

"I, A.B. do swear in the name of God/solemnly affirm that I will faithfully execute solemnly affirm the office of Governor (or discharge the functions of the Governor) of..... and will to the best of my ability preserve, protect and defend the Constitution and the law and that I will devote myself to the service and well being of the people of....

(Part VI, Article 159)

160. Discharge of the functions of the Governor in certain contingencies: The President may make such provision as he thinks fit for the discharge of the function of the Governor of a State in any contingency not provided for in this Chapter.

(Part VI, Article 160)

161. Power of Governor to grant pardons, etc. and to suspend, remit or commute sentence in certain cases: The Governor of a State shall have the power to grant pardons, reprieves, respites or remissions of punishment or to suspend, remit or commute the sentence of any person convicted of any offence against any law relating to a matter to which the executive power of the State extends.

(Part VI, Article 161)

COMMENTS

The power of pardoning of the Governor is on the same pattern as that of the President. The power of the Governor extends to the executive power of the State. It was held that the Governor's order should not come in conflict with the rules of the Supreme Court made under Article 145 in regard to criminal appeals. The Governor cannot exercise his power of suspension of the sentence for the period when the Supreme Court is seized of the case.[19] "The court would also be justified in interfering with an order passed by the Governor in exercise of power if the Governor is found to have exercised the power himself without being advised by the Government or if the Governor transgresses the jurisdiction in exercising the same or it is established that the Governor has passed the order without application of mind or the order in question is a mala fide one or the Governor has passed the order on same extraneous consideration."[20]

The Court invalidated the remission of the sentence by the Governor based on wrong information and incomplete facts. The Governor has power to grant pardons, reprieves and respites in all cases where the sentence is not a sentence of death to reconcile with power of President under article 72. It, therefore, follows that the Governor has the power to grant a pardon or remit the sentence of a person who is sentenced to life imprisonment. However, the Governor, in his order of pardon, is not expected to express any opinion on the innocence or guilt of the concerned person because that is the matter to be determined by the Court. The Government should ensure that all facts are placed before him, e.g. other cases pending against the petitioner in other courts or the petition has been brought before him by the convict just to delay his hanging or to misuse the legal procedure. For instance, in case of Dhananjoy Chatterjee,[21] a petition for clemency was filed before the Governor of West Bengal, though he was condemned to death. The Supreme Court held that failure to bring all the material facts including the mitigating factors to the notice of the Governor vitiates his decision.

It was not Dhananjoy Chatterjee directly praying for mercy or clemency, but few NGOs influenced by the Western thoughts were pursuing his mercy petitions at various levels and even protested when he was hanged in Alipore Central Jail, Kolkata for raping and murdering a teenaged girl in her flat which he was guarding. As a result, his hanging was delayed for a number of years on flimsy grounds and in fact, he enjoyed life for, few years more rather than he suffered agony for delay due to procedural wrangles at various forums including hearing of multifarious litigations in courts.

162. Extent of Executive Power of State: Subject to the provisions of this Constitution, the executive power of a State shall extend to the matters with respect to which the Legislature of the State has power to make laws: Provided that in any matter with respect to which the Legislature of a State and Parliament have power to make laws, the executive power of the State shall be subject to, and limited by, the executive power expressly conferred by this Constitution or by any law made by the Parliament upon the Union or authorities thereof.

(Part VI, Article 162)

COMMENTS

The power extends to matters with respect to which the State Legislature has authority to make laws, i.e. the subjects enumerated in the State List and the Concurrent List. But in relation to the subjects enumerated in the Concurrent List, the executive power of the State is subject to the executive power expressly conferred by the Constitution or by any law made by the Parliament, upon the Union or its authorities. "Any exercise of executive power by the State in such case will be unconstitutional."[22] It was held that there are limitations on exercise of power by the State executive. "A tax or compulsory ejection of money from any person can also not be justified in the exercise of executive power without the authority of law."[23] Proper functioning of State administration should not be jeopardised owing to ego clashes between high officers. Such officers should be aware that power should be exercised for public good, and not for personal benefit."[24] In the similar vein, the higher court observed that the senior officers should not be unnecessarily asked to be present in the court to explain certain matters or in frequent cases of contempt of court.[25] The Supreme Court further observed, "In general, the court would not exercise its power of judicial review to interfere with a policy made by the Government in exercise of its power under Article 162, particularly where it involves technical, scientific or economic expertise."[26]

Thus, the checks and balance is the key principle in exercise of power by any wing of the State i.e. executive, Legislative or judiciary.

A Minister who for any period of six consecutive months is not a member of the Legislature of the State shall at the expiration of that period cease to be a Minister.

The salaries and allowances to Ministers shall be such as the Legislature of the State may from time to time by law determine and, until the Legislature of the State so determines, shall be as specified in the Second Schedule.

163. Council of Ministers to aid and advise Governor: (1) There shall be a Council of Ministers with the Chief Minister at the head to aid and advise the Governor in the exercise of his functions, except insofar as he is by or under this Constitution required to exercise his functions or any of them in his discretion.

(2) If any question arises whether any matter is or is not a matter as respects which the Governor is by or under this Constitution required to act in his discretion, the decision of the Governor in his discretion shall be final, and the validity of anything done by the Governor shall not be called in question on the ground that he ought or ought not to have acted in his discretion.

(3) The question whether any, and if so what, advice was tendered by Ministers to the Governor shall not be inquired into any court.

164. Other Provisions as to Ministers: (1) the Chief Minister shall be appointed by the Governor and the other Ministers shall be appointed by the Governor on the advice of the Chief Minister, and the Ministers shall hold office during the pleasure of the Governor.

Provided that in the States of Bihar, Madhya Pradesh and Orissa, there shall be a Minister in charge of tribal welfare who may in addition be in charge of the welfare of the Scheduled Castes and backward classes or any other work.

(2) The Council of Ministers shall be collectively responsible to the Legislative Assembly of the State.

(3) Before a Minister enters upon his office, the Governor shall administer to him the oaths of office and of secrecy according to the forms set out for the purpose in the Third Schedule.

(4) A Minister who for any period of six consecutive months is not a member of the Legislature of the State shall at the expiration of that period cease to be a Minister.

(5) The salaries and allowances of Ministers shall be such

as the Legislature of the State may from time to time by law determine and, until the Legislature of the State so determines, shall be as specified in the Second Schedule.

(Part VI, Articles 163 & 164)

165. Advocate-General for the State: (1) The Governor of each State shall appoint a person who is qualified to be appointed a Judge of a High Court to be Advocate-General for the State.

(2) It shall be the duty of the Advocate-General to give advice to the Government of the State upon such legal matters, and to perform such other duties of a legal character, as may from time to time be referred or assigned to him by or under this Constitution or any other law for the time being in force.

(3) The Advocate-General shall hold office during the pleasure of the Governor, and shall receive such remuneration as the Governor may determine.

(Part VI Article 165)

COMMENTS

There is one Constitutional post of Advocate-General in a State. The State may appoint other counsels for looking after the legal matters of the States and may give them any designation, including the designation of Additional Advocate-General. But such counsels are appointed and their designations are assigned in the exercise of executive power of the State. A Statement made by the Advocate-General in the Court binds the government while that may not be true about the Statement of a counsel appearing for the State unless such counsel has a written instruction from the State.[29]

It was held that the person beyond the age of 62 years can be appointed as Advocate General. In fact, advocates generally in a few States are still working beyond the age of 62 years.

166. Conduct of business of the Government of a State: (1) All executive action of the Government of a State shall be expressed to be taken in the name of the Governor.

(2) Orders and other instruments made and executed in the name of the Governor shall be authenticated in such manner as may be specified in rules to be made by the Governor, and the validity of an order or instrument which is so authenticated shall not be called in question on the ground that it is not an order or instrument made or executed by the Governor.

(3) The Governor shall make rules for the more convenient transaction of the business of the Government of the State, and for the allocation among Ministers of the said business insofar as it is not business with respect to which the Governor is by or under this Constitution required to act in his discretion.

(Part VI, Article 166)

COMMENTS

Under our Constitution, the Governor or President is essentially a constitutional head. The administration of the State is run by the Council of Ministers. But in view of multifarious matters in volume, it is impossible to refer all matters to the Governor which come before the Government. In order to remove that difficulty, the Constitution has authorised the Governor under clause (3) of Article 166 to make rules for the more convenient transaction of business of the Government of the State and for the allocation among its ministers of the business of Government. Therefore, all actions of the Governor under the allocation of business rules mean the action of the State Government.

Once the order has been made in accordance with the rules, it is conclusive and beyond challenge in the courts. The rules of business framed under Article 166(3) do not create or confer any right upon a person to be enforced in a court of law.[30] However, such orders are open for adjudication whether these are passed in accordance with the law.

167. Duties of Chief Minister as respects the furnishing of information to Governor, etc. It shall be the duty of the Chief Minister of each State:

(a) To communicate to the Governor of the State all decisions of the Council of Ministers relating to the administration of the affairs of the State and proposals for legislation;

(b) To furnish such information relating to the administration of the affairs of the State and proposals for legislation as the Governor may call for; and

(c) If the Governor so requires, to submit for the consideration of the Council of Ministers any matter on which a decision has been taken by a Minister but which has not been considered by the Council.

(Part VI, Article 167)

COMMENTS

The Governor is to act with the aid or advice of the Council of Ministers. Therefore, till the advice is accepted by the Governor, views of the Council of Ministers do not get crystallised into action of the State.[31] However, except where the Governor is to exercise his functions in his discretion, the Governor has to accept the advice of the State Council of Ministers, as per rulings.[32]

Government action is routed through officers, or officials. Hence, they should be answerable for illegal acts. Further, a policy directed by the Minister can be examined by the court to see if it is meant for the public good or whether it fritters away public property.[33]

REFERENCES

1. S.P. Anand vs. H.D. Deve Gowda, AIR 1997 SC 272.
2. P.A. Sangma vs. Pranab Mukherjee, AIR 2013 SC 372.
3. Charan Lal Sahu vs. Neelam Sanjeeva Reddy, (1978) 2 SCC 500.
4. AIR 1975 SC 2299.
5. AIR 1957 SC 694.
6. Kehar Singh vs. Union of India, (1989) 1 SCC 204.
7. Mani Ram vs. Union of India, AIR 1980 SC 214 7.
8. E P. Sudhakar vs. Govt. of AP (2006) 8 SCC 161; State of U.P. vs. Sanjay Kumar, (2012) 8 SCC 537.
9. Sriharan alias Murugan vs. Union of India, (2014) 4 SCC 242, D.P.S. Bhullar vs. State (NCT of Delhi (2013) 6 SCC 195.
10. Union of India Vs. Azadi Bachao Andolan (2004) 10 SCC 1.
11. S.P. Gupta vs. President of India, AIR 1982 SC 149.

12. State of Rajasthan vs. Union of India, (1977) 3 SCC 592.
13. Kartar Singh vs. State of Punjab (1994) 3 SCC 569.
14. Common Cause vs. Union of India, (1999) 6 SCC 667.
15. Ram Jawaya Vs. State of Punjab, (1955) 2 SCR 225(238-39).
16. Arun Kumar Agrawal vs. Union of India, (2013) 7 SCC 1 (24).
17. Arvind Gupta vs. Union of India, (2013) 1 SCC 393 (394).
18. Constituent Assembly Debates, Vol VII, p-455.
19. K.M. Nanavati vs. State of Bombay, AIR 1961 SC 112.
20. Satpal vs. State of Haryana, (2000) 5 SCC 170.
21. Dhananjoy Chatterjee vs. State of West Bengal (2004) 9 SCC 751.
22. Bharat Coking Coal Ltd. vs. State of Bihar, (1990) 4 SCC 557.
23. Hindustan Times vs. State of U.P., (2003) 1 SCC 591.
24. State of Assam vs. P.C. Mishra, AIR 1996 SC 430.
25. Shri Sitaram Sugar Co. Ltd. vs. Union of India, (1990) 3 SCC 223.
29. P & P Rubbers, Ltd. vs. State of Kerala, (1991) 4 SCC 195.
30. Arun Kumar Bhattacharjee vs. State of W.B. AIR 1968 Cal.

□

Chapter 7
THE LEGISLATURE

1. Introduction

India is a federal state and the Constitution of India provides for a legislature each for the Union and in States. Two out of seven Union Territories are having a legislative assembly. These are the National Capital Territory of Delhi and Puducherry (earlier name was Pondicherry).

Parliament comprises of the President and two Houses of Parliament. All States do not have both legislative assemblies and a legislative council but major States do have both a legislative assembly and a legislative council. Thus, by and large the structure of legislature at Union and in States have identical provisions. The State of Jammu and Kashmir has its own Constitution and all central laws do not automatically apply to the State of Jammu and Kashmir.

The number of States since independence have increased mainly due to reorganisation of States first in 1956 on linguistic lines and subsequent reorganisation of States took place for creating smaller States. Major States in recent years have been bifurcated e.g. Uttar Pradesh, Madhya Pradesh, Bihar and Andhra Pradesh and new States created are Uttaranchal, Jharkhand, Chattisgarh and Telegana. All States in north east which were earlier part of Assam and north east frontier agency are now States e.g. Assam, Meghalaya, Manipur, Mizoram, Nagaland, Arunachal Pradesh, Tripura and Sikkim. Sikkim was first admitted as associate state and later on became a full fledged state of Union of India. In 1960, Goa, Daman and Diu became part of India first as Union Territories and subsequently Goa attained full statehood whereas Daman and Diu remains a union territory. The other union Territories are Chandigarh, Andaman and Nicobar Island, Lakshadweep and Minicoy Island. The administration of a union territory vests with Lt Governor and the President has power to promulgate regulations for the peace, order and good governance of a union territory (Article 240 of the Constitution).

As the provisions of the Parliament and State Legislature are similar in most of the Articles, therefore, the repetition has been avoided.

(A) Parliament

79. Constitution of Parliament: There shall be a Parliament for the Union which shall consist of the President and two Houses to be known respectively as the Council of States and the House of the People.

81. Composition of the House of the People: (1) Subject to the provisions of Article 331, the House of the People shall consist of—(a) not more than five hundred and thirty members chosen by direct election from territorial constituencies in the States, and (b) not more than twenty members to represent the union Territories, chosen in such manner as Parliament may by law provide.

(2) For the purposes of sub-clause (a) of clause (1)—(a) there shall be allotted to each state a number of seats in the House of the People in such manner that the ratio between that number and the population of the state is, so far as practicable, the same for all States; and

(b) Each state shall be divided into territorial constituencies in such manner that the ratio between the population of each constituency and the number of seats allotted to it is, so far as practicable, the same throughout the state: provided that the provisions of sub-clause (a) of this clause shall not be applicable for the purpose of allotment of seats in the house of the people to any state so long as the population of that state does not exceed six millions.

(3) In this Article, the expression "population" means the population as ascertained at the last preceding census of which the relevant figures have been published, provided that the reference in this clause to the last preceding census of which the relevant figures have been published shall, until the relevant figures for the first census taken after the year 2026 have been published, be construed:

(i) for the purposes of sub-clause (a) of clause (2) and the proviso to that clause, as a reference to the 1971 census; and (ii) for the purposes of sub-clause (b) of clause (2) as a reference to the 2001 census.

82. Re-adjustment after each Census: Upon the completion of each census, the allocation of seats in the house of the people to the States and the division of each state into territorial constituencies shall be readjusted by such authority and in such manner as the Parliament may by law determine:

Provided that such readjustment shall not affect representation in the House of the People until the dissolution of the then existing House:

Provided further that such readjustment shall take effect from such date as the President may, by order, specify and until such readjustment takes effect, any election to the house may be held on the basis of the territorial constituencies existing before such readjustment: provided also that until the relevant figures for the first census taken after the year 2026 have been published, it shall not be necessary to readjust— (i) the allocation of seats in the house of people to the States as readjusted on the basis of the 1971 census; and (ii) the division of each state into territorial constituencies as may be readjusted on the basis of the 2001 census, under this Article.

(Part V, Article 79-82)

COMMENTS

Article 81 as originally enacted provided that each Parliamentary constituency shall have a population of 7.5 lakhs. However, Article 81 of the Constitution was amended soon after the Constitution came into force and more prominently by the Constitution (Forty-second amendment) Act, 1976. The Constitution (Forty-second amendment) Act, 1976 declared a freeze on number of seats each state has in the house of the people and, thus, total number of seats in the house of the people remains five hundred and thirty from major States, although the population in those States has trebled during the last 40 years.

Article 82 of the Constitution provides for delimitation of territorial constituencies after every 10 years. The first delimitation of constituencies was undertaken based upon a Presidential notification. Thereafter, the Parliament enacted Delimitation Acts in 1952, 1962, 1972 and in 2002 respectively. As stated above that by the Constitution (Forty-second amendment) Act, 1976 the delimitation of the constituencies was frozen for a period of 30 years. Based upon the Delimitation Act, 2002, the territorial constituencies were readjusted by the Fourth Delimitation Commission headed by Justice Kuldeep Singh. The next delimitation of constituencies shall be undertaken after the year 2026 as the number of seats as well as the readjustment of seats has been frozen by the Constitution (Eighty-Seventh Amendment) Act, 2003.

Rationale for freezing of delimitation of constituencies: As originally envisaged in the Constitution, the population is the sole basis of delimitation of constituencies. In India the population policy of the Union Government mandated that among other measures for controlling population in the country, one measure could be to neutralise the impact of population in a state or a region by freezing the number of seats a State is entitled be based on its population till such time the growth of population shows negative results.

Evil effects of freezing of delimitation of constituencies: One result of freezing of delimitation of constituencies has been unduly large size of a Parliamentary constituency. Many major States have Parliamentary constituency having a population of 25 lakhs and above. This goes against the concept of one person one vote. It seems that the population as the sole basis for delimitation of constituencies has lost its significance and a time has come to take into account other factors apart from population to determine the basis of delimitation of constituencies. The freeze of delimitation of constituencies for 30 years in 1976 and again for 30 years in 2002 may be constitutionally valid but it goes against the principle of one person-one vote.

84. Qualification for Membership of Parliament: A person shall not be qualified to be chosen to fill a seat in the Parliament unless he—

(a) is a citizen of India, and makes and subscribes before some person authorised in that behalf by the Election Commission an oath or affirmation according to the form set out for the purpose in the third schedule;

(b) is, in the case of a seat in the Council of States, not less than thirty years of age and, in the case of a seat in the House of the People, not less than twenty-five years of age; and

(c) possesses such other qualifications as may be prescribed in that behalf by or under any law made by the Parliament.

(Part V, Article 84)

COMMENTS

Any person desirous of contesting an election must be not be less than twenty-five years of age in case of a seat in Lok Sabha; and not less than thirty years of age in the case of a seat in the Rajya Sabha. Such person must be a citizen of India. A person acquires citizenship either by birth or may acquire citizenship afterwards. The Citizenship Act, 1955 provides in detail the modes of acquiring citizenship more particularly when both, the parents are not citizens of India or one of them is a citizen of India. By an amendment of the Representation of People Act, 1950, a non-resident Indian may be enrolled as a voter in India, although such, a person is not eligible to contest an election.

80. Composition of the Council of States: (1) The Council of States shall consist of:

(a) twelve members to be nominated by the President in accordance with the provisions of clause (3); and

(b) not more than two hundred and thirty eight representatives of the States and of the Union Territories.

(2) the allocation of seats in the Council of States to be filled by the representatives of the States and of the Union Territories shall be in accordance with the provisions in that behalf contained in the Fourth Schedule.

(3) The members to be nominated by the President under sub-clause (a) of clause (1) shall consist of persons having special knowledge or practical experience in respect of such matters as the following, namely: Literature, science, art and social services.

(4) The representatives of each State in the Council of States shall be elected by the elected members of the Legislative Assembly of the State in accordance with the system of proportional representation by means of the single transferable vote.

(5) The representatives of the Union Territories in the Council of States shall be chosen in such the manner as Parliament may by law prescribe.

(Part V, Article 80)

COMMENTS

Article 80 of the Constitution lays down the maximum strength of Rajya Sabha as 250, out of which 12 members are nominated by the President and 238 are representatives of the States and of the two Union Territories. The present strength of Rajya Sabha, however, is 245, out of which 233 are representatives of the States and union Territories of Delhi and Puducherry and 12 are nominated by the President. The members nominated by the President are persons having special knowledge or practical experience in respect of such matters as literature, science, art and social service.

Allocation of seats: The Fourth Schedule to the Constitution provides for the allocation of seats to the States and union Territories in Rajya Sabha. The allocation of seats is made on the basis of the population of each state. Consequent on the reorganisation of States and formation of new States, the number of elected seats in the Rajya Sabha allotted to States and union Territories has changed from time to time since 1952.

Recent Amendments as to Election to Rajya Sabha: Rajya Sabha is a permanent house and members are elected for a term of six years and approximately one-third members retire every two years. Till 2003, it was incumbent on a person seeking election to, Rajya Sabha to be an ordinary resident of a State or union territory, as the case may be, and other requirements were that of secrecy of voting. By an amendment of 2003, the requirements of ordinary resident and of secrecy in voting were dispensed. The amendments made in 2003 were challenged in the Supreme Court and were held constitutionally valid.

The constitutional validity of the amendment was upheld by the Supreme Court in the case of Kuldip Nayar vs. Union of India and ors(1). The Court observed as under:

'...it is provided in Article 80(2) that allocation of seats in the Council of States to be filled by the representatives of States and the Union Territories shall be in accordance with the provisions in that behalf contained in the fourth schedule. In Article 80(4), it is provided that the representatives of each state shall be elected by the elected members of the legislative assemblies of the States in accordance with the system of proportional representation by means of a single transferable vote. Apart from this, the Constitution does not put any restriction on the legislative powers of the Parliament in this regard. The amendments in Sections 3, 59, 94 and 128 of the Representation of the People Act, 1951 by the Representation of the People (Amendment) Act, 2003 (40 of 2003) has been made in exercise of the powers conferred on the Parliament under Article 246 read with Articles 84 and 327 and entry 72 of the union list of the seventh schedule to the Constitution. The impugned amendment does not infringe any constitutional provision. It cannot be found to be violative of fundamental rights in part (iii) of the Constitution. It is not disputed that Parliament has legislative competence to enact the amending act. In these facts and circumstances, the impugned legislation cannot be struck down as unconstitutional. All the writ petitions questioning the constitutional validity of the amendments brought about in the Representation of People Act, 1951 through the Representation of the People (Amendment) Act, 2003 (Act no. 40 of 2003), being devoid of merits are hereby dismissed.[1]

102. Disqualification of membership: (1) A person shall be disqualified for being chosen as, and for being, a member of either House of Parliament—(a) if he holds any office of profit under the Government of India or the Government of any State, other than an office declared by the Parliament by law not to disqualify its holder; (b) if he is of unsound mind and stands so declared by a competent court; (c) if he is an undischarged insolvent; (d) if he is not a citizen of India, or has voluntarily acquired the citizenship of a foreign State, or is under any acknowledgement of allegiance or adherence to a foreign State; (e) if he is so disqualified by or under any law made by the Parliament.

Explanation: For the purposes of this clause the person shall not be deemed to hold an office of profit under the Government of India or the Government of any State by reason only that he is a Minister either for the Union or for such State.

(2) A person shall be disqualified for being a member of either House of Parliament if he is so disqualified under the Tenth Schedule.

(Part V, Article 102)

103. Decision on questions as to disqualifications of members: (1) If any question arises as to whether a member of either House of Parliament has become subject to any of the disqualifications mentioned in clause (1) of Article 102, the question shall be referred for the decision of the President and his decision shall be final.

(2) Before giving any decision on any such question, the President shall obtain the opinion of the Election Commission and shall act according to such opinion.

(Part V, Article 103)

COMMENTS

No other subject in constitutional law has attracted more attention than that of electoral disqualifications. Quite often nomination of a candidate at an election is challenged on the ground that a particular candidate does not possess necessary qualifications or suffers from some disqualification for being a candidate in the election. These disputes do continue after the elections are over and there are instances where an election was held void on the ground of lack of qualification or disqualification of a candidate.

Any post-election dispute of a Member of Parliament on the ground of "holding an office of profit under the government" or any other disqualification shall be referred to the President and the President shall decide the issue of disqualification after the consultation of the Election Commission of India. Any post-election dispute as to disqualification of a member of State Assembly on the ground of "holding an office of profit under the government" or any other disqualification shall be referred to the Governor and the Governor shall decide the issue of disqualification after the consultation of the Election Commission of India.

In Jaya Bachchan case (2), the facts leading to the order of the President were as under:

"Smt. Jaya Bachchan, who was elected to the Council of States from Uttar Pradesh in June 2004, was appointed as Chairperson of the Uttar Pradesh Films Development Council on 14th July, 2004 by the Uttar Pradesh Government. A petition was filed before the President by Sh. Madan Mohan, under Article 103(1) of the Constitution, raising the question of disqualification of Smt. Bachchan on the ground that she was holding an office of profit under the Uttar Pradesh Government following her appointment as Chairperson of the said Council, with the status of a Cabinet Minister, and entitled to certain benefits and facilities. The President referred the petition to the Election Commission for its Opinion under Article 103(2). The main question which falls for determination of the Commission is whether the office of the Chairperson of the Uttar Pradesh Films Development Council to which the opposite party has been appointed on 14.7.2004 is an 'office of profit under the Government of Uttar Pradesh' within the meaning of Article 102(1)(a) of the Constitution. The Election Commission held that the honorarium of ₹ 5,000/- per month payable to the Chairperson of the Council was 'pecuniary gain' to the holder of that office and was not by way of any compensatory allowance to defray out-of-pocket expenses and finally vide its opinion dated 2nd March, 2006 the Commission held that Smt. Jaya Bachchan was disqualified.

The petitioner Jaya Bachchan moved to the Supreme Court. Before the Supreme Court, the phrase "office of profit" fell for interpretation within the meaning of Article 102 and other provisions of the Constitution with regard to use of the expression "honorarium" and its effect regarding the financial status of the holder of office or interest of the holder in profiting from the office. It was observed that what was relevant was whether the office was capable of yielding a profit or pecuniary gain, other than reimbursement of out-of-pocket/actual expenses, and not whether the person actually received monetary gain or did not withdraw the emoluments to which she was entitled. The three Judges Bench, which heard the matter, held that an office of profit is an office which is capable of yielding profits of pecuniary gain and that holding an office under the Central or State Government, to which some pay, salary, emolument, remuneration or non-compensatory allowance is attached is "holding an office of profit."

In Sibu Soren case the Supreme Court had before it a controversy, which revolved around two issues. Firstly, the nature of payment of ₹ 1,750/- per month as "honorarium" to the appellant. And, secondly, whether the 'office' of the Chairman Interim, Jharkhand Area Autonomous Council; was an "office under the State Government".

The question now is what is pecuniary gain? Does the receipt of "honorarium at the rate of ₹ 1,750/- per month by the appellant, besides other allowances and perquisites, amount to causing any "pecuniary gains" to the appellant?

The Supreme Court agreed with the High Court that the appellant, as Chairman of the Interim JAA Council, was in receipt of pecuniary gain in the form of honorarium and he, thus, held an "office of profit." It was observed by the court that the expression "profit" connotes an idea of some pecuniary gain other than "compensation." Neither the quantum of amount paid, nor the label under which the payment is made, may always be material to determine whether the office is one of profit. The Court went on further to observe that mere use of the word "honorarium" cannot take the payment out of the concept of profit, if there is some pecuniary gain for the recipient. The payment of an honorarium, in addition to daily allowances in the nature of compensatory allowances, rent-free accommodation and chauffeur-driven car at State expense, were in the nature of remuneration and, thus, is a source of pecuniary gain and, hence, constituted profit.

In Shibu Soren and Jaya Bachchan, the issue that in what manner appointment to the office would have been prejudicial to the constituency or affect the independence of the member was neither raised nor argued and thus remained undetermined. How by virtue of honorarium either Shibu Soren or Jaya Bachchan were beholden to the executive government of a State (Jharkhand and Uttar Pradesh and not to the Central Government) and lost their independence of thought and action in the discharge of their public duties as representatives of the people in the Parliament was also neither raised/argued nor determined.

Parliament to declare certain offices of profit not to disqualify their holders: In pursuance of its power under Article 102(1)(a) of the Constitution, Parliament has exempted a number of offices from being an office of profit through a Parliamentary enactments, namely:

1. The Parliament (Prevention of Disqualification) Act, 1959;
2. Section 12 of the Salary and Allowances of Leaders of Opposition in the Parliament Act, 1977;
3. The Parliament (Prevention of Disqualification) Amendment Act, 1993;
4. Section 5 of the Leaders and Chief Whips of Recognised Parties and Groups in the Parliament (Facilities) Act, 1998;

5. The Leaders and Chief Whips of Recognised Parties and Groups in the Parliament (Facilities) Amendment Act, 2000; and
6. The Parliament (Prevention of Disqualification) Amendment Act, 2006.

Constitutional validity of the Parliament (Prevention of Disqualification) Amendment Act, 2006 was challenged and the Supreme Court in a case, namely the Consumer Education & Research Society vs. Union of India & Ors (4)(2009) 9 SCC 648 framed two issues as under:

(i) Whether the Amendment Act retrospectively exempting certain offices of profit from disqualification violates Articles 101 to 104 of the Constitution and is, therefore, invalid?

(ii) Whether exemption of as many as 55 offices relating to statutory bodies/non-statutory bodies, without referring the proposal to the Joint Committee would render the Amendment a colourable legislation which violated any 'Constitutional convention' or Article 14 of the Constitution?

On the first issue, the court observed as under:

"...upon a proper construction of the provisions of Articles 101 to 103, it is evident that a declaration by the President under Article 103(1) in the case of a disqualification under Article 102(1) and a declaration by the Speaker or the Chairman under Para. 6 of Tenth Schedule in the case of a disqualification under Article 102(2) is a condition precedent for the vacancy of the seat. If Article 101(3)(a) is interpreted otherwise, it will lead to absurd results, thereby making it impossible to implement or enforce the relevant provisions of the Constitution or the RP Act."

The Court held that while a disqualification results in the vacation of the seat of a Member, the vacancy occurs only when the President decides and declares the disqualification under Article 103.

On the second issue, the court observed that which 'offices' should be excluded for the purpose of disqualification is a question that properly lies in the legislative domain. The plea regarding violation of Article 14 merely because several other similar offices of profit are not included in the exempted category has no basis in the opinion of the court. As each office of profit may have different effects and consequences on the Member, there is no viable basis for the assumption that all offices of profit are equal and that all offices of profit should be excluded. The court found that the argument based on Article 14 of the Constitution is highly illogical and without any force.

The court upheld the impugned legislation, i.e. the Parliament (Prevention of Disqualification) Amendment Act, 2006 as constitutionally valid and in Para 77, the subject was explained as under:

"...what kind of office would amount to an 'office of profit' under the Government and whether such an office of profit is to be exempted is a matter to be considered by the Parliament. The key concern that certain offices or places held by an MP may be either incompatible with his/her duty as an elected representative of the people or affect his/her independence and thus weaken his/her loyalty to his/her constituency and, therefore, should disqualify the holder thereof, is a matter to be addressed by the Parliament. It is also not possible to classify and include the offices exempted from the said disqualification in a generic sense. While making the legislation exempting any office, the question whether such office is incompatible with his/her position as an MP and whether his/her independence would be compromised and whether his/her loyalty to his/her constituency will be affected should no doubt be kept in mind to safeguard the independence of the Members of the legislature and to ensure that they are free from any kind of undue influence from the executive."

Guidelines for future: The court expressed its view that while making the legislation exempting any office, the question whether such office is incompatible with his/her position as an MP and whether his/her independence would be compromised and whether his/her loyalty to his/her constituency will be affected should no doubt be kept in mind to safeguard the independence of the Members of the legislature and to ensure that they are free from any kind of undue influence from the executive. However, the observations of the court that the learned counsel for the petitioners have not advanced any contention that any of the newly exempted 'offices' suffer from any such impropriety or will be prejudicial to the constituency or affect the independence of the member are significant to note.

105. Powers, privileges, etc. of the Houses of Parliament and of the members and committees thereof: (1) Subject to the provisions of this Constitution and the rules and standing orders regulating the procedure of Parliament, there shall be freedom of speech in the Parliament.

(2) No member of the Parliament shall be liable to any proceedings in any court in respect of anything said or any vote given by him in the Parliament or any committee thereof, and no person shall be so liable in respect of the publication by or under the authority of either House of Parliament of any report, paper, votes or proceedings.

(3) In other respects, the powers, privileges and immunities of each House of Parliament, and of the members and the committees of each House, shall be such as may from time to time be defined by the Parliament by law, and, until so defined, shall be those of that House and of its members and committees immediately before the coming into force of Section 15 of the Constitution (Forty-fourth Amendment) Act, 1978.

(4) The provisions of clauses (1), (2) and (3) shall apply in relation to persons who by virtue of this Constitution have the right to speak in, and otherwise to take part in the proceedings of, a House of Parliament or any committee thereof as they apply in relation to the members of the Parliament."

(Part V, Article 105)

COMMENTS

The power, privileges and immunities of each House of Parliament and of the Members and the Committees of each House are set out in Article 105 of the Constitution. The Article comprises four clauses. Article 194 similarly sets out the powers, privileges and immunities of the House of the Legislature of a

State, of its members and the committees of the House of such Legislature.

Clause (1) of Article 105 has been interpreted by the Supreme Court in MSM Sharma vs. Shrikrishna Sinha[5] in re Keshav Singh's[6] case and in P.V. Narasimha Rao vs. State.[7] It has been held by the Court in MSM Sharma case that the freedom of speech guaranteed by clause (1) to the Members of the Parliament is in addition to the freedom of speech and expression guaranteed to the citizens of this country by Article 19(1)(a) and that the said freedom guaranteed to the Members of Parliament is not subject to the reasonable restrictions contemplated by clause (2) of Article 19. In MSM Sharma case, Pandit Sharma, was editor of an English Daily Newspaper "Searchlight" of Patna. He invited the wrath of the legislative assembly of Bihar by publishing extracts from proceedings of the legislative assembly including certain parts which had been ordered to be expunged by the Speaker. In this context, the Speaker had referred the matter to the Privileges Committee of the assembly, which, in turn, issued a show cause notice to him. Pandit Sharma brought writ petition in this court under Article 32 of the Constitution of India, alleging that the proceedings initiated by the legislative assembly had violated his fundamental right of speech and expression under Article 19(1) (a) as also the fundamental right of protection of his personal liberty under Article 21. The court concluded that the fundamental right of free speech and expression under Article 19(1)(a) being general in nature must yield to Article 194(1) and the latter part of Article 194(3) which are special provisions.

In re Keshav Singh case: The legislative assembly of Uttar Pradesh had committed one Keshav Singh, who was not one of its members, to prison for its contempt. The warrant of committal did not contain the facts constituting the alleged contempt. Keshav Singh moved a petition, inter alia, under Article 226 of the Constitution through his advocate challenging his committal as being in breach of his fundamental rights. A division bench of the High Court sitting at Lucknow gave notice to the Government counsel and on the appointed day, proceeded to hear the application for bail. At that stage, the Government Counsel did not appear. The division bench heard the application and ordered release of Keshav Singh on interim bail pending decision on his writ petition. The legislative assembly found that Keshav Singh and his advocate in moving the High court and the two Judges of the High Court in entertaining the petition and granting bail had committed contempt of the legislative assembly. The assembly passed a resolution that all of them, including the two High Court Judges, be produced before it in custody. The High Court Judges and the advocate in question thereupon filed writ petitions before the High Court at Allahabad. A full bench of the High Court admitted the writ petitions and ordered the stay of execution of the assembly's resolution against them. Subsequently, the legislative assembly passed a clarificatory resolution modifying its earlier stand and asking the Judges and the advocate to appear before the House and offer their explanation. It was against this backdrop that the President made a reference under Article 143(1) of the Constitution, seeking opinion mainly as to the Constitutional relationship between the High Court and the State Legislature in matters of the powers and privileges of the latter.

The court dealt with the main privileges claimed by the House of Commons as under:

"Freedom of speech is a privilege essential to every free council or legislature, and that is claimed by both the Houses as a basic privilege. This privilege was from 1541 included by established practice in the petition of the Commons to the King at the commencement of the Parliament. It is remarkable that notwithstanding the repeated recognition of this privilege, the Crown and the Commons were not always agreed upon its limits. This privilege received final statutory recognition after the Revolution of 1688. By the 9th Article of the Bill of Rights, it was declared "that the freedom of speech, and debates or proceedings in the Parliament ought not to be impeached or questioned in any court or place out of the Parliament. May's Parliamentary Practice, p. 52."

Amongst the other privileges are the right to exclude strangers, the right to control publication of debates and proceedings, the right to exclusive cognizance of proceedings in the Parliament, the right of each House to be the sole judge of the lawfulness of its own proceedings, and the right implied to punish its own Members for their conduct in the Parliament ibid, p. 52-53.

Besides these privileges, both the Houses of the Parliament were possessed of the privilege of freedom from arrest or molestation, and from being impleaded, which was claimed by the Commons on the ground of prescription.

Clause (2) is in two parts. The first part confers an immunity upon a Member of the Parliament in respect of anything said or any vote given by him in the Parliament or any committee thereof; the immunity protects him from being proceeded against in a court of law. The second part confers an immunity upon the person who publishes such proceedings by or under the authority of either House of the Parliament; the publication may be of any report, paper, vote or proceedings. This clause is aimed to provide the Members of the Parliament an unrestricted freedom of speech and expression within the House.

The interpretation of clause (2) arose most prominently in P.V. Narasimha's Case. A chargesheet was filed against Shri P.V. Narasimha Rao and some other Members of the Parliament and others under Section 120B IPC and Sections 7, 12, 13(2) read with section 13(1)(d)(iii) of the Prevention of Corruption Act, 1988. The charge was that a criminal conspiracy was entered into to vote against the motion of 'no confidence' moved against Shri P.V. Narasimha Rao's government in Lok Sabha. Both the bribe givers and bribe takers were chargesheeted.

On the question of interpretation of clause (2) of Article 105, there was a division of opinion. Two judges, S.C. Agrawal and A.S. Anand, J.J. held that "a Member of the Parliament does not enjoy immunity under Article 105(2) or Article 105(3) of the Constitution from being prosecuted before a criminal court for an offence involving offer or acceptance of bribe for the purpose of speaking or by giving his vote in the Parliament or in any committees thereof". On the other hand, S.P. Barucha and Rajendra Babu, J.J. held that while bribe-givers (who are the Members of the Parliament) cannot invoke the immunity conferred by clause (2) of Article 105, the bribe-takers (Members of the Parliament) can invoke that immunity if they have actually spoken or voted in the House pursuant to the bribe taken by them. If, however, a Member of the Parliament takes a bribe for speaking or voting in the House in a particular manner, but does not so speak or vote, the immunity cannot be invoked by him. The conclusion follows the construction of the words "in respect of" occurring in the said clause. The learned judges held that the said words were of wide amplitude and, therefore, the integral connection between the bribe-taking and the vote in the House cannot be dissected or separated. G.N. Ray, J. agreed with Barucha and Rajendra Babu, J.J. on this question.

Article 105(3) underwent a change in terms of Section 15 of the Constitution (44th Amendment) Act, 1978. In Article 105(3), the words "shall be those of the House of Commons of the Parliament of the United Kingdom, and of its members and committees at the commencement of this Constitution" were substituted by the words "shall be those of that House and of its members and committees immediately before the coming into force of Section 15 of the Constitution (fourty-fourth Amendment) Act, 1978."

In Raja Ram Pal case (2007)[8], the question was whether in exercise of the powers, privileges and immunities as contained in Article 105, are the Houses of the Parliament competent to expel their respective Members from membership of the House. If such a power exists, is it subject to judicial review, and if so, the scope of such judicial review. The Raja Ram Pal case considered the powers of the Parliament to expel their members as eleven members from both the houses were unseated as they were caught on camera taking bribes from journalists for raising questions in the Parliament. The Supreme Court held that the Houses of the Parliament had acted within their jurisdiction.

In Raja Ram Pal case (2007), it was the petitioners' contention that the Houses of the Parliament had no power of expulsion of a sitting member. They pleaded that the petitioners could not be debarred from membership of the House by or under the impugned notifications pursuant to proceedings consequent upon the media reports inasmuch as substantive and adjectival law had been disregarded and the Constitutional inhibition placed on the exercise of power of debarment had been defeated.

A constitution bench of five judges observed that in the constitutional scheme that has been adopted in India, the Legislatures play a significant role in pursuit of the goals set before the nation and command the position of grandeur and majesty. The Legislatures undoubtedly have plenary powers but such powers are controlled by the basic concepts of the written constitution and can be exercised within the legislative fields allotted to their respective jurisdiction under the Seventh Schedule. They have the plenary legislative authority and discharge their legislative functions by virtue of the powers conferred on them by the relevant provisions of the Constitution. But, the basis of that power is the Constitution itself. Expulsion is related to the conduct of the member that lowers the dignity of the House, which may not have been necessarily known at the time of election. It is not a capricious exercise of the House, but an action to protect its dignity before the people of the country. This is also an integral aspect of our democratic set-up. Thus, the Court held that the power of expulsion is not contrary to a democratic process. It is rather part of the guarantee of a democratic process. Expulsion is not a decision by a single person. It is a decision taken by the representatives of the rest of the country. Finally, the power of expulsion does not bar a member from standing for re-election or the constituency from electing that member once again.

The Parliament has not yet catalogued the powers, privileges and immunities of each House of the Parliament and of their members and committees. Thus, the second part of Article 105(3) shall come to an end as soon as the Parliament defined by law its powers, privileges and immunities.

Clause (4) reads thus:

"(4) The provisions of clauses (1), (2) and (3) shall apply in relation to persons who by virtue of this Constitution have the right to speak in, and otherwise to take part in the proceedings of, a House of the Parliament or any committee thereof as they apply in relation to the members of the Parliament."

107. Provisions as to introduction and passing of Bills: (1) Subject to the provisions of Articles 109 and 117 with respect to Money Bills and other financial Bills, a Bill may originate in either House of the Parliament.

(2) Subject to the provisions of Articles 108 and 109, a Bill shall not be deemed to have been passed by the Houses of the Parliament unless it has been agreed to by both the Houses, either without amendment or with such amendments only as are agreed to by both Houses.

(Part V, Article 107)

COMMENTS

Article 107 and other Articles of the Constitution broadly classify a Bill as an ordinary Bill, a Financial Bill, a Money Bill. A further category of Money Bill is an Appropriation Bill. Except in case of Money Bill, the Constitution does not stipulate any time-limit for the passing of a Bill. A money Bill also requires prior recommendation of President for its introduction and also for its consideration and passing. A financial Bill also requires recommendation of the President for its introduction and passing.

108. Joint sitting of both the Houses in certain cases: (1) If after a Bill has been passed by one House and transmitted to the other House—(a) the Bill is rejected by the other House; or (b) the Houses have finally disagreed as to the amendments to be made in the Bill; or (c) more than six months elapse from the date of the reception of the Bill by the other House without the Bill being passed by it, the President may, unless the Bill has elapsed by reason of a dissolution of the House of the People, notify to the Houses by message if they are sitting or by public notification if they are not sitting, his intention to summon them to meet in a joint sitting for the purpose of deliberating and voting on the Bill: Provided that nothing in this clause shall apply to a Money Bill. (2) In reckoning any such period of six months as is referred to in clause (1), no account shall be taken of any period during which the House referred to in sub-clause (c) of that clause is prorogued or adjourned for more than four consecutive days. (3) Where the President has under clause (1) notified his intention of summoning the Houses to meet in a joint sitting, neither House shall proceed further with the Bill, but the President may at any time after the date of his notification summon the Houses to meet in a joint sitting for the purpose specified in the notification and, if he does so, the Houses shall meet accordingly. (4) If at the joint sitting of the two Houses the Bill, with such amendments, if any, as are agreed to in joint sitting, is passed by a majority of the total number of members of both the Houses present and voting, it shall be deemed for the purposes of this Constitution to have been passed by both the Houses: Provided that at a joint sitting—(a) if the Bill, having been passed by one House, has not been passed by the other House with amendments and returned to the House in which it originated, no amendment shall be proposed to the Bill other than such amendments (if any) as are made necessary by the delay in the passage of the Bill; (b) if the Bill has been so passed and returned, only such amendments as aforesaid shall be proposed to the Bill and such other amendments as are relevant to the matters with respect to which the Houses have not agreed; and the decision of the person presiding as to the amendments which are admissible under this clause shall be final. (5) A joint sitting may be held under this Article and a Bill passed thereat, notwithstanding that a dissolution of the House of the People has intervened since the President notified his intention to summon the Houses to meet therein.

(Part V, Article 108)

COMMENTS

In order to resolve a deadlock between the two houses, in case of an ordinary legislation, the Constitution provides for the joint sitting of both the Houses. In fact, there have been three occasions in the past when the Houses of the Parliament had met in joint sitting to resolve differences between them.

The following bills have been passed at the joint sitting:

(1) The Dowry Prohibition Bill.

(2) The Banking Service Commission.

(3) The Prevention of Terrorism Bill.

The Houses of the Parliament (Joint Sittings and Communications) Rules were made by the President, after consultation with the chairman of the council of States and the speaker of the house of the people, in exercise of the powers conferred by clause (3) of Article 118 of the Constitution of India. Under the rules, issues in joint sitting are decided by a majority of the total number of members of both the Houses present and voting. However, in the case of a money bill, there is no provision in the Constitution for a joint sitting of both the Houses as Lok Sabha clearly enjoys pre-eminence over Rajya Sabha in financial matters. Further, there is no provision for resolving a deadlock between the two houses in regard to a Constitution amendment bill as the Constitution provides for a special procedure for the passing of a Constitution Amendment Bill.

109. Special Procedure in respect of Money Bills: (1) A Money Bill shall not be introduced in the Council of States.

(2) After a Money Bill has been passed by the House of the People, it shall be transmitted to the Council of States for its recommendations and the Council of States shall within a period of fourteen days from the date of its receipt of the Bill return the Bill to the House of the People with its recommendations and the House of the People may thereupon either accept or reject all or any of the recommendations of the Council of States.

(3) If the House of the People accepts any of the recommendations of the Council of States, the Money Bill shall be deemed to have been passed by both the Houses with the amendments recommended by the Council of States and accepted by the House of the People.

(4) If the House of the People does not accept any of the recommendations of the Council of States, the Money Bill shall be deemed to have been passed by both the Houses in the form in which it was passed by the House of the People without any of the amendments recommended by the Council of States.

(5) If a Money Bill passed by the House of the People and transmitted to the Council of States for its recommendations is not returned to the House of the People within the said period

of fourteen days, it shall be deemed to have been passed by both the Houses at the expiration of the said period in the form in which it was passed by the House of the People.

110. Definition of "Money Bills": (1) For the purposes of this Chapter, a Bill shall be deemed to be a Money Bill if it contains only provisions dealing with all or any of the following matters, namely: (a) the imposition, abolition, remission, alteration or regulation of any tax; (b) the regulation of the borrowing of money or the giving of any guarantee by the Government of India, or the amendment of the law with respect to any financial obligations undertaken or to be undertaken by the Government of India; (c) the custody of the Consolidated Fund or the Contingency Fund of India, the payment of moneys into or the withdrawal of moneys from any such Fund; (d) the appropriation of moneys out of the Consolidated Fund of India; (e) the declaring of any expenditures to be expenditures charged on the Consolidated Fund of India or the increasing of the amount of any such expenditures; (f) the receipt of money on account of the Consolidated Fund of India or the public account of India or the custody or issue of such money or the audit of the accounts of the Union or of a State; or (g) any matter incidental to any of the matters specified in sub-clauses (a) to (f).

(2) A Bill shall not be deemed to be a Money Bill by reason only that it provides for the imposition of fines or other pecuniary penalties, or for the demand or payment of fees for licenses or fees for the services rendered, or by reason that it provides for the imposition, abolition, remission, alteration or regulation of any tax by any local authority or body for local purposes.

(Part V, Article 109 & 110)

COMMENTS

There are categories of Money Bill. The first is an Appropriation Bill and the other is a Finance Bill. A Finance Bill is introduced each year as mandated by Section 4 of the Income Tax Act, 1961 that the rates of income tax to be determined each year by a Finance Bill. A Finance Bill also prescribes the rates of custom duties, excise duties and other levies including the levy of a cess. Except in case of a Finance Bill the Constitution does not stipulate any time-limit for the passing of a Bill. The reason for passing of Finance Bill within the stipulated period of 75 days is because of a provision of the Provisional Collection of Tax Act, 1931. Section 3 of this Act is important and states that where a Bill to be introduced in the Parliament on behalf of Government provides for the imposition or increase of a duty of customs or excise, the Central Government may cause to be inserted in the Bill a declaration that it is expedient in the public interest that any provision of the Bill relating to such imposition or increase shall have immediate effect under this Act. Thus, by virtue of the declaration, the provision of a Finance bill takes effect immediately on the introduction of the Finance bill in Lok Sabha and unless the Finance bill is passed or defeated earlier then on the expiry of the seventy-fifth day after the day on which the Bill containing it was introduced it will cease to have effect.

From time to time, a Finance Bill also contained amendment of the Income Tax Act, the Central Excise Act, the Customs Act and other Acts administered by the Department of Revenue and Department of Expenditures of Ministry of Finance, Government of India. New taxes were levied by a law as part of the Finance Bill. The most important example is the levy of Service Tax by the Finance Act, 1994 which continues to be amended by the subsequent Finance Acts including the Finance Act, 2016. The other Act which has been amended in the past has been the Post-Office Act, 1898 so far the postal rates are concerned. The recent trend of inclusion of a number of financial legislations either incorporating a new legislation or amending an existing legislation as a part of the Finance Bill puts certain questions to policy-makers including putting pressure of time on draftsperson of legislative department in the Ministry of Law and justice to finish the drafting of the Finance Bill in less than three week time. Should a Finance Bill containing rates of tax and other substantive legislative proposals of a new law or substantially amending an existing law be referred to the Standing Committee of the Parliament of the Ministry of Finance so far as those legislative proposals are concerned as is the current practice in U.K.?

It is instructive to look experienced in U.K. Very recently in the United Kingdom, the House of Lords Economic Affairs Committee has set up a Finance Bill Sub-Committee (the FBSC) to inquire into the draft Finance Bill, 2016, which was published on 9 December, 2015. The FBSC's inquiries focus on technical issues of tax administration, clarification and simplification rather than on rates or incidence of tax. The practice started in 2003 when the House of Lord's Select Committee on Economic Affairs first appointed a Sub-Committee to inquire into the selected aspects of that year's Finance Bill. The Finance Bill Sub-Committee's inquiries address technical issues of tax administration, clarification and simplification, rather than rates or incidence of tax.

A Finance Bill is constitutionally valid if it has obtained prior recommendation of President for its introduction and also for its consideration and passing and a certificate from the Speaker that the bill in question is a Money Bill. On this question, the decision of the Speaker is final.

112. Annual financial statement: (1) The President shall in respect of every financial year cause to be laid before both the Houses of the Parliament a statement of the estimated receipts and expenditures of the Government of India for that year, in this Part referred to as the "annual financial statement."

(2) The estimates of expenditures embodied in the annual financial statement shall show separately:

(a) the sums required to meet expenditures described by this Constitution as expenditures charged upon the Consolidated Fund of India; and

(b) the sums required to meet other expenditures proposed to be made from the Consolidated Fund of India, and shall distinguish expenditures on revenue account from other expenditures.

(3) The following expenditures shall be expenditures charged on the Consolidated Fund of India:

(a) the emoluments and allowances of the President and other expenditures relating to his office;

(b) the salaries and allowances of the Chairman and the Deputy Chairman of the Council of States and the Speaker and the Deputy Speaker of the House of the People;

(c) debt charges for which the Government of India is liable, including interest, sinking fund charges and redemption charges, and other expenditures relating to the raising of loans and the service and redemption of debt;

(d) (i) the salaries, allowances and pensions payable to or in respect of Judges of the Supreme Court;

(ii) the pensions payable to or in respect of Judges of the Federal Court;

(iii) the pensions payable to or in respect of Judges of any High Court, which exercises jurisdiction in relation to any area included in the territory of India or which, at any time before the commencement of this Constitution, exercised jurisdiction in relation to any area included in 1a Governor's Province of the Dominion of India;

(e) the salary, allowances and pension payable to or in respect of the Comptroller and Auditor-General of India;

(f) any sums required to satisfy any judgement, decree or award of any court or arbitral tribunal;

(g) any other expenditures declared by this Constitution or by the Parliament by law to be so charged.

(Part V, Article 112)

COMMENTS

The following expenditures shall be expenditures charged on the Consolidated Fund of India as per Article 112(3) which States as under:

(a) the emoluments and allowances of the President and other expenditures relating to his office;

(b) the salaries and allowances of the Chairman and the Deputy Chairman of the Council of States and the Speaker and the Deputy Speaker of the House of the People;

(c) debt charges for which the Government of India is liable, including interest, sinking fund charges and redemption charges, and other expenditures relating to the raising of loans and the service and redemption of debt;

(d) (i) the salaries, allowances and pensions payable to or in respect of Judges of the Supreme Court;

(ii) the pensions payable to or in respect of Judges of the Federal Court,

(iii) the pensions payable to or in respect of Judges of any High Court which exercises jurisdiction in relation to any area included in the territory of India or which, at any time before the commencement of this Constitution exercised jurisdiction in relation to any area included in a Governor's Province of the Dominion of India;

(e) the salary, allowances and pension payable to or in respect of the Comptroller and Auditor-General of India;

(f) any sums required to satisfy any judgement, decree or award of any court or arbitral tribunal;

(g) any other expenditures declared by this Constitution or by the Parliament by law to be so charged.

113. Procedure in the Parliament with respect to estimates: (1) So much of the estimate as relates to expenditures charged upon the Consolidated Fund of India shall not be submitted to the vote of the Parliament, but nothing in this clause shall be construed as preventing the discussion in either House of the Parliament of any of those estimates.

(2) So much of the said estimates as relates to other expenditures shall be submitted in the form of demands for grants to the House of the People, and the House of the People shall have power to assent, or to refuse to assent, to any demand,

or to assent to any demand subject to a reduction of the amount specified therein.

(3) No demand for a grant shall be made except on the recommendation of the President.

(Part V, Article 113)

COMMENTS

The Annual Financial Statement or the Statement of the Estimated Receipts and Expenditures of the Government of India in respect of each financial year is popularly known as the Budget. Estimated expenditures is either charged upon the consolidated Fund of India or is submitted in the form of demands for grants for vote of the Parliament.

114. Appropriation Bills: (1) As soon as may be after the grants under Article 113 have been made by the House of the People, there shall be introduced a Bill to provide for the appropriation out of the Consolidated Fund of India of all moneys required to meet—

(a) the grants so made by the House of the People; and

(b) the expenditures charged on the Consolidated Fund of India but not exceeding in any case the amount shown in the statement previously laid before the Parliament.

(2) No amendment shall be proposed to any such Bill in either House of the Parliament which will have the effect of varying the amount or altering the destination of any grant so made or of varying the amount of any expenditures charged on the Consolidated Fund of India, and the decision of the person presiding as to whether an amendment is inadmissible under this clause shall be final.

(Part V, Article 114)

COMMENTS

A Bill to provide for the appropriation out of the Consolidated Fund of India of all moneys required to meet the grants and the expenditures charged on the Consolidated Fund of India is introduced, considered and passed after the demands for grants have been passed by the House. The introduction of the Appropriation Bill cannot be opposed. The Constitution expressly prohibits an amendment to the Appropriation Bill. It also provides for a fund known as Consolidated Fund of India. Moneys can be appropriated from the Consolidated Fund of India for the expenditures which are classified as Charged Expenditures and Voted Expenditures.

118. Rules of Procedure: (1) Each House of the Parliament may make rules for regulating, subject to the provisions of this Constitution, its procedure and the conduct of its business.

(2) Until rules are made under clause (1), the rules of procedure and standing orders in force immediately before the commencement of this Constitution with respect to the Legislature of the Dominion of India shall have effect in relation to the Parliament subject to such modifications and adaptations as may be made therein by the Chairman of the Council of States or the Speaker of the House of the People, as the case may be.

(3) The President, after consultation with the Chairman of the Council of States and the Speaker of the House of the People, may make rules as to the procedure with respect to joint sittings of, and communications between, the two Houses.

(4) At a joint sitting of the two Houses, the Speaker of the House of the People, or in his absence, such person as may be determined by the rules of procedure made under clause (3), shall preside.

(Part V, Article 118)

119. Regulation by law of procedure in the Parliament in relation to financial business: The Parliament may, for the purpose of the timely completion of financial business, regulate by law the procedure of, and the conduct of business in, each House of the Parliament in relation to any financial matter or to any Bill for the appropriation of moneys out of the Consolidated Fund of India, and, if and so far as any provision of any law so made is inconsistent with any rule made by a House of the Parliament under clause (1) of Article 118 or with any rule or standing order having effect in relation to the Parliament under clause (2) of that Article, such provision shall prevail.

(Part V, Article 119)

COMMENTS

For timely completion of financial business, the Parliament may enact a law under this Article. What is a financial business is not defined in the Constitution. Thus, a wide variety of legislation which may not fall within the definition of money bill may be considered as falling within the term 'financial business'. A law relating to monetary policy or restructuring the finances of companies may be considered within the term 'financial business'.

123. Power of the President to promulgate Ordinances during recess of the Parliament: (1) If at any time, except when both the Houses of the Parliament are in session, the President is satisfied that the circumstances exist which render it necessary for him to take immediate action, he may promulgate such Ordinances as the circumstances appear to him to require. (2) An Ordinance promulgated under this Article shall have the same force and effect as an Act of the Parliament, but every such Ordinance—(a) shall be laid before both the Houses of the Parliament and shall cease to operate at the expiration of six weeks from the reassembly of the Parliament, or, if before the expiration of that period, resolutions disapproving it are passed by both the Houses, upon the passing of the second of those resolutions; and (b) may be withdrawn at any time by the President.

Explanation: Where the Houses of the Parliament are summoned to reassemble on different dates, the period of six weeks shall be reckoned from the latter of those dates for the purposes of this clause. (3) If and so far as an Ordinance under this Article makes any provision, which, the Parliament would not under this Constitution be competent to enact, it shall be void.

(Part V, Article 123)

COMMENTS

Article 123 confers powers on the President to promulgate a law by issuing an Ordinance to enable the executive to deal with the emergent situation, which might well include a situation created by a law being declared void by a court of law. The President has the legislative power under Article 123 to promulgate an Ordinance and this legislative power is coextensive with the power of the Parliament to make laws. If the Parliament can by enacting legislation alter or amend tax laws, equally can the President do so by issuing an Ordinance under Article 123. There have been, in fact, numerous instances where the President has issued an Ordinance replacing with retrospective effect a tax law declared void by the High Court or the Supreme Court. In R.K. Garg vs. Union of India(9), the Constitutional validity of the Special Bearer Bonds Ordinance, 1980 was upheld. Prior to that, in A.K. Roy vs. Union of India,[10] the validity of the National Security Ordinance, 1980 which dealt with preventing detention was upheld.

In D.C. Wadhwa vs. State of Bihar[11], the repeated promulgation of the same Ordinance(s) was held a fraud on the Constitution. In this case, the writ petitions were filed by four petitioners challenging the practice of the State of Bihar in promulgating and repromulgating. Ordinances on a massive scale and in particular, they challenged the Constitutional validity of three different Ordinances issued by the Governor of Bihar, namely (i) Bihar Forest Produce (Regulation of Trade) Third Ordinance, 1983, (ii) The Bihar Intermediate Education Council Third Ordinance, 1983, and (iii) The Bihar Bricks Supply (Control) Third Ordinance, 1983. The Court held as under:

"The power conferred on the Governor to issue ordinances is in the nature of an Emergency power which is vested in the Governor for taking immediate action where such action may become necessary at a time when the legislature is not in session. The primary law-making authority under the Constitution is the legislature and not the executive but it is possible that when the legislature is not in session circumstances may arise, which render it necessary to take immediate action and in such a case in order that public interest may not suffer by reason of the inability of the legislature to make law to deal with the emergent situation, the Governor is vested with the power to promulgate ordinances. But every ordinance promulgated by the Governor must be placed before the legislature and it would cease to operate at the expiration of six weeks from the reassembly of the legislature or, if before the expiration of that period, a resolution disapproving it is passed by the Legislative Assembly and agreed to by the Legislative Council, if any. The object of this provision is that since the power conferred on the Governor to issue ordinances is an emergent power exercisable when the legislature is not in session, an ordinance promulgated by the Governor to deal with a situation, which requires immediate action and which cannot wait until the legislature reassembles, must necessarily have a limited life.

...The law-making function is entrusted by the Constitution to the legislature consisting of the representatives of the people and if the executive were permitted to continue the provisions of an ordinance in force by adopting the methodology of repromulgation without submitting to the voice of the legislature, it would be nothing short of usurpation by the executive of the law-making function of the legislature. The executive cannot by taking resort to an Emergency power exercisable by it only when the legislature is not in session, take over the law-making function of the legislature. That would be clearly subverting the democratic process which lies at the core of our Constitutional scheme, for then the people would be governed not by the laws made by the legislature as provided in the Constitution but by the laws made by the executive. The Government cannot bypass the legislature and without enacting the provisions of the ordinance into an Act of the legislature, repromulgate the ordinance as soon as the legislature is prorogued. Of course, there may be a situation where it may not be possible for the government to introduce and push through in the legislature a Bill containing the same provisions as in the ordinance, because the legislature may have too much legislative business in a particular session or the time at the disposal of the legislature in a particular session may be short, and in that event, the Governor may legitimately find that it is necessary to repromulgate the ordinance. Where such is the case, repromulgation of the ordinance may not be open to attack. But, otherwise, it would be a colourable exercise of power on the part of the executive to continue an ordinance with substantially the same provisions beyond the period limited by the Constitution, by adopting the methodology of repromulgation. It is settled, law that a Constitutional authority cannot do indirectly what it is not permitted to do directly. If there is a Constitutional provision inhibiting the Constitutional authority from doing an act, such provision cannot be allowed to be defeated by adoption of any subterfuge. That would be clearly a fraud on the Constitutional provision.

The Court also held that it is significant to note that so far as the President of India is concerned, though he has the same power of issuing an ordinance under Article 123 as the Governor has under Article 213, there is not a single instance in which the President has, since 1950 till today, repromulgated any ordinance after its expiry.

Promulgation and Repromulgation of Ordinances by the President:

The Narasimha Rao Government from year 1991-1996 had promulgated an average of 21 ordinances per year and the following Ordinances were promulgated after summoning of both the Houses.

1. The Payment of Bonus (Amendment) Ordinance, 1995 (8 of 1995)
2. The Union Duties of Excise (Goods of Special Importance) Amendment Ordinance, 1995 (9 of 1995)
3. The Additional Duties of Excise (Goods of Special Importance) Amendment Ordinance, 1995 (10 of 1995)
4. The Constitution (Scheduled Tribes) Order (Amendment) Third Ordinance, 1996 (30 of 1996)
5. The Income-tax (Amendment) Ordinance, 1996 (31 of 1996)

In the 16th Lok Sabha, a number of Ordinances were promulgated, including the amendment of the Telecom Regulatory Authority of India Act, 1997 and the amendment of the new Land Acquisition Act, 2013.

B. State Legislatures

The provisions of States are similar to that of Union. Only two Articles have been commented upon in this part.

"194. Powers, privileges, etc, of the House of Legislatures and of the members and committees thereof:

(3) In other respects, the powers, privileges and immunities of a House of the Legislature of a State, and of the members and the committees of a House of such Legislature shall be such as may from time to time be defined by the Legislature by law, and, until so defined, shall be those of that House and of its members and committees immediately before the coming into force of Section 26 of the Constitution Forty fourth Amendment Act, 1978."

(Part VI, Article 194)

COMMENTS

Article 194 (i) & (ii) is similar to Article 105 of the Constitution, which provides for the privileges of the Parliament and its Members. The said Articles provide that the privileges enjoyed by the legislature shall be such as may from time to time be defined by the legislature by law. It is relevant to mention that any law made by the Parliament or the legislature is subject to the discipline contained in Part III of the Constitution. The privileges have not been defined but the above Article provides that until the same are so defined (i.e. by the legislature by law), they shall be those which the House or its members and committees enjoyed immediately before the coming into force of Section 26 of the Constitution Forty-fourth Amendment Act, 1978.

The privileges are available only insofar as they are necessary in order that the House may freely perform its functions but do not extend to the activities undertaken outside the House on which the legislative provisions would apply without any differentiations. The scope of the privileges enjoyed depends upon the need for privileges, i.e., why they have been provided for. The basic premise for the privileges enjoyed by the members is to allow them to perform their functions as members and no hindrance is caused to the functioning of the House. The basic concept is that the privileges are those rights without which the House cannot perform its legislative functions. They do not exempt the Members from their obligations under any statute, which continue to apply to them like any other law applicable to ordinary citizens. Thus, enquiry or investigation into an allegation of corruption cannot be said to interfere with the legislative functions of the Assembly. No one enjoys any privilege against criminal prosecution.

Codification of Privileges: The question of codification of privileges has engaged the attention of the Presiding Officers of the Parliament and State Legislatures in India since 1921. On the subject, the Committee of Privileges of the Tenth Lok Sabha noted as follows:

"(i) the Parliamentary privileges are intended to be enjoyed on behalf of the people, in their interests and not against the people opposed to their interests;

(ii) the concept of privileges for any class of people is anachronistic in a democratic society and, therefore, if any, these privileges should be the barest minimum – only those necessary for functional purposes – and invariably defined in clear and precise terms;

(iii) sovereignty of the Parliament has increasingly become a myth, and a fallacy for sovereignty, if any, vests only in the people of India who exercise it at the time of general elections to the Lok Sabha and to the State Assemblies;

(iv) in a system wedded to freedom and democracy – rule of law, rights of the individual, independent judiciary and constitutional government – it is only fair that the fundamental rights of the citizens enshrined in the Constitution should have primacy over any privileges or special rights of any class of people, including the elected legislators, and that all such claims should be subject to judicial scrutiny, for situations may arise where the rights of the people may have to be protected even against the Parliament or against captive or capricious Parliamentary majorities of the moment;

(v) the Constitution specifically envisaged privileges of the Houses of Parliament and State Legislatures and their members and committees being defined by law by the respective legislatures and as such the Constitution makers definitely intended these privileges being subject to the fundamental rights, provisions of the Constitution and the jurisdiction of the courts;

(vi) The basic law that all citizens should be treated equally before the law holds good in the case of members of the Parliament as well. They have the same rights and liberties as ordinary citizens except when they perform their duties in the Parliament. The privileges, therefore, do not, in any way, exempt members from their normal obligation to the society which apply to them as much and, perhaps, more closely in that as they apply to others.

In any case, there is no question of any fresh privileges being added inasmuch as (a) under the Constitution, even at present, the Parliamentary privileges in India continue in actual practice to be governed by the precedents of the House of Commons as they existed on the day our Constitution came into force; and (b) in the House of Commons itself, creation of new privileges is not allowed."

200. Assent to Bills: When a Bill has been passed by the Legislative Assembly of a State or, in the case of a State having a Legislative Council, has been passed by both the Houses of the Legislature of the State, it shall be presented to the Governor and the Governor shall declare either that he assents to the Bill or that he withholds assent therefrom or that he reserves the Bill for the consideration of the President:

Provided that the Governor may, as soon as possible after the presentation to him of the Bill for assent, return the Bill if it is not a Money Bill together with a message requesting that the House or Houses will reconsider the Bill or any specified provisions thereof and, in particular, will consider the desirability of introducing any such amendments as he may recommend in his message and, when a Bill is so returned, the House or Houses shall reconsider the Bill accordingly, and if the Bill is passed again by the House or Houses with or without amendment and presented to the Governor for assent, the Governor shall not withhold assent therefrom:

Provided further that the Governor shall not assent to, but shall reserve for the consideration of the President, any Bill which in the opinion of the Governor would, if it became law, so derogate from the powers of the High Court as to endanger the position which that Court is by this Constitution designed to fill.

(Part VI, Article 200)

COMMENTS

Article 200 of the Constitution empowers the Governor of a State to reserve any Bill passed by the Legislature for consideration of the President. The other provisions in the Constitution like Articles 31A, 31C, 254 (2), 288, 304(b) and 360 also make it mandatory for the State laws to be reserved for the consideration of the President.

Under Article 200 of the Constitution, the Governor has the option either to assent the Bill or withhold his assent therefrom or reserve the Bill for consideration of the President. Governor has power to return a Bill, other than a Money Bill, to the Legislature for reconsideration. Where a Bill is reserved by the Governor for consideration of the President, the President has the option of either assenting the Bill or withholding his assent therefrom.

The Supreme Court of India in case P. Nambudiri vs. State of Kerala[12] held that the Constitution does not stipulate to that the assent of the Governor or the President must be given during the life term of the Assembly which passed the Bill. The Constitution does not impose any time limit within which the Governor or the President should make a declaration for giving or refusing the assent.

REFERENCES

1. Kuldip Nayar vs. Union of India & Ors (2006) 7 SCC 1.
2. Jaya Bachchan vs. Union of India & Ors (2006) 5 SCC 266.
3. Sibu Soren vs. Dayanand Sahay & Ors (2001) 7 SCC 425.
4. Consumer Education & Research Society vs. Union of India & Ors. (2009) 9 SCC 648.

5. MSM Sharma vs. Shrikrishna Sinha AIR 1959 SC 395.
6. In re Keshav Singh's 1965 AIR 745.
7. P.V. Narasimha Rao vs. State (1998) 4 SCC 626.
8. Raja Ram Pal Prasad vs. Hon'ble Speaker, Lok Sabha (2007)3 SCC 184.
9. R.K. Garg vs. Union of India, Air 1981 Sc 2138.
10. A.K. Roy vs. Union of India, (1982) 1 SCC 271.
11. D.C. Wadhwa vs. State of Bihar, 1987 AIR 579.
12. P. Nambudiri vs. State of Kerala, 1962 AIR 694.

□

Chapter 8
THE JUDICIARY

A. The Supreme Court

124. Establishment and constitution of Supreme Court: (1) There shall be a Supreme Court of India consisting of a Chief Justice of India and, until the Parliament by law prescribes a larger number, of not more than seven other Judges.

(2) Every Judge of the Supreme Court shall be appointed by the President by warrant under his hand and seal after consultation with such of the Judges of the Supreme Court and of the High Courts in the States as the President may deem necessary for the purpose and shall hold office until he attains the age of sixty-five years:

Provided that in the case of appointment of a Judge other than the Chief Justice, the Chief Justice of India shall always be consulted:

Provided further that—

(a) a Judge may, by writing under his hand addressed to the President, resign his office;

(b) a Judge may be removed from his office in the manner provided in clause (4).

(2A) The age of a Judge of the Supreme Court shall be determined by such authority and in such manner as the Parliament may by law provide.

(3) A person shall not be qualified for appointment as a Judge of the Supreme Court unless he is a citizen of India and—

(a) has been for at least five years a Judge of a High Court or of two or more such Courts in succession; or

(b) has been for at least ten years an advocate of a High Court or of two or more such Courts in succession; or

(c) is, in the opinion of the President, a distinguished jurist.

Explanation I: In this clause, "High Court" means a High Court which exercises, or which at any time before the commencement of this Constitution exercised, jurisdiction in any part of the territory of India.

Explanation II: In computing for the purpose of this clause, the period during which a person has been an advocate, any period during which a person has held judicial office not inferior to that of a district judge after he became an advocate shall be included.

(4) A Judge of the Supreme Court shall not be removed from his office except by an order of the President passed after an address by each House of the Parliament supported by a majority of the total membership of that House and by a majority of not less than two-thirds of the members of that House present and voting has been presented to the President in the same session for such removal on the ground of proved misbehaviour or incapacity.

(5) The Parliament may by law regulate the procedure for the presentation of an address and for the investigation and proof of the misbehaviour or incapacity of a Judge under clause (4).

(6) Every person appointed to be a Judge of the Supreme Court shall, before he enters upon his office, make and subscribe before the President, or some person appointed in that behalf by him, an oath or affirmation according to the form set out for the purpose in the Third Schedule.

(7) No person who has held office as a Judge of the Supreme Court shall plead or act in any court or before any authority within the territory of India.

(Part V, Article 124)

COMMENTS

The manner in which judges of the Supreme Court and High Court are appointed has been and still remains an issue of constitutional significance. The striking down of the

Constitution (Ninety-ninth Amendment) Act, 2014 and the National Judicial Appointment Commission Act, 2014 has raised issues on the power of the appointment of judges and more significantly whether the executive should have any role in the appointment of judges or not. For a long time the judiciary recognised the role of executive in appointment of judges. The first controversy arose in S.P. Gupta vs. Union of India[1], wherein a letter from the Union Law Minister to the Governor of Punjab and to the Chief Ministers of all other States and the addressees was questioned by way of writ under Article 32 of the Constitution. The letter informed the addressee, inter alia, that "...one-third of the Judges of the High Court, should as far as possible be from outside the State in which the High Court is situated..." and the addressees were requested to obtain from all additional Judges working in the High Courts their consent to be appointed as permanent Judges in any other High Court in the country. In response to the letter, quite a few additional Judges gave their consent to be appointed outside their parent State. The primacy of the executive was accepted by the majority though the judgement was rendered by a majority of 4:3. In the First Judges case, as it is known on issue of independence of judiciary and on the interpretation of the word 'consultation', the judges observed as under:

(a) P.N. Bhagwati, J. (as he then was) opined on independence of judiciary and on the meaning of the term 'consultation' and on consultation process as under:

(i) On the subject of independence of the judiciary, it was opined, that:

"...The concept of independence of judiciary is a noble concept which inspires the constitutional scheme and constitutes the foundation on which rests the edifice of our democratic polity. If there is one principle which runs through the entire fabric of the entire Constitution, it is the principle of the rule of law and under the Constitution, it is the judiciary which is entrusted with the task of keeping every organ of the State within the limits of the law and, thereby, making the rule of law meaningful and effective...The judiciary stands between the citizen and the State as a bulwark against executive excesses and misuse or abuse of power by the executive, and, therefore, it is absolutely essential that the judiciary must be free from executive pressure or influence and this has been secured by the Constitution makers by making elaborate provisions in the Constitution. It had many dimensions, namely fearlessness of other power centers, economic or political, and freedom from prejudices acquired and nourished by the class to which the Judges belong (paragraph 27).

(ii) On the question of the meaning of the term "consultation" expressed in Article 124(2) and Article 217(1), it was held that this question was no longer res integra, as the issue stood concluded by the decision of the Supreme Court in Union of India vs. Sankalchand Himatlal Sheth, wherein its meaning was determined with reference to Article 222(1).

Each of the constitutional functionaries, required to be consulted under Article 124 and Article 217, must have for his consideration, full and identical facts bearing upon appointment or non-appointment of the person concerned, and the opinion of each of them taken on identical material, must be considered by the Central Government, before it takes a decision, whether or not to appoint the person concerned as a Judge. It was open to the Central Government to take its own decision, in regard to the appointment or non-appointment of a Judge to a High Court or the Supreme Court, after taking into account and giving due weight to the opinions expressed. It was also observed that the only ground on which such a decision could be assailed was that the action was based on mala fides or irrelevant considerations. In case of a difference of opinion amongst the constitutional functionaries, who were to be consulted, it was felt that it was for the Central Government to decide, whose opinion should be accepted. The contention raised on behalf of the petitioners, that in the consultative process, primacy should be that of the Chief Justice of India, since he was the head of the Indian judiciary and pater families of the judicial fraternity, was rejected for the reason that each of the constitutional functionaries was entitled to equal weightage. With reference to appointment of Judges of the Supreme Court, it was held that the Chief Justice of India was required to be consulted, but the Central Government was not bound to act in accordance with the opinion of the Chief Justice of India, even though his opinion was entitled to great weight. It was, therefore, held that the ultimate power of appointment rested with the Central Government (paragraph 30).

(iii) On the issue of appointment of Judges of the Supreme Court, it was concluded that consultation with the Chief Justice of India was a mandatory requirement. But while making an appointment, consultation could extend to such other Judges of the Supreme Court, and of the High Courts, as the Central Government may deem necessary. It was felt that consultation with the Chief Justice of India alone, with reference to the appointment of Judges to the Supreme Court, was not a very satisfactory mode of appointment because wisdom and experience demanded that no power should rest in a single individual howsoever, high and great he may be, and howsoever honest and well-meaning. It was suggested that it would be more appropriate if a collegium would make the recommendations to the President with regard to appointments to the higher judiciary, and the recommending authority should be more broad-based. If the collegium was comprised of persons who had knowledge of persons, who may be fit for appointment to the Bench, and possessed the qualities required for such appointment, it would go a long way towards securing the right kind of Judges, who would be truly independent (paragraph 31).

(b) The observation of other judges was as under:

1. A.C. Gupta, J.:

(i) On the subject of the "independence of the judiciary", it was opined that the same did not mean freedom of Judges to act arbitrarily. It only meant that the Judges must be free while discharging their judicial functions. In order to maintain "independence of the judiciary", it was felt that Judges had to be protected against interference, direct or indirect. It was concluded that the constitutional provisions should not be construed in a manner that would tend to undermine the concept of "independence of the judiciary" (paragraph 119).

(ii) On the question whether the opinion of the Chief Justice of India would have primacy in case of a difference of opinion between the Chief Justice of a High Court and the Chief Justice of India, the view expressed was that the President should accept the opinion of the Chief Justice of India, unless such opinion suffered from any obvious infirmity. And that the President could not act as an umpire, and choose between the two opinions (paragraph 134).

2. V.D. Tulzapurkar, J.

(i) Insofar as the question of "independence of the judiciary" is concerned, it was asserted that all the Judges who had expressed their opinions in the matter had emphasised that the framers of the Constitution had taken the utmost pains to secure the "independence of the Judges" of the higher judiciary (paragraph 639).

3. R.S. Pathak, J. (as he then was):

(i) With reference to the issue of "independence of the judiciary", it was observed that while the administration of justice drew its legal sanction from the Constitution, its credibility rested in the faith of the people. Indispensable to such faith was the "independence of the judiciary". An independent and impartial judiciary, it was felt, gives character and content to the constitutional milieu (paragraph 874).

4. E.S. Venkataramiah, J. (as he then was):

(i) With reference to the "independence of the judiciary", it was opined that the same was one of the central values on which the Constitution was based. It was pointed out that in all countries, where the rule of law prevailed, and the power to adjudicate upon disputes between a man and a man, and a man and the State, and a State and another State, and a State and the Centre, was entrusted to a judicial body, it was natural that such body should be assigned a status, free from capricious or whimsical interference from outside, so that it could act without fear and in consonance with judicial conscience (paragraph 1068).

The First judges case held the field from 1981 to 1993 and appointment of judges by a 'collegium' was followed and the role of the executive including the Union Law Minister was recognised.

The Second Judges Case: The First judges case was overruled by a nine judge bench in the Second judges case. The correctness of the First Judges case was doubted by a three judges Bench in Subhash Sharma vs. Union of India[2], which opined that the majority view in the First judges case should be considered by a larger Bench. In Subhash Sharma vs. U.O.I., doubts were expressed about the correctness of the interpretation of the word "consultation" in regard to the appointment of judges in S.P. Gupta vs. U.O.I., popularly known as First judges case.

In the Supreme Court Advocate on Record Association vs. Union of India[3] popularly referred to as Second judges case, the petitioners alleged that the Executive had failed to properly discharge its duty to fill judicial appointments in the High Courts in a timely manner, and failed to select the most qualified judges. The Chief Justice of India constituted a nine judges Bench to examine two questions. Firstly, whether the opinion of the Chief Justice of India in regard to the appointment of Judges to the Supreme Court and to the High Courts as well as transfer of Chief Justices and Judges of High Courts was entitled to primacy? And secondly, whether the fixation of the judge-strength in High Courts was justiciable? By a majority of 7:2, a nine judges bench of this Court, in the Second judges case, overruled the judgement in the First Judges case. The judgement was rendered on 6.10.1993.

The conclusions drawn by the majority view were as under:

"(1) The process of appointment of judges to the Supreme Court and the High Courts is an integrated 'participatory consultative process' for selecting the best and most suitable persons available for appointment; and all the constitutional functionaries must perform this duty collectively with a view primarily to reach an agreed decision, subserving the constitutional purpose, so that the occasion of primacy does not arise.

(2) Initiation of the proposal for appointment in the case of the Supreme Court must be by the Chief Justice of India, and in the case of a High Court by the Chief Justice of that High Court, and for transfer of a Judge/Chief Justice of a High Court, the proposal has to be initiated by the Chief Justice of India.

This is the manner in which proposals for appointments to the Supreme Court and the High Courts as well as for the transfers of Judges/Chief Justices of the High Courts must invariably be made.

(3) In the event of conflicting opinions by the constitutional functionaries, the opinion of the judiciary 'symbolised by the view of the Chief Justice of India', and formed in the manner indicated, has primacy.

(4) No appointment of any Judge to the Supreme Court or any High Court can be made unless it is in conformity with the opinion of the Chief Justice of India.

(5) In exceptional cases alone, for stated strong cogent reasons, disclosed to the Chief Justice of India, indicating that the recommendee is not suitable for appointment, that appointment recommended by the Chief Justice of India may not be made. However, if the stated reasons are not accepted by the Chief Justice of India and the other Judges of the Supreme Court who have been consulted in the matter, on reiteration of the recommendation by the Chief Justice of India, the appointment should be made as a healthy convention.

(6) Appointment to the office of the Chief Justice of India should be of the seniormost Judge of the Supreme Court considered fit to hold the office.

(7) The opinion of the Chief Justice of India has not mere primacy, but is determinative in the matter of transfers of High Court judges/Chief Justices.

(8) Consent of the transferred Judge/Chief Justice is not required for either the first or any subsequent transfer from one High Court to another.

(9) Any transfer made on the recommendation of the Chief Justice of India is not to be deemed to be punitive, and such transfer is not justiciable on any ground.

(10) In making all appointments and transfers, the norms indicated must be followed. However, the same do not confer any justiciable right in anyone.

(11) Only limited judicial review on the grounds specified earlier is available in matters of appointments and transfers.

(12) The initial appointment of Judge can be made to a High Court other than that for which the proposal was initiated.

(13) Fixation of Judges' strength in the High Courts is justiciable, but only to the extent and in the manner indicated.

(14) The majority opinion in S.P. Gupta vs. Union of India (1982) 2 SCR 365: AIR 1982 SC 149, insofar as it takes the contrary view relating to primacy of the role of the Chief Justice of India in matters of appointments and transfers, and the justifiability of these matters as well as in relation to Judges strength does not commend itself to us as being the correct view. The relevant provisions of the Constitution including the constitutional scheme must now be construed, understood and implemented in the manner indicated herein by us."

Consequent upon doubts having arisen with the Union of India about the interpretation of the Second Judges' case, the President of India, in exercise of his power under Article 143, referred nine questions to the Supreme Court, for its opinion.[4] A nine Judges' Bench answered the reference unanimously, on 28.10.1998.

In the Third judges case, it was held:

"1. The expression "consultation with the Chief Justice of India" in Articles 217(1) of the Constitution of India requires consultation with a plurality of judges in the formation of the opinion of the Chief Justice of India. The sole individual opinion of the Chief Justice of India does not constitute "consultation" within the meaning of the said Articles.

2. The transfer of puisne judges is judicially reviewable only to this extent that the recommendation that has been made by the Chief Justice of India in this behalf has not been made in consultation with the four seniormost puisne Judges of the Supreme Court and/or that the views of the Chief Justice of the High Court from which the transfer is to be effected and of the Chief Justice of the High Court to which the transfer is to be effected have not been obtained.

3. The Chief Justice of India must make a recommendation to appoint a Judge of the Supreme Court and to transfer a Chief Justice or puisne judge of a High Court in consultation with the four seniormost puisne judges of the Supreme Court.

Insofar as an appointment to the High Court is concerned, the recommendation must be made in consultation with two seniormost puisne Judges of the Supreme Court.

4. The Chief Justice of India is not entitled to act solely in his individual capacity, without consultation with other judges of the Supreme Court, in respect of materials and information conveyed by the Government of India for non-appointment of a judge recommended for appointment.

5. The requirement of consultation by the Chief Justice of India with his colleagues who are likely to be conversant with the affairs of the concerned High Court does not refer only to those judges who have that High Court as a parent High Court. It does not exclude judges who have occupied the office of a Judge or Chief Justice of that High Court on transfer.

6. "Strong cogent reasons" do not have to be recorded as justification for a departure from the order of seniority, in respect of each senior Judge who has been passed over. What has to be recorded is the positive reason for the recommendation.

7. The views of the judges consulted should be in writing and should be conveyed to the Government of India by the Chief Justice of India along with his views to the extent set out in the body of this opinion.

8. The Chief Justice of India is obliged to comply with the norms and the requirement of the consultation process, as aforestated, in making his recommendations to the Government of India.

9. Recommendations made by the Chief Justice of India without complying with the norms and requirements of the consultation process, as aforestated, are not binding upon the Government of India."

Memorandum of Procedure for Appointment of Judges

After the judgement in the Second judges case was rendered in 1993, and the advisory opinion of this Court was tendered to the President of India in 1998, the Union of India then framed a Memorandum of Procedure on 30.6.1999 for the appointment of Judges and Chief Justices to the High Courts and the Supreme Court in consonance with the above two judgements. Later on, three judgements of the Supreme Court were reviewed by the Law Commission of India in its Report titled 'Proposal for Reconsideration of Judges cases I, II and III – S. P. Gupta vs. UOI reported in AIR 1982 SC 149, Supreme Court Advocates-on-Record Association vs. UOI reported in 1993 (4) SCC 441 and Special Reference 1 of 1998 reported in 1998 (7) SCC 739' dated 21st November, 2008.[5] The Report recommended that two alternatives are available to the Government of the day. One is to seek a reconsideration of the three judgements aforesaid before the Hon'ble Supreme Court. Otherwise a law may be passed restoring the primacy of the Chief Justice of India and the power of the executive to make the appointments. After a gap of almost 6 years in the year 2014, a Constitution Amendment Bill followed by a the Parliamentary legislation titled the National Judicial Appointment Commission Act, 2014 were enacted by the Parliament. The validity of the Constitution Amendment Act and of the NJCA was challenged by the Supreme Court Bar Association and others.[6]

The question which arose for consideration related to the constitutional validity of the Constitution (Ninety-ninth Amendment) Act, 2014 and also that of the National Judicial Appointments Commission Act, 2014. The core issue that arose for consideration related to the validity of the process of selection and appointment of Judges to the higher judiciary (i.e., Chief Justices and Judges of the High Courts and the Supreme Court), and transfer of Chief Justices and Judges of one High Court to another.

The Constitution (Ninety-ninth Amendment) Act, 2014 added new Articles 124A, 124B and 124C after Article 124 of the Constitution. An enabling legislation titled National Judicial Appointments Commission Act, 2014 was also enacted. It is significant to note that the Statement of Objects and Reasons appended with the Bill stated, inter alia, that the proposed Bill seeks to broadbase the method of appointment of Judges in the Supreme Court and High Courts, enables participation of judiciary, executive and eminent persons and ensures greater transparency, accountability and objectivity in the appointment of the Judges in the Supreme Court and High Courts. However, no reference in the Statement of Objects and Reasons was given of the recommendation contained in the Report 214 dated 21st November, 2008 of the Law Commission of India as the said report had its basis in various recommendations of the Parliamentary Standing Committees and law of foreign jurisdiction like America, Australia, Canada and Kenya, where the executive is the sole authority to appoint Judges or the executive appoints in consultation with the Chief Justice of the Country and the reference of the same could have provided better understanding for the enactment of the Constitution (Ninety-ninth Amendment) Act, 2014 and the National Judicial Appointment Commission Act, 2014. The following paragraph of the Report 214 of the Law Commission of India is most relevant, which reads as under:

'Indian Constitution provides a beautiful system of checks and balances under Articles 124(2) and 217(1) for the appointment of Judges of the Supreme Court and High Courts where both the executive and judiciary have been given a balanced role. As already stated, this delicate balance has been upset by the 2nd Judges case (Advocate on Record Association vs. Union of India 1993(4) SCC 4412 and the opinion of the Supreme Court in the Presidential Reference (Special Reference No. 1 of 1998). It is time the original balance of power is restored'.

The newly inserted Article 124A(1) provided for the constitution and the composition of the National Judicial Appointments Commission and as per the Constitution (Ninety-ninth Amendment) Act, 2014. The composition provided was as under:

(a) the Chief Justice of India, Chairperson, ex officio;
(b) two other senior Judges of Supreme Court, next to the Chief Justice of India – Members, ex officio;
(c) the Union Minister in charge of Law and Justice – Member, ex officio;
(d) two eminent persons, to be nominated – Members.

In the Supreme Court Bar Association and Others vs. Union of India (7) The constitution bench of five judges speaking through Justice Khehar held that clauses (a) and (b) of Article 124A(1) do not provide an adequate representation to the judicial component in the NJAC and clauses (a) and (b) of Article 124A(1) are insufficient to preserve the primacy of the judiciary, in the matter of selection and appointment of Judges, to the higher judiciary (as also transfer of Chief Justices and Judges, from one High Court to another), hence, the same were held violative of the principle of "independence of the judiciary". Justice Khehar further observed that clause (c) of Article 124A(1) is ultra vires the provisions of the Constitution because of the inclusion of the Union Minister in charge of Law and Justice as an exofficio Member of the NJAC. Clause (c) of Article 124A(1), in view of the court, impinges upon the principles of "independence of the judiciary", as well as, "separation of powers". It was further held that clause (d) of Article 124A(1) which provides for the inclusion of two "eminent persons" as Members of the NJAC is ultra vires the provisions of the Constitution, for a variety of reasons and one of them being as violative of the "basic structure" of the Constitution. Thus, clauses (a) to (d) of Article 124A(1) were set aside by the court and were struck down. One effect of striking down of Article 124A(1) was that the entire Constitution (99th Amendment) Act, 2014 was set aside and struck down in its entirety, as being ultra vires the provisions of the Constitution.

In paragraph 5 of the Order of the Court dated 16th October, 2014, it was decided to consider the incorporation of additional appropriate measures, if any, for an improved working of the "collegium system". In the Supreme Court Advocates-on-Record Association and Anrs vs. Union of India dated December 16, 2015[8]. broad suggestions for consideration and supplementing the Memorandum of Procedure for the faithful implementation of the principles laid down in the Second Judges case and the Third Judges case were made by the constitution bench of five judges to the Union Government. Thus, a fresh Memorandum of Procedure is to be brought into place, so that new appointments to the higher judiciary could be made.

Hopefully, the fresh Memorandum for Appointment of Judges would be based on the conclusion, inter alia, drawn by the majority view that the process of appointment of Judges to the Supreme Court and the High Courts is an integrated 'participatory consultative process' for selecting the best and most suitable persons available for appointment; and all the constitutional functionaries must perform this duty collectively with a view primarily to reach an agreed decision. Thus, for selecting the best and most suitable person, it is hoped that the fresh Memorandum of Appointment will contain elaborate mechanism.

125. Salaries, etc. of Judges: (1) There shall be paid to the Judges of the Supreme Court such salaries as may be determined by the Parliament by law and, until provision in that behalf is so made, such salaries as are specified in the Second Schedule.

(2) Every Judge shall be entitled to such privileges and allowances and to such rights in respect of leave of absence and pension as may from time to time be determined by or under law made by the Parliament and, until so determined, to such privileges, allowances and rights as are specified in the Second Schedule:

Provided that neither the privileges nor the allowances of a Judge nor his rights in respect of leave of absence or pension shall be varied to his disadvantage after his appointment.

(Part V, Article 125)

COMMENTS

Judges of the Supreme Court are paid salaries and other allowances as determined by an Act of the Parliament. The Supreme Court Judges (Salary and Conditions of Service) Act,1985 has been amended from time to time and more recently in 2015. With effect from January 1, 2006, the salaries shall be as follows:

Chief Justice of India – from ₹ 33,000/pm to ₹ 1,00,000/pm; (b) Judge of Supreme Court – from ₹ 30,000/pm to ₹ 90,000/pm; (c) Chief Justice of High Court – from ₹ 30,000/pm to ₹ 90,000/pm; and (d) Judges of High Court – from ₹ 26,000/pm to ₹ 80,000/pm.

129. Supreme Court to be a court of record: The Supreme Court shall be a court of record and shall have all the powers of such a court including the power to punish for contempt of itself.

(Part V, Article 129)

COMMENTS

The meaning of the word 'contempt' has often come up for its interpretation before the courts. According to the Black's Law Dictionary[9], 'Contempt' is defined as "Conduct that defies the authority or dignity of a Court or legislature." It also adds that "because such conduct interferes with the administration of justice, it is punishable."

The Supreme Court in the following cases observed on power of the contempt as under:

(a) In the case of Aligarh Municipal Board vs. Ekka Tonga Mazdoor Union,[10] Court said that it is the seriousness of the irresponsible acts of the contemners and the degree of harm caused to the administration of justice, which would decisively determine whether the matter should be tried as a criminal contempt or not.

(b) In the case of L.D. Jaikwal vs. State of U.P.,[11] Court held as under:

"6. We do not think that merely because the appellant has tendered his apology, we should set aside the sentence and allow him to go unpunished. Otherwise, all that a person wanting to intimidate a Judge by making the grossest imputations against him has to do, is to go ahead and scandalise him, and later on, tender a formal empty apology which costs him practically nothing. If such an apology were to be accepted, as a rule, and not as an exception, we would in fact be virtually issuing a "licence" to scandalise courts and commit contempt of court with impunity......"

(c) In the case of M.B. Sanghi Advocate vs. High Court of Punjab & Haryana,[12] the court cautioned against the growing tendency of maligning the reputation of judicial officers by disgruntled elements who fail to secure desired orders. While observing that it was high time that such tendency is to be nipped in the bud, this Court said, "Such causes raise larger issues touching the independence of not only the concerned Judge, but the entire institution... It is high time that we realise that the much cherished judicial independence has to be protected not only from the executive or the legislature, but also from those who are an integral part of the system."

(d) In Re: Vinay Chandra Mishra,[13] it was held that the power of the Supreme Court to punish for contempt was not limited by any statute. In this case, the court awarded exemplary punishment and observed:

"The facts and circumstances of the present case justify our invoking the power under Article 129 read with Article 142 of the Constitution to award to the contemner a suspended sentence of imprisonment together with the suspension of his practice as an advocate as directed herein. The contemner shall stand suspended for practising as an advocate for tree years."

The decision of debarring from practice was challenged by the Supreme Court Bar Association[14] and the only question before the constitution bench of five judges was whether the punishment for established contempt of Court committed by an Advocate can include punishment to debar the concerned advocate from practice by suspending his license (sanad) for a specified period, in exercise of its powers under Article 129 read with Article 142 of the Constitution of India. The court held as under:

"We are of the opinion that this court cannot in exercise of its jurisdiction under Article 142 read with Article 129 of the Constitution, while punishing a contemner for committing contempt of court, also impose a punishment of suspending his licence to practice, where the contemner happens to be an Advocate. Such a punishment cannot even be imposed by taking recourse to the appellate powers under Section 38 of the Act while dealing with a case of contempt of court (and not an appeal relating to professional misconduct as such). To that extent, the law laid down in Re: Vinay Chandra Mishra, (1995) 2 S.C.C. 584 is not good law and we overrule it."

133. Appellate jurisdiction of Supreme Court in appeals from High Courts in regard to civil matters: (1) An appeal shall lie to the Supreme Court from any judgement, decree or final order in a civil proceeding of a High Court in the territory of India if the High Court certifies under Article 134A—

(a) that the case involves a substantial question of law of general importance; and

(b) that in the opinion of the High Court, the said question needs to be decided by the Supreme Court.

(2) Notwithstanding anything in Article 132, any party appealing to the Supreme Court under clause (1) may urge as one of the grounds in such appeal that a substantial question of law as to the interpretation of this Constitution has been wrongly decided.

(Part V, Article 133)

COMMENTS

In the case of James Joseph vs. State of Kerala[15], the following principles with reference to appeals were laid down, namely:

"(i) An appeal is a proceeding where a higher forum reconsiders the decision of a lower forum, on questions of fact and questions of law, with jurisdiction to confirm, reverse, modify the decision or remand the matter to the lower forum for fresh decision in terms of its directions;

(ii) The appellate jurisdiction can be limited or regulated by the legislature and its extent has to be decided with reference to the language employed by the statute conferring the appellate jurisdiction;

(iii) The width of jurisdiction or the limitations on jurisdiction with reference to an appeal, does not depend on whether the appeal is a first appeal or a second appeal, but depends upon the limitations, if any, placed by the statute conferring the right of appeal;

(iv) If the Legislature's intention is to limit the jurisdiction in an appeal, it may indicate such limits in the provision providing for appeal. Alternatively, it may expressly or impliedly incorporate the provisions of Section 100 of the Code into the provision for appeals;

(v) Generally, statutory provisions for appeals against original orders or decrees (that is, first appeals) will not have any limitations and, therefore, rehearing on both law and fact is contemplated; and statutory provisions for appeals against appellate orders (that is, second appeals) will be restricted to questions of law. But such restriction is not on account of any legal principle that all second appeals should always be with reference to questions of law, but would depend upon the wording of the statute placing the restrictions upon the scope of second appeal;

(vi) Where the statute does not place any limitations or restrictions in regard to the scope and width of the appeal, it shall be construed that the appeal provides a right of rehearing on law as well as facts. If the Legislature enacts a self-contained provision for second appeals, without any limitation upon the scope of the second appeal and excludes the possibility of reading the provision of Section 100 of the Code, into such provision, then, it will not be permissible to read the limitations of Section 100 of the Code into the special provision."

136. Special leave to appeal by the Supreme Court: (1) Notwithstanding anything in this Chapter, the Supreme Court may, in its discretion, grant special leave to appeal from any judgement, decree, determination, sentence or order in any cause or matter passed or made by any court or tribunal in the territory of India.

(2) Nothing in clause (1) shall apply to any judgement, determination, sentence or order passed or made by any court or tribunal constituted by or under any law relating to the Armed Forces.

(Part V, Article 136)

COMMENTS

Under Article 136 of the Constitution of India any person aggrieved by any judgement, decree, determination or order in any cause or matter passed or made by any Court or Tribunal in the territory of India may appeal to the Supreme Court of India. Accordingly a person aggrieved by any order or judgement of High Court or of Tribunal may appeal to the Supreme Court by filing a Special Leave Petition.

The rules governing SLP are contained in Order XVI of the Supreme Court Rules, 1966. Under the said Rules, SLP can be filed against either the Order of High Court rejecting petition for Leave to Appeal to the Supreme Court of India i.e., on High Court refusing to grant Certificate of Fitness for Leave to Appeal to the Supreme Court or against the Order/Judgement itself. It is also possible to file SLP against the Judgement of the High Court either in Writ Petition or in the Income-tax Reference. If the Petition is filed against the Judgement of the High Court, the time limit is 90 days from the date of Judgement/Order and if the Petition is filed against the Order of High Court refusing to grant Certificate of Fitness for Appeal, the time limit is 60 days from the date of Order refusing to grant Certificate. The above time limit is subject to the time taken for obtaining certified copy of the Judgement/Order, i.e., subject to Sections 4, 5, 12 and 14 of the Limitation Act, 1963.

The discretionary power of the Supreme Court may be used where it considers appropriate against any order of High court in civil or criminal matters where such High Court has not issued a certificate under Article 133 or Article 134 of the Constitution. Under Article 136 an application for special leave to appeal lies against orders of a court or tribunal including Industrial Tribunal. Powers under Article 136 is to be exercised in exceptional circumstances only.

137. Review of judgements or orders by the Supreme Court: Subject to the provisions of any law made by the Parliament or any rules made under Article 145, the Supreme Court shall have power to review any judgement pronounced or order made by it.

(Part V, Article 137)

COMMENTS

Part VIII Order XL of the Supreme Court Rules, 1966 deals with the review and consists of four rules. Rule 1 reads as under:

"The Court may review its judgement or order, but no application for review will be entertained in a civil proceeding except on the ground mentioned in Order XLVII Rule 1 of the Code and in a criminal proceeding except on the ground of an error apparent on the face of the record."

Order XLVII, Rule 1(1) of the Code of Civil Procedure, 1908 provides for an application for review, which reads as under:

"Any person considering himself aggrieved:

(a) by a decree or order from which an appeal is allowed, but from which no appeal has been preferred,

(b) by a decree or order from which no appeal is allowed, or

(c) by a decision on a reference from a Court of Small Causes, and who, from the discovery of new and important matter or evidence which, after the exercise of due diligence, was not within his knowledge or could not be produced by him at the time when the decree was passed or order made, or on account of some mistake or error apparent on the face of the record, or for any other sufficient reason, desires to obtain a review of the decree passed or order made against him, may apply for a review of judgement to the court which passed the decree or made the order."

In a criminal proceeding, review is permissible on the ground of an error apparent on the face of the record.

To sum up, a review will be maintainable on:

(i) discovery of new and important matter or evidence which, after the exercise of due diligence, was not within the knowledge of the petitioner or could not be produced by him;

(ii) Mistake or error apparent on the face of the record;

(iii) Any other sufficient reason.

141. Law declared by the Supreme Court to be binding on all courts: The law declared by the Supreme Court shall be binding on all courts within the territory of India.

(Part V, Article 141)

COMMENTS

The binding essence of a judicial decision is traditionally summed up in the phrase ratio decidendi ('reason for deciding'). In legal theory, there are two leading views of the ratio decidendi of a case. One is the classical theory which holds that the ratio is the rule or principle that the court deciding a case considers necessary for the result reached in the case. The other view is the Goodhart theory, which is that the ratio consists of the facts the judge in the precedent case believed were material, and the judge's decision based on those facts.

In India, a decision of the Supreme Court on identical facts and law binds the Court on the same points of law in a later case. The doctrine of binding precedents has been settled by several pronouncements of the Supreme Court. The Constitution Bench of this Court in the case of Union of India vs. Raghubir Singh,[16] observed as under:

"8. Taking note of the hierarchical character of the judicial system in India, it is of paramount importance that the law declared by this Court should be certain, clear and consistent. It is commonly known that most decisions of the courts are of significance not merely because they constitute an adjudication on the rights of the parties and resolve the dispute between them, but also because in doing so, they embody a declaration of law operating as a binding principle in future cases. In this latter aspect lies their particular value in developing the jurisprudence of the law.

9. The doctrine of binding precedent has the merit of promoting a certainty and consistency in judicial decisions, and enables an organic development of the law, besides providing assurance to the individual as to the consequence of transactions forming part of his daily affairs. And, therefore, the need for a clear and consistent enunciation of legal principle in the decisions of a court.

In Municipal Corporation of Delhi vs. Gurnam Kaur,[17] it was observed that the decisions of the Supreme Court have no binding force firstly, where it is obiter dicta, i.e. statements which are not part of ratio decidendi; secondly, where a decision is per incurium, i.e. given in ignorance of the term of a statute or rule having the force of a statute; thirdly, where a decision is passed sub-silentio, i.e. without any argument or debate on the relevant question; and fourthly, where an order is made with the consent of the parties, and with the reservation that it should not be treated as precedent."

The latin expression 'per incuriam' literally means 'through inadvertence'. In State of U.P. vs. Synthetics and Chemicals Ltd.,[18] it was explained as follows:

"40. 'Incuria' literally means 'carelessness'. In practice 'per incuriam' appears to mean per ignoratium. English courts have developed this principle in relaxation of the rule of stare decisis....

On another exception of the rule of precedent, i.e. sub-silention, the court observed in as under:

"41. Does this principle extend and apply to a conclusion of law, which was neither raised nor preceded by any consideration. In other words, can such conclusions be considered as declaration of law? Here again the English courts and jurists have carved out an exception to the rule of precedents. It has been explained as rule of sub-silentio. A decision passes sub-silentio in the technical sense that has come to be attached to that phrase, when the particular point of law involved in the decision is not perceived by the court or present to its mind."

142. Enforcement of decrees and orders of Supreme Court and orders as to discovery, etc.: (1) The Supreme Court in the exercise of its jurisdiction may pass such decree or make such order as is necessary for doing complete justice in any case or matter pending before it, and any decree so passed or order so made shall be enforceable throughout the territory of India in such a manner as may be prescribed by or under any law made by the Parliament and, until provision in that behalf is so made, in such a manner as the President may by order prescribe.

(2) Subject to the provisions of any law made in this behalf by the Parliament, the Supreme Court shall, as respects the whole of the territory of India, have all and every power to make any order for the purpose of securing the attendance of

any person, the discovery or production of any documents, or the investigation or punishment of any contempt of itself.

(Part V, Article 142)

COMMENTS

The main purpose of Article 142 is to do complete justice. In Manohar Lal Sharma vs. Principal Secy, & Ors.,[19] the court held that the Supreme Court has been conferred with very wide powers for proper and effective administration of justice. In many matters of environment protection, family law and for the welfare of downtrodden, the Supreme Court invoked its powers under Article 142 of the Constitution.

143. Power of President to consult the Supreme Court: (1) If, at any time, it appears to the President that a question of law or fact has arisen, or is likely to arise, which is of such a nature and of such public importance that it is expedient to obtain the opinion of the Supreme Court upon it, he may refer the question to that Court for consideration and the Court may, after such hearing as it thinks fit, report to the President its opinion thereon.

(2) The President may, notwithstanding anything in the proviso to Article 131, refer a dispute of the kind mentioned in the said proviso to the Supreme Court for opinion and the Supreme Court shall, after such hearing as it thinks fit, report to the President its opinion thereon.

(Part V, Article 143)

COMMENTS

The minimum number of Judges to give such opinion shall be five. The important references under Article 143 are Kerala Education Bill, 1958[20], In Re Berubari's case in 1960,[21] In Re Sea Customs Act case in 1962,[22] In Re Keshav Singh's case in 1965,[23] In Re President Poll,[24] In Re the Special Court's Bill,[25] In Re Cauvery Water Disputes Tribunals,[26] In Re Principles and Procedure regarding appointment of Supreme Court and High Court Judges,[27] Gujarat Assembly[28] and in Re Special Reference No. 1 of 2012 (2G Spectrum Case).[29] In 2G Spectrum case, the court observed that no part of the natural resource can be dissipated as a matter of largess, charity, donation or endowment, for private exploitation. Each bit of natural resource expended must bring back a reciprocal consideration. The consideration may be in the nature of earning revenue or may be to "best subserve the common good". It may well be the amalgam of the two. There cannot be a dissipation of material resources free of cost or at a consideration lower than their actual worth. One set of citizens cannot prosper at the cost of another set of citizens, for that would not be fair or reasonable.

144. Civil and judicial authorities to act in aid of the Supreme Court: All authorities, civil and judicial, in the territory of India, shall act in aid of the Supreme Court.

(Part V, Article 144)

COMMENTS

Article 144 is to be read with Article 141 of the Indian Constitution which enacts that the law declared by the Supreme Court shall be binding on 'all courts' in the territory of India. Under the Constitution, the rule of precedent is followed which is also known as the doctrine of stare decisis. Under this doctrine, even the single judgement of a higher court must be followed by lower courts and other authorities.

145. Rules of Court, etc.: (1) Subject to the provisions of any law made by Parliament, the Supreme Court may from time to time, with the approval of the President, make rules for regulating generally the practice and procedure of the Court including—

(a) rules as to the persons practising before the Court;

(b) rules as to the procedure for hearing appeals and other matters pertaining to appeals including the time within which appeals to the Court are to be entered;

(c) rules as to the proceedings in the Court for the enforcement of any of the rights conferred by Part III;

(cc) rules as to the proceedings in the Court under Article 139A;

(d) rules as to the entertainment of appeals under sub-clause (c) of clause (1) of Article 134;

(e) rules as to the conditions subject to which any judgement pronounced or order made by the Court may be reviewed and the procedure for such review including the time within which applications to the Court for such review are to be entered;

(f) rules as to the costs of and incidental to any proceedings in the Court and as to the fees to be charged in respect of proceedings therein;

(g) rules as to the granting of bail;

(h) rules as to stay of proceedings;

(i) rules providing for the summary determination of any appeal, which appears to the Court to be frivolous or vexatious or brought for the purpose of delay;

(j) rules as to the procedure for inquiries referred to in clause (1) of Article 317.

(2) Subject to the provisions of clause (3), rules made under this Article may fix the minimum number of Judges who are to sit for any purpose, and may provide for the powers of single Judges and Division Courts.

(3) The minimum number of Judges who are to sit for the purpose of deciding any case involving a substantial question of law as to the interpretation of this Constitution or for the purpose of hearing any reference under Article 143 shall be five:

Provided that, where the Court hearing an appeal under any of the provisions of this Chapter other than Article 132 consists of less than five Judges and in the course of the hearing of the appeal, the Court is satisfied that the appeal involves a substantial question of law as to the interpretation of this Constitution, the determination of which is necessary for the disposal of the appeal, such Court shall refer the question for opinion to a Court constituted as required by this clause for the purpose of deciding any case involving such a question and shall on receipt of the opinion dispose of the appeal in conformity with such opinion.

(4) No judgement shall be delivered by the Supreme Court save in open Court, and no report shall be made under

Article 143 save in accordance with an opinion also delivered in open Court.

(5) No judgement and no such opinion shall be delivered by the Supreme Court save with the concurrence of a majority of the Judges present at the hearing of the case, but nothing in this clause shall be deemed to prevent a Judge who does not concur from delivering a dissenting judgement or opinion.

(Part V, Article 145)

COMMENTS

In its initial years, on an average, one hundred cases were heard by a bench of five judges or more. After Emergency, the number of cases heard by five judges or more declined. In an illuminating Article published in Economic and Political weekly (30) titled Interpreting the Constitution: Supreme Court Constitution Benches since Independence (February 26, 2011), it is stated that as of November 2010, there were 754 five-judge or larger matters pending to be heard for regular hearing in the Supreme Court. Although many of these matters could be clubbed together to be heard in fewer hearings, this still represents a major backlog of vital constitution bench matters.

146. Officers and servants and the expenses of the Supreme Court: (1) Appointments of officers and servants of the Supreme Court shall be made by the Chief Justice of India or such other Judge or officer of the Court as he may direct:

Provided that the President may by rule require that in such cases, as may be specified in the rule, no person not already attached to the Court shall be appointed to any office connected with the Court, save after consultation with the Union Public Service Commission.

(2) Subject to the provisions of any law made by the Parliament, the conditions of service of officers and servants of the Supreme Court shall be such as may be prescribed by rules made by the Chief Justice of India or by some other Judge or officer of the Court authorised by the Chief Justice of India to make rules for the purpose:

Provided that the rules made under this clause shall, so far as they relate to salaries, allowances, leave or pensions, require the approval of the President.

(3) The administrative expenses of the Supreme Court, including all salaries, allowances and pensions payable to or in respect of the officers and servants of the Court, shall be charged upon the Consolidated Fund of India, and any fees or other moneys taken by the Court shall form part of that Fund.

(Part V, Article 146)

147. Interpretation: In this Chapter and in Chapter V of Part VI, references to any substantial question of law as to the interpretation of this Constitution shall be construed as including references to any substantial question of law as to the interpretation of the Government of India Act, 1935 (including any enactment amending or supplementing that Act), or of any Order in Council or order made thereunder, or of the Indian Independence Act, 1947, or of any order made thereunder.

(Part V, Article 147)

(B) High Courts

214. High Courts for States: There shall be a High Court for each State.

(Part VI, Article 214)

COMMENTS

The Indian High Courts Act, 1861; the Indian High Courts Act, 1911 and the Indian High Courts Act, 1921 established High Courts in pre-independence in India. After independence, at other places, High Courts were established by separate Acts of the Parliament or under the Re-organisation Acts.

By the Indian High Courts Act, 1861, the Queen in England was empowered to establish by letters Patent, High Courts of Judicature at Calcutta, Madras and Bombay. High Courts at three places were established on December 28, 1865. Jurisdictions and powers of the abolished courts (Supreme Court and Sadar Court) were transferred to the new Courts. As the abolished Supreme Court was a court of record, so the High Courts were also conferred the status of a court of record. Later on, in 1866, in exercise of its powers under Section 16 of the Act, the High Court for the North-West Provinces of then British India was established (presently High Court of Judicature at Allahabad).

The chartered High Court at Bombay exercises jurisdiction over Maharashtra, Goa, and Daman and Diu having benches at Nagpur, Aurangabad and Panjim. Nagpur was the capital of the Central provinces and Berar and was seat of the High Court before reorganisation of States in the year 1956.

Under the Charter Act of 1861 enacted by the British the Parliament, a High Court for North-Western Provinces of then British India was set up by a Letters Patent dated 17th March, 1866 at Agra. In 1869, the principal seat of the High Court shifted to Allahabad and by a supplementary Letters Patent dated March 11, 1919, the name given was of the High Court of Judicature at Allahabad. After independence, on July 1948 by the Uttar Pradesh High Court Amalgamation Order, the territorial jurisdiction of Allahabad High Court established in 1866 was augmented by amalgamation of Oudh Chief Court with it. The Oudh Chief Court was established after the then United Provinces Legislature passed the Oudh Court Act, 1925. Since then, the principal seat of the High Court of Judicature had been at Allahabad with a bench at Lucknow. After the Uttar Pradesh Reorganisation Act, 2000, its jurisdiction diminished with the creation of a High Court at Nainital for the State of Uttarakhand. For more than one State in the country, there are High Courts at Chandigarh, Guwahati and Hyderabad, namely the High Court of Punjab and Haryana, the High court of Guwahati and the High Court of Andhra Pradesh.

215. High Courts to be courts of record: Every High Court shall be a court of record and shall have all the powers of such a court including the power to punish for contempt of itself.

(Part VI, Article 215)

216. Constitution of High Courts: Every High Court shall consist of a Chief Justice and such other Judges as the President may from time to time deem it necessary to appoint.

(Part VI, Article 216)

217. Appointment and conditions of the office of a Judge of a High Court: (1) Every Judge of a High Court shall be appointed by the President by warrant under his hand and seal after consultation with the Chief Justice of India, the Governor of the State, and, in the case of appointment of a Judge other than the Chief Justice, the Chief Justice of the High Court, and shall hold office, in the case of an additional or acting Judge, as provided in Article 224, and in any other case, until he attains the age of sixty-two years.

(Part VI, Article 217)

COMMENTS

Enquiry from various sources and recorded statements would be valid.[29]

222. Transfer of a Judge from one High Court to another: (1) The President may, after consultation with the Chief Justice of India, transfer a Judge from one High Court to any other High Court.

(2) When a Judge has been or is so transferred, he shall, during the period he serves, after the commencement of the Constitution (Fifteenth Amendment) Act, 1963, as a Judge of the other High Court, be entitled to receive in addition to his salary such compensatory allowance as may be determined by Parliament by law and, until so determined, such compensatory allowance as the President may by order fix.

(Part VI, Article 222)

225. Jurisdiction of the existing High Courts: Subject to the provisions of this Constitution and to the provisions of any law of the appropriate Legislature made by virtue of powers conferred on that Legislature by this Constitution, the jurisdiction of, and the law administered in, any existing High Court, and the respective powers of the Judges thereof in relation to the administration of justice in the Court, including any power to make rules of Court and to regulate the sittings of the Court and of members thereof sitting alone or in

Division Courts, shall be the same as immediately before the commencement of this Constitution:

Provided that any restriction to which the exercise of original jurisdiction by any of the High Courts with respect to any matter concerning the revenue or concerning any act ordered or done in the collection thereof was subject immediately before the commencement of this Constitution shall no longer apply to the exercise of such jurisdiction.

(Part VI, Article 225)

226. Power of High Courts to issue certain writs: (1) Notwithstanding anything in Article 32, every High Court shall have power, throughout the Territories in relation to which it exercises jurisdiction, to issue to any person or authority, including, in appropriate cases, any Government, within those Territories, directions, orders or writs, including writs in the nature of habeas corpus, mandamus, prohibition, quo warranto and certiorari, or any of them, for the enforcement of any of the rights conferred by Part III and for any other purpose.

(2) The power conferred by clause (1) to issue directions, orders or writs to any Government, authority or person may also be exercised by any High Court exercising jurisdiction in relation to the Territories within which the cause of action, wholly or in part. arises for the exercise of such power, notwithstanding that the seat of such Government or authority or the residence of such person is not within those Territories.

(3) Where any party against whom an interim order, whether by way of injunction or stay or in any other manner, is made on, or in any proceedings relating to, a petition under clause (1), without—

(a) furnishing to such party copies of such petition and all documents in support of the plea for such interim order; and

(b) giving such party an opportunity of being heard, makes an application to the High Court for the vacation of such order and furnishes a copy of such application to the party in whose favour such order has been made or the counsel of such party, the High Court shall dispose of the application within a period of two weeks from the date on which it is received or from the date on which the copy of such application is so furnished, whichever is later, or where the High Court is closed on the last day of that period, before the expiry of the next day afterwards on which the High Court is open; and if the application is not so disposed of, the interim order shall, on the expiry of that period, or, as the case may be, the expiry of the said next day, stand vacated.

(4) The power conferred on a High Court by this Article shall not be in derogation of the power conferred on the Supreme Court by clause (2) of Article 32.

(Part VI, Article 226)

COMMENTS

Any person aggrieved by an order of any authority-judicial, quasi-judicial or administrative – may approach the High Court having jurisdiction over the subject-matter to issue any writ, order, direction. Under Article 226 a the High Court may judge the constitutionality of any legislation-whether primary or secondary (subordinate). It may give direction to any administrative authority under its jurisdiction in all matters – civil, criminal, revenue, tax etc. Thus, against a tax notice, an aggrieved person may approach High Court.However, the power exercised by a the High Court under Article 226 is known as the power of judicial review and is subject to limits laid down by the courts from time to time.

In the United Kingdom, the development of the principles of judicial review was slow and gradual. Earlier, the Courts could interfere only with the decisions of judicial and quasi-judicial authorities but not with administrative decisions. The decision in Associated Provincial Picture Houses Ltd. vs. Wednesbury Corporation altered this position. In this case, the plaintiff – company was granted license under the Cinematograph Act subject to the condition that "no children under the age of 15 years shall be admitted to any entertainment whether accompanied by an adult or not." This condition was challenged as unreasonable and the provisions of Sunday

Entertainments Act were also challenged. The Court held that it cannot interfere as an appellate authority overriding the decisions of such authority but only as a judicial authority concerned to see whether it has contravened the law by acting in excess of its power. Lord Greene enunciated—"principles of reasonableness." This was described to mean actions based on illegality, irrelevancy and the like. It was not within the courts' constitutional role to criticise executive decisions on their merits – they could intervene only in cases of unreasonableness.

Later on, Lord Diplock in the case of Council of Civil Services Unions vs. Minister for the Civil Services widened the grounds of judicial review. He particularly emphasised the principles of proportionality in addition to three grounds upon which administrative action is subject to control by judicial review, namely first "illegality", the second "irrationality" and the third 'procedural impropriety'.

Professor Jowell describes the proportionality test to involve a four-stage process posing the following questions:

(1) Did the action pursue a legitimate aim?
(2) Were the means employed suitable to achieve that aim?
(3) Could the aim have been achieved by a less restrictive alternative?
(4) Is the derogation justified overall in the interests of a democratic society?

The recent decision of the UK Supreme Court in Pham v Secretary of State for the Home Department 2015 UKSC 19 marks a turning-point in the role of proportionality as a common-law ground of judicial review.

India: In India, the Supreme Court at Calcutta was established by the Charter of 1774, which was issued under the Regulating Act, 1773 and had the powers of judicial review. The powers of the judges of that court were the same as those of the judges of the court of Kings Bench in England. Later on, with the establishment of High Courts, the power of judicial review has been exercised by the High Courts in all matters including contractual matters.

Contractual matters: It is also well settled that a contract is subject to judicial review on the touchstone of fairness, relevance, natural justice, non-discrimination, equality and proportionality. The petitioner could not be denied participation in tender just because he has not furnished latest I.T. Returns.

Rashmi Metaliks Ltd. & Anr. vs. Kolkata Metropolitan Development Authority & Ors.[31]

The Hon'ble Supreme Court after considering the judgement on the subject held in TATA Cellular vs. Union of India[32].

"It cannot be denied that the principles of judicial review would apply to the exercise of contractual powers by Government bodies in order to prevent arbitrariness and favouritism. However, it must be clearly stated that there are inherent limitations in exercise of that power of judicial review. Government is the guardian of the finances of the state. It is expected to protect the financial interest of the state. The right to refuse the lowest or any other tender is always available to the Government. But the principle laid down in Article 14 of the Constitution have to be kept in view while accepting or refusing a tender. There can no question of infringement of Article 14 if Government tries to get the best person, the best quotation. The right to choose cannot be considered to be an arbitrary power. Of course, if the said power is exercised for any collateral purpose, the exercise of that power will be struck down."

Subsequent to the above, the Hon'ble Supreme Court in Asia Foundation and Construction Ltd. vs. Trafalgas House Construction (I) Ltd.[33] held that "Though the principle of judicial review cannot be denied as far as exercise of contractual powers of Government bodies is concerned but it is intended to prevent arbitrariness or favouritism and is exercised in the larger public interest and is brought to the notice of the court if the power has been exercised for any collateral purpose."

Tax Matters: Where an Act provides for a complete machinery to challenge an order of assessment, and the impugned orders of assessment can only be challenged by the mode prescribed by the Act and not by a petition under Article 226 of the Constitution. The rule that where a right or liability is created by a statute which gives a special remedy for enforcing it, the remedy provided by that statute only must be availed of. This rule was stated by Willes J., in Wolverhampton New Water Works Co. vs. Hawkesford (1859) 6 CB (NS) 336 at p. 356 as under:

"There are three classes of cases in which a liability may be established founded upon statute.... But there is a third class, viz., where a liability not existing at common law is created by a statute which, at the same time, gives a special and particular remedy for enforcing it..... the remedy provided by the statute must be followed, and it is not competent to the party to pursue the course applicable to cases of the second class. The form given by the statute must be adopted and adhered to."

The above rule was approved by the House of Lords in Neville vs. London "Express" Newspaper Ltd. (1919) AC 368 (HL) and has been reaffirmed by the Privy Council in Attorney-General of Trinidad and Tobago vs. Gordon Grant & Co. (1935) AC 532 (PC) and Secretary of State vs. Mask & Co., AIR 1940 PC 105 and has also been held in to be equally applicable to enforcement of rights, and has been followed by courts in India.

Thus, the High Court will not interfere when there is alternative remedy and a Court did not interfere. The Court held:[35]

"The show-cause notice was issued on the allegation that salary had been paid to four employees who were working with the appellants in India. These employees were Japanese and the salary in question had been paid by a Japanese company in Japan. In addition thereto, the appellants had also paid salaries to these four employees but tax had been deducted at source. The show-cause notice stated that what was paid to these four employees in Yen currency was also taxable under Section 9 of the Income-tax Act and tax should have been deducted at source. Instead of filing a reply to the show-cause notice, the appellants chose to file a writ petition. The singe judge dismissed the writ petition on the ground that alternative remedy was available to the appellants. In appeal, the Division Bench took the same view. Hence this appeal by special leave. It is contended by Dr. Pal, on behalf of the appellants, that during the pendency of this appeal, taking advantage of the Voluntary Disclosure Scheme, Asahi Glass Co. Ltd., Japan had filed returns of income e-tax in respect of the four employees in question and had paid the entire amount of income-tax payable in respect of what was paid to these four employees in Yen currency. This and the other facts cannot be taken up for consideration by this Court for the first time. In our opinion, the High Court was right in coming to the conclusion that it is appropriate for the appellants to file a reply to the show-cause notice and take whatever defence is open to them. While affirming the decision of the High Court, we, therefore, grant ten weeks' time to the appellants to file a reply to the aforesaid show-cause notice dated May 16, 1996. On the reply being so filed, the Income-tax Officer will take a decision, after giving an opportunity of hearing to the Appellants. The decision should be taken within four months of the reply being so filed. It will be open to the appellants to place on record the subsequent facts, the effect of which will be for the Income Tax Officer to decide."

In Criminal Matters: A large number of writ petitions were filed in High Court for quashing of First Information Report (FIR), Charge-sheet, etc. The position was explained in Kunisetty Sathyanarayana[35] by the Hon'ble Supreme Court as under:

"It is well settled by a series of decisions of this Court that ordinarily no writ lies against a charge-sheet or show-cause notice vide Executive Engineer, Bihar State Housing Board vs. Ramdesh Kumar Singh and others.[36] Special Director and another vs. Mohd. Ghulam Ghouse and another.[37] Ulagappa and others vs. Divisional Commissioner, Mysore and others,[38] State of U.P. vs. Brahm Datt Sharma and another.[39]

"The reason why ordinarily a writ petition should not be entertained against a mere show-cause notice or charge-sheet is that at that stage, the writ petition may be held to be premature. A mere charge-sheet or show-cause notice does not give rise to any cause of action, because it does not amount to an adverse order which affects the rights of any party unless the same has been issued by a person having no jurisdiction to do so. It is quite possible that after considering the reply to the show-cause notice or after holding an enquiry, the authority concerned may drop the proceedings and/or hold that the charges are not established. It is well settled that a writ lies when some right of any party is infringed. A mere show-cause notice or charge-sheet does not infringe the right of anyone. It is only when a final order imposing some punishment or otherwise adversely affecting a party is passed that the said party can be said to have any grievance.

No doubt, in some very rare and exceptional cases, the High Court can quash a charge-sheet or show-cause notice if it is found to be wholly without jurisdiction or for some other reason, if it is wholly illegal however, ordinarily the High Court should not interfere in such a matter."

Conduct of the Petitioner: It is settled that when a party approaches High Court, he must place all the facts before the Court without any reservation. Hon'ble Supreme Court in Prestige Lights Ltd. vs. State Bank of India[40] observed as under:

"It is thus clear that though the Appellant Company had approached the High Court under Article 226 of the Constitution-it had not candidly stated all the facts to the Court. The High Court is exercising discretionary and extraordinary jurisdiction under Article 226 of the Constitution. Over and above, a Court of Law is also a Court of Equity. It is, therefore, of utmost necessity that when a party approaches the High Court, he must place all the facts before the Court without any reservation. If there is suppression of material facts on the part of the Applicant or twisted facts have been placed before the Court, the Writ Court may refuse to entertain the Petition and dismiss it without entering into merits of the matter."

"The object underlying the above principle has been succinctly stated by Scrutton, L.J. in R.V. Kinsington Income Tax Commissioners (1917) 1 KB 486: 86b LJ KB 257: 116 LT 136 in the following words:

"It has been for many years the rule of the Court, and one which, it is of the greatest importance to maintain, that when an applicant comes to the Court to obtain relief on an exparte statement he should make a full and fair disclosure of all the material facts – facts, not law. He must not mis-state the law if he can help it – the Court is supposed to know the law. But it knows nothing about the facts, and the applicant must sate fully and fairly the facts, and the penalty by which the Court enforces that obligation is that if it finds out that the facts have not been fully and fairly stated to it, the Court will set aside, any action which it has taken on the faith of the imperfect statement."

It is well settled that a prerogative remedy is not a matter of course. In exercising extraordinary power, therefore, a Writ Court will indeed bear in mind the conduct of the party who is invoking such jurisdiction. If the Applicant does not disclose full facts or suppresses relevant materials or is otherwise guilty of misleading the Court, the Court may dismiss the action without adjudicating the matter. The rules have been evolved in larger public interest to deter unscrupulous litigants from abusing the process of Court by deceiving it. The very basis of the writ jurisdiction rests in disclosure of true, complete and correct facts. If the material facts are not candidly stated or are suppressed or are distorted, the very functioning of the writ courts would become impossible."

227. Power of superintendence over all courts by the High Court: (1) Every High Court shall have superintendence over all courts and tribunals throughout the Territories in relation to which it exercises jurisdiction.

(2) Without prejudice to the generality of the foregoing provision, the High Court may—

(a) call for returns from such courts;

(b) make and issue general rules and prescribe forms for regulating the practice and proceedings of such courts; and

(c) prescribe forms in which books, entries and accounts shall be kept by the officers of any such courts.

(3) The High Court may also settle tables of fees to be allowed to the sherif and all clerks and officers of such courts and to attorneys, advocates and pleaders practising therein:

Provided that any rules made, forms prescribed or tables settled under clause (2) or clause (3) shall not be inconsistent with the provision of any law for the time being in force, and shall require the previous approval of the Governor.

Nothing in this Article shall be deemed to confer on a High Court powers of superintendence over any court or tribunal constituted by or under any law relating to the Armed Forces.

(Part VI, Article 227)

COMMENTS

As High Courts have full power of superintendence over all courts and tribunals under their respective jurisdiction. It is hoped that Hon'ble Judges of High Courts will find time to do inspection of various Courts, District Courts and tribunals and gear them up to fulfill the aspirations of people specially the litigants, so that people have not to wait for with very long time to have decisions in their cases. This will also do away lot of violence and unrest in the society which is being caused due to undecided disputes or unjust decisions. People tend to take law in their own hands when there is no decision.

228. Transfer of certain cases to High Court: If the High Court is satisfied that a case pending in a court subordinate to it involves a substantial question of law as to the interpretation of this Constitution, the determination of which is necessary for the disposal of the case, it shall withdraw the case and may—

(a) either dispose of the case itself, or

(b) determine the said question of law and return the case to the court from which the case has been so withdrawn together with a copy of its judgement on such question, and the said court shall on receipt thereof proceed to dispose of the case in conformity with such judgement.

(Part VI, Article 228)

228A. Repealed.

229. Officers and servants and the expenses of High Courts: (1) Appointments of officers and servants of a High Court shall be made by the Chief Justice of the Court or such other Judge or officer of the Court as he may direct:

Provided that the Governor of the State may by rule require that in such cases, as may be specified in the rule, no person not already attached to the Court shall be appointed to any office connected with the Court save after consultation with the State Public Service Commission.

(2) Subject to the provisions of any law made by the Legislature of the State, the conditions of service of officers and servants of a High Court shall be such as may be prescribed by rules made by the Chief Justice of the Court or by some other Judge or officer of the Court authorised by the Chief Justice to make rules for the purpose:

Provided that the rules made under this clause shall, so far as they relate to salaries, allowances, leave or pensions, require the approval of the Governor of the State.

(3) The administrative expenses of a High Court, including all salaries, allowances and pensions payable to or in respect of the officers and servants of the Court, shall be charged upon the Consolidated Fund of the State, and any fees or other moneys taken by the Court shall form part of that Fund.

(Part VI, Article 229)

230. Extension of jurisdiction of High Courts to Union Territories: (1) the Parliament may by law extend the jurisdiction of a High Court to, or exclude the jurisdiction of a High Court from, any Union territory.

(2) Where the High Court of a State exercises jurisdiction in relation to a Union Territory—

(a) nothing in this Constitution shall be construed as empowering the Legislature of the State to increase, restrict or abolish that jurisdiction; and

(b) the reference in Article 227 to the Governor shall, in relation to any rules, forms or tables for subordinate courts in that territory, be construed as a reference to the President.

(Part VI, Article 230)

231. Establishment of a common High Court for two or more States: (1) Notwithstanding anything contained in the preceding provisions of this Chapter, the Parliament may by law establish a common High Court for two or more States or for two or more States and a Union territory.

(2) In relation to any such High Court,—

(a) the reference in Article 217 to the Governor of the State shall be construed as a reference to the Governors of all the States in relation to which the High Court exercises jurisdiction;

(b) the reference in Article 227 to the Governor shall, in relation to any rules, forms or tables for subordinate courts, be construed as a reference to the Governor of the State in which the subordinate courts are situated; and

(c) the references in Articles 219 and 229 to the State shall be construed as a reference to the State in which the High Court has its principal seat:

Provided that if such principal seat is in a Union Territory, the references in Articles 219 and 229 to the Governor, Public Service Commission, Legislature and Consolidated Fund of the State shall be construed respectively as references to the President, Union Public Service Commission, the Parliament and Consolidated Fund of India.

(c) Subordinate Courts

233. Appointment of district judges: (1) Appointments of persons to be, and the posting and promotion of, district judges in any State shall be made by the Governor of the State in consultation with the High Court exercising jurisdiction in relation to such State.

(2) A person not already in the service of the Union or of the State shall only be eligible to be appointed a district judge if he has been for not less than seven years an advocate or a pleader and is recommended by the High Court for appointment.

(Part VI, Article 233)

233A. Validation of appointments of, and judgements, etc., delivered by certain district judges: Notwithstanding any judgement, decree or order of any court—

(a) (i) no appointment of any person already in the judicial service of a State or of any person who has been for not less than seven years an advocate or a pleader, to be a district judge in that State, and

(ii) no posting, promotion or transfer of any such person as a district judge, made at any time before the commencement of the Constitution (Twentieth Amendment) Act, 1966, otherwise than in accordance with the provisions of Article 233 or Article 235 shall be deemed to be illegal or void or ever to have become illegal or void by reason only of the fact that such appointment, posting, promotion or transfer was not made in accordance with the said provisions;

(b) no jurisdiction exercised, no judgement, decree, sentence or order passed or made, and no other act or proceeding done or taken, before the commencement of the Consiitution (Twentieth Amendment) Act, 1966 by, or before, any person appointed, posted, promoted or transferred as a district judge in any State otherwise than in accordance with the provisions of Article 233 or Article 235 shall be deemed to be illegal or invalid or ever to have become illegal or invalid by reason only of the fact that such appointment, posting, promotion or transfer was not made in accordance with the said provisions.

(Part VI, Article 233A)

234. Recruitment of persons other than district judges to the judicial service: Appointments of persons other than district judges to the judicial service of a State shall be made by the Governor of the State in accordance with rules made by him in that behalf after consultation with the State Public Service Commission and with the High Court exercising jurisdiction in relation to such State.

(Part VI, Article 233)

COMMENTS

Pursuant to the directions in the All India Judges' Association[37] (2) Case, the Central Government appointed a

Commission under the Chairmanship of Justice Shetty known as First National Judicial Pay Commission. Recommendations of the Commission were considered by the Supreme Court in All India Judges' Assn. (3).[38] The Court hardly took cognizance of objections by the Central Government and approved most of the recommendations of the Commission including the much higher pay scales making the State Judicial Service even higher than I.A.S. The Court also accepted many of the measures of Judicial Reforms like increase in the number of Judges to 50 for every 10 lakh of population and early filling of all vacancies in the Subordinate Courts which are yet to be implemented.[39]

235. Control over subordinate courts: The control over district courts and courts subordinate thereto including the posting and promotion of, and the grant of leave to, persons belonging to the judicial service of a State and holding any post inferior to the post of district judge shall be vested in the High Court, but nothing in this Article shall be construed as taking away from any such person any right of appeal which he may have under the law regulating the conditions of his service or as authorising the High Court to deal with him otherwise than in accordance with the conditions of his service prescribed under such law.

(Part VI, Article 234)

236. Interpretation: In this Chapter—

(a) the expression "district judge" includes judge of a city civil court, additional district judge, joint district judge, assistant district judge, chief judge of a small cause court, chief presidency magistrate, additional chief presidency magistrate, sessions judge, additional sessions judge and assistant sessions Judge;

(b) the expression "judicial service" means a service consisting exclusively of persons intended to fill the post of district judge and other civil judicial posts inferior to the post of district judge.

(Part VI, Article 236)

237. Application of the provisions of this Chapter to certain class or classes of magistrates: The Governor may by public notification direct that the foregoing provisions of this Chapter and any rules made thereunder shall with effect from such date as may be fixed by him in that behalf apply in relation to any class or classes of magistrates in the State as they apply in relation to persons appointed to the judicial service of the State, subject to such exceptions and modifications as may be specified in the notification.

(Part VI, Article 237)

REFERENCES

1. AIR 1982 SC 149.
2. 1991(1)Supp. SCC 594.
3. (1993) 4 SCC 441.
4. Special Reference 1of 1998 1998 (7) SCC 739.
5. Report no. 214 dated November 2008, Law Commission of India.
6. Supreme Court Bar Association and Ors vs. Union of India.
7. Ibid.
8. Supreme Court Bar Association vs. Union of India.
9. 8th edn., 1999.
10. (1970) 3 SCC 98.
11. (1984) 3 SCC 405.
12. (1991) 3 SCC 600.
13. (1995) 2 SCC 584.
14. Supreme Court Bar Association vs. Union of India-1998 (4)SCC 409.
15. Civil Appeal No. 7207 of 2010 judgement delivered on 31st August, 2010.
16. (1989) 2 SCC 754.
17. (1989) 1 SCC 101.
18. (1991) 4 SCC 139.
19. (2014) 2 SCC 532.
20. (AIR 1958 SC 996).
21. (AIR 1960 SC 845).
22. (AIR 1963 SC 1760).
23. (AIR 1965 SC 745).
24. (AIR 1974 SC 1682).
25. (AIR 1979 SC 478).
26. (AIR 1992 SC 522).
27. (AIR 1999 SC 1).

28. (AIR 2003 SC 8).
29. In Re Special Reference No 1 of 2012 (2G Spectrum Case).
30. Civil Appeal No. 6772 of 2013, decided on September 11, 2013.
31. (1994) 6 SCC 651.
32. (197)(1) SCC 738.
34. Indo Aashi Glass Company Ltd., & Anr vs. ITO & others (2002) (10)SCC 444.
35. AIR 2007 SC 906.
36. (2007) 139 Comp. Cases 169 (SC).
37. (1993)4 SCC 288.
38. All India Judges' Assn (3) vs. Union of India, (2002)4 SCC 24.
39. All India Judge's Assn vs. Union of India, (2010) 15 SCC 170.

□

Chapter 9
THE UNION TERRITORIES

239. Administration of Union Territories: (1) Save as otherwise provided by the Parliament by law, every Union Territory shall be administered by the President acting, to such extent as he thinks fit, through an administrator to be appointed by him with such designation as he may specify.

(2) Notwithstanding anything contained in Part VI, the President may appoint the Governor of a State as the administrator of an adjoining Union Territory, and where a Governor is so appointed, he shall exercise his functions as such administrator independently of his Council of Ministers.

(Part VIII, Article 239)

COMMENTS

All the Union Territories are administered by an Administrator as the agent of the President and not by the Governor acting as the head of a State. At present, there are seven Union Territories, viz. Andaman and Nicobar Islands, Lakshadweep, Dadra and Nagar Haveli, Daman and Diu, Puducherry, Chandigarh and Delhi (First Schedule).

239A. Creation of Local Legislatures or Council of Ministers or both for certain Union Territories: (1) The Parliament may by law create for the Union Territory of Puducherry—

(a) a body, whether elected or partly nominated and partly elected, to function as a Legislature for the Union Territory, or

(b) a Council of Ministers, or both with such constitution, powers and functions, in each case, as may be specified in the law.

(2) Any such law as is referred to in clause (1) shall not be deemed to be an amendment of this Constitution for the purposes of Article 368 notwithstanding that it contains any provision which amends or has the effect of amending this Constitution.

(Part VIII, Article 239 A)

COMMENTS

Parliament is now empowered to create a Legislature or Council of Ministers or both for some of the Union Territories. But the President can override the legislative power of the Parliament inasmuch as a regulation made by the President as regards UTs. He may repeal or amend any Act of the Parliament which is for the time being applicable to the Union Territory by virtue of Article 240(2). Legislatures and Council of Ministers exist for the Union Territories of Puducherry, and for the National Capital Territory of Delhi.

239AA. Special Provisions with respect to Delhi: (1) As from the date of commencement of the Constitution (Sixty-ninth Amendment) Act, 1991, the Union Territory of Delhi shall be called the National Capital Territory of Delhi (hereafter in this Part referred to as the National Capital Territory) and the administrator thereof appointed under Article 239 shall be designated as the Lieutenant Governor.

(2) (a) There shall be a Legislative Assembly for the National Capital Territory and the seats in such Assembly shall be filled by members chosen by direct election from territorial constituencies in the National Capital Territory.

(b) The total number of seats in the Legislative Assembly, the number of seats reserved for Scheduled Castes, the division of the National Capital Territory into territorial constituencies (including the basis for such division) and all other matters relating to the functioning of the Legislative Assembly shall be regulated by law made by the Parliament.

(c) The provisions of Articles 324 to 327 and 329 shall apply in relation to the National Capital Territory, the Legislative Assembly of the National Capital Territory and the members thereof as they apply, in relation to a State, the Legislative Assembly of a State and the members thereof respectively; and any reference in Articles 326 and 329 to "appropriate Legislature" shall be deemed to be a reference to the Parliament.

(3) (a) Subject to the provisions of this Constitution, the Legislative Assembly shall have power to make laws for the whole or any part of the National Capital Territory with respect to any of the matters enumerated in the State List or in the Concurrent List insofar as any such matter is applicable to Union Territories except matters with respect to Entries 1, 2 and 18 of the State List and Entries 64, 65 and 66 of that List insofar as they relate to the said Entries 1, 2 and 18.

(b) Nothing in sub-clause (a) shall derogate from the powers of the Parliament under this Constitution to make laws with respect to any matter for a Union Territory or any part thereof.

(c) If any provision of a law made by the Legislative Assembly with respect to any matter is repugnant to any provision of a law made by the Parliament with respect to that matter, whether passed before or after the law made by the Legislative Assembly, or of an earlier law, other than a law made by the Legislative Assembly, then, in either case, the law made by the Parliament, or, as the case may be, such earlier law, shall prevail and the law made by the Legislative Assembly shall, to the extent of the repugnancy, be void:

Provided that if any such law made by the Legislative Assembly has been reserved for the consideration of the

President and has received his assent, such law shall prevail in the National Capital Territory:

Provided further that nothing in this sub-clause shall prevent the Parliament from enacting at any time any law with respect to the same matter including a law adding to, amending, varying or repealing the law so made by the Legislative Assembly.

(4) There shall be a Council of Ministers consisting of not more than ten per cent of the total number of members in the Legislative Assembly, with the Chief Minister at the head to aid and advise the Lieutenant Governor in the exercise of his functions in relation to matters with respect to which the Legislative Assembly has power to make laws, except insofar as he is, by or under any law, required to act in his discretion:

Provided that in the case of difference of opinion between the Lieutenant Governor and his Ministers on any matter, the Lieutenant Governor shall refer it to the President for decision and act according to the decision given thereon by the President and pending such decision, it shall be competent for the Lieutenant Governor in any case where the matter, in his opinion, is so urgent that it is necessary for him to take immediate action, to take such action or to give such direction in the matter as he deems necessary.

(5) The Chief Minister shall be appointed by the President and other Ministers shall be appointed by the President on the advice of the Chief Minister and the Ministers shall hold office during the pleasure of the President.

(6) The Council of Ministers shall be collectively responsible to the Legislative Assembly.

(7) (a) The Parliament may, by law, make provisions for giving effect to, or supplementing the provisions contained in the foregoing clauses and for all matters incidental or consequential thereto.

(b) Any such law as is referred to in sub-clause (a) shall not be deemed to be an amendment of this Constitution for the purposes of Article 368 notwithstanding that it contains any provision which amends or has the effect of amending, this Constitution.

(8) The provisions of Article 239B shall, so far as may be, apply in relation to the National Capital Territory, the Lieutenant Governor and the Legislative Assembly, as they apply in relation to the Union Territory of Puducherry, the administrator and its Legislature, respectively; and any reference in that Article to "clause (1) of Article 239A" shall be deemed to be a reference to this Article or Article 239AB, as the case may be.

(Part VIII, Article 239AA)

COMMENTS

At the time of Independence, Delhi was allowed to be governed through the Chief Commissioner under the overall control of the Government of India. After the States Reorganisation Act, 1956, Delhi was converted into a Union Territory and the Chief Commissioner was replaced by the Lieutenant Governor. However, more powers were decentralised by the 69th Amendment of the Constitution in 1991 when the UT of Delhi was conferred a status of NCT of Delhi having its own elected Legislative Assembly of Delhi like Puducherry. But the Legislatrue Assembly of Delhi was not to have any power with respect to public order, police and land contained in the State List of Second Schedule of the Constitution. Thus, the NCT of Delhi has been conferred only limited autonomy keeping the basic framework of the Constitution in mind to preserve the strong Centre. The President has been given further dominant powers in all matters, where there will be difference of opinion between Ministers and the Lieutenant Governor (Article 239 AA (4) Provision) whereas in States, the Governor is bound to act on the aid and advice of the Council of Ministers.

According to constitutional expert, Ivory Jennings, India is a federation with strong centralised tendencies. In a practical situation, the Central Government at Delhi will not be able to function with peace and free mind if its Ministers, Officers and staff are constantly scared of the local Government of Delhi on the score of vigilance or law and order. The Transaction of Business Rules, which emanate from the Constitution and law provide that the Lieutenant Governor has to keep the President informed beforehand about the appointment of Chief Secretary, Police Commissioner, Secretary (Home) and Secretary (Land), matters affecting the interests of minorities, Scheduled Castes and backward classes and important matters affecting the peace and order of the NCT of Delhi. On the other hand, the Delhi NCT administration has to ensure as a representative of governance of the Union of India that people from all States and regions are not discriminated against. Thus, the Delhi NCT is basically a city State, which was not made even 'C' category State after due consideration. The Sarkaria-Balakrishnan Committee also opposed a separate State status for Delhi. Without the present framework, the Government of Delhi-NCT has lot of subjects and works relating to public welfare and city management.

More autonomy and decentralisation of power are well accepted principles of good governance but these are to be based on history, past practices and experiences. In the present scenario, where States are not able to manage their finances, maintain law and order and discipline their public servants, it is better than the present constitutional status of Delhi-NCT continues. Even though this Article confers special status on the Union Territory of Delhi, Delhi remains a Union Territory and does not acquire the status of a State.[1]

In matters of disciplinary action against the members of subordinate judiciary under Article 235, the Lieutenant Governor must act on the recommendation of the High Court and not on the aid and advice of the Council of Ministers.[2]

239AB. Provision in case of failure of constitutional machinery: If the President, on receipt of a report from the Lieutenant Governor or otherwise, is satisfied—

(a) that a situation has arisen in which the administration of the National Capital Territory cannot be carried on in accordance with the provisions of Article 239AA or of any law made in pursuance of that Article; or

(b) that for the proper administration of the National Capital Territory, it is necessary or expedient so to do, the President may by order suspend the operation of any provision of Article 239AA or of all or any of the provisions of any law made in pursuance of that Article for such period and subject to such conditions as may be specified in such law and make such incidental and consequential provisions as may appear to him to be necessary or expedient for administering the National Capital Territory in accordance with the provisions of Article 239 and Article 239AA.

239B. Power of administrator to promulgate Ordinances during recess of Legislature: (1) If, at any time, except when the Legislature of the Union Territory of Puducherry is in session, the administrator thereof is satisfied that circumstances exist, which render it necessary for him to take immediate action, he may promulgate such Ordinances as the circumstances appear to him to require:

Provided that no such Ordinance shall be promulgated by the administrator except after obtaining instructions from the President in that behalf:

Provided further that whenever the said Legislature is dissolved, or its functioning remains suspended on account of any action taken under any such law as is referred to in clause (1) of Article 239A, the administrator shall not promulgate any Ordinance during the period of such dissolution or suspension.

(2) An Ordinance promulgated under this Article in pursuance of instructions from the President shall be deemed to be an Act of the Legislature of the Union Territory which has been duly enacted after complying with the provisions in that behalf contained in any such law as is referred to in clause (1) of Article 239A, but every such Ordinance—

(a) shall be laid before the Legislature of the Union Territory and shall cease to operate at the expiration of six weeks from the reassembly of the Legislature or if, before the expiration of that period, a resolution disapproving it is passed by the Legislature, upon the passing of the resolution; and

(b) may be withdrawn at any time by the administrator after obtaining instructions from the President in that behalf.

(3) If and so far as an Ordinance under this Article makes any provision, which would not be valid if enacted in an Act of the Legislature of the Union Territory made after complying with the provisions in that behalf contained in any such law as is referred to in clause (1) of Article 239A, it shall be void.

240. Power of President to make regulations for certain Union Territories: (1) The President may make regulations for the peace, progress and good government of the Union Territory of—

(a) the Andaman and Nicobar Islands;
(b) Lakshadweep;
(c) Dadra and Nagar Haveli;
(d) Daman and Diu;
(e) Puducherry;

Provided that when any body is created under Article 239A to function as a Legislature for the Union Territory of Puducherry, the President shall not make any regulation for the peace, progress and good governance of that Union Territory with effect from the date appointed for the first meeting of the Legislature:

Provided further that whenever the body functioning as a Legislature for the Union Territory of Puducherry is dissolved, or the functioning of that body as such Legislature remains suspended on account of any action taken under any such law as is referred to in clause (1) of Article 239A, the President may, during the period of such dissolution or suspension, make regulations for the peace, progress and good governance of that Union Territory.

(2) Any regulation so made may repeal or amend any Act made by the Parliament or any other law which is for the time being applicable to the Union Territory and, when promulgated by the President, shall have the same force and effect as an Act of the Parliament which applies to that territory.

(Part VIII, Article 240)

241. High Courts for Union Territories: (1) The Parliament may by law constitute a High Court for a Union Territory or declare any court in any such Territory to be a High Court for all or any of the purposes of this Constitution.

(2) The provisions of Chapter V of Part VI shall apply in relation to every High Court referred to in clause (1) as they apply in relation to a High Court referred to in Article 214 subject to such modifications or exceptions as the Parliament may by law provide.

(3) Subject to the provisions of this Constitution and to the provisions of any law of the appropriate Legislature made by virtue of powers conferred on that Legislature by or under this Constitution, every High Court exercising jurisdiction immediately before the commencement of the Constitution (Seventh Amendment) Act, 1956, in relation to any Union Territory, shall continue to exercise such jurisdiction in relation to that Territory after such commencement.

(4) Nothing in this Article derogates from the power of the Parliament to extend or exclude the jurisdiction of a High Court for a State to, or from, any Union Territory or part thereof.

(Part VIII, Article 241)

COMMENTS

The High Court for a Union Territory has the same status as the High Court for a State.

242. Repealed.

REFERENCES

1. Govt. (NCT of Delhi) vs. All India Central Civil Accounts, JAU's ASSN, (2002) 1 SCC 344, 348.
2. Rajendra Singh Verma vs. Lt. Governor (NCT of Delhi), (2011) 10 SCC 1, 50-51.

Chapter 10

THE PANCHAYATS, THE MUNICIPALITIES AND THE COOPERATIVE SOCIETIES

Part IX – The Panchayats

243. Definitions: In this Part, unless the context otherwise requires—

(a) "District" means a district in a State;

(b) "Gram Sabha" means a body consisting of persons registered in the electoral rolls relating to a village comprised within the area of Panchayat at the village level;

(c) "Intermediate level" means a level between the village and district levels specified by the Governor of a State by public notification to be the intermediate level for the purposes of this Part;

(d) "Panchayat" means an institution (by whatever name called) of self-government constituted under Article 243B, for the rural areas;

(e) "Panchayat area" means the territorial area of a Panchayat;

(f) "Population" means the population as ascertained at the last preceding census of which the relevant figures have been published;

(g) "Village" means a village specified by the Governor by public notification to be a village for the purposes of this Part and includes a group of villages so specified.

(Part IX, Article 243)

Introduction: The main object of inserting of Part IX in the Constitution by the 73rd Amendment in 1992 is to make constitutional provisions for setting up institutions of self government in rural area to be called Panchayats and to give these institutions constitutional status, continuity, certainty and strength. Earlier, Article 40 as one of the Directive Principles of the State Policy provided to organise village Panchayats. Since the Directive principle is not justiciable and enforceable, the States had the option to set up the Panchayat System and to give them adequate powers, functions and finance. After independence, most of the States set up Panchayat system and few even Nyaya Panchayat, but in the course of time, these units of self-government gradually became defunct except in few States, like Gujarat, Maharashtra, etc. because they were not given grants in aid by the State administration. Secondly, as corruption spread, the members of legislative assemblies did not want them as they treated them as their rivals to share power. Thus, introduction of Part IX gave the Panchayat system new life and energy and now they have become fourth organ of the State after legislature, executive and judiciary and none can afford to overlook them.

While moving the Constitutional Amendment, the then Prime Minister Rajiv Gandhi said that the independent people are those who know their people are governed according to their will and with their consent. It was to make the rural people as real partners in governance. The States are still free to make Panchayat Act according to their tradition and requirement, keeping the overall structure of three-tier Panchayat system intact with jurisdiction and power as per Part IX read with Eleventh Schedule of the Constitution.

Due sanctity to the Panchayat System has been reiterated by the Supreme Court in many cases which come up before it. In one of the cases before it in WGC No. 719/95, the Supreme Court observed. "The States cannot be permitted to postpone the elections of Panchayats except in cases of floods, earthquake or other natural disasters or compelling and real difficulties in holding Panchayat election by the State." Thus, the Supreme

Court did not allow the Bihar Government to postpone the Panchyat Election and warned that even the President's Rule can be imposed for failure to place in position this constitutional machinery. Such is the importance of incorporation of Panchayat System or Panchayat Raj institutions (PRIs) in the Constitution.

The Gram Sabha has been defined afresh. All the voters within the village registered in the electoral rolls relating to a village comprised within the area of a Panchayat is 'Gram Sabha'. The Gram Panchayat or village Panchayat shall have to convene the meeting of Gram Sabha at least once a year to place all its activities. In this way, real representative democracy has been introduced at the grass roots.

243A. Gram Sabha: A Gram Sabha may exercise such powers and perform such functions at the village level as the Legislature of a State may, by law, provide.

(Part IX, Article 243A)

COMMENTS

Most of the State Legislatures have provided convening of the meeting of Gram Sabha at least once a year to know and comment on the performance of the Panchayats.

The notification of the Governor is conclusive as regards definition of village.[1]

However, this Panchayat System is not mandatory in Jammu & Kashmir, Meghalaya, Mizoram, Nagaland and National Capital Territory of Delhi, hilly areas in Manipur and Darjeeling in West Bengal.

243B. Constitution of Panchayats: (1) There shall be constituted in every State the Panchayats at the village, intermediate and district levels in accordance with the provisions of this Part.

(2) Notwithstanding anything in clause (1), Panchayats at the intermediate level may not be constituted in a State having a population not exceeding twenty lakhs.

(Part IX, Article 243B)

COMMENTS

The Constitution envisages a three-tier system of Panchayats, namely:

The village level, known as Gram Panchayat or Gram Sabha;

The Intermediate, known as Panchayat Samiti or Block Panchayat or Khand Panchayat.

The District Panchayat at the district level known as Zilla Parishad or District Panchayat.

The intermediate level Panchayats will be constituted in a State having a population of twenty lakhs or above.

243C. Composition of Panchayats: (1) Subject to the provisions of this Part, the Legislature of a State may, by law, make provisions with respect to the composition of Panchayats:

Provided that the ratio between the population of the territorial area of a Panchayat at any level and the number of seats in such Panchayat to be filled by election shall, so far as practicable, be the same throughout the State.

(2) All the seats in a Panchayat shall be filled by persons chosen by direct election from territorial constituencies in the Panchayat area and, for this purpose, each Panchayat area shall be divided into territorial constituencies in such manner that the ratio between the population of each constituency and the number of seats allotted to it shall, so far as practicable, be the same throughout the Panchayat area.

(3) The Legislature of a State may, by law, provide for the representation—

(a) of the Chairpersons of the Panchayats at the village level, in the Panchayats at the intermediate level or, in the case of a State not having Panchayats at the intermediate level, in the Panchayats at the district level;

(b) of the Chairpersons of the Panchayats at the intermediate level, in the Panchayats at the district level;

(c) of the members of the House of the People and the members of the Legislative Assembly of the State representing constituencies which comprise wholly or partly a Panchayat area at a level other than the village level, in such Panchayat;

(d) of the members of the Council of States and the members of the Legislative Council of the State, where they are registered as electors within—

(i) a Panchayat area at the intermediate level, in Panchayat at the intermediate level;

(ii) a Panchayat area at the district level, in Panchayat at the district level.

(4) The Chairperson of a Panchayat and other members of a Panchayat, whether or not chosen by direct election from territorial constituencies in the Panchayat area, shall have the right to vote in the meetings of the Panchayats.

(5) The Chairperson of—

(a) a Panchayat at the village level shall be elected in such manner as the Legislature of a State may, by law, provide; and

(b) a Panchayat at the intermediate level or district level shall be elected by, and from amongst, the elected members thereof.

(Part IX, Article 243C)

COMMENTS

The Constitution provides number of seats or members equally according to the population in each tier of the Panchayat. The Chairperson of the Panchayat at the village level can be elected directly along with other members or by the members of the Gram Panchayat. However, at the intermediate and district level, the Chairman or President of the Panchayat shall be elected by, and from amongst, the elected members. It is debatable whether ex-officio members like MLAs or MPs can also vote during such elections.

243D. Reservation of seats: (1) Seats shall be reserved for—

(a) the Scheduled Castes; and

(b) the Scheduled Tribes,

in every Panchayat and the number of seats so reserved shall bear, as nearly as may be, the same proportion to the total number of seats to be filled by direct election in that Panchayat as the population of the Scheduled Castes in that Panchayat area or of the Scheduled Tribes in that Panchayat area bears to the total population of that area and such seats may be allotted by rotation to different constituencies in a Panchayat.

(2) Not less than one-third of the total number of seats reserved under clause (1) shall be reserved for women belonging to the Scheduled Castes or, as the case may be, the Scheduled Tribes.

(3) Not less than one-third (including the number of seats reserved for women belonging to the Scheduled Castes and the Scheduled Tribes) of the total number of seats to be filled by direct election in every Panchayat shall be reserved for women and such seats may be allotted by rotation to different constituencies in a Panchayat.

(4) The offices of the Chairpersons in the Panchayats at the village or any other level shall be reserved for the Scheduled Castes, the Scheduled Tribes and women in such manner as the Legislature of a State may, by law, provide:

Provided that the number of offices of Chairpersons reserved for the Scheduled Castes and the Scheduled Tribes in the Panchayats at each level in any State shall bear, as nearly as may be, the same proportion to the total number of such offices in the Panchayats at each level as the population of the Scheduled Castes in the State or of the Scheduled Tribes in the State bears to the total population of the State:

Provided further that not less than one-third of the total number of offices of Chairpersons in the Panchayats at each level shall be reserved for women:

Provided also that the number of offices reserved under this clause shall be allotted by rotation to different Panchayats at each level.

(5) The reservation of seats under clauses (1) and (2) and the reservation of offices of Chairpersons (other than the reservation for women) under clause (4) shall cease to have effect on the expiration of the period specified in Article 334.

(6) Nothing in this Part shall prevent the Legislature of a State from making any provision for reservation of seats in any

Panchayat or offices of Chairpersons in the Panchayats at any level in favour of backward class of citizens.

(Part IX, Article 243D)

COMMENTS

As per provisions, seats in Panchayats are to be reserved for Scheduled Castes and Scheduled Tribes.

The reservation shall be in proportion of population in that Panchayat area. Out of the seats so reserved, not less than 1/3rd of the seats shall be reserved for women belonging to Scheduled Castes and Scheduled Tribes respectively. Not less than 1/3rd of the total number of seats to be filled by direct elections in every Panchayat shall be reserved for women. Thus, some states like Bihar have increased the percentage of reservation of seats to capture female votes which are about 50%.

A State may by law make provision for similar reservation of the Offices of chairpersons in the Panchayats at the village and other levels, which is working well. The rotation system of reservation of seats is an innovative idea and has given relief to the majority population.

In reservation of seats for sarpanchs in Gram Panchayat under the Haryana Panchayati Raj Act, 1994, this principle is a safeguard against the possibility of particular office being reserved in perpetuity.[37]

243E. Duration of Panchayats, etc.: (1) Every Panchayat, unless sooner dissolved under any law for the time being in force, shall continue for five years from the date appointed for its first meeting and no longer.

(2) No amendment of any law for the time being in force shall have the effect of causing dissolution of a Panchayat at any level, which is functioning immediately before such amendment, till the expiration of its duration specified in clause (1).

(3) An election to constitute a Panchayat shall be completed—

(a) before the expiry of its duration specified in clause (1);

(b) before the expiration of a period of six months from the date of its dissolution:

Provided that where the remainder of the period for which the dissolved Panchayat would have continued is less than six months, it shall not be necessary to hold any election under this clause for constituting the Panchayat for such period.

(4) A Panchayat constituted upon the dissolution of a Panchayat before the expiration of its duration shall continue only for the remainder of the period for which the dissolved Panchayat would have continued under clause (1) had it not been so dissolved.

(Part IX, Article 243 E)

COMMENTS

By this provision, the duration of Panchayats has been made continuous so that local self-governance may not be denied to some areas on some alibi or others. In the past, the government in power manipulated not to re-elect the Panchayats in mid-term if they were held by the opposition or likely to be held by the opposition. As Panchayats are now active part of administration, their elections should be held along with the Legislative Assembly Election or immediately after their Assembly Election so that the Panchayats may not be discriminated against by the State administration. It would be an ideal situation if the term of Panchayats is four years so that they can come and go with the Council of Ministers. It will be even better if the Panchayat elections are held without the explicit party support or symbol.

243F. Disqualification for membership: (1) A person shall be disqualified for being chosen as, and for being, a member of a Panchayat—

(a) if he is so disqualified by or under any law for the time being in force for the purposes of elections to the Legislature of the State concerned:

Provided that no person shall be disqualified on the ground that he is less than twenty-five years of age, if he has attained the age of twenty-one years;

(b) if he is so disqualified by or under any law made by the Legislature of the State.

(2) If any question arises as to whether a member of a Panchayat has become subject to any of the disqualifications mentioned in clause (1), the question shall be referred for the decision of such authority and in such manner as the Legislature of a State may, by law, provide.

(Part IX, Article 243 F)

COMMENTS

The State Government has quite wide powers to prescribe qualification for membership of Panchayat bodies. It is but natural that qualified persons should administer Panchayats because they have to do lot of implementation of schemes and have to send reports and returns to the government. But that cannot be very rigid because an educated bureaucracy only indulged into corruption. Local reputed and honest persons though illiterate should be perhaps considered due to this factor in mind. The Haryana Government has boldly prescribed minimum qualification for contesting elections of office bearers of Panchayats at three tiers and the Apex Court has upheld the legislation as valid.

243G. Powers, Authorities and Responsibilities of Panchayats: Subject to the provisions of this Constitution, the Legislature of a State may, by law, endow the Panchayats with such powers and authorities as may be necessary to enable them to function as institutions of self-government and such law may contain provisions for the devolution of powers and responsibilities upon Panchayats at the appropriate level, subject to such conditions as may be specified therein, with respect to—

(a) the preparation of plans for economic development and social justice;

(b) the implementation of schemes for economic development and social justice as may be entrusted to them including those in relation to the matters listed in the Eleventh Schedule.

(Part IX, Article 243G)

COMMENTS

The State will make such law that the Panchayats will function smoothly to ensure economic development of the area and deliver social justice. Under this Article, the Eleventh Schedule to the Constitution demarcates a large area of activities to Panchayats. They will work in the areas of agriculture, land and reforms, minor irrigation, watershed development, dairying and poultry fisheries, social forestry, minor forest produce, small scale industries, Khadi, village and cottage industries, rural housing, drinking water, roads, bridges, waterways, etc., rural electrification, non-conventional energy, poverty alleviation programme, like MNREGA, education, specially primary and secondary schools, vocational education, non-formal education, libraries, markets and fairs, healthy, sanitation family welfare, primary health centres, women and child development, social welfare, welfare of the Scheduled Castes and the Scheduled Tribes, public distribution system and maintenance of community assets.

For such a wide scope of work, the chairperson alone cannot deliver results especially because he is not a full-time paid public servant. Secondly, the local people have to be associated at each and every level of Panchayats. For that purpose, most of the State Panchayat Acts contain provisions to constitute sub-committees at the block and district level Panchayats, specially for areas like rural employment and public distribution system agriculture, irrigation, forests, implementation of land reforms, health and family welfare, roads and electrification, education and finance. Out of these finance sub-committee is very important, which is presided over generally by the chairperson of the Panchayat. The sub-committees discuss the relevant issues threadbare and forward their minutes approved for by the chairperson or the full body of the Panchayat. However, this decision-making process takes a long time. This requires to be reduced to make Panchayat bodies more effective. They are becoming like Legislative Assembly. Secondly, officers concerned do not attend the meetings of Panchayats regularly. As a result, the Panchayats are becoming debating platforms, rather than work execution bodies, which is the object of the Constitution.

However, at Gram Panchayat level, the chairperson known as Pradhan or Sarpanch is directly elected by his constituency and has unfettered power of execution of works as there is no system of sub-committees at the Gram Panchayat level. He has powers and discretion like the President of USA. Sometimes, this is resulting into corruption and partisan working.

The Panchayats are body corporate and can sue and be sued in their own name. They can also file a petition in the High Court of their States against an order or decision of a State authority which aggrieves them. But the Panchayats should be controlled in wasting precious public revenue in litigation. The Panchayat representatives and Panchayat officials function as public servants under the Prevention of Corruption Act as they function like public servants and government assets are in their custody.[3]

243H. Powers to impose Taxes and Funds of the Panchayats: The Legislature of a State may, by law,—

(a) authorise a Panchayat to levy, collect and appropriate such taxes, duties, tolls and fees in accordance with such procedure and subject to such limits;

(b) assign to a Panchayat such taxes, duties, tolls and fees levied and collected by the State Government for such purposes and subject to such conditions and limits;

(c) provide for making such grants-in-aid to the Panchayats from the Consolidated Fund of the State; and

(d) provide for constitution of such Funds for crediting all moneys received, respectively, by or on behalf of the Panchayats and also for the withdrawal of such moneys therefrom, as may be specified in the law.

(Part IX, Article 243H)

COMMENTS

It is observed that the Panchayats are gradually becoming dependent on government finance. They spend a lot on allowances, pay and facilities to elected Panchayat's office bearers and governmental officials working in Panchayats. The Panchayats should be self-dependent and autonomous in respect of finance. Then only they can afford to take a position against government action. Real autonomy comes from financial self-sufficiency. If any Panchayat Office bearer whether elected or deputed is found indulging into misappropriating Panchayat fund or corruption, he should be prosecuted under the IPC and the Prevention of Corruption Act, 1988 as a public servant.

243I. Constitution of Finance Commission to review financial position: (1) The Governor of a State shall, as soon as may be within one year from the commencement of the Constitution (Seventy-third Amendment) Act, 1992, and thereafter at the expiration of every fifth year, constitute a Finance Commission to review the financial position of the Panchayats and to make recommendations to the Governor as to—

(a) the principles which should govern—

   (i) the distribution between the State and the Panchayats of the net proceeds of the taxes, duties, tolls and fees leviable by the State, which may be divided between them under this Part and the allocation between the Panchayats at all levels of their respective shares of such proceeds;

   (ii) the determination of the taxes, duties, tolls and fees, which may be assigned to, or appropriated by, the Panchayats;

   (iii) the grants-in-aid to the Panchayats from the Consolidated Fund of the State;

(b) the measures needed to improve the financial position of the Panchayats;

(c) any other matter referred to the Finance Commission by the Governor in the interests of sound finance of the Panchayats.

(2) The Legislature of a State may, by law, provide for the composition of the Commission, the qualifications which shall be requisite for appointment as members thereof and the manner in which they shall be selected.

(3) The Commission shall determine their procedure and shall have such powers in the performance of their functions as the Legislature of the State may, by law, confer on them.

(4) The Governor shall cause every recommendation made by the Commission under this Article together with an explanatory memorandum as to the action taken thereon to be laid before the Legislature of the State.

(Part IX, Article 243I)

COMMENTS

Appointment of a Finance Commission after every fifth year is the base for success of the Panchayat System. Some State Governments delay in constitution of the Finance Commission to delay allocation of funds to the Panchayats. Even if the report is received, additional funds are not released firstly because the financial position of many State governments is precarious and secondly because the bureaucracy and political executive at the State Secretariat don't want to part with their powers which emanate from finance. This amounts to violation of the Constitution as this is mandatory under Article 243I.

243J. Audit of Accounts of Panchayats: The Legislature of a State may, by law, make provisions with respect to the maintenance of accounts by the Panchayats and the auditing of such accounts.

(Part IX, Article 243J)

COMMENTS

Even the audit officials, who visit Panchayats, are managed by the Panchayats to give their favourable report. The audit officials, therefore, should be equally accountable for incomplete or biased audit report, known as audit paras.

243K. Election to the Panchayats: (1) The superintendence, direction and control of the preparation of electoral rolls for, and the conduct of, all elections to the Panchayats shall be vested in a State Election Commission consisting of a State Election Commissioner to be appointed by the Governor.

(2) Subject to the provisions of any law made by the Legislature of a State, the conditions of service and tenure of office of the State Election Commissioner shall be such as the Governor may, by rule, determine:

Provided that the State Election Commissioner shall not be removed from his office except in like manner and on the like grounds as a Judge of a High Court and the conditions of service of the State Election Commissioner shall not be varied to his disadvantage after his appointment.

(3) The Governor of a State shall, when so requested by the State Election Commission, make available to the State Election Commission such staff as may be necessary for the discharge of the functions conferred on the State Election Commission by clause (1).

(4) Subject to the provisions of this Constitution, the Legislature of a State may, by law, make provision with respect to all matters relating to, or in connection with, elections to the Panchayats.

(Part IX, Article 243K)

COMMENTS

The system of election envisaged under the Constitution is as foolproof as the general election of the country. However, persons accused of rigging during elections are not duly prosecuted and punished after the results are declared. The action against persons indulging in malpractices will keep the subsequent election problem free. Once the Rural Development and Panchayats Department converted the post of Panch or Pradhan from BC category into SC category and the petitioner was declared as a Panch in SC category, the respondents were statutorily duty-bound to notify election of Panch of the petitioners in SC category under the Punjab State Election Commission Act, 1994.[4]

—

243L: Application to Union Territories: The provisions of this Part shall apply to the Union Territories and shall, in their application to a Union Territory, have effect as if the references to the Governor of a State were references to the Administrator of the Union Territory appointed under Article 239 and references to the Legislature or the Legislative Assembly of a State were references, in relation to a Union Territory having a Legislative Assembly, to that Legislative Assembly:

Provided that the President may, by public notification, direct that the provisions of this Part shall apply to any Union Territory or part thereof subject to such exceptions and modifications as he may specify in the notification.

(Part IX, Article 243L)

COMMENTS:

The Panchayat system is not there in Union Territory of Delhi as the Part IX of the Constitution has not been extended to the urban agglomerations of Delhi.

243M. Part not to apply to certain areas: (1) Nothing in this Part shall apply to the Scheduled Areas referred to in clause (1), and the tribal areas referred to in clause (2) of Article 244.

(2) Nothing in this Part shall apply to—

(a) the States of Nagaland, Meghalaya and Mizoram;

(b) the hilly areas in the State of Manipur for which District Councils exist under any law for the time being in force.

(3) Nothing in this Part—

(a) relating to Panchayats at the district level shall apply to the hilly areas of the District of Darjeeling in the State of West Bengal for which Darjeeling Gorkha Hill Council exists under any law for the time being in force;

(b) shall be construed to affect the functions and powers of the Darjeeling Gorkha Hill Council constituted under such law.

(3A) Nothing in Article 243D, relating to reservation of seats for the Scheduled Castes, shall apply to the State of Arunachal Pradesh.

(4) Notwithstanding anything in this Constitution—

(a) the Legislature of a State referred to in sub-clause (a) of clause (2) may, by law, extend this part to that State, except the areas, if any, referred to in clause (1), if the Legislative Assembly of that State passes a resolution to that effect by a majority of the total membership of that House and by a majority of not less than two-thirds of the members of that House present and voting;

(b) the Parliament may, by law, extend the provisions of this Part to the Scheduled Areas and the tribal areas referred to in clause (1) subject to such exceptions and modifications as may be specified in such law, and no such law shall be deemed to be an amendment of this Constitution for the purposes of Article 368.

(Part IX, Article 243M)

COMMENTS

In pursuance of this Article, the Parliament has enacted the Panchayats (Extension to the Scheduled Areas) Act, 1996, known as PESA, which provide inter alia of at least 50 percent seats for the STs. It also requires reservation of all seats of chairpersons at all levels for the STs. The validity of this Act as well as the Jharkhand Panchayati Raj Act, 2001 made in pursuance of it, under which in some Scheduled Areas, reservation could reach upto 80 per cent for the SCs and backward classes, was upheld by the Supreme Court with the following observation;

"It is our considered view that total reservation exceeding 50% of the seats in Panchayats located in Scheduled Areas are permissible on account of the exceptional treatment mandated under Article 243 M (4) (b)."[5]

243N. Continuance of existing laws and Panchayats: Notwithstanding anything in this part any provisions of any law relating to Panchayats in force in a State immediately before the commencement of the Constitution (Seventy-third Amendment) Act, 1992, which is inconsistent with the provisions of this part, shall continue to be in force until amended or repealed by a competent Legislature or other competent authority or until the expiration of one year from such commencement, whichever is earlier.

Provided that all the Panchayats existing immediately before such commencement shall continue till the expiration of their duration, unless sooner dissolved by a resolution passed to that effect by the Legislative Assembly of that State or, in the case of a State having a Legislative Council, by each house of the Legislature of that State.

(Part IX, Article 243N)

COMMENTS

Accordingly, most of the States have amended their Panchayat Acts to bring them in line with the Constitution (Seventy-Third Amendment) Act, 1992.

243O. Bar to interferences by courts in electoral matters: Notwithstanding anything in this Constitution:

(a) The validity of any law relating to the delimitation of constituencies or the allotment of seats to such constituencies, made or purporting to be made under Article 243K shall not be called in question in any court.

(b) No election to any Panchayat shall be called in question except by an election petition presented to such authority and in such manner as is provided for by or under any law made by the Legislature of a State.

(Part IX, Article 243O)

COMMENTS

Once the election process has started, the High Court cannot direct the election officer to stall the proceedings or to conduct the election process afresh or direct him not to declare the result of the election of the Gram Panchayat.[6]

Part IXA – The Municipalities

243P. Definitions: In this Part, unless the context otherwise requires—

(a) "Committee" means a Committee constituted under Article 243S;

(b) "district" means a district in a State;

(c) "Metropolitan area" means an area having a population of ten lakhs or more, comprised in one or more districts and consisting of two or more Municipalities or Panchayats or other contiguous areas, specified by the Governor by public notification to be a Metropolitan area for the purposes of this Part;

(d) "Municipal area" means the territorial area of a Municipality as is notified by the Governor;

(e) "Municipality" means an institution of self-government constituted under Article 243Q;

(f) "Panchayat" means a Panchayat constituted under Article 243B;

(g) "Population" means the population as ascertained at the last preceding census, of which the relevant figures have been published.

(Part IX-A, Article 243P)

COMMENTS

Part IX-A, which has come into force on 01.06.1993 gives a Constitutional status to the local self-government units in urban areas. In fact, such institutions have been in existence all over the country for a long time.

Some of the provisions are similar to Part IX, e.g. Reservation of seats. Finance Commission, Election Commission, etc.

243Q. Constitution of Municipalities: There shall be constituted in every State:

(a) a Nagar Panchayat (by whatever name called) for a transitional area, that is to say, an area in transition from a rural area to an urban area.

(b) a Municipal Council for a smaller urban area; and

(c) a Municipal Corporation for a larger urban area.

In accordance with the provisions of this Part:

Provided that a Municipality under this clause may not be constituted in such urban area or part thereof as the Governor may, having regard to the size of the area and the municipal services being provided or proposed to be provided by an industrial establishment in that area and such other factors as he may deem fit, by public notification, specify to be an industrial township.

(1) In this Article "a transitional area", "a smaller urban area" or " larger urban area" means such on area as the Governor may, having regard to the population of the area, the density of the population therein, the revenue generated for local administration, the percentage of employment in non-agricultural activities, the economic importance or such other factors as he may deem fit, specify by public notification for the purposes of this Part.

(Part IX-A, Article 243Q)

COMMENTS

The State Government and, in turn, Governor has all the powers to constitute an area as municipal area or to exempt one in favour of a development authority like NOIDA in U.P. or industrial township like Durgapur and Asansal in West Bengal. The Governor has to issue public notification considering the population of the area, density of the population therein with other factors mentioned in the above Article for declaring any area as "transitional area."[7]

243R. Composition of Municipalities: (1) Save as provided in clause (2), all the seats in a Municipality shall be filled by persons chosen by direct election from the territorial constituencies in the Municipal area and for this purpose, each Municipal area shall be divided into territorial constituencies to be known as wards.

(2) The Legislature of a State may, by law, provide—

(a) for the representation in a Municipality of—

(i) persons having special knowledge or experience in Municipal Administration;

(ii) the members of the House of the People and the members of the Legislative Assembly of the State representing constituencies which comprise wholly or partly the Municipal area;

(iii) the members of the Council of States and the members of the Legislative Council of the State registered as electors within the Municipal area;

(iv) the Chairpersons of the Committees constituted under clause (5) of Article 243S: Provided that the persons referred to in paragraph (i) shall not have the right to vote in the meetings of the Municipality;

(b) the manner of election of the Chairperson of a Municipality.

(Part IX-A, Article 243R)

COMMENTS

There is special provision that persons having special knowledge or experience in Municipal administration can be nominated as members. But they will not be entitled to vote. Thus, there is a scope to co-opt experts in the fields like Municipal Administration, etc. Thus, specialist knowledge will flow into Municipal Administration.

243S. Constitution and composition of wards committees, etc.: (1) There shall be constituted Wards Committees, consisting of one or more wards, within the territorial area of a Municipality having a population of three lakhs or more.

(2) The Legislature of a state may, by law, make provisions with respect to:

(a) the composition and the territorial area of a Wards Committee.

(b) the manner in which the seats in a Wards Committee shall be filled.

(3) A member of a Municipality representing a ward within the territorial area of the Wards Committee shall be a member of that Committee.

(4) where a Wards Committee consists of:

(a) one ward, the member representing that ward in the Municipality; or

(b) two or more wards, one of the members representing such wards in the Municipality elected by the members of the Wards Committee, shall be the Chairperson of that Committee.

(5) Nothing in this Article shall be deemed to prevent the Legislature of a State from making any provisions for

the constitution of Committees in addition to the Wards Committees.

(Part IX-A, Article 243S)

COMMENTS

Constitution of Ward Committees in a municipality having a population of three lakhs or more is further decentralisation of power at the ground level. In Panchayats, there is a system of sub-committees at the intermediate or district level by State Government's Act but in case of urban bodies, there is the constitutional mandate. The State Legislature shall further make provision with respect to its composition, territorial area and the manner in which the seats in a Ward Committees shall be filled. But this provision of the Constitution has not been practically implemented in the field. The citizens in a municipal area also do not take required interest in the functioning of municipality interest in the functioning of municipality or its committees, whereas in rural areas, the Panchayats function like Legislative Assembly in the State. Wherever there is undue delay in decision-making, the Committees may be bypassed.

243T. Reservation of Seats: (1) Seats shall be reserved for the Scheduled Castes and the Scheduled Tribes in every Municipality and the number of seats so reserved shall bear, as nearly as may be, the same proportion to the total number of seats to be filled by direct elections in that Municipality as the population of the Scheduled Castes in the Municipal area or of the Scheduled Tribes in the Municipal area bears to the total population of that area and such seats may be allotted by rotation to different constituencies in a Municipality.

(2) Not less than one-third of the total number of seats reserved under clause (1) shall be reserved for women belonging to the Scheduled Castes or, as the case may be, the Scheduled Tribes.

(3) Not less than one-third (including the number of seats reserved for women belonging to the Scheduled Castes and the Scheduled Tribes) of the total number of seats to be filled by direct elections in every Municipality shall be reserved for

women and such seats may be allotted by rotation to different constituencies in a Municipality.

(4) The offices of Chairpersons in the Municipalities shall be reserved for the Scheduled Castes, the Scheduled Tribes and women in such manner as the Legislature of a State may, by law, provide

(5) The reservation of seats under clauses (1) and (2) and the reservations of offices of Chairpersons (other than the reservation for women) under clause (4) shall cease to have effect on the expiration of the period specified in Article 334.

(6) Nothing in this Part shall prevent the Legislature of a State from making any provisions for reservation of seats in any Municipality or offices of Chairpersons in the Municipalities in favour of backward class of citizens.

(Part IX-A, Article 243T)

COMMENTS

Reservations have been provided on the same pattern as in Panchayats. Additionally, reservation for backward classes is permissible in municipalities as few STs will be available in municipalities for reservation. A member from the reserved category can seek election for the post of chairperson under clause (4), even though he was elected as member from an unreserved constituency. It is not necessary that he should be elected from a reserved category.[8]

243U. Duration of Municipalities, etc.: (1) Every Municipality, unless sooner dissolved under any law for the time being in force, shall continue for five years from the date appointed for its first meeting and no longer:

Provided that a Municipality shall be given a reasonable opportunity of being heard before its dissolution.

(2) No amendment of any law for the time being in force shall have the effect of causing dissolution of a Municipality at any level, which is functioning immediately before such amendment, till the expiration of its duration specified in clause (1).

(3) An election to constitute a Municipality shall be completed—

(a) Before the expiry of its duration specified in clause (1).

(b) Before the expiration of a period of six months from the date of its dissolution.

Provided that where the remainder of the period for which the dissolved Municipality would have continued its less than six months, it shall not be necessary to hold any election under this clause for constituting the Municipality for such period.

(4) A Municipality constituted upon the dissolution of a Municipality before the expiration of its duration shall continue only for the remainder of the period for which the dissolved Municipality would have continued under clause (1) had it not been so dissolved.

(Part IX-A, Article 243U)

COMMENTS:

In the present constitutional scheme, the life of municipalities will be continuous and will not depend on whims and fancies of the Government of State in power. 'Elections for the Constitution of a new municipality must be held before the expiry of five years."[9]

243V. Disqualification for Membership: (1) A person shall be disqualified for being chosen as, and for being, a member of a Municipality—

(a) if he is so disqualified by or under any law for the time being in force for the purposes of elections to the Legislature of the State concerned.

Provided that no person shall be disqualified on the ground that he is less than twenty-five years of age, if he has attained the age of twenty-one years;

(b) If he is so disqualified by or under any law made by the Legislature of the State.

(2) If any question arises as to whether a member of a Municipality has become subject to any of the disqualifications mentioned in clause (1), the question shall be referred for the

decision of such authority and in such manner as the Legislature of a State may, by law, provide.

(Part IX-A, Article 243V)

COMMENTS

There is a difference. These persons who have attained the age of 21 years will be eligible to be members of the municipality, whereas for membership of State Assembly or House of People, minimum age is 25 years.

243W. Powers authority and responsibilities of Municipalities, etc.: Subject to the provisions of this Constitution, the Legislature of a State may, by law, endow—

(a) The Municipalities with such powers and authority as may be necessary to enable them to function as institutions of self-government and such law may contain provisions for the devolution of powers and responsibilities upon Municipalities, subject to such conditions as may be specified therein, with respect to:

(i) The preparation of plans for economic development and social justice;

(ii) The performance of functions and the implementation of schemes as may be entrusted to them including those in relation to the matters listed in the Twelfth Schedules;

(b) The Committees with such powers and authority as may be necessary to enable them to carry out the responsibility conferred upon them including those in relation to the matters listed in the Twelfth Schedule.

(Part IX-A, Article 243W)

COMMENTS:

The municipalities are required to prepare plan and perform functions for economic development and social justice within their jurisdiction. The municipalities have been entrusted with elaborate functions as regards eighteen items in the 12th Schedule of the Constitution, namely Urban planning, Regulation of land use and construction of buildings, Roads and bridges, Water supply, Public health, fire services, urban forestry, welfare of slums and the handicapped, urban poverty alleviation, urban amenities, Promotion of culture, Burials, Cattle ponds, registration of births & deaths, street lighting, bus stops, Public conveniences and Regulation of slaughter houses and tanneries. It is high time that the important units of urban self-government will come out with their excessive preoccupation with passing plans for construction of buildings and collection of property tax and to pay salaries to their employees.

They should now priortise the areas mentioned in the Constitution including the 12th Schedule of the Constitution. Then the poverty from the urban areas will be reduced and the municipal areas will be a tidy and suitable place for development.

243X. Power to impose taxes by, and funds, of the Municipalities: The Legislature of a State may, by law:

(a) Authorise a Municipality to levy, collect and appropriate such taxes, duties, tolls and fees in accordance with such procedure and subject to such limits;
(b) Assign to a Municipality such taxes, duties, tolls and fees levied and collected by the State Government for such purposes and subject to such conditions and limits;
(c) Provide for making such grants-in-aid to the Municipalities from the Consolidated Fund of the State; and
(d) Provide for Constitution of such Funds for crediting all moneys received, respectively, by or on behalf of the Municipalities and also for the withdrawal of such moneys therefrom, as may be specified in the law.

(Part IX-A, Article 243X)

243Y. Finance Commission: (1) The Finance Commission constituted under Article 243I shall also review the financial position of the Municipalities and make recommendations to the Governor as to:

(a) The principles which should govern:

(i) The distribution between the State and the Municipalities of the net proceeds of the taxes, duties, tolls and fees by the State, which may be divided between them under this Part and the allocation between the Municipalities at all levels of their respective shares of such proceeds;

(ii) The determination of the taxes, duties, tolls and fees, which may be assigned to, or appropriated by, the Municipalities;

(iii) The grants-in-aid to the Municipalities from the Consolidated Fund of the State;

(b) The measures needed to improve the financial position of the Municipalities;

(c) Any other matter referred to the Finance Commission by the Governor in the interests of sound finance of the Municipalities.

(2) The Governor shall cause every recommendation made by the Commission under this Article together with an explanatory memorandum as to the action taken thereon to be laid before the Legislature of the State.

(Part IX-A, Article 243Y)

243Z. Audit of accounts of Municipalities: The Legislature of a State may, by law, make provisions with respect to the maintenance of accounts by the Municipalities and the auditing of such accounts.

(Part IX-A, Article 243 Z)

COMMENTS

The Legislature of a State may, by law, make provisions with respect to the maintenance of accounts by the Municipalities and the auditing of such accounts.

243ZA. Elections to the Municipalities: (1) The superintendence, direction and control of the preparation of electoral rolls for, and the conduct of, all elections to the Municipalities shall be vested in the State Election Commission referred to in Article 243K.

(2) Subject to provisions of this Constitution, the Legislature of a State may, by law, make provision with respect to all matters relating to, or in connection with, elections to the Municipalities.

(Part IX-A Article 243ZA)

COMMENTS

The fact that the President is qualified to participate in the election of Vice-President as provided in the Act and Rules framed thereunder, does not make him an elected Councillor.[10]

243ZB. Application to Union Territories: The provisions of this Part shall apply to the Union Territories and shall, in their application to a Union Territory, have effect as if the references to the Governor of a State were references to the Administrator of the Union Territory appointed under Article 239 and references to the Legislature or the Legislative Assembly of a State were references in relations to a Union Territory having a Legislative Assembly, to that Legislative Assembly.

Provided that the President may, by public notification, direct that the provisions of this Part shall apply to any Union Territory or part thereof subject to such exceptions and modifications as he may specify in the notification.

COMMENTS

The Provisions of this part shall apply to the Union Territories and shall, in their application to a Union Territory, have effect as if the references to the Governor of a State were references to the Administrator of the Union Territory appointed under Article 239 and references to the Legislature or the Legislature Assembly of a State were references in relation to a Union Territory having a Legislative Assembly, to that Legislative Assembly:

Provided that the President, may, by public notification, direct that the provisions of this Part shall apply to any Union Territory or part thereof subject to such exceptions and modifications as he may specify in the notification.

(Part IX-A, Article 243ZB)

COMMENTS

President has power to issue notification whether this Article will be applicable to a particular Union Territory or group of Union of Territories.

243ZC-Part not to apply to certain areas: (1) Nothing in this Part shall apply to the Scheduled Areas referred to in Clause (1), and the tribal areas referred to in Clause (2), of Article 244.

(2) Nothing in this part shall be construed to affect the functions and powers of the Darjeeling Gorkha Hill Council constituted under any law for the time being in force for the hilly areas of the district of Darjeeling in the State of West Bengal.

(3) Notwithstanding anything in this Constitution, the Parliament may, by law, extend the provisions of this Part to the Scheduled Areas and the Tribal Areas referred to in clause (1) subject to such exceptions and modifications as may be specified in such law, and no such law shall be deemed to be an amendment of this Constitution for the purposes of Article 368.

(Part IX-A, Article 243-ZC)

COMMENTS

Article 243ZC (3) has empowered the State to provide extensive privileges for Scheduled Tribes in the Scheduled Areas which are dominated by the tribal population, who are still behind other parts or castes in India. Secondly, it is essential to preserve their ethnic culture and particular way of life. This privilege is being accorded to the aboriginal population in other countries, who have been pushed or are being habituated in reserved areas like in USA, Australia, etc.

243ZD. Committee for District Planning: (1) There shall be constituted in every State at the district level a District Planning Committee to consolidate the plans prepared by the Panchayats and the Municipalities in the district and to prepare a draft development plan for the district as a whole.

(2) The Legislatiure of a State may, by law, make provision with respect to:

(a) the composition of the District Planning Committees.

(b) the manner in which the seats in such Committees shall be filled:

Provided that not less than four-fifths of the total number of members of such Committee shall be elected by, and from amongst, the elected members of the Panchayat at the district level and of the Municipalities in the district in proportion to the ratio between the population of the rural areas and of the urban areas in the district:

(c) the functions relating to district planning which may be assigned to such Committees;

(d) the manner in which the Chairpersons of such Committees be chosen.

(3) Every District Planning Committee shall, in preparing the draft development plan—

(a) have regard to:

(i) matters of common interest between the Panchayats and the Municipalities including spatial planning, sharing of water and other physical and natural resources, the integrated development of infrastructure and environmental conservation;

(ii) the extent and type of available resources whether financial or otherwise;

(b) consult such institutions and organisations as the Governor may, by order, specify.

(4) The Chairperson of every District Planning Committee shall forward the development plan, as recommended by such Committee, to the Government of the State.

(Part IX-A, Article 243ZD)

COMMENTS

The Article contains basic guidelines for constitution and functioning of the District Planning Committee. This Article is the bulwark of decentralised planning in India and its functioning. The details regarding composition of the District Planning Committee, its functioning and the manner in which the seats are to be filled are to be provided by a law to be made by the State Legislature. The District Planning Committee symbolises decentralised planning in India in practice at the grass root level.

The DPC will prepare a draft development plan for matters of common interests between the Panchayats and the municipalities to avoid conflict. They will deal with:

Spatial planning,
Sharing of water and other physical resources,
Integrated development of infrastructure, and
Environmental conservation.

The Chairman of every DPC will be as per the law of State and shall forward the development plan to the State Government to incorporate in the State Plan which will be then forwarded to the Union Government to consider allocation of available resources to the State, which will then allocate to the Districts either through the Collector or through the Zilla Panchayat or District Panchayat for devolution, among block and gram Panchayats and municipalities. The State can also directly allocate to municipalities or through the earlier channel of the District Collector. Before the District Development Plan is prepared, the intermediate Panchayats will collect and collate the plans of Gram Panchayats and will send to the DPC for incorporation in the District Development Plan. At district level, all other line departments and municipalities will also submit their plans to DPC Thus, the real voice and suggestions from the grassroot levels will be echoed and will find place in the District Development Plan. Thus, it will not be a plan from the top to the lowest level. It will be a decentralised planning from the lowest level to the highest level. However, there is always room and scope to associate specialised persons and opinion at every level. There will be lot of autonomy and transparency in the process of planning and thereafter, none can complain that his voice or opinion was not be given heed to. The process of planning will start from the meeting of Gaon Sabha in which all the people will participate. However, if there is delay in submission of schemes or shelf of schemes at any level, it cannot blame the State that it was left out in the process to solve its specific problem or its specific concerns were not addressed to. This will help to maintain law and order because everyone is now partner in the development.

If there are abnormal requirements of development schemes, the concerned Panchayat or municipality can meet from their own funds or through Shramdan or mutual co-operation at the grass root level. Earlier, local MLA or MP used to dictate in planning process through bureaucrats whom they controlled through weapon of transfer from the State level.

Now, it will not be possible. They can always participate in the meeting of DPC as ex-officio members and get their proposals incorporated at that level. However, success of District Planning or decentralised planning will depend on the following factors.

The Planning process at every level is undertaken in time and forwarded onward in time. For that shelf or Bank of schemes should be kept ready before hand.

The District Development Plan is prepared moderately which is feasible, otherwise State will have discretion to cut down schemes on budget allocation according to its resources.

The Finance Commission should be active and should ensure placement of fund to the District which can then sub-allocate according to the inter se priorities.

There should be a mechanism of monitoring at district level which can also fix up accountability of a government functionary or the Panchayat functionary. It is now laid down generally that sub-divisional officer can taken action against a Gram Panchayat member or Pradhan or Sarpanch, District Collector against the member or chairperson of block level Panchayat or municipality and Divisional Commissioner against district Panchayat member or chairperson including Municipal Corporation. However, such a system may differ from State to State but the system is in place, though it is not being implemented with required seriousness.

243ZE: Committee for Metropolitan Planning: (1) Here shall be constituted in every metropolitan area a Metropolitan Planning Committee to prepare a draft development plan for the Metropolitan area as a whole.

(2) The Legislature of a State may, by law, make with respect to:

(a) The composition of the Metropolitan Planning Committees;

(b) The manner in which the seats in such Committees shall be filled: Provided that not less than two-thirds of the members of such Committee shall be elected by, and from amongst, the elected members of the Municipalities and Chairpersons of the Panchayats in the Metropolitan area in proportion to the ratio between the population of the Municipalities and of the Panchayats in that area;

(c) The representation, in such Committees of the Government of India and the Government of the State and of such organisations and institutions as may be deemed necessary for carrying out the functions assigned to such Committees;

(d) The functions relating to planning and coordination for the Metropolitan area which may be assigned to such Committees;

(e) The matter in which the Chairpersons of such Committees shall be chosen.

(3) Every Metropolitan Planning Committee shall, in preparing the draft development plan:

(a) Have regard to:

(i) The plans prepared by the Municipalities and the Panchayats in the Metropolitan area;

(ii) Matters of common interest between the Municipalities and the Panchayats, including co-ordinate spatial planning of the area, sharing of water and other physical and natural resources, the integrated development of infrastructure and environmental conservation;

(iii) The overall objectives and priorities set by the Government of India and the Government of the State;

(iv) The extent and nature of investments likely to be made in the Metropolitan area by agencies of the

Government of India and of the Government of the State and other available resources whether financial or otherwise;

(b) Consult such institutions and organisations as the Governor may, by order, specify.

(4) The Chairperson of every Metropolitan Planning Committee shall forward the development plan, as recommended by such Committee, to the Government of the State.

(Part IX-A, Article 243ZE)

COMMENTS

Like in Panchayat area, Article 243ZE has provided for Constitution of Committee for Metropolitan Planning for every metropolitan area. In this case, not less than two-third members will be elected. The Metropolitan Planning Committee may have representations from State Government, Government of India and of various organisations and institutions as may be deemed necessary. State Government will provide how its chairperson will be elected.

The members of the Committee shall be elected by the members of the Municipalities and chairpersons of the Panchayats in the Metropolitan area among themselves. The proportion of seats to be showed by them would be based on the ratio of the population of the Municipalities and of the Panchayats in the area. The Metropolitan Planning Committee will prepare a development plan for the whole Metropolitan area; the State Legislation may, by law, prescribe. The Committee will have functions relating to planning and co-ordination for the Metropolitan area. The Committee, inter alia, will take care of overall objectives of Government of India and State Government and will attract investments.

It is a fact that the planning of Metropolitan area, like Delhi, Mumbai, Kolkata, Chennai, Hyderabad, and Bengaluru will be quite different from the planning of the rural areas. In Metropolitan areas, the citizens don't want to participate in its local administration. Therefore, only 2/3rd representation of elected members is provided for. Secondly, these are important centres for investment and development of the country having lot of international ramifications. Therefore, more specialised inputs are required for such areas. All these factors have been included in the Constitution. However, after the Constitutional mandate in 1993, the feedback is not on record how these Metropolitan Committees have been in place and what has been their performance. A Constitutional mandate without implementation attracts lot of Constitutional accountability before the people of India and even before the Supreme Court who is the guardian of the Constitution.

243ZF. Continuance of existing laws and Municipalities: Notwithstanding anything in this Part, any provision of any law relating to Municipalities in force in a State immediately before the commencement of the Constitution (Seventy-fourth Amendment) Act, 1992, which is inconsistent with the provisions of this Part, shall continue to be in force until amended or repealed by a competent Legislature or other competent authority or until the expiration of one year from such commencement, whichever is earlier.

Provided that all the Municipalities existing immediately before such commencement shall continue till the expiration of their duration, unless sooner dissolved by a resolution passed to that effect by the Legislative Assembly of that State or, in the case of a State having a Legislative Council, by each House of the Legislature of that State.

(Part IX-A, Article 243ZF)

COMMENTS

'The purpose of Article 243 ZF of the Constitution, an existing law is to enable necessary amendments to be made to the existing law to make it in consonance with Part IX-A of the Constitution."[11]

243ZG. Bar to interference by Courts in electoral matters: Notwithstanding anything in this Constitution:

(a) The validity of any law relating to the delimitation of constituencies or the allotment of seats to such constituencies, made or purporting to be made under Article 243ZA, shall not be called in question in any court;

(b) No election to any Municipality shall be called in question except by an election petition presented to such authority and in such manner as is provided for by or under any law made by the Legislature of a State.

(Part IX-A, Article 243ZG)

COMMENTS

The jurisdiction of regular courts in the country has been barred relating to validity of a law relating to delimitation of constituencies or the allotment of seats made under Article 243ZA because during past, many Panchayats and municipalities couldn't function for years just because the cases pending in courts could not be disposed of. In view of pendency of more than 2.5 crores cases in various courts in the country, such a provision has justification.

(C) The Co-Operative Societies

243ZH. Definitions: In this Part, unless the context otherwise requires—

(a) "Authorised person" means a person referred to as such in Article 243ZQ;

(b) "Board" means the board of directors or the governing body of a co-operative society, by whatever name called, to which the direction and control of the management of the affairs of a society is entrusted to;

(c) "Co-operative society" means a society registered or deemed to be registered under any law relating to co-operative societies for the time being in force in any State;

(d) "Multi-State co-operative society" means a society with objects not confined to one State and registered or deemed to be registered under any law for the time being in force relating to such co-operatives;

(e) "Officer bearer" means a President, Vice-President, Chairperson, Vice-Chairperson, Secretary or Treasurer of a co-operative society and includes any other person to be elected by the board of any co-operative society;

(f) "Registrar" means the Central Registrar appointed by the Central Government in relation to the multi-State co-operative societies and the Registrar for co-operative societies appointed by the State Government under the law made by the Legislature of a State in relation to co-operative societies;

(g) "State Act" means any law made by the Legislature of a State;

(h) "State level co-operative society" means a co-operative society having its area of operation extending to the whole of a State and defined as such in any law made by the Legislature of a State.

243ZI. Incorporation of co-operative societies: Subject to the provisions of this Part, the Legislature of a State may, by law, make provisions with respect to the incorporation, regulation and winding up of co-operative societies based on the principles of voluntary formation, democratic member-control, member-economic participation and autonomous functioning.

243ZJ. Number and term of members of board and its office bearers: (1) The board shall consist of such number of directors as may be provided by the Legislature of a State, by law:

Provided that the maximum number of directors of a co-operative society shall not exceed twenty-one:

Provided further that the Legislature of a State shall, by law, provide for the reservation of one seat for the Scheduled Castes or the Scheduled Tribes and two seats for women on board of every co-operative society consisting of individuals as members and having members from such class or category of persons.

(2) The term of office of elected members of the board and its office bearers shall be five years from the date of election and the term of office bearers shall be conterminous with the term of the board:

Provided that the board may fill a casual vacancy on the board by nomination out of the same class of members in respect of which the casual vacancy has arisen, if the term of office of the board is less than half of its original term.

(3) The Legislature of a State shall, by law, make provisions for co-option of persons to be members of the board having experience in the field of banking, management, finance or specialisation in any other field relating to the objects and activities undertaken by the co-operative society, as members of the board of such society:

Provided that the number of such co-opted members shall not exceed two in addition to twenty-one directors specified in the first proviso to clause (1):

Provided further that such co-opted members shall not have the right to vote in any election of the co-operative society in their capacity as such member or to be eligible to be elected as office bearers of the board:

Provided also that the functional directors of a co-operative society shall also be the members of the board and such members shall be excluded for the purpose of counting the total number of directors specified in the first proviso to clause (1).

243ZK. Election of members of board: (1) Notwithstanding anything contained in any law made by the Legislature of a State, the election of a board shall be conducted before the expiry of the term of the board so as to ensure that the newly elected members of the board assume office immediately on the expiry of the office of members of the outgoing board.

(2) The superintendence, direction and control of the preparation of electoral rolls for, and the conduct of, all elections to a co-operative society shall vest in such an authority or body, as may be provided by the Legislature of a State, by law:

Provided that the Legislature of a State may, by law, provide for the procedure and guidelines for the conduct of such elections.

243ZL. Supersession and suspension of board and interim management: (1) Notwithstanding anything contained in any law for the time being in force, no board shall be superseded or kept under suspension for a period exceeding six months:

Provided that the board may be superseded or kept under suspension in case—

(i) of its persistent default; or

(ii) of negligence in the performance of its duties; or

(iii) the board has committed any act prejudicial to the interests of the co-operative society or its members; or

(iv) there is stalemate in the constitution or functions of the board; or

(v) the authority or body as provided by the Legislature of a State, by law, under clause (2) of Article 243ZK, has failed to conduct elections in accordance with the provisions of the State Act: Provided further that the board of any such co-operative society shall not be superseded or kept under suspension where there is no Government shareholding or loan or financial assistance or any guarantee by the Government:

Provided also that in case of a co-operative society carrying on the business of banking, the provisions of the Banking Regulation Act, 1949 (10 of 1949) shall also apply:

Provided also that in case of a co-operative society, other than a multi-State co-operative society, carrying on the business of banking, the provisions of this clause shall have the effect as if for the words "six months", the words "one year" had been substituted.

(2) In case of supersession of a board, the administrator appointed to manage the affairs of such co-operative society shall arrange for conduct of elections within the period specified in clause (1) and handover the management to be elected board.

(3) The Legislature of a State may, by law, make provisions for the conditions of service of the administrator.

243ZM. Audit of accounts of co-operative societies: (1) The Legislature of a State may, by law, make provisions with respect to the maintenance of accounts by the co-operative societies and the auditing of such accounts at least once in each financial year.

(2) The Legislature of a State shall, by law, lay down the minimum qualifications and experience of auditors and auditing firms that shall be eligible for auditing accounts of the co-operative societies.

(3) Every co-operative society shall cause to be audited by an auditor or auditing firms referred to in clause (2) appointed by the general body of the co-operative society:

Provided that such auditors or auditing firms shall be appointed from a panel approved by the State Government or an authority authorised by the State Government in this behalf.

(4) The accounts of every co-operative society shall be audited within six months of the close of the financial year to which such accounts relate.

(5) The audit report of the accounts of an apex co-operative society, as may be defined by the State Act, shall be laid before the State Legislature in the manner, as may be provided by the State Legislature, by law.

243ZN. Convening of general body meetings: The Legislature of a State may, by law, make provisions that the annual general body meeting of every co-operative society shall be convened within a period of six months of close of the financial year to transact the business as may be provided in such law.

243ZO. Right of a member to get information: (1) The Legislature of a State may, by law, provide for access to every member of a co-operative society to the books, information and accounts of the co-operative society kept in regular transaction of its business with such member.

(2) The Legislature of a State may, by law, make provisions to ensure the participation of members in the management of the co-operative society providing minimum requirement of attending meetings by the members and utilising the minimum level of services as may be provided in such law.

(3) The Legislature of a State may, by law, provide for co-operative education and training for its members.

243ZP. Returns: Every co-operative society shall file returns, within six months of the close of every financial year, to the authority designated by the State Government including the following matters, namely—

(a) annual report of its activities;
(b) its audited statement of accounts;
(c) plan for surplus disposal as approved by the general body of the co-operative society;
(d) list of amendments to the bye-laws of the co-operative society, if any;
(e) declaration regarding date of holding of its general body meeting and conduct of elections when due; and
(f) any other information required by the Registrar in pursuance of any of the provisions of the State Act.

243ZQ. Offences and penalties: (1) The Legislature of a State may, by law, make provisions for the offences relating to the co-operative societies and penalties for such offences.

(2) A law made by the Legislature of a State under clause (1) shall include the commission of the following act or omission as offences, namely—

(a) a co-operative society or an officer or member thereof wilfully makes a false return or furnishes false information, or any person wilfully does not furnish any information required from him by a person authorised in this behalf under the provisions of the State Act;
(b) any person wilfully or without any reasonable excuse disobeys any summons, requisition or lawful written order issued under the provisions of the State Act;
(c) any employer who, without sufficient cause, fails to pay to a cooperative society amount deducted by him from its employee within a period of fourteen days from the date on which such deduction is made;
(d) any officer or custodian who wilfully fails to handover custody of books, accounts, documents, records, cash, security and other property belonging to a co-operative society of which he is an officer or custodian, to an authorised person; and

(e) whoever, before, during or after the election of members of the board or office bearers, adopts any corrupt practice.

243ZR. Application to multi-State co-operative societies: The provisions of this Part shall apply to the multi-State co-operative societies subject to the modification that any reference to "Legislature of a State", "State Act" or "State Government" shall be construed as a reference to "the Parliament", "Central Act" or "the Central Government" respectively.

243ZS. Application to Union Territories: The provisions of this Part shall apply to the Union Territories and shall, in their application to a Union Territory, having no Legislative Assembly as if the references to the Legislature of a State were a reference to the administrator thereof appointed under Article 239 and, in relation to a Union Territory having a Legislative Assembly, to that Legislative Assembly:

Provided that the President may, by notification in the Official Gazette, direct that the provisions of this Part shall not apply to any Union Territory or Part thereof as he may specify in the notification.

243ZT. Continuance of existing laws: Notwithstanding anything in this Part, any provision of any law relating to co-operative societies in force in a State immediately before the commencement of the Constitution (Ninety-seventh Amendment) Act, 2011, which is inconsistent with the provisions of this Part, shall continue to be in force until amended or repealed by a competent Legislature or other competent authority or until the expiration of one year from such commencement, whichever is less.

(Part IX B, Articles 243ZH to 243ZT)

COMMENTS

The provisions relating to Co-operative Societies have been added by the Constitution (Ninety-seventh Amendment) Act, 2011. The Cooperative Societies are also forms of grass root institutions, having full participation of people. Now co-operative societies have their foray into various fields and dimensions from credit societies, milk co-operatives, sugar co-operative, fertiliser cooperatives, retail cooperatives, etc. for the agricultural sector to the housing complexes in urban areas. These are governed by some State laws but there was lot of variance Statewise. These co-operative societies sometimes become instruments of exploitation lacking in transparency. Therefore, this Part in the Constitution is added to ensure that the co-operative societies in the country function in a democratic autonomous and professional manner. To tide over the malfunctioning of cooperative societies, following special features have been provided in the Constitution, which will find place in State laws gradually within one year as per the Constitution.

- Multi-State Cooperative Society is one whose objects are not confined to one State.
- There will be at least one seat reserved for the Scheduled Castes as Director or the Scheduled Tribes and two seats for women.
- There will be continuation of Board of Directors.
- The Board of such Co-operative Society shall not be superseded or kept under suspension, where there is no Government shareholding or loan or financial assistance or any guarantee by the Government.
- Participation of members is to be ensured in the management of the co-operative society.

Co-operative is an important sector in the country. Now, even the informal groups known as 'self help groups' are very active in the country but they cannot be regulated by law. The socialist countries are run by the co-operative societies in various fields, like, farming, etc. but the cooperative societies in Soviet Russia, having constitutional status, failed because there was lot of bureaucratisation of these societies in farming sector. This was one of the causes of disintegration of Russia and eclipse of socialism in Russia. It is hoped that these Constitutional provisions will save the co-operative societies to go into oblivion and continue to contribute towards the development of the country. Other provisions relating to the co-operative societies are similar to Panchayats and municipalities as contained in Part IX and IX-A of the Constitution. However, it is held that the bye-laws of co-operative society must be brought at par with the laws and statutory provisions of the Societies Act.[12]

REFERENCES

1. State of U.P. vs. Pradhan Sangh Kshettra Samiti, AIR 1995 SC 1512.
2. Pawan Kumar vs. State of Haryana, AIR 2011 P & H, 102.
3. State of M.P. vs. Narsimham (1975) 2 SCC 377.
4. Joginder Singh vs. State of Punjab, AIR 2012, P & H. 28.
5. Union of India vs. Rakesh Kumar, (2010 4 SCC 50.
6. Boddule Krishnaiah vs. State Election Commissioner, Andhra Pradesh, (1996), 3 SCC 416.
7. B.I.M.A. Office Premises Co-Operative Society vs. Kala Kalamboli Village Panchayat, AIR 2001 Bom. 81.
8. Kasambhai F. Ghanchi vs. Chandubhai D. Rajput, (1998) 1 SCC 285.
9. Kisha Sing Tomar vs. Municipal Corporation of the City of Ahmedabad, (2006) 8 SCC 352.
10. Sangeeta Bansal vs. State of Madhya Pradesh, AIR 2015, SC 51.
11. Sundergarh Adivasi Advocates Association vs. State of Odisha, (2013) 14 SCC 217 (220).
12. Rajkot Distt. Co-operative Bank vs. State of Gujarat, AIR 2015 SC 489.

□

Chapter 11
THE SCHEDULED TRIBAL AREAS

244. Administration of Scheduled Areas and Tribal Areas: (1) The provisions of the Fifth Schedule shall apply to the administration and control of the Scheduled Areas and Scheduled Tribes in any State other than the States of Assam, Meghalaya, Tripura and Mizoram.

(2) The provisions of the Sixth Schedule shall apply to the administration to the tribal areas in the States of Assam, Meghalaya, Tripura and Mizoram.

(Part X, Article 244)

COMMENTS

The Constitution makes special provisions for the administration of certain areas called 'Scheduled Areas' in States even though such areas are situated within a State or Union Territory because of the backwardness of the people of these areas and their special way of living.

The President has made the Scheduled Areas Order, 1950 with the approval of the Parliament. These areas inhabit the Tribes specified as 'Scheduled Tribes' in the 5th Schedule of the Constitution.

"The Governor is competent to enact provision restricting transfer of land situated in scheduled area between the Tribal and Non-Tribals.[1] A question arose for consideration before the Supreme Court that whether the Bihar Regulation I of 1951 was in excess of the Governor's powers. It was held that the regulation is an instance of valid piece of legislation emanating from legislative authority in its plenitude of Governor's power and there is no aspect of delegated or conditional legislation. The Governor had full power to make regulations which are laws and just as the Parliament can enact that a piece of legislation will apply to a particular State. Similarly, the Governor under Paragraph 5 of the Fifth Schedule can apply specified laws to a Scheduled Area.

244A. Formation of an Autonomous State comprising certain tribal areas in Assam, and creation of local Legislature or Council of Ministers or both therefor: (1) Notwithstanding anything in this Constitution, the Parliament may, by law, form within the State of Assam an autonomous State comprising (whether wholly or in part) all or any of the tribal areas specified in part I of the table appended to paragraph 20 of the Sixth Schedule and create therefor:

(a) a body, whether elected or partly nominated and partly elected, to function as a Legislature for the autonomous State, or

(b) a Council of Ministers, or both with such constitution, powers and functions, in each case, as may be specified in the law.

(2) Any such law as is referred to in clause (1) may, in particular—

(a) specify the matters enumerated in the State List or the Concurrent List with respect to which the Legislature of the autonomous State shall have power to make laws for the whole or any part thereof, whether to the exclusion of the Legislature of the State of Assam or otherwise;

(b) define the matters with respect to which the executive power of the autonomous State shall extend;

(c) provide that any tax levied by the State of Assam shall be assigned to the autonomous State insofar as the proceeds thereof are attributable to the autonomous State;

(d) provide that any reference to a State in any Article of this Constitution shall be construed as including a reference to the autonomous State; and

(e) make such supplemental, incidental and consequential provisions as may be deemed necessary.

(3) An amendment of any such law as aforesaid insofar as such amendment relates to any of the matters specified in sub-clause (a) or sub-clause (b) of clause (2) shall have no effect unless the amendment is passed in each House of the Parliament by not less than two-thirds of the members present and voting.

(4) Any such law as is referred to in this Article shall not be deemed to be an amendment of this Constitution for the purposes of Article 368 notwithstanding that it contains any provision which amends or has the effect of amending this Constitution.

(Part X, Article 244A)

COMMENTS

Scheduled Tribes (STs) mean such tribes or parts of groups within such tribes or tribal communities mentioned in the Scheduled Tribes Order under Article 342. The Tribal Areas in the States of Assam, Meghalaya, Tripura, and Mizoram are separately dealt with and provisions for their administration are to be found in the Sixth schedule to the Constitution. Originally, Table in the Sixth Schedule consisted of three Parts as follows:

Part I: 1. The North Cachar Hills District, 2. The Karbi Anglong District, 3. The Bodoland Territorial Areas District.

Part II: 1. The Khasi Hills, District, 2. The Jaintia Hills District, 3. The Gora Hills, District (in Meghalaya)

Part IIA: Tripura Tribal Areas District

Part III: 1. The Chakma District, 2. The Mara District, 3. The Lai District.

But since the creation of the State of Nagaland, the table includes nine areas in four parts.

These Tribal Areas are to be administered as autonomous districts through creation of District Councils and Regional Councils. These Councils are primarily representative bodies and they have got the power of law making in certain specified fields, such as management of a forest other than a reserved forest, inheritance of property, marriage and social customs, and the Governor may also confer upon these Councils the power to try certain suits or offences. These Councils have also the power to assess and collect land revenue and to impose certain specified taxes. The laws made by the Councils shall have, however, no effect unless assented to by the Governor.

With respect to the matters belonging to Councils, Acts of the State Legislature shall not extend to such Areas unless the concerned District Council so directs by public notification. As regards other matters, the President with respect to a Central Act and the Governor with respect to State Act may direct that or Act of the Parliament or of the State Legislature shall not apply to an autonomous district or shall apply only subject to exceptions or notifications as may be specified thereon. These Councils shall also possess judicial power, civil and criminal, subject to the jurisdiction of the High Court as the Governor may from time to time specify. Corruption has crept into the functioning of these Councils. It is high time that some 'Lokayukta' is appointed covering a group of District or Regional Councils and the Prevention of Corruption Act, 1988 should be extended to these Councils before lot of harm is caused to the ecology of these preserved Areas. The Supreme Court held that the "powers of the District Councils is confined to the distribution or setting a part of the land mentioned therein only for the purpose of occupation or use as expressly stated in Paragraph 3 (1) (a) of the Sixth Schedule. It is clear that the District Councils unlike the Parliament and the State Legislatures are not intended to be clothed with plenary powers of legislation. Thus, power to make laws is expressly limited by the provisions of the Sixth Schedule which has created them, and they can do nothing beyond the limit which circumscible their powers.

REFERENCES

1. Sudhakar B. Kadu vs. State of Madhya Pradesh, AIR 2014 MP 69(DB).
2. District Council of United Khasi and Jaintia Hills vs. Sitimou Sawian, (1971) 3 SCC 708.

□

Chapter 12
RELATIONS BETWEEN THE UNION AND THE STATES

(A) Legislative Relations

Distribution of Legislative Powers

245. Extent of laws made by the Parliament and by the Legislatures of States: (1) Subject to the provisions of this Constitution, the Parliament may make laws for the whole or any part of the Territory of India, and the Legislature of a State may make laws for the whole or any part of the State.

(2) No law made by the Parliament shall be deemed to be invalid on the ground that it would have extra-territorial operation.

(Part XI, Article 245)

COMMENTS

The framers of the Constitution have created a federation where cooperation between the Union and the States is very essential. This is called cooperative federalism. The Parliament and State Legislatures have plenary powers of legislation in their territorial jurisdiction which is limited by the distribution of Legislature powers. However, the Indian Constitution is not true to any traditional pattern of federation.[1]

There can be no quarrel with the proposition that the Indian model is broadly based on a federal form of governance but with a tilt towards the centre.[2] All authority and power must be exercised in conformity with the Constitution. Neither the Union nor the State should encroach upon the power or jurisdiction, which is exclusively vested in the other unit of the federation. All Constitutional and statutory powers must be exercised for the purpose for which they are intended.

Delegated Legislation: The essential power of legislation cannot be delegated. The conferment of unfettered, uncanalysed powers without laying down certain norms for enforcement of the Act tantamounts to abdication of legislative power by the legislature. It is not permissible in law.[3] If the legislature has left enunciation of policy and principle including prescribing criteria to the delegate, there is excessive delegation which is not permissible. The legislature may leave all incidental and ancillary provisions to make the law effective mainly procedural in nature. An Act of the legislature represents the will of the people and cannot be lightly declared as unconstitutional.[4] Legislature can even render a judicial decision by enacting a valid law retrospectively. But it cannot declare a particular judgement of the Court as invalid as that would amount to exercise of judicial power.[5]

Even the delegate can further delegate, provided the administrative authority retains general control over his sub-delegate or subordinate authority.

However, a legislature cannot legislate and cannot ignore the march of events and the Constitutional rights accrued in the course of time. That would be most arbitrary, unreasonable and a negation of history.

246. Subject matter of laws made by the Parliament or by the Legislatures of States: (1) Notwithstanding anything in clauses (2) and (3), the Parliament has exclusive power to make laws with respect to any of the matters enumerated in List I in the Seventh Schedule in this Constitution referred to as the "Union List".

(2) Notwithstanding anything in clause (3), the Parliament, and, subject to clause (1), the Legislature of any State also have power to make laws with respect to any of the matters enumerated in List III in the Seventh Schedule (in this Constitution referred to as the "Concurrent List".

(3) Subject to clauses (1) and (2), the Legislature of any State has exclusive power to make laws for such State or any part thereof with respect to any of the matters enumerated in List II in the Seventh Schedule in this Constitution referred to as the "State List".

(4) the Parliament has power to make laws with respect to any matter for any part of the Territory of India not included in a State notwithstanding that such matter is a matter enumerated in the State List.

(Part XI, Article 246)

COMMENTS

The scheme of distribution of legislative powers is based on three lists in the Seventh Schedule of the Constitution. The Union Parliament to have exclusive jurisdiction to make laws in regard to items in the Union List, i.e. List I, the State Legislature has exclusive power to make laws in respect of items enumerated in the State List, e.g. List II and both the Union and State Legislatures, could Legislate in areas of items included in the Concurrent list, i.e. List III. The residuary power of legislation is with the Union and as regards Union Territories; the Parliament has plenary power to legislate with regard to any subject.

Doctrine of Pith and Substance: In case of overlapping of the jurisdiction of two statutes, it is essential to take resort to the doctrine of Pith and Substance. The court looks to the substance of the matter. Thus, if the substance falls within the Union List, then the incidental encroachment by the law on the State List does not make it invalid. For example, the power to levy tax would not include the power to confiscate goods as ancillary thereto.[7] The power to tax, which also includes the power to prevent evasion of tax, cannot be used to cover those who have nothing to do with the transaction like transporters of goods.[8] Thus, the transporters are smuggling lot of goods. The Legislatures cannot resort to colourable legislation indirectly which they cannot do directly. The Legislatures cannot pass a taxing statute which is confiscatory in character.

The power of the State Legislature as regards industries other than those falling under the Union List is exclusive. However, entries in the State List regarding 'money –lending' as per entry 30 cannot fall within Union List entry 46, Bill of Exchange etc.

In the field of mining, if the Parliament as declared to make regulation in the public interest under entry 54, Union List, the State Legislature cannot legislate any further. [10] In the latest judgement on Coal-gate it was held that the Union Government cannot be allowed to indulge in arbitrary or unbridled action under the Mines and Minerals (Regulation and Development) Act, 1957 in case of distribution of State largesses.[11]

247. Power of the Parliament to provide for the establishment of certain Additional Courts: Notwithstanding anything in this Chapter, the Parliament may by law provide for the establishment of any additional courts for the better administration of laws made by the Parliament or of any existing laws with respect to a matter enumerated in the Union List.

(Part XI, Article 247)

COMMENTS

This power of Parliament to establish courts has acquired additional impetus with the introduction of Entry 11-A in List III by the Constitution (42nd Amendment) Act, 1976, which authorises the Parliament to make laws with respect to "administration of justice, Constitution and organisation of all courts, except the Supreme Court and the High Court." Thus, the Parliament may now constitute courts even for the administration of State laws.

In fact, some courts have been constituted. One of them may be 'Family Courts', 'Fast Track Courts' in the States. More courts will be required to be constituted by the Union Government to address problem of large pendency of cases in subordinate courts, whereas some specific cases require special attention, specially in cases of corruption, election, commercial or tax disputes, offences against women and cases against juveniles, etc.

248. Residency powers of Legislation: (1) The Parliament has exclusive power to make any law with respect to any matter not enumerated in the Concurrent List or State List.

(2) Such power shall include the power of making any law imposing a tax not mentioned in either of those Lists.

(Part IX, Article 248)

COMMENTS

This Article assigns residuary powers of legislation exclusively to, the Parliament. This is in line with other federal countries, like Canada, USA and Australia.

Since the three lists in the Seventh Schedule attempt an exhaustive enumeration of all possible subjects of "legislation", and the Courts interpret the ambit of the enumerated powers literally, the scope for the application of the residuary power will be very narrow."[12]

But human ingenuity is boundless. Everyday new problems and new types of offences are arising. Demands of welfare State, hopes, aspiration and expectations in developing society necessitate legislation on topics that were not within the contemplation of the Constitution makers.

"The Terrorist and Disruptive Activities (Prevention) Act, 1987 and Armed Forces (Special Powers) Act, 1958 were also upheld under Article 248 with Entry 97 of List I."[13]

Expressing the wide amplitude of the legislative power of the Parliament, including its residuary power, in the Harbhajan Singh Dhillon cases[14] Sikri CJ also made the following sweeping remark:

"If a Central Act is challenged as being beyond the legislative competence of the Parliament, it is enough if it is law with respect to matters or taxes enumerated in State List. It is not, no further question arises."

249. Power of the Parliament to legislate with respect to matter in the State List in the National Interest: (1) Notwithstanding anything in the foregoing provisions of this Chapter, if the Council of States has declared by resolution supported by not less than two-thirds of the members present and voting that it is necessary or expedient in national interest that the Parliament should make laws with respect to any matter enumerated in the State List specified in the resolution, it shall be lawful for the Parliament to make laws for the whole or any part of the Territory of India with respect to the matter while the resolution remains in force.

(2) A resolution passed under clause (1) shall remain in force for such period not exceeding one year as may be specified therein. Provided that if and so often as a resolution approving the continuance in force of any such resolution is passed in the manner provided in clause (1), such resolution shall continue in force for a further period of one year from the date on which under this clause, it would otherwise have ceased to be in force.

(3) A law made by the Parliament which the Parliament would not but for the passing of a resolution under clause (1) have been competent to make shall, to the extent of the incompetency, cease to have effort on the expiration of a period of six months after the resolution has ceased to be in force, except as respect things done or omitted to be done before the expiration of the said period.

(Part XI, Article 249)

COMMENTS

The Constitution confers on State Legislatures exclusive law-making power on subjects in the State List. However when a subject assumes national importance, the Parliament can legislative only if the Council of State, which may be said to represent the States as units, passes a resolution to that effect by a two-third majority. The resolution of the Council of States may be further renewed.

It demonstrates that in-spite of federal structure, the national interest is uppermost. If the nation survives, then only federal structure can survive.

250. Power of the Parliament to legislate with respect to any matter in the State List if a Proclamation of Emergency is in operation: (1) Notwithstanding anything in this Chapter, the Parliament shall, while a Proclamation of Emergency is in operation, have power to make laws for the whole or any part of the Territory of India with respect to any of the matters enumerated in the State List.

(2) A law made by the Parliament which the Parliament would not but for the issue of a Proclamation of Emergency have been competent to make shall, to the extent of the incompetency, cease to have effect on the expiration of a period of six months after the Proclamation has ceased to operate, except as respect things done or omitted to be done before the expiration of the said period.

(Part XI, Article 250)

COMMENTS

The Parliament is empowered to make laws on any item included in the State List for the whole or any part of India while a Proclamation of Emergency is in operation. The maximum duration of validity of such laws will be six months after the expiry of the Emergency under Article 352 of the Constitution.

251. Inconsistency between laws made by the Parliament under Articles 249 and 250 and laws made by the Legislatures of States: Nothing in Articles 249 and 250 shall restrict the power of the Legislature of a State to make any law which, under this Constitution it has power to make, but if any provision of a law made by the Legislature of a State is repugnant to any provision of a law made by the Parliament which the Parliament has under either of the said Articles power to make, the law made by the Parliament, whether passed before or after the law made by the Legislature of the State, shall prevail, and the law made by the Legislature of the State shall to the extent of the repugnancy, but so long only as the law made by the Parliament continues to have effect, be inoperative.

(Part –XI, Article 251)

COMMENTS

In case of a conflict between a Union and a State law, the Union law will prevail under Article 249. So also, it will prevail when, during the Proclamation of Emergency, the Union Parliament is enabled to make laws on matters in the State List.

252. Power of the Parliament to Legislate: (1) If it appears to the Legislatures of two or more States to be desirable that any of the matters with respect to which the Parliament has no power to make laws for the States except as provided in Articles 249 and 250 should be regulated in such States by the Parliament by law, and if resolutions to that effect are passed by all the Houses of the Legislatures of those States, it shall be lawful for the Parliament to pass an Act for regulating that matter accordingly, and any Act so passed shall apply to such States and to any other State by which it is adopted afterwards by resolution passed in that behalf by the House or, where there are two Houses, by each of the Houses of the Legislature of that State.

(2) Any Act so passed by the Parliament may be amended or repealed by an Act of the Parliament passed or adopted in like manner but shall not, as respect any State to which it applies, be amended or repealed by an Act of the Legislature of that State.

(Part XI, Article 252)

COMMENTS

If two or more States are desirous that on any particular matter in the State List, there should be a common Act, which would apply in those States, they can approach the Parliament to make such an Act for them. The effect is that the Parliament, which has no power to legislate with respect to the matter which is the subject of the resolution, becomes entitled to legislate with respect to it. On the other hand, the State Legislature ceases to have a power to make a law relating to that matter.

The Parliament could so structure the law that it applied uniformly in entire India, if later adopted by all the States and that it could take into account its suitability to the States which adopt it later on.

The Supreme Court upheld the validity of the Urban Land (Ceiling and Regulation) Act, 1976, which was enacted by the

Parliament on the resolution of 11 States under this Article and was adopted by the other States later.

The resolution by the Legislature of the State operates as abdication or surrender of the power of the State Legislature with respect to the matter, which is subject matter of the resolution and such matter is placed entirely with the Parliament and the Parliament alone can legislate with respect to it.

"However, it does not deprive the State Legislature from making laws under that entry in respect of other matters such as resolution of relation between landlord and tenant or regulation of agrarian relations."[15]

253. Legislation for giving effect to international agreements: Notwithstanding anything in the foregoing provisions of this Chapter, the Parliament has power to make any law for the whole or any part of the Territory of India for implementing any treaty, agreement or convention with any other country or countries or any decision made at any international conference, association or other body.

(Part XI, Article 253)

COMMENTS

The normal distribution of powers will not stand in the way of the Parliament to enact legislation for carrying out the international obligations, even though such legislation may be necessary in relation to a State subject. But the law so made cannot override the fundamental rights. This has become more essential because many laws are being made to implement globalisation like TRIPS to ensure India's conformity with WTO membership. Legislative intervention through enactment of a law is required only if the implementation of the treaty comes in conflict with individual rights or any existing laws.

254. In-consistency between laws made by the Parliament and laws made by the Legislature of State: (1) If any provision of a law made by the Legislature of a State is repugnant to any provision of a law made by the Parliament which the Parliament is competent to enact, or to any provision of an existing law with respect to one of the matters enumerated in the Concurrent List, then, subject to the provisions of clause (2), the law made by the Parliament, whether passed before or after the law made by the Legislature of such State, or, as the case may be, the existing law, shall prevail and the law made by the Legislature of the State shall, to the extent of the repugnancy, be void.

(2) Where a law made by the Legislature of a State with respect to one of the matters enumerated in the Concurrent List contains any provision repugnant to the provisions of an earlier law made by the Parliament or an existing law with respect to that matter, then, the law so made by the Legislature of such State shall, if it has been reserved for the consideration of the President and has received his assent, prevail in that State. Provided that nothing in this clause shall prevent the Parliament from enacting at any time any law with respect to the same matter including a law adding to, amending, varying or repealing the law so made by the Legislature of the State.

(Part XI, Article 254)

COMMENTS

Article 254 contains mechanism for resolution of conflict between Union and State legislation enacted with respect to any matter enumerated the Concurrent List of the 7th Schedule of the Constitution.[16]

In case of any conflict or in constancy between laws made by the Parliament and those made by the Legislature of a State in respect of items in the Concurrent list, the Union law shall prevail and the State law shall be void to the extent of inconsistency or repugnancy except where a State law is reserved for the consideration of the President and receives his assent.

The test of 'pith and substance' has to be applied to determine whether the State law has substantially transgressed the field, occupied by the law of the Parliament. There is no repugnance where the encroachment is not substantial, or the subject-matter of the legislation is not the same.

'A Tamil Nadu Act which is repugnant to Section 10A of the Indian Medical Council Act, 1956 is void as repugnant to the latter. The latter Act covers the entire field for establishing a new medical college, leaving no scope for State legislation.[17]

"However, the Court found that the Tamil Nadu Public men (Criminal Misconduct) Act, 1974 was not repugnant to the Penal Code, 1860 or the Prevention of Corruption Act, 1947 was not repugnant but complementary because it provided for severe punishment than provided in the Central laws."[18] However, the President's assent can be obtained to regularise action taken under a State law, which subsequently come in conflict with the Central Act from the time the Central Act came into operation.[19]

255. Requirements as to recommendations and previous sanctions to be regarded as matters of procedure only: No Act of the Parliament or of the Legislature of a State, and no provision in any such Act, shall be invalid by reason only that some recommendation or previous sanction required by this Constitution was not given, if assent to that Act was given—(a) where the recommendation required was that of the Governor, either by the Governor or by the President; (b) where the recommendation required was that of the Rajpramukh, either by the Rajpramukh or by the President; (c) where the recommendation or previous sanction required was that of the President, by the President.

(Part XI, Article 255)

COMMENTS

No Act of the Parliament or of the Legislature of a State and no provision in any such Act shall be invalid by reason only that some recommendation or previous sanction required by this Constitution was not given, if assent to that Act was given.

Where the recommendation required was that of the Governor, either by the Governor or by the President;

Where the recommendation required was that of the Rajpramukh, either by the Rajpramukh or by the President;

Where the recommendation or previous sanction required was that of the President, by the President.

The assent of the President or Governor can cure the defect for future action under the Act. But neither the Legislature nor the President has the power to declare that the non-compliance with Article 255 of the Constitution was of no effect.[20]

(B) Administrative Relations

256. Obligation of States and the Union: The executive power of every State shall be so exercised as to ensure compliance with the laws made by the Parliament and any existing laws which apply in that State, and the executive power of the Union shall extend to the giving of such directions to a State as may appear to the Government of India to be necessary for that purpose.

(Part XI, Article 256)

COMMENTS

The administrative relation generally follows the scheme of distribution of the legislative powers. The executive power of a State shall extend only to its own Territory and with respect to those subjects over which it has legislative competence. However, the Central Government can direct how its laws or executive power shall be implemented in that State because within the State, government of the State is all powerful. 'A failure to comply with Article 250 may attract serious consequences but no court is likely to entertain a grievance at the instance of a private party that Article 256 has not been complied with by a State Government.'[21]

257. Control of the Union over States in certain cases: (1) The executive power of every State shall be so exercised as not to impede or prejudice the exercise of the executive power of the Union, and the executive power of the Union shall extend to the giving of such directions to a State as may appear to the Government of India to be necessary for that purpose.

(2) The executive power of the Union shall also extend to the giving of directions to a State as to the construction and maintenance of means of communication declared in the direction to be of national or military importance:

Provided that nothing in this clause shall be taken as restricting the power of the Parliament to declare highways or waterways to be national highways or national waterways so declared or the power of the Union to construct and maintain means of communication as part of its functions with respect to naval, military and air-force works.

(3) The executive power of the Union shall also extend to the giving of directions to a State as to the measures to be taken for the protection of the railways within the State.

(4) Where in carrying out any direction given to a State under clause (2) as to the construction or maintenance of any means of communication or under clause (3) as to the measures to be taken for the protection of any railway, costs have been incurred in excess of those which would have been incurred in the discharge of the normal duties of the State if such direction had not been given, there shall be paid by the Government of India to the State such sum as may be agreed, or, in default of agreement, as may be determined by an arbitrator appointed by the Chief Justice of India, in respect of the extra costs so incurred by the State.

(Part XI, Article 257)

COMMENTS

The Union Government can issue directions to the State in the following matters:

The manner in which the executive power of the State shall be exercised so as not to impede or abridge the executive power of the Union.

The construction and maintenance of means of communication, declared to be of national or military importance, and

Measures to be taken for the protection of railways within the State.

Thus, the Central Government can give directions to a State as to the measures to be taken by it for the protection of railways within the State.

258. Power of the Union to confer powers, etc. on States in certain cases: (1) Notwithstanding anything in this Constitution, the President may, with the consent of the Governor of a State, entrust either conditionally or unconditionally to that Government or to its officers functions in relation to any matter to which the executive power of the Union extends.

(2) A law made by the Parliament which applies in any State may, notwithstanding that it relates to a matter with respect to which the Legislature of the State has no power to make laws, confer powers and impose duties, or authorise the conferring of powers and the imposition of duties, upon the State or officers and authorities thereof.

(3) Where, by virtue of this Article, powers and duties have been conferred or imposed upon a State or officers or authorities thereof, there shall be paid by the Government of India to the State such sum as may be agreed, or, in default of agreement, as may be determined by an arbitrator appointed by the Chief Justice of India, in respect of any extra costs of administration incurred by the State in connection with the exercise of those powers and duties.

(Part XI, Article 258)

COMMENTS

The Central Government can delegate executive power to the State with its consent or by law made by the Parliament. In the latter case, the administrative control of the Union remains with it to issue necessary directions to State.

When the executive power is conferred by the Union, by law, the State is entitled to be compensated for the extra costs which it has to incur on account of the delegation. However, powers like power to promulgate ordinances, under Article 123, powers under Emergency (Article 352), make rules, regarding service conditions under Article 309 cannot be delegated as these are not powers of the Union, but are vested in the President by the Constitution.

It was held that the order by Government of J & K to deport a foreigner under the Foreigners Act, 1946 is valid because the

Central Government had validtiy delegated its administrative powers under the Foreigners Act.[22]

259. Deleted.

260. Jurisdiction of the Union in relation to Territories outside India: The Government of India may by agreement with the Government of any Territory not being part of the Territory of India undertake any executive, legislative or judicial functions vested in the Government of such Territory, but every such agreement shall be subject to, and governed by, any law relating to the exercise of foreign jurisdiction for the time being in force.

(Part XI, Article 260)

COMMENTS

The Government of India can an exercise jurisdiction over Territories outside India in respect of which the Government of India has acquired jurisdiction by treaty, agreement, grant, usage, political sufferance or other lawful means, for example, the Government of India has some powers to involve itself in the administration of Bhutan.

261. Public Acts, records and judicial proceedings: (1) Full faith and credit shall be given throughout the Territory of India to public acts, records and judicial proceedings of the Union and of every State.

(2) The manner in which, and the conditions under which, the acts, records and proceedings referred to in clause (1) shall be proved and the effect thereof determined shall be as provided by the law made by the Parliament.

(3) Final judgements or orders delivered or passed by civil courts in any part of the Territory of India shall be capable of execution anywhere within that Territory according to law.

(Part XI, Article 261)

COMMENTS

The final judgements or orders of civil courts in any part of the Territory of India, shall be executable anywhere within the Territory without the necessity of a fresh suit upon the judgement. The rule applies only to civil judgements. It does not require the courts of a State to enforce the penal laws of another State.

Disputes relating to Waters

262. Adjudication of disputes relating to water of inter-state rivers or river valleys: (1) The Parliament may by law provide for the adjudication of any dispute or complaint with respect to the use, distribution or control of the waters of, or in, any inter-state river or river valley.

(2) Notwithstanding anything in this Constitution, the Parliament may by law provide that neither the Supreme Court nor any other court shall exercise jurisdiction in respect of any such dispute or complaint as is referred to in clause (1).

(Part XI, Article 262)

COMMENTS

The Water Disputes Act, 1956 empowers the Central Government to set up a tribunal for the adjudication of the dispute on a complaint from a State Government. The tribunal shall consist of one person only nominated in this behalf by the Chief Justice of India from amongst persons who are, or have been, judges of the Supreme Court or judges of a High Court.

The decision given by the tribunal shall be final and binding on the parties to the dispute and shall be given effect to by them. Neither the Supreme Court nor any other Court shall exercise jurisdiction in respect of any water dispute which may be referred to a tribunal under this Act.[23]

However, the Supreme Court can direct that Central Government is to fulfill its statutory obligation under Section 4 of the Act, which is mandatory particularly when the State of Tamil Nadu supported the writ petition filed for the purpose by a registered society.[24] The Supreme Court directed the Central Government to refer the dispute to the tribunal under a writ of mandamus.

The Constitution Commission (NCRWC) has further recommended as follows:

Appropriate Parliamentary legislation should be made for repealing the River Boards Act, 1956 and replacing it by another comprehensive enactment under Entry 56 of List I in the national interest treating the inter-state rivers as national resources of the community.

In resolving problems and coordinating policy and action, the Union as well as the States should more effectively utilise the forum of inter-state Council.

263. Provision with respect to an inter-state Council: If at any time it appears to the President that the public interests would be served by the establishment of a Council charged with the duty of—

(a) inquiring into and advising upon disputes which may have arisen between States;

(b) investigating and discussing subjects in which some or all of the States, or the Union and one or more of the States, have a common interest; or

(c) making recommendations upon any such subject and, in particular, recommendations for the better co-ordination of policy and action with respect to that subject, it shall be lawful for the President by order to establish such a Council, and to define the nature of the duties to be performed by it and its organisation and procedure.

(Part XI, Article 263)

COMMENTS

The Supreme Court has jurisdiction to hear disputes between the States involving the existence or extent of a legal right.[25] But experience of the working of federations has shown that inter-state disputes of a non-legal character sometimes arise.

It was considered desirable to provide some Constitutional machinery for disposing of such differences. The States Reorganisation Act, 1956 has set up five Zonal Councils, namely the Northern Zone Council, the Council of the Central Zone, the Eastern Zone Council, the Western Zone Council and the Council of the Southern Zone. A sixth Council named as the North-Eastern Council was set up under the North-Eastern Council Act, 1971. Each of these Councils consists of the Home Minister of the Govternment of India as ex-officio Chairman, Chief Minister, of the member states and two other ministers nominated by the Governor of the States concerned. These Councils are intended to foster inter-state concord and thereby to strengthen the Centre and the States. They would work to promote co-operation, successful implementation and execution of development projects and would also act as advisory bodies in matters of common interest, particularly in respect of economic and social planning. They would also provide a forum for settling border disputes and other problems relating to linguistic minorities or inter-state transport, etc.

However, the meetings of Inter-state Council are occasionally held and they are not effective as is expected of them.

REFERENCES

1. State of West Bengal vs. Union of India. AIR 1963 SC 1241.
2. Kuldeep Nayar vs. Union of India, (2006) 7 SCC 1.
3. State of Tamil Nadu vs. M. Seshachelam, (2011) 12 SCC.
4. State of Bihar vs. Bihar Distillery Ltd. (1997) 2 SCC 453.
5. S.S. Bole vs. B.D. Sardane, (1997) 8 SCC 522.
6. A.P. Dairy Development Corporation Federation vs. B. Narasimha Reddy, (2011) 9 SCC 286.
7. Check Post Officer V.K.P. Abdulla and Bros (1970) 3 SCC 355.
8. State of Haryana vs. Sant Lal, (1993) 4 SCC 380.
9. B. Viswanathiah & Co. vs. State of Karnataka, (1991), 3 SCC 358.
10. Baijnath Kedia vs. State of Bihar, (1969) 3 SCC 838.
11. Common Cause vs. Union of India, 838 (1996) 6 SCC 530.
12. Azam vs. Expenditures Tax Office, (1971) 3 SCC 621.
13. Kartar Singh vs. State of Punjab, (1994) 3 SCC 569.
14. Naga People's Movement of Human Rights vs. Union of India, (1998) 2 SCC 109.
15. Union of India vs. Harbhajan Singh Dhillon, (1971) 2 SCC 779.
16. Central Bank of India vs. State of Kerala, (2009) 4 SCC 94.
17. TKVTSS Medical Education and Charitable Trust vs. State of Tamil Nadu, (1996) 3 SCC 15.

18. M. Karuna Nidhi vs. Union of India, (1979) 3 SCC 431.
19. Deep Chand vs. State of U.P. AIR 1959 SC 648.
20. Utkal Contractors and Joinery (P) Ltd. vs. State of Orissa, AIR 1987 SC 2310.
21. Additional District Magistrate, Jabalpur vs. Shivkant Shukla, (1976) 2 SCC 521.
22. Anwar vs. State of J & K, (1971) 3 SCC 104.
23. Re. Cauvery Water Disputes Tribunal, AIR 1992 SC 522.
24. T.N. Cauvery NVVNUP Sangam vs. Union of India, (1990) 3SCC 440.
25. Article 131.

□

Chapter 13

FINANCE, PROPERTY, CONTRACTS AND SUITS

264. Interpretation: In this Part, 'Finance Commission' means a Finance Commission constituted under Article 280.

(Part XII, Article 264)

265. Taxes not to be imposed save by authority of law: No tax shall be levied or collected except by authority of law.

(Part XII, Article 265)

COMMENTS

The object is the equitable distribution of the financial resources between the States and the Union instead of dividing the resources into two water-tight compartments. The Union and States together form one organic whole for the purpose of utilisation of the resources of Territories of India as a whole. Article 265 upholds the faith in the elected representatives and categorically declares that no taxes can be imposed without the authority of law. Also it adds: taxes can be 'collected' only according to law.

Tax illegally levied must be refunded. Tax will be refunded which is paid under mistake of law.

The authorisation made by the statute to levy tax must be express. Taxing power cannot be derived from the delegation of mere regulating power. The power to tax is not incidental or ancillary to the power to legislate on a matter.[1] However, a tax law may be invalidated when it violates the fundamental right to equality or to practise any profession or to carry on any occupation, trade or business in Article 19(1)(g).

Taxation is a matter of compulsion to run the State. Taxation is an imposition made for a public purpose. The quantum of imposition depends generally upon the capacity of tax payer to pay. Fee is levied against the services. There should be a reasonable 'relationship' between levy of fee and the services rendered. When there is no such co-relation, the levy, despite its nomenclature is, in, fact, a tax.[2] For regulatory fee, the service to be rendered is not a condition precedent.

Any compulsory exaction of money by the Government like a tax or cess has to be according to the law and strictly constructed in accordance with law.[3] The substantive taxing provisions in parent statute cannot be amended or enlarged by a notification.[4]

266. Consolidated Funds and public accounts of India and of the States: (1) Subject to the provisions of Article 267 and to the provisions of this Chapter with respect to the assignment of the whole or part of the net proceeds of certain taxes and duties to States, all revenues received by the Government of India, all loans raised by that Government by the issue of treasury bills, loans or ways and money advances and all moneys received by that Government in repayment of loans shall form one consolidated fund to be entitled "the Consolidated Fund of India", and all revenues received by the Government of a State, all loans raised by that Government by the issue of treasury bills, loans or ways and money advances and all moneys received by that Government in repayment of loans shall form one consolidated fund to be entitled "the Consolidated Fund of the State".

(2) All other public moneys received by or on behalf of the Government of India or the Government of a State shall be credited to the public account of India or the public account of the State, as the case may be.

(3) No moneys out of the Consolidated Fund of India or the Consolidated Fund of a State shall be appropriated except

in accordance with law and for the purposes and in the manner provided in this Constitution.

(Part XII, Article 266)

COMMENTS

Public Account: All revenues collected, and all moneys received on loan, and all repayments of loans shall be credited to the respective consolidated funds of the Union and the States. All other public moneys received by on behalf of the Government of India or the Government of State shall be credited to the Public Account of India, or the Public Account of the State, as the case may be.

267. Contingency Fund: (1) The Parliament may by law establish a Contingency Fund in the nature of an interest to be entitled "the Contingency Fund of India" into which shall be paid from time to time such sums as may be determined by such law, and the said Fund shall be placed at the disposal of the President to enable advances to be made by him out of such Fund for the purposes of meeting unforeseen expenditures pending authorisation of such expenditures by the Parliament by law under Article 115 or Article 116.

(2) The Legislature of a State may by law establish a Contingency Fund in the nature of an impurest to be entitled "the Contingency Fund of the State" into which shall be paid from time to time such sums as may be determined by such law, and the said Fund shall be placed at the disposal of the Governor of the State to enable advances to be made by him out of such Fund for the purposes of meeting unforeseen expenditures pending authorisation of such expenditures by the Legislature of the State by law under Article 205 or Article 206.

(Part XII, Article 267)

COMMENTS

This fund shall be placed at the disposal of the President to enable advances to be made by him out of the fund for the purpose of meeting unforeseen expenditures. The expenditures, however, must subsequently be authorised by the Parliament. Similar fund is also established by the State Legislature.

Distribution of Revenues between the Union and the States

268. Duties levied by the Union but collected and appropriated by the State: (1) Such stamp duties and such duties of exercise on medicinal and toilet preparations as are mentioned in the Union List shall be levied by the Government of India but shall be collected:

(a) in the case where such duties are leviable within any Union Territory, by the Government of India, and

(b) in other cases, by the States within which such duties are respectively leviable.

(2) The proceeds in any financial year of any such duty leviable within any State shall not form part of the Consolidated Fund of India, but shall be assigned to that State.

(Part XII, Article 268)

COMMENTS

These are stamp duties on Bills of Exchange and Excise Duties on medicinal and toilet preparations containing alcohol, etc.

268A. Service tax levied by Union and collected and appropriated by the Union and the States: (1) Taxes on services shall be levied by the Government of India and such tax shall be collected and appropriated by the Government of India and the States in the manner provided in clause (2).

(2) The proceeds in any financial year of any such tax levied in accordance with the provisions of clause (1) shall be—(a) collected by the Government of India and the States; (b) appropriated by the Government of India and the States, in accordance with such principles of collection and appropriation as may be formulated by the Parliament by law.

(Part XII, Article 268A)

COMMENTS

The Service Tax was introduced by the Constitution (88th Amendment) Act, 2003. It is now in force and is being collected.

269. Taxes levied & collected by the Union but assigned to the States: (1) The following duties and taxes shall be levied and collected by the Government of India but shall be assigned to the States in the manner provided in clause (2), namely:

(a) duties in respect of succession to property other than agricultural land;

(b) estate duty in respect of property other than agricultural land;

(c) terminal taxes on goods or passengers carried by railway, sea or air;

(d) taxes on railway fares and freights;

(e) Taxes other than stamp duties on transaction in stock exchanges and futures markets;

(f) taxes on the sale or purchase of newspapers and on advertisements published therein;

(g) taxes on the sale or purchase of goods other than newspapers, where such sale or purchase takes place in the course of inter-state trade or commerce;

(h) taxes on the consignment of goods (whether the consignment is to the person making it or to any other person), where such consignment takes place in the course of inter-state trade or commerce.

(2) The net proceeds in any financial year of any such duty or tax, except, insofar as those proceeds represent proceeds attributable to Union Territories, shall not form part of the Consolidated Fund of India, but shall be assigned to the States within which that duty or tax is leviable in that year, and shall be distributed among those States in accordance with such principles of distribution as may be formulated by the Parliament by law.

(3) The Parliament may by law formulate principles for determining when a sale or purchase of, or consignment of goods takes place in the course of inter-state or commerce.

(Part XII, Article 269)

COMMENTS

Duties and Taxes are:

Duties on succession to property,
Estate duty,
Terminal taxes except on road transport,
Taxes on railway fare and freights,
Taxes on stock exchange,
Taxes on advertisements in newspapers,
Sale Tax on inter-state trade or commerce, and consignment of goods.

270. Taxes levied and collected by the Union and distributed between the Union and the States: (1) Taxes on income other than agricultural income shall be levied and collected by the Government of India and distributed between the Union and the States in the manner provided in clause (2).

(2) Such percentage, as may be prescribed, of the net proceeds in any financial year of any such tax, except insofar as those proceeds represent proceeds attributable to Union Territories or to taxes payable in respect of Union emoluments, shall not form part of the Consolidated Fund of India, but shall be assigned to the States within which that tax or duty is leviable in that year, and shall be distributed among those states in such manner and from such time as may be prescribed.

(Part XII, Article 270)

COMMENTS

Following are major taxes levied & collected by the Union and distributed between the Union and the States:

Taxes on income other than on agricultural income;
Duties of excise.

Corporation tax is a super tax on the profits of companies. Corporation tax is not liable to be shared with the States.[5]

The income tax attributed to Union Territories forms part of the Consolidated Fund of India. It is not necessary to make any distribution of income tax with respect to Union Territories, as UTs are centrally administered through the President.[6]

271. Surcharge on certain duties and taxes for purposes of the Union: Notwithstanding anything in Articles 269 and 270, the Parliament may at any time increase any of the duties or taxes referred to in those Articles by a surcharge for purposes of the Union and the whole proceeds of any such surcharge shall form part of the Consolidated Fund of India.

(Part XII, Article 271)

COMMENTS

"All proceeds from such surcharges are to form part of the Consolidated Fund of India and are not liable to be distributed among the States. There is nothing to prevent the Parliament from imposing a surcharge any number of times."[7]

272. Deleted.

(Part XII, Article 272)

273. Grants in lieu of exports duty on jute and jute products: (1) There shall be charged on the Consolidated Fund of India in each year as grants-in-aid of the resources of states of Assam, Bihar, Odisha and West Bengal in lieu of assignment of any share of the net proceeds in each year of export duty on jute and jute products to those States, such sums as may be prescribed.

(2) The sums so prescribed shall continue to be charged on the Consolidated Fund of India so long as any export duty on jute or jute products continues to be levied by the Government of India or until the expiration of ten years from the commencement of this Constitution, whichever is earlier.

(3) In this Article, the expression "prescribed" has the same meaning as in Article 270.

(Part XII, Article 273)

COMMENTS

Under the present provision, the States of Bihar, Odisha, and West Bengal, Assam are not entitled to any share of net proceeds of the jute export duty.

274. Prior recommendation of President required to Bills affecting taxation in which States are interested: (1) No Bill or amendment which imposes or varies any tax or duty in which States are interested, or which varies the meaning of the expression "agricultural income" as defined for the purposes of the enactments relating to Indian Income-Tax, or which affects the principles on which under any of the foregoing provisions of this Chapter, moneys are or may be distributable to State, or which imposes any surcharge for the purposes of the Union as is mentioned in the foregoing provisions of this Chapter, shall be introduced or moved in either House of the Parliament except on the recommendation of the President.

(2) In this Article, the expression "tax or duty in which States are interested" means:

(a) a tax or duty, the whole or part of the net proceeds whereof are assigned to any State; or

(b) a tax or duty by reference to the net proceeds, whereof sums are for the time being payable out of the Consolidated Fund of India to any State.

(Part XII, Article 274)

COMMENTS

A bill varying any tax or duty, in which States are interested, cannot be moved without prior recommendation from the President.

275. Grants from the Union to certain States: (1) Such sums as the Parliament may by law provide shall be charged on the Consolidated Fund of India in each year as grants-in-aid of the revenues of such States as the Parliament may determine to be in need of assistance, and different sums may be fixed for different States:

Provided that there shall be paid out of the Consolidated Fund of India as grants-in-aid of the revenues of a State such capital and recurring sums as may be necessary to enable that State to meet the costs of such schemes of development as may be undertaken by the State with the approval of the Government of India for the purpose of promoting the welfare of the Scheduled

Tribes in that State or raising the level of administration of the Scheduled Areas therein to that of the administration of the rest of the areas of that State:

Provided further that there shall be paid out of the Consolidated Fund of India as grants-in-aids of the revenues of the State of Assam sums, capital and recurring, equivalent to:

(a) The average excess of expenditures over the revenues during the two years immediately preceding the commencement of this Constitution in respect of the administration of the tribal areas specified in Part I of the table appended to paragraph 20 of the Sixth Schedule; and

(b) The costs of such schemes of development as may be undertaken by that State with the approval of the Government of India for the purpose of raising the level of administration of the said areas to that of the administration of the rest of the areas of that State.

(1A) On and from the formation of the autonomous State under Article 244A:

(i) Any sums payable under clause (a) of the second proviso to clause (1) shall, if the autonomous State therein, be paid to the autonomous State, and, if the autonomous State comprises only some of those tribal areas, be apportioned between the State of Assam and the autonomous State as the President may, by order, specify;

(ii) There shall be paid out of the Consolidated Fund of India as grants-in-aid of the revenues of the autonomous State sums, capital and recurring, equivalent to the costs of such schemes of development as may be undertaken by the autonomous State with the approval of the Government of India for the purpose of raising the level of administration of that State to that of the administration of the rest of the State of Assam.

(2) Until provision is made by the Parliament under clause (1), the powers conferred on the Parliament under that clause shall be exercisable by the President under this clause shall have effect subject to any provision so made by the Parliament.

Provided that after a Finance Commission has been constituted, no order shall be made under this clause by the President except after considering the recommendations of the Finance Commission.

(Part XII, Article 275)

COMMENTS

Grants-in-aid shall be made in each year by the Union to such States as the Parliament may determine to be in need of assistance, particularly, for the promotion of welfare of tribal areas, including special grants to Assam in this respect.

276. Taxes on professions, trades, callings and employments: (1) Notwithstanding anything in Article 246, no law of the Legislature of a State relating to taxes for the benefit of the State or of a municipality, district board, local board or other local authority therein in respect of professions, trades, callings or employments shall be invalid on the ground that it relates to a tax on income.

(2) The total amount payable in respect of any one person to the State or to any one municipality, district board, local board or other local authority in the State by way of taxes on professions, trades, callings and employments shall not exceed two thousand and five hundred rupees per annum.

(3) The power of the Legislature of a State to make laws as aforesaid with respect to taxes on professions, trades, callings & others.

(Part XII, Article 276)

COMMENTS

The power to levy taxes on professions, trades, callings and employments is conferred on the State Legislatures. A tax upto ₹ 2,500 can be imposed by the State, a municipality, district board, local board or other local authority on any profession, trade, calling, or employment.

277. Savings: Any taxes, duties, cesses or fees which, immediately before the commencement of this Constitution, were being lawfully levied by the Government of any State or by any municipality or other local authority or body for the purposes of the State, municipality, district or other local area may, notwithstanding that those taxes, duties, cesses or fees are mentioned in the Union List, continue to be levied and to be applied to the same purposes until provision to the contrary is made by the Parliament by law.

(Part XII, Article 277)

COMMENTS

Article 277 saves all pre-constitution valid laws in regards to taxes, duties, cesses or fees lawfully levied immediately before the Constitution.

278. Deleted.

(Part XII, Article 278)

279. Calculation of "net proceeds" etc.: (1) In the foregoing provisions of this Chapter, "net proceeds" mean in relation to any tax or duty, the proceeds thereof reduced by the cost of collection, and for the purposes of those provisions the net proceeds of any tax or duty, or of any part of any tax or duty, in or attributable to any area shall be ascertained and certified by the Comptroller and Auditor-General of India, whose certificate shall be final.

(2) Subject as aforesaid, and to any other express provision of this Chapter, a law made by the Parliament or an order of the President may, in any case where under this Part, the proceeds of any duty or tax are, or may be, assigned to any State, provide for the manner in which the proceeds are to be calculated, for the time from or at which and the manner in which any payments are to be made, for the making of adjustments between one financial year and another, and for any other incidental or ancillary matters.

(Part XII, Article 279)

COMMENTS

This Article defines 'net profits' of a tax. It means all the proceeds of tax reduced by the cost of collection. The certificate of the Comptroller and Auditor General of India of net proceeds of a tax in a State shall be final.

280. Finance Commission: (1) The President shall, within two years from the commencement of this Constitution and thereafter at the expiration of every fifth year or at such earlier time as the President considers necessary, by order constitute a Finance Commission which shall consist of a Chairman and four other members to be appointed by the President.

(2) The Parliament may by law determine the qualifications which shall be requisite for appointment as members of the Commission and the manner in which they shall be selected.

(3) It shall be the duty of the Commission to make recommendations to the President as to:

(a) The distribution between the Union and the States of the net proceeds of taxes which are to be, or may be, divided between them under this Chapter and the allocation between the States of the respective shares of such proceeds;

(b) The principles which should govern the grants-in-aid of the revenues of the States out of the Consolidated Fund of India;

(bb) The measures needed to augment the Consolidated Fund of a State to supplement the resources of the Panchayats in the State on the basis of the recommendations made by the Finance Commission of the State;

(c) The measures needed to augment the Consolidated Fund of a State supplement the resources of the Municipalities in the State on the basis of the recommendations made by the Finance Commission of the State;

(d) Any other matter referred to the Commission by the President in the interests of sound finance.

(4) The Commission shall determine their procedure and shall have such powers in the performance of their functions as the Parliament may by law confer on them.

(Part XII, Article 280)

COMMENTS

The Finance Commission at five years intervals is to recommend to the President certain measures relating to the distribution of financial resources between the Union and the States. The Chairman must be a person having 'experience in public affairs' and the other four members must be a High Court Judge and three experts in finance, administration and economics.

281. Recommendation of the Finance Commission: The President shall cause every recommendation made by the Finance Commission under the provisions of this Constitution together with an explanatory memorandum as to the action taken thereon to be laid before each House of the Parliament.

(Part XII, Article 281)

COMMENTS

The President shall cause every recommendation made by the Finance Commission under the provisions of this Constitution together with an explanatory memorandum as to the action taken therein to be laid before each House of the Parliament.

282. Miscellaneous Financial Provisions: The Union or a State may make any grants for any public purpose, notwithstanding that the purpose is not one with respect to which the Parliament or the Legislature of the State, as the case may be, may make laws.

(Part XII, Article 282)

COMMENTS

According to this Article, the spending power of the Union or a State is not coterminous with its legislative power. The Union or a State may make grants for any public purpose, although that public purpose does not relate to a subject over which it can make laws. Thus, the Union may give grants to hospitals or to schools, although neither public health nor education is a Union subject.

283. Custody, etc. of Consolidated Funds, Contingency Funds and moneys credited to the Public accounts: (1) The custody of the Consolidated Fund of India and the Contingency Fund of India, the payment of moneys into such Funds, the withdrawal of moneys therefrom, the custody of public moneys other than those credited to such Funds received by or on behalf of the Government of India, their payment into the public account of India and the withdrawal of moneys from such account and all other matters connected with or ancillary to matters aforesaid shall be regulated by law made by the Parliament, and until provision in that behalf is so made, shall be regulated by rules and made by the President.

(2) The custody of the Consolidated fund of a State and the Contingency Fund of a State, the payment of moneys into such Funds, the withdrawal of moneys therefrom, the custody of public moneys other than those credited to such Funds, received by or on behalf of the Government of the State, their payment into the public account of the State and withdrawal of moneys from such account and all other matters connected with or ancillary to matters aforesaid shall be regulated by law made by the Legislature of the State, and until provision in that behalf is so made, shall be regulated by rules made by the Governor of the State.

(Part XII, Article 283)

COMMENTS

This Article aims at placing the custody as well as the expenditures of all public moneys under the control of the Parliament or the State Legislature as the case may be. These matters shall be regulated by law.

284. Custody of suitors' deposits and other moneys received by public servants and courts: All moneys received by or deposited with:

(a) Any officer employed in connection with the affairs of the Union or of a State in his capacity as such, other than revenues or public moneys raised or received by the Government of India or the Government of the State, as the case may be, or

(b) Any court within the Territory of India to the credit of any cause, matter, account or persons, shall be paid into the public account of India or the public account of the State, as the case may be.

(Part XII, Article 284)

COMMENTS

This Article contains that all moneys received by public servants and courts shall be paid into the Public Account of India or the Public Account of the State, as the case may be. Private Custody of such moneys is illegal.

285. Exemption of property of the Union from State taxation: (1) The property of the Union shall, save insofar as the Parliament may by law otherwise provide, be exempt from all taxes imposed by a State or by any authority within a State.

(2) Nothing in clause (1) shall, until the Parliament by law otherwise provides, prevent any authority within a State from levying any tax on any property of the Union to which such property was immediately before the commencement of this Constitution liable or treated as liable, so long as that tax continues to be levied in that State.

(Part XII, Article 285)

COMMENTS

Property of the Union is exempted under Article 285 Writ Petition by the Union of India was accepted.[8]

However, the property owned or vested in an independent statutory authority like the International Airport Authority is not the property of the Union for the purposes of exemption from municipal taxes.[9]

286. Restriction as to imposition of tax on the sale or purchase of goods: (1) No law of a State shall impose, or authorise the imposition of, a tax on the sale or purchase or goods where such sale or purchase takes place:

(a) Outside the State; or

(b) in the course of the import of the goods into, or export of the goods out of, the Territory of India.

(2) The Parliament may by law formulate principles for determining when a sale or purchase of goods takes place in any of the ways mentioned in clause (1).

(3) Any law of a State shall, insofar as it imposes, or authorises the imposition of:

(a) a tax on the sale or purchase of goods declared by the Parliament by law to be of special importance in inter-state trade or commerce, or

(b) a tax on the sale or purchase of goods, being a tax of the nature referred to in sub-clause (b), sub-clause (c) or sub-clause (d) of clause (29A) of Article 366, be subject to such restrictions and conditions in regard to the system of levy, rates and other incidents of the tax as the Parliament may by law specify.

(Part XII, Article 286)

COMMENTS

A State could impose sales tax on goods except for inter-state trade or commerce or in the course of export or import.

Accordingly, the Central Sales Tax, 1956 is in usage all over the country. The tax payable by any dealer under the Central Act is levied & collected in the same manner and through the same authorities as are empowered under the general sales tax law of the appropriate State.

The Sales Tax Act has a territorial nexus "In case of electricity, its sale cannot be separated from its consumption. Therefore, if sale and consumption of electricity were to take place in different States, territorial nexus for the State in which the sale took place is lost. Therefore, the State in which sale takes place cannot tax such a sale."[10]

Section 4 of Central Sales Tax Act, 1956 lays down that the goods shall be deemed to be sold or purchased inside a State if the goods are within the State at the time the contract of sale is made.

The important criteria are that the sale or purchase must occasion the movement of goods from one State to another.[11]

'When the contract of inter-state sale was entered into, it would be the first sale in the State. Once that sale had taken place, and when the goods were delivered in the States of Andhra Pradesh and Kerala, there was no further sale to the company when it transferred to its branches those goods which had already been subject to tax in Madras.[12]

The Parliament is empowered to declare certain goods of special importance in inter-state trade or commerce to lay down the restrictions and conditions subject to which any State law may regulate the tax on sales or purchases of such goods in the State.

287. Exemption from taxes on electricity: Save insofar as the Parliament may by law otherwise provide, no law of a State shall impose, or authorise the imposition of, a tax on the consumption or sale of electricity (whether produced by a Government or other persons) which is—

(a) consumed by the Government of India, or sold to the Government of India for consumption by that Government; or

(b) consumed in the construction, maintenance or operation of any railway by the Government of India or a railway company operating that railway, or sold to that Government or any such railway company for consumption in the construction, maintenance or operation of any railway, and any such law imposing, or authorising the imposition of, a tax on the sale of electricity shall secure that the price of electricity sold to the Government of India for consumption by that Government, or to any such railway company as aforesaid for consumption in the construction, maintenance or operation of any railway, shall be less by the amount of the tax than the price charged to other consumers of a substantial quantity of electricity.

(Part XII, Article 287)

COMMENTS

Entry 53, List-II of Seventh Schedule empowers a State Legislature to levy taxes on the consumption or sale of electricity. But no State Legislature unless authorised by a Union Law can impose any tax on electricity consumed by the Government of India or utilised for the construction, maintenance or operation of any Railway. The Union law can authorise a State to levy such tax with concessions.

(Part XII, Article 287)

288. Exemption from taxation by States in respect of water or electricity in certain cases: (1) Save insofar as the President may by order otherwise provide, no law of a State in force immediately before the commencement of this Constitution shall impose, or authorise the imposition of, a tax in respect of any water or electricity stored, generated, consumed, distributed or sold by any authority established by any existing law or any law made by the Parliament for regulating or developing any inter-state river or river-valley.

Explanation: The expression "law of a State in force" in this clause shall include a law of a State passed or made before the commencement of this Constitution and not previously repealed, notwithstanding that it or parts of it may not be then in operation either at all or in particular areas.

(2) The Legislature of a State may by law impose, or authorise the imposition of, any such tax as is mentioned in clause (1), but no such law shall have any effect unless it has, after having been reserved for the consideration of the President, received his assent; and if any such law provides for the fixation of the rates and other incidents of such tax by means of rules or orders to be made under the law by any authority, the law shall provide for the previous consent of the President being obtained to the making of any such rule or order.

(Part XII, Article 288)

COMMENTS

The State Legislature may impose a tax on interstate river or river valley bodies, provided it has received the assent of the President.

289. Exemption of property and income of a State from Union Taxation: (1) The property and income of a State shall be exempt from Union Taxation.

(2) Nothing in clause (1) shall prevent the Union from imposing, or authorising the imposition of, any tax to such extent, if any, as the Parliament may by law provide in respect of a trade or business of any kind carried on by, or on behalf of, the Government of a State, or any operations connected therewith, or any property used or occupied for the purposes of such trade or business, or any income accruing or arising in connection therewith.

(3) Nothing in clause (2) shall apply to any trade or business, or to any class of trade or business, which the Parliament may by law declare to be incidental to the ordinary functions of the Government.

(Part XII, Article 289)

COMMENTS

Conversely, the property and income of a State shall be exempt from Union taxation except in there where a State enters into a trade or business, other than a trade or business, which is declared by the Parliament to be incidental to the ordinary business of government; it shall not be exempt from Union Taxation. The privilege relates to a tax on property. Hence, the property of a State through sea route is not immune from customs duty.[13]

In a well contested matter, a decision has one in favour of the State, whereas State of Punjab claimed exemption from tax on their property situated within Delhi. It was held that the taxes imposed by Delhi Municipal Corporation Act, 1957 and the New Delhi Municipal Council Act, 1994 amounted to Union taxation. It was accordingly exempt under the above laws. The decision by 5:4 judges recognised greater autonomy of the States in the federation of India.

290. Adjustment in respect of certain expenses and pensions: Where under the provisions of this Constitution the expenses of any court or commission, or the pension payable to or in respect of a person who has served before the commencement of this Constitution under the Crown in India or after such commencement in connection with the affairs of the Union or of a State, are charged on the Consolidated Fund of India or the Consolidated Fund of a State, then, if:

(a) in the case of a charge on the Consolidated Fund of India, the court or Commission serves any of the separate needs of a State, or the person has served wholly or in part in connection with the affairs of a State; or

(b) in the case of a charge on the Consolidated Fund of a State, the court or Commission serves any of the separate needs of the Union or another State, or the person has served wholly or in part in connection with the affairs of the Union or another State, there shall be charged on and paid out of the Consolidated Fund of the State or, as the case may be, the Consolidated Fund of India or the Consolidated Fund of the other State, such contribution in respect of the expenses or pension as may be agreed, or as may in default of agreement be determined by an arbitrator to be appointed by the Chief Justice of India.

(Part XII, Article 290)

COMMENTS

The Article provides for adjustment, by agreement or arbitration, of certain expenses, pensions, etc. which under the Constitution are liable to be shared between the Union and the States or the States inter se.

290A: Annual payment to certain Devaswom Funds: A sum of forty-six lakhs and fifty thousand rupees shall be charged on, and paid out of, the Consolidated Fund of the State of Kerala every year to the Travancore Devaswom Fund; and a sum of thirteen lakhs and fifty thousand rupees shall be charged on, and paid out, of the consolidated fund of the State of Tamil Nadu every year to the Devaswom Fund established in that State for the maintenance of Hindu temples and shrines in the

Territories transferred to that State on the 1st day of November, 1956, from the State of Travancore-Cochin.

(Part XII, Article 290A)

COMMENTS

The Devaswom or Devasthan funds are given by governments to run old trusts of religious and charitable purposes in every State. However, the trusts or temples have gold and other properties in abundance but many of them do not come forward to change into gold bonds. It is hoped that with the change of wind, these trusts or temples will have faith in Government, who is the representative of God, and will put their funds or valuables with the government treasury. They will, however, not be able to protect these valuables in times to come as anti-social and robbers are inventing new methods of stealing or robbing.

291. Deleted

COMMENTS

GST Bill: The Goods and Services Tax Bill or GST Bill, officially known as the Constitution (122nd Amendment) Bill, 2014, would be a Value Added Tax (VAT) to be implemented in India. GST stands for "Goods and Services Tax" and is proposed to be a comprehensive indirect tax levied on manufacture, sale and consumption of goods as well as services at the national level. It will replace all indirect taxes levied on goods and services by the Centrai and State governments. It is aimed to cover most of the goods and services. This is a step towards economic reforms and has been on avail after protracted discussions and consultation among the Central Government and State Governments, etc. This will save the trade and business of the country from high-handedness of tax officials. But however, outer limit should be reasonably fixed so that it does not become a similar instrument of exploitation of the business community. However, after it is passed, many of the preceding Articles of Part XII of the Constitution will stand amended for future.

Borrowing

292. Borrowing by the Government of India: The executive power of the Union extends to borrowing upon the security of the Consolidated Funds of India within such limits if any, as may from time to time be fixed by the Parliament by law and to the giving of guarantees, within such limits if any, as may be so fixed.

(Part XII, Articles 292)

COMMENTS

The provision permits the Government of India to borrow money on the security of the Consolidated Fund of India. The Parliament may by law fix the limits of borrowing. Efforts were made to fix outer limit of borrowing by the Government of India because political executives, Ministers and Prime Minister may try to borrow beyond financial prudence and norms to give heavy doles to the public to win elections and to remain in power. Thus, such a law by the Parliament is a need of the hour to protect India. It is learnt that one such bill is long pending in the Parliament

293. Borrowing by States: (1) Subject to the provisions of this Article, the executive power of a State extends to borrowing within the Territory of India upon the security of the Consolidated Fund of the State within such limits, if any, as may from time to time be fixed by the Legislature of such State by law and to the giving of guarantees within such limits, if any, as may be so fixed.

(2) The Government of India may, subject to such conditions as may be laid down by or under any law made by the Parliament, make loans to any State or, so long as any limits fixed under Article 292 are not exceeded, give guarantees in respect of loans raised by any State, and any sums required for the purpose of making such loans shall be charged on the Consolidated Fund of India.

(3) A State may not without the consent of the Government of India raise any loan if there is still outstanding any part of a loan which has been made to the State by the

Government of India or by its predecessor Government, or in respect of which a guarantee has been given by the Government of India or by its predecessor Government. (4) A consent under clause (3) may be granted subject to such conditions, if any, as the Government of India may think fit to impose.

(Part XII, Article 293)

COMMENTS

A State could also borrow subject to limits set by law by the State Legislature. However, a State cannot borrow from outside India. The Government of India, within its borrowing powers, could make loans to any State or give guarantees in respect of loans raised by the State. So long as any of such loans remained outstanding, the State Government could not raise any further loans without consent of Government of India.

294. Succession to property, assets, rights, liabilities and obligations in certain cases: As from the commencement of this Constitution:

(a) All property and assets which immediately before such commencement were vested in His Majesty for the purposes of the Government of the Dominion of India and all property and assets which immediately before such commencement were vested in His Majesty for the purposes of the Government of each Governor's Province shall vest respectively in the Union and the corresponding State, and

(b) All rights, liabilities and obligations of the Government of the Dominion of India and of the Government of each Governor's Province, whether arising out of any contract or otherwise, shall be the rights, liabilities and obligations respectively of the Government of India and the Government of each corresponding State.

Subject to any adjustment made or to be made by reason of the creation before the commencement of this Constitution of the dominion of Pakistan or of the Provinces of West Bengal, East Bengal, West Punjab and East Punjab.

(Part XII, Article 294)

COMMENTS

The provisions provide for substitution of one Government in place of the other.

295. Succession to property, assets, rights, liabilities and obligations in other cases: (1) As from the commencement of this Constitution:

(a) all property and assets which immediately before such commencement were vested in any Indian State corresponding to a State specified in Part B of the First Schedule shall vest in the Union, if the purposes for which such property and assets were held immediately before such commencement will thereafter be purposes of the Union relating to any of the matters enumerated in the Union List, and

(b) all rights, liabilities and obligations of the Government of any Indian State corresponding to a State specified in Part B of the First Schedule, whether arising out of any contract or otherwise, shall be the rights, liabilities and obligations of the Government of India, if the purposes for which such rights were acquired or liabilities or obligations were incurred before such commencement will thereafter be purposes of the Government of India relating to any of the matters enumerated in the Union List, subject to any agreement entered into in that behalf by the Government of India with the Government of that State.

(2) Subject as aforesaid, the Government of each State specified in Part B of the First Schedule shall, as from the commencement of this Constitution, be the successor of the Government of the corresponding Indian State as regards all property and assets and all rights, liabilities and obligations, whether arising out of any contact or otherwise, other than those referred to in clause (1).

(Part XII, Article 295)

COMMENTS

There is no question of any constitutional obligation being cast by the provisions contained in Article 295 (1) (b) on the

Government of India to fulfill the contracts irrespective of whether they were binding on the original State, which entered into contracts and whether they can be affected by law validtiy passed after the Constitution came into force.

296. Property accruing by escheat or lapse or as *bona vacantia*: Subject as hereinafter provided any property in the Territory of India which, if this Constitution had not come into operation, would have accrued to His Majesty or, as the case may be, to the Ruler of an Indian State by escheat or lapse, or as bona vacantia for want of a rightful owner, shall, if it is property situated in a State, vest in such State, and shall, in any other case, vest in the Union:

Provided that any property which at the date when it would have so accrued to His Majesty or to the Ruler of an Indian State was in the possession or under the control of the Government of India or the Government of a State shall, according as the purposes for which it was then used or held were purposes of the Union or a State, vest in the Union or in that State.

Explanation: In the Article, the expressions "Ruler" and "Indian State" have the same meanings as in Article 363.

(Part XII, Article 296)

COMMENTS

Any property by escheat, lapse or bona vacantia, if the property is situated in a State, vest in such State. In other cases, such property is to vest in the Union.

297. Things of value within territorial waters or continental shelf and resources of the exclusive economic zone to vest in the Union: (1) All lands, minerals and other things of value underlying the ocean within the territorial waters, or the continental shelf, or the exclusive economic zone, of India shall vest in the Union and be held for the purposes of the Union.

(2) All other resources of the exclusive economic zone of India shall also vest in the Union and be held for the purposes of the Union.

(3) The limits of the territorial waters, the continental shelf, the exclusive economic zone, and other maritime zones, of India shall be such as may be specified, from time to time, by or under any law made by the Parliament.

(Part XII, Article 297)

COMMENTS

Things of value within territorial waters or continental shelf and resources of the exclusive economic zone shall vest in the Union.

298. Power to carry on trade, etc.: The executive power of the Union and of each State shall extend to the carrying on of any trade or business and to the acquisition, holding and disposal of property and the making of contracts for any purpose:

Provided that:

(a) The said executive power of the Union shall, insofar as such trade or business or such purpose is not one with respect to which the Parliament may make laws, be subject in each State to legislation by the State; and

(b) The said executive power of each State shall, insofar as such trade or business or such purpose is not one with respect to which the State Legislature may make laws, be subject to legislation by the Parliament.

(Part XII, Article 298)

COMMENTS

The Government can carry on any business or trade and does not require any additional powers and whatever is necessary for its purpose, including entering into contracts, is within the ambit of its executive power. "Therefore, it is not correct to hold that the carrying on the business of printing and publishing textbooks was beyond the competence of the executive government without a specific legislation sanctioning such course."[15]

The Supreme Court held that the power of a State under Article 298 to carry on trade, etc. extends to carrying on a trade in other States also.[16]

299. Contracts: (1) All contracts made in the exercise of the executive power of the Union or of a State shall be expressed to be made by the President, or by the Governor of the State, as the case may be, and all such contracts and all assurances of property made in the exercise of that power shall be executed on behalf of the President or the Governor by such persons and in such manner as he may direct or authorise.

(2) Neither the President nor the Governor shall be personally liable in respect of any contract or assurance made or executed for the purposes of this Constitution, or for the purposes of any enactment relating to the Government of India heretofore in force, nor shall any person making or executing any such contracts or assurance on behalf of any of them be personally liable in respect thereof.

(Part XII, Article 299)

COMMENTS

Government Contracts: All contracts made in the exercise of the executive power of the Union or of a State will be in the name of the President or the Governor as the case may be. No personal liability is to be attached to the President or the Governor or to the persons executing the contracts, etc.

Secondly, the government contracts must be executed by the competent person and in the prescribed manner. If it is not done, the Government will not be bound by the contract as these provisions are mandatory.

The Government, however, if it enjoys the benefit of performance by the other party to the contract, would be bound to give recompense on the principle of quantum ment or quantum valebat (service or goods received). Besides this, the doctrine of promissory estoppel may apply to on the facts of the case.

Doctrine of Indoor Management: In case of Government contracts and contracts of Government Corporation, doctrine of indoor management cannot be applied so as to remove the need to observe the formalities regarding drawing of the contract or essential terms of the contracts.[17]

'This has no application to a case where a particular statutory authority enters into a contract which is statutory in nature like, grant of license or exclusive privilege by an auction sale etc.[18]

Fairness in government contracts: 'However, government contract must observe the propriety of fairness in consonance with the Preamble of the Constitution, fundamental rights and the directive principles of State policy'.[19] 'The exercise of power by Government should not be unreasonable or arbitrary actuated by mala-fide, affected by bias or is in disregard of the prescribed mandatory procedures'.[20]

Leading cases in this regard are allotment of spectrum case or 2G case in which allocation of spectrum to mobile operators on first-come-first t-serve basis was invalidated because that denied equal opportunity to all aspirants which could be given by allocation through auction."[21] It was followed up in Coalgate case in which the Court accepting the principle of fairness in the allocation of natural resources, held that auction may not be the only method of ensuring fairness. It should be under a transparent and valid policy, law, rules or procedure.[22]

300. Suits and proceedings: (1) The Government of India may sue or be sued by the name of the Union of India and the Government of a State may sue or be sued by the name of the State and may, subject to any provisions which may be made by the Act of the Parliament or of the Legislature of such State enacted by virtue of powers conferred by this Constitution, sue or be sued in relation to their respective affairs in the like cases as the Dominion of India and the corresponding Provinces or the corresponding Indian States might have sued or been sued if this Constitution had not been enacted.

(2) If at the commencement of this Constitution:

(a) any legal proceedings are pending to which the Dominion of India is a party, the Union of India shall be deemed to be substituted for the Dominion in those proceedings; and

(b) any legal proceedings are pending to which a Province or an Indian State is a party, the corresponding State shall be deemed to be substituted for the Province or the Indian State in those proceedings.

(Part XII, Article 300)

COMMENTS

Act of State: The main principle is that Government is not liable for torts of its employees committed in the course of performance of sovereign functions.

The courts now interpret 'sovereign functions' narrowly.

In Vidhyawati Case,[23] the Court expressed displeasure but followed doctrine of Sovereign function and allowed immunity to government for accident by its driver.

But in Kasturi Lal case,[24] the Supreme Court reversed its decision. The Court found gross negligence on the part of police authorities for misappropriation of gold by its head constable who fled away to Pakistan.

'Similarly, a suit lies against the Government for wrongs done by public servants in the course of business such as death or injury caused to a person by police authorities.[25]

Right to Property

300A. Persons not to be deprived of property save by authority of law: No person shall be deprived of his property save by authority of law.

(Part XII, Article 300A)

COMMENTS

The right to property has been made a constitutional right from the fundamental right under erstwhile Article 19(f) read with Article 31. As a result, the violation of the right under Article 32 cannot be invoked. The High Court can certainly be approached under Article 226.

The Supreme Court held that the controversial aspects of Article 31, because of which it was deleted from the Constitution, should not be brought back by judicial interpretation. The Court admitted that the exercise of power of eminent domain recognised in Article 300-A requires existence of public purpose and payment of money for acquisition of property, but the payment must not be illusory and the principles for determining the compensation must be relevant for the purpose of arriving at a non-illusory or fair compensation.[26] Wherever the Constitution requires payment of compensation at market price, it has provided for it such as in Articles 31(1-A) and 31A(1) second proviso.[27]

Thus, the right to property will be available against the executive interference but not against the legislative interference.[28] However, public purpose is still a precondition for deprivation of a person from his property and the right to claim compensation is inbuilt. 'It was held that the respondents cannot take law into their own hands and with Police help can evict the petitioner.[29] If the State intends to appropriate the private property without the owners' consent, 'thus authorised by law' has to be mandatory and compulsorily followed. Police cannot arrest a person without adequate background of crime.

Validity of a law passed under Article 300A can be challenged on the ground of no provision being made for payment of compensation for depriving citizen of his property.[30]

REFERENCES

1. Synthetics and Chemicals Ltd. vs. State of Uttar Pradesh, (1990) 1 SCC 109.
2. State of U.P. vs. Vam Organic Chemicals Ltd. (2004) 1 SCC 225.
3. Diwan Chand Builders & Contractors vs. Union of India, (2012) 1 SCC 101.
4. Tata Sky Ltd. vs. State of Madhya Pradesh, (2013) 4 SCC 656.
5. ITO vs. T.S. Devinath Nadar, AIR 1968 SC 623.
6. T.N. Kanniyan vs. ITO, AIR 1968 SC 637.
7. Ved Vyas Chawla vs. ITO, AIR, 1965 All 37.
8. Union of India vs. State of Punjab, AIR 1990 P & H 183.
9. Municipal Commissioner of Dum Dum Municipality vs. Indian Tourism Development Corp. (1995), 5 SCC 251.
10. State of A.P. vs. NTPC Ltd., (2002) 5 SCC 203.
11. TISCO vs. S.R. Sarkar, AIR 1961 SC 65.
12. State of T.N. vs. Madurai South Indian Corp. (P) Ltd. (1973) 1 SCC 65.
13. Coffee Board vs. CTO, AIR 1971 SC 870.

14. New Delhi Municipal Council vs. State of Punjab, (1997) 7 SCC 339.
15. Ram Jawaya Kapoor vs. State of Punjab, AIR 1951 SC 549.
16. Khazan Singh vs. State of UP, AIR 1974, SC 669 and also see Anraj vs. State of Maharashtra, AIR 1984 SC 781.
17. U.P. Rajkiya Nirman Nigam Ltd. vs. Indure Pvt. Ltd., (1996) 2 SCC 667.
18. State of Haryana vs. Lal Chand ((1984) 3 SCC 634.
19. LIC vs. Consumer Education & Research, (1995) 5SCC 482.
20. Tata Cellular vs. Union of India (1994) 6SCC 651.
21. Centre for Public Interest Litigation vs. Union of India (2012) 3 SCC 1.
22. Natural Resources Allocation, (2012) 10 SCC 1.
23. State of Rajasthan vs. Vidhyawati, AIR 1962 SC 933.
24. Kasturi Lal vs. State of U.P. AIR 1965 SC 1039.
25. Saheli vs. Commissioner of Police, (1990) 1 SCC 422.
26. Jilubhai Nanbhai Khachar vs. State of Gujarat, AIR 1995 SC 142.
27. K.T. Plantation (P) Ltd. vs. State of Karnataka (2011) 9 SCC 1.
28. Devindar Singh vs. State of Punjab, (2008)1 SCC 728.
29. Indra Pratap Singh vs. State of Bihar, AIR 2015 Page 20.
30. Bishamber vs. State of U.P., AIR 1982 SC 33.

□

Chapter 14
TRADE, COMMERCE AND INTERCOURSE

301. Freedom of Trade, Commerce and Intercourse: Subject to the other provision of this Part, trade, commerce and intercourse throughout the Territory of India shall be free.

(Part XIII, Article 301)

COMMENTS

The object of this Article in a federal Constitution is to break down the trade barriers between the constituent States and to make the entire Territory of the country as one unit with a view to encouraging trade and commerce in the country. A right is guaranteed by this Article to free movement of persons or things, tangible or intangible, commercial or non-commercial, unobstructed by barriers, Inter-state or intrastate or any other impediments operating as such barriers. All obstructions or impediments except taxation, whatever shape they may take, to the free flow or movement of trade or non-commercial intercourse offend Article 301 of the Constitution. Regulatory measures or a legislation imposing taxes facilitating trade cannot be considered violative of the freedom of trade. Trade, commerce and intercourse include movement of goods and persons.[1] The restrictions are contained in Articles 302 to 305.

The Supreme Court in Atiabari Tea Co.[2] held that tax laws are not outside the purview of Article 301. In the case, the appellants carried on the business of growing tea and exporting it to Calcutta via Assam. In the course of its passing through the State of Assam, the tea was liable to tax under the Assam Taxation Act, 1954, which imposed tax, on goods carried by road or inland waterways in the State of Assam. The Supreme Court held that the tax imposed on the goods directly restricted their transport or movement and thus violated Article 301.

The Act can be held to be valid only if it is shown that the restrictions imposed by it are reasonable and in the public interest. If a tax was compensatory in nature, it will be valid. Money lending as such is not extra-commercium, it is only the manner in which certain class of persons were operating, made it pernicious and extra-commercium.[3] In Jindal Stainless Ltd.[4] the Supreme Court held that the freedom is not from all laws but freedom from such laws which restrict or affect activities of trade and commerce among the States. These laws go beyond regulation which burdens, restricts or prevents the trade movement between States and within States.

The word 'intercourse' covers all those things which are not included in the words 'trade and commerce'. It would cover non-commercial dealings for personal use.

302. Power of the Parliament to impose restrictions on trade, commerce and intercourse: The Parliament may by law impose such restrictions on the freedom of trade, commerce or intercourse between one State and another or within any part of the Territory of India as may be required in the public interest.

(Part III, Article 302)

COMMENTS

The restrictions can be imposed in the public interest. The restrictions however must bear a reasonable nexus with the need to serve public interest. Thus, restrictions on the movement of foodgrains under the Defence of India Rules were held in the interests of general public.[5]

This law in the public interest is not justiciable. The Parliament is given the sole power to decide what restrictions can be imposed in the public interest as authorised by Article 302. A law prohibiting transmission of stolen or of harmful substances would be saved under this exception.

303. Restrictions on the legislative powers of the Union and of the States with regard to trade and commerce: (1) Notwithstanding anything in Article 302, neither the Parliament nor the Legislature of a State shall have power to make any law giving, or authorising the giving of, any preference to one State over another, or making, or authorising the making of, any discrimination between one State and another, by virtue of any entry relating to trade and commerce in any of the Lists in the Seventh Schedule.

(2) Nothing in clause (1) shall prevent the Parliament from making any law giving, or authorising the giving of, any preference or making, or authorising the making of, any discrimination if it is declared by such law that it is necessary to do so for the purpose of dealing with a situation arising from scarcity of goods in any part of the Territory of India.

(Part III, Article 303)

COMMENTS

The Parliament can impose restrictions if there is scarcity of goods. Such a declaration would normally be not justiciable. Where an assesse is purchasing scrap from outside State and locally were taxed differently for manufactured steel, it was held violative of scheme of the Constitution and was discriminatory.

304. Restrictions on trade, commerce and intercourse among States: Notwithstanding anything in Article 301 or Article 303, the Legislature of a State may by law:

(a) impose on goods imported from other States or the Union Territories any tax to which similar goods manufactured or produced in that State are subject, so, however, as not to discriminate between goods so imported and goods so manufactured or produced; and

(b) impose such reasonable restrictions on the freedom of trade, commerce or intercourse with or within that Sate as may be required in the public interests.

Provided that no Bill or amendment for the purposes of

clause (b) shall be introduced or moved in the Legislature of a State without the previous sanction of the President.

(Part XIII, Article 304)

COMMENTS

If the levy of a tax is a condition precedent to the entry of a commodity in the taxable area, it impedes the free flow of trade and as such is in violation of Article 301. But it is not so if the dual requirements of Article 304 (b) are met, that is, if the restrictions are reasonable and in public interest.[6]

Taxation by a State on goods imported from outside is valid provided it is non-discriminatory and this includes sales tax along as it is non-discriminatory.[7] As action which furthers the economic development of the whole of India and its unity by removing economic barriers cannot be said to be discriminatory.[8]

The illegal felling of trees may be regulated by requiring that no forest produce should be transported from one place to another without obtaining a permit from a specified officer. Even the law regarding State monopoly in a particular sphere of trade or commerce, law might have to be justified before the courts as being in the public interest under Article 301 or as amounting to a 'reasonable restriction' under Article 304 (b).

305. Saving of existing laws and laws providing for State monopolies: Nothing in Articles 301 and 303 shall affect the provisions of any existing law except insofar as the President may by order otherwise direct; and nothing in Article 301 shall affect the operation of any law made before the commencement of the Constitution (fourth Amendment) Act, 1955, insofar as is relates to, or prevent the Parliament or the Legislature of a State from making any law relating to, any such matter as is referred to in sub-clause (ii) of clause (6) of Article 19.

(Part XIII, Article 305)

COMMENTS

The protection to pre-existing Act is not available insofar as the amending Act makes any additional provisions.[9] The rules made under an existing law after the commencement of the Constitution should not be deemed to be existing law. Every such rule will have to stand the test laid down in Article 304.[10]

306. Power of certain States in Part B of the First Schedule to impose restrictions on trade and commerce: Rep. by the Constitution (Seventh Amendment) Act, 1956, sec. 29 and Schedule.

307. Appointment of authority for carrying out the purposes of Articles 301 to 304: The Parliament may by law appoint such authority as it considers appropriate for carrying out the purposes of Articles 301, 302, 303 and 304, and confer on the authority so appointed such powers and such duties as it thinks necessary.

(Part XIII, Article 307)

COMMENTS

In view of regulatory authorities in vogue in India like the Competition Commission, Telecom Regulatory Authority and many more to come as similar to authorities around the world, this provision is forward-looking provision which requires to be implemented in the present fierce competition scenario among the State units in the backdrop of globalisation.

The Constitution Commission (NCRWC) recommended that to eliminate interstate barriers to inter state trade and commerce. The Parliament should by law, establish an authority to be named the 'Inter-State Trade and Commerce Commission'.

REFERENCES

1. Automobile Transport Ltd., vs. State of Rajasthan, AIR 1962 SC 1406.
2. Atiabari Tea Co. Ltd., vs. State of Assam, AIR 1961 SC 232.
3. B.R. Enterprises vs. State of U.P. (1999) 9 SCC 700.
4. Jindal Stainless Ltd., vs. State of Haryana (2006) 7 SCC 241.
5. Surajmal Roopchand & Co. vs. State of Rajasthan, AIR 1967 Raj 104.
6. State of Bihar vs. Bihar Chamber of Commerce, (1996) 9 SCC 136.

7. Indian Cement vs. State of Andhra Pradesh, (1988) 1 SCC 743.
8. Video Electronics Pvt. Ltd. vs. State of Punjab, (1990) 3 SCC 87.
9. Punjab Traders vs. State of Punjab, (1991) 1 SCC 86.
10. State of Mysore vs. H. Sanjeev Viahar, AIR 1967 SC 1189.

□

Chapter 15
SERVICES UNDER THE UNION AND THE STATES

308. Interpretation: In this Part, unless the context otherwise requires, the expression "State" does not include the 'State' of Jammu and Kashmir.

(Part I, Article 308)

COMMENTS

The definition of "State" in this Part is different from and narrower than the definition of 'State' in Article 12.[1]

Thus, the provisions of this Part shall not apply to a post held under local bodies like municipalities or Panchayats or to posts held in the statutory corporations.

309. Recruitment and conditions of service of persons serving the Union or a State: Subject to the provisions of this Constitution, Act of the appropriate Legislature may regulate the recruitment, and conditions of service of persons appointed to public services and posts in connection with the affairs of the Union or of any State:

Provided that it shall be competent for the President or such person as he may direct in the case of services and posts in connection with the affairs of the Union, and for the Governor of a State or such persons as he may direct in the case of services and posts in connection with the affairs of the Union, and for the Governor of a State or such person as he may direct in the case of services and posts in connection with the affairs of the State, to make rules regulating the recruitment, and the conditions of service of persons appointed, to such services and posts until provision in that behalf is made by or under an Act of the appropriate Legislature under this Article, and any rules so made shall have effect subject to the provisions of any such Act.

(Part IVX, Article 309)

COMMENTS

The rules providing terms of service can be altered unilaterally by the Government and this is so because once appointed to his office or post, the Government servant acquires status and his rights and obligations are no longer determined by consent of both parties but by statute or statutory rules which may be framed and altered unilaterally by Government. The legal position of a Government servant is more of a status than of contract.[2]

A rule validating past illegal retirements is not a rule falling within the scope of the proviso to this Article, since it does not concern either the recruitment or conditions of service of the employees and also conflicts with Article 311[3] Similarly, the rule relating to compulsory retirement does not contravene either Article 309 or 311 of the Constitution.

As regards retirees from the Armed forces, the Supreme Court has not accepted the demand of retirees, of armed forces for "One rank one pension"[3]. But the retirees realised their demand in 2015 after resorting to hunger strike at the Jantar Mantar, New Delhi, on the basis of assurance of the BJP, party-in-power during the General Election, in the year 2014.

The rule of 'equal pay for equal work' is a golden rule but weightage for relevant higher qualification or for additional duties can be given. A selection by written test or interview alone cannot be held to be illegal. Mandamus would issue to give the petitioner the same pay scale as has been given to employees of the same cadre without any justification.[5] Under a pension scheme, Government has a continuing obligation so long as the retiree is alive. Courts can only examine service matters from the point of fundamental rights, statutory provisions, rules & instructions & fairness.[6]

310. Tenure of office of persons serving the Union or a State: (1) Except as expressly provided by this Constitution, every person who is a member of a defense service or of a civil service of the Union or of an all-India service or holds any post connected with defense or any civil post under the Union, holds office during the pleasure of the President, and every person, who is a member of a civil service of a State or holds any civil post is a member of a civil service of a State or holds any civil post under a State, holds office during the pleasure of the Governor of the State.

(2) Notwithstanding that a person holding a civil post under the Union or a State holds office during the pleasure of the President or, as the case may be, of the Governor of the State, any contract or of an all-India service or of a civil service or of a civil service of the Union or a State, is appointed under this Constitution as the case may be, deems it necessary in order to secure the services of a person having special qualifications, provide for the payment to him of compensation, if before the expiration of an agreed period, that post is abolished or he is, for reasons not connected with any misconduct or his part required to vacate that post.

(Part XIV, Article 310)

COMMENTS

Doctrine of Pleasure: Tenure of a public servant is guided by the Doctrine of Pleasure. The Constitution of India in this Article, accepts and adopts the Common Law doctrine of pleasure, though by cognate provisions of Article 311, its ill effects and the chances of its misuse have been minimised to a very great extent. The doctrine of pleasure connotes that there is no contract that gives the employee a remedy for its breach. The doctrine of pleasure is based upon the public policy that a public servant, whose continuance in office is not required or is against the public interest, must be relieved of his duties.

There is no doubt that the pleasure of the President has lost some of its majesty and power because it is clearly controlled by provisions of Article 311 and so the field, i.e. covered by Article

311 would be excluded from the operation of the absolute doctrine of pleasure.[7]

There are certain posts described in the Constitution, the tenure of which has not been made dependent upon the head of State, i.e. tenure of the judges of High Courts and the Supreme Court, the Comptroller and Auditor General of India, Chief Election Commissioner and the Chairman and members of the Public Service Commissions.

The doctrine of pleasure further is subject to the Fundamental Rights. Moreover, a specific contract can override the doctrine of pleasure.

311. Dismissal, removal or reduction in rank of persons employed in civil capacities under the Union or a State: (1) No person who is a member of a civil service of the Union or an all-India service or a civil service of a State or holds a civil post under the Union or a State shall be dismissed or removed by a authority subordinate to that by which he was appointed.

(2) No such person as aforesaid shall be dismissed or removed or reduced in rank except after an inquiry in which he has been informed of the charges against him and given a reasonable opportunity of being heard in respect of those charges:

Provided that where it is proposed after such inquiry, to impose upon him any such penalty, such penalty may be imposed on the basis of the evidence adduced during such inquiry and it shall not be necessary to give such person any opportunity of making representation on the penalty proposed:

Provided further that this clause shall not apply:

(a) Where a person is dismissed or removed or reduced in rank on the ground of conduct which has led to his conviction on a criminal charge; or

(b) Where the authority empowered to dismiss or remove a person or to reduce him in rank is satisfied that for some reason, to be recorded by that authority in writing, it is not reasonably practicable to hold such inquiry, or

(c) Where the President or the Governor, as the case may be, is satisfied that in the interest of the security of the State, it is not expedient to hold such inquiry.

(1) If, in respect of any such person as aforesaid, a question arises whether it is reasonably practicable to hold such inquiry as is referred to in clause (2), the decision thereon of the authority empowered to dismiss or remove such person or to reduce him in rank shall be final.

(Part XIV, Article 311)

COMMENTS

Article 311 places two restrictions on the prerogative of dismissal at pleasure. These restrictions are the Constitutional safeguards of the civil servants. These apply only to the persons who are members of a civil service of the Union or of an All India Service or of a civil service of a State or to the persons who hold services of a State or to the persons who hold civil post under the Union or a State. These safeguards are not applicable to members of defence forces or to any post connected with defence. Their employment can be terminated without assigning any reasons.

The expression 'civil post' means an appointment, office or employment, on the civil side of the administration. There must exist a relationship of master and servant between the State and a person said to be holding a post under it.

The provisions are applicable both to permanent and temporary servants. A person employed in police holds a 'civil post'. However, it has been held that the employees of statutory corporations or Government Companies registered under the Companies Act are not civil servants.[8]

Article 311, however, does not apply to probationers. It applies to them only after they are confirmed in the post on the expiry of the period of probation or otherwise.[9]

Suspension of a government servant from service is neither dismissal nor removal and is not, therefore, covered by Article 311.

No removal by subordinate authority: A civil servant cannot be dismissed or removed by any authority subordinate to the authority by which he was appointed. For example, Dy. Inspector General (Police) cannot dismiss a person who was appointed by the Inspector General of Police (IG). This does not mean that the removal or dismissal must be by the same authority who made the appointment or by his direct superior. It is enough if the removing authority is of the same or co-ordinate rank as the appointing authority.

Reasonable Opportunity to defend: The second safeguard given to a civil servant is that he shall not be dismissed or removed or reduced in rank except after an enquiry, he has been informed of the charges against him and given a reasonable opportunity of being heard in respect of those charges according to the principle of natural justice that no man should be condemned without hearing. The protection of Article 311(2) can be available where dismissal, removal or reduction in rank is sought to be inflicted by way of punishment and not otherwise when he is guilty of misconduct or is lacking in ability or capacity or the will to discharge his duties, as he should do.

Compulsory Retirement: The compulsory retirement without any element of charge or imputation, does not attract provisions of Article 311. But the present trend is that the court may, in appropriate cases, lift the veil to find out whether the order is based on any misconduct of the government servant or whether it is bonafide[10] and not colourable to weed out the dead wood to increase efficiency in the public interest. Adverse remarks in Annual Confidential Report or otherwise is one way to control employees by the superior officer as regards his performance. Where there is no rule requiring the competent authority to record or communicate reasons for rejecting a representation against adverse remarks, such order of rejection can not be challenged merely on the ground of non-recording of reasons, provided it was passed in a fair and just manner, after considering the materials on records. The competent authority may show the reasons from the notings in the file and other materials on the record.[11] However, the adverse remarks should be recorded by the superior officer after recording of reasons consistent with the principles of natural justice. This is an instrument of infusing discipline and work culture in an organisation or government office/department. But sometimes, few of superior officers are eccentric or whimsical and record adverse comments based on their subjective considerations external to the work. This dampens motivation in a government organisation. Therefore, if reasons are recorded for adverse comments in a Performance Appraisal Report, it will serve all purpose. It is learnt that Government of India in the Department of Personnel and Administrative Reforms has issued such instructions on one representation.

Earlier remarks of corruption against an officer cannot be expunged on the ground that he earned good remarks in subsequent years.[12]

Disciplinary Proceedings: Disciplinary proceeding is another method by which government servants are made accountable. The proceedings commence only when charge-sheet is issued. But administration in government departments generally complain that they have lost control and government officials and officers because of opportunities of hearing to be accorded to government servants to draw up disciplinary proceedings against them for infraction of discipline or misconduct or even poor performance at work. If the government offices are made courts, they will be as slow as courts in decision-making. The Supreme Court also supported this line of thinking and held that without undermining the importance of the principles of natural justice, the application of the principles of natural justice may be excluded by legislation or by a constitutional provision such as the second proviso to Article 311(2).[13]

An inquiry into the chargesheet may be conducted either by the disciplinary authority or by an inquiry officer appointed by the disciplinary authority. But the delinquent civil servant should be given an opportunity to make a representation against any adverse remarks in it. Further, he should be allowed to cross-examine the witnesses. However, the Court should examine before reversing the decision whether giving opportunity of hearing would have made difference in decision-making.

Temporary Post: The protection of Article 311 is not available to public servants on temporary or adhoc posts, unless it is so specified in the terms of contract or a specific rule but stigma should not be attached on his competency which may affect his future career. Similarly, a reduction in rank for administrative reasons will not amount to punishment and Article 311(2) will not be attracted. A public servant who is officiating on a higher rank in a leave vacancy or otherwise and is reverted back, cannot say that he has been reduced in rank within the meaning of Article 311. Likewise, discharge of a probationer found unfit for the post does not attract Article 311(2). The motive behind termination is immaterial. If the order visits the public servant with any evil consequences or casts an aspersion against his character or integrity, it must be considered to be one by way of punishment, no matter whether he was a mere probationer or temporary servant. In any case, the public servant can demand arrears of salary.

Reliefs: An employee can be reinstalled in service as per the service rules and not as a matter of right.[14]

Date of Birth: Where an employee has throughout his career accepted a particular date of birth, he cannot apply for its change near about his date of superannuation.

Withholding a material information or meeting false representation itself amounts to moral turpitude and is a separate and district matter altogether than what is involved in the criminal case. Thus, the departmental proceedings and criminal case can run side by side.[15]

Double Jeopardy: It was held that rule of double jeopardy is not applicable. The proceedings under the Army Act for Court-Martial deal with personal aspect of the misconduct while proceedings under the Central Rules deal with the disciplinary aspect of the misconduct. The two proceedings do not overlap.[16]

It was held by the Supreme Court that even, the question of security of State under Article 311(2) (c) is also subject to judicial review and its validity can be examined by the court on the ground that the satisfaction of the President or the Governor is vitiated by malafides or is based on wholly extraneous or irrelevant grounds.[17]

Thus, the Supreme Court and High Courts have been taking cognizance of cases filed by civil servants under Articles

32, 136 and 226 over & above departmental remedies as judicial remedy under the well-established principles of judicial review of administrative action.

312. All-India Services: (1) Notwithstanding anything in Chapter VI of Part VI or Part XI, if the Council of States has declared by resolution supported by not less than two-thirds of the members present and voting that it is necessary or expedient in the national interest so to do, the Parliament may by law provide for the creation of one or more all-India services (including an all-India judicial service) common to the Union and the States, and subject to the other provisions of this Chapter, regulate the recruitment, and the conditions of service of persons appointed, to any such service.

(2) The services known at the commencement of this Constitution as the Indian Administrative Service and the Indian Police Service shall be deemed to be services created by Parliament under this article.

(Part XIV, Article 312)

COMMENTS

All-India Services are active agents to control fissiparous tendencies in India. All-India Services officers have been well established in the country during the last 66 years and every citizen has faith in their impartiality and efficiency over and above State civil service officers. The All India Services represent unity in diversity. One can visit any district in the country and find that amidst regional feelings or sentiments, the heads of two most important departments, i.e. revenue and general administration, and police are officers from outside that State belonging to the Indian Administrative Service and Indian Police Service respectively. That creates further faith in the citizens of India to move freely and peaceably in any part of India as envisaged in the Constitution of India. Secondly, All India Services have cream of officers of the country and are less prone to political influence and part of political bickering within the State and even at the Centre. They have steel security and State governments cannot play with their service-conditions because they are also controlled by the Union. This double control reaffirms India as a federal country with a powerful Union.

Without the concurrence of the Union Public Service Commission, members of All India Services cannot be dismissed or reduced in rank. The Supreme Court appreciated the All India Services and wanted judiciary to have an all India level-such service. By the 42nd Amendment of the Constitution in pursuance of judgement of the Supreme Court in All India Judges Association case,[18] an All of India Judicial Service was created in 1977 to ensure uniform standards throughout the country in matters of judicial service, such as hierarchy and designations, age of superannuation, pay scales, allowances, residential accommodation, provision for conveyance, library allowances, and in-service training. It is high time that this constitutional mandate be implemented as one of the measures of judicial reforms to ensure better accountability and speedy disposal of cases by providing to judges more security and better service conditions for apex jobs. This service will be left under the control of the judiciary and not under the Government. This would be essential for maintaining independence and impartiality of the judiciary.

The Central Government can make rules and regulations for the recruitment and conditions of service for persons appointed to the All India services.[19]

313. Transitional provisions: Until other provision is made in this behalf under this Constitution, all the laws in force immediately before the commencement of this Constitution and applicable to any public service or any post which continues to exist after the commencement of service or post under the Union or a State shall continue in force so far as consistent with the provisions of this Constitution.

(Part XIV, Article 313)

315. Public Service Commissions for the Union and for the States: (1) Subject to the provisions of this Article, there shall be a Public Service Commission for the Union and a Public Service Commission for each State.

(2) Two or more States may agree that there shall be one Public Service Commission for that group of States, and if a resolution to that effect is passed by the House or, where there are two Houses, by each House of the Legislature of each of those States, the Parliament by law provides for the appointment of a Joint State Public Service Commission (referred to in this Chapter as Joint Commission) to serve the needs of those States.

(3) Any such law provisions as may be necessary or desirable for giving effect to the purposes of the law.

(4) The Public Service Commission for the Union, if requested so to do by the Governor of a State, may, with the approval of the President, agree to serve all or any of the needs of the State.

(5) References in this Constitution to the Union Public Service Commission or a State Public Service Commission shall, unless the context otherwise requires, be construed as references to the Commission serving the needs of the Union or, as the case may be, the State as respects the particular matter in question.

(Part XIV, Article 315)

COMMENTS

The Public Service Commissions are envisaged as independent constitutional institutions not subject to governmental or political interference or control and vested with the responsibility of recruitment and advising respective government to manage the public services.

The functions of Public Service Commissions are:

(i) To conduct examinations for appointment to the services of the Union/State;

(ii) To make recommendations to the Union/State Government for appointment of persons to its services;

(iii) To be consulted in regard to method of recruitment, principles in matters of appointments, promotions, transfers from one service to another and disciplinary matters of civilian employees;

(iv) To advise on any other matter that may be referred to by the President/Governor;

(v) On request to assist two or more States in regard to schemes for joint recruitment;

(vi) To advise on disciplinary matters affecting a person in service;

(vii) To present an annual report to the President/ Governor who shall cause it to be laid before the Houses of the Parliament/State Legislatures;

(viii) Any other function that the Parliament/State Assembly may by law assign.

The Supreme Court has held that the function of the Commission is purely advisory and if the Government fails to consult it in any matter, specified for consultation, a public servant affected thereby cannot expect a remedy in a court of law under Article 320. But where consultation is provided for by law or regulation, it will be a legal obligation like under Articles 320, 321 & 323.[20]

The Public Service Commission can relax essential qualification only if it is expressly given power of relaxation.[21] Candidates belonging to competitive examination of earlier year selected illegally by lowering norms cannot claim seniority over candidates, selected legally from competitive examination held in subsequent year.[22]

316. Appointment and term of office of members: (1) The Chairman and other members of a Public Service Commission shall be appointed, in the case of the Union Commission or a Joint Commission, by the President, and in the case of a State Commission, by the Governor of the State:

Provided that as nearly as may be one-half of the members of every Public Service Commission shall be persons who at the dates of their respective appointments have held office for at least ten years either under the Government of India or under the Government of a State, and in computing the said period of ten years any period before the commencement of this Constitution during which a person has held office under the

Crown in India or under the Government of an Indian State shall be included.

(1A) If the office of the Chairman of the Commission becomes vacant or if any such Chairman is by reason of absence or for any other reason unable to perform the duties of his office, those duties shall, until some persons appointed under clause (1) to the vacant office have entered on the duties thereof or, as the case may be, until the chairman has resumed his duties, be performed by such one of the other members of the Commission as the President, in the case of the Union Commission or a Joint Commission, and the Governor of the State in the case of a State in the case of a State Commission, may appoint for the purpose.

(2) A member of a Public Service Commission shall hold office for a term of six years from the date on which he enters upon his office or until he attains, in the case of the Union Commission, the age of sixty-five years, and in the case of a State Commission or a Joint Commission, the age of sixty-two years, whichever is earlier:

Provided that:

(a) A member of a Public Service Commission may, by writing under his hand addressed, in the case of the Union Commission or a Joint Commission, to the President, and in the case of a State Commission, to the Governor of the State, resign his office;

(b) A member of a Public Service Commission may be removed from his office in the manner provided in clause (1) or clause (3) of Article 317.

(3) A person who holds office as a member of a Public Service Commission shall, on the expiration of his term of office, be ineligible for re-appointment to that office.

(Part XIV, Article 316)

COMMENTS

At least, one-half of members of every Public Service Commission will be public servants who have served at least for ten years. However, it is not of paramount importance. It was held that if a member, when appointed as Chairman in the middle of his term, starts a new six-year term subject to other provisions of the Constitution.[23]

The Governor of a State has not only the express power of appointing the Chairman and other Members of the Public Service Commission but also has implied power to lay down the procedure for appointment.[24]

317. Removal and suspension of a member of a Public Service Commission: (1) Subject to the provisions of clause (3), the Chairman or any other member of a Public Service Commission shall only be removed from his office by order of the President on the ground of misbehaviour after the Supreme Court, on reference being made to it by the President, has, on inquiry held in accordance with the procedure prescribed in that behalf under Article 145, reported that the Chairman or such other member, as the case may be, ought on any such ground to be removed.

(2) The President, in the case of the Union Commission or a Joint Commission, and the Governor in the case of a State Commission, may suspend from office the Chairman or any other member of the Commission in respect of whom a reference has been made to the Supreme Court under clause (1) until the President has passed receipt of the report of the Supreme Court on such reference.

(3) Notwithstanding anything in clause (1), the President may by order remove from office the Chairman or any other member of a Public Service Commission if the chairman or such other member, as the case may be:

(a) Is adjudged an insolvent; or
(b) Engages during his term of office in any paid employment outside the duties of his office; or
(c) Is, in the opinion of the President, unfit to continue in office by reason of infirmity of mind or body.

(4) If the Chairman or any other member of a Public Service Commission is or becomes in any way concerned or interested in any contract or agreement made by or on behalf of the Government of India or the Government of a State or participates in any way in the profit thereof or in any benefit

or emolument arising therefrom otherwise than as a member and in common with the other members of an incorporated company, he shall, for the purposes of clause (1), be deemed to be guilty of misbehaviour.

(Part XIV, Article 317)

COMMENTS

The member of a Public Service Commission can be removed on the basis of proved misbehaviour on a reference by the President to the Supreme Court. Finding the allegations against the member to be true that he tried to influence the Commission and temper with the examination to get favour for his nephew and, that when he failed in his efforts, he made baseless allegations against the Chairman and Secretary of the Commission, the Supreme Court answered the reference in the affirmative.[25]

For the exercise of power of supervision under clause (2) the President or the Governor is not required to serve a notice and give hearing to the chairperson or a member of the Commission.[26]

319. Prohibition as to the holding of offices by members of Commission on ceasing to be such members: On ceasing to hold office—

(a) the Chairman of the Union Public Service Commission shall be ineligible for further employment either under the Government of India or under the Government of a State;

(b) the Chairman of a State Public Service Commission shall be eligible for appointment as the Chairman or any other member of the Union Public Service Commission or as the Chairman of any other State Public Service Commission, but not for any other employment either under the Government of India or under the Government of a State;

(c) a member other than the Chairman of the Union Public Service Commission shall be eligible for appointment as the Chairman of the Union Public Service Commission, or as the Chairman of a State Public Service Commission, but not for any other employment either under the Government of India or under the Government of a State;

(d) a member other than the Chairman of a State Public Service Commission shall be eligible for appointment as the Chairman or any other member of the Union Public Service Commission or as the Chairman of that or any other State Public Service Commission, but not for any other employment either under the Government of India or under the Government of a State.

(Part XIV, Article 319)

COMMENTS

The law on employment applied even to employment on contract basis.

320. Functions of Public Service Commissions: (1) It shall be the duty of the Union and the State Public Service Commissions to conduct examinations for appointments to the services of the Union and the services of the State respectively.

(2) It shall also be the duty of the Union Public Service Commission, if requested by any two or more States, so to do, to assist those States in framing and operating schemes of joint recruitment for any services for which candidates possessing special qualifications are required.

(3) The Union Public Service Commission or the State Public Service Commission, as the case may be, shall be consulted—

(a) on all matters relating to methods of recruitment to civil services and for civil posts;

(b) on the principles to be followed in making appointments to civil services and posts and in making promotions and transfers from one service to another and on the suitability of candidates for such appointments, promotions or transfers;

(c) on all disciplinary matters affecting a person serving under the Government of India or the Government of a State in a civil capacity, including memorials or petitions relating to such matters;

(d) on any claim by or in respect of a person who is serving or has served under the Government of India or the Government of a State or under the Crown in India or under the Government of an Indian State, in a civil capacity, that any costs incurred by him in defending legal proceedings instituted against him in respect of acts done or purporting to be done in the execution of his duty should be paid out of the Consolidated Fund of India, or, as the case may be, out of the Consolidated Fund of the State;

(e) on any claim for the award of a pension in respect of injuries sustained by a person while serving under the Government of India or the Government of a State or under the Crown in India or under the Government of an Indian State, in a civil capacity, and any question as to the amount of any such award, and it shall be the duty of a Public Service Commission to advise on any matter so referred to them and on any other matter which the President, or, as the case may be, the Governor of the State, may refer to them:

Provided that the President as respects the all-India services and also as respects other services and posts in connection with the affairs of the Union, and the Governor, as respects other services and posts in connection with the affairs of a State, may make regulations specifying the matters in which either generally, or in any particular class of case or in any particular circumstances, it shall not be necessary for a Public Service Commission to be consulted.

(4) Nothing in clause (3) shall require a Public Service Commission to be consulted as respects the manner in which any provision referred to in clause (4) of Article 16 may be made or as respects the manner in which effect may be given to the provisions of Article 335.

(5) All regulations made under the proviso to clause (3) by the President or the Governor of a State shall be laid for not less than fourteen days before each House of the Parliament or

the House or each House of the Legislature of the State, as the case may be, as soon as possible after they are made, and shall be subject to such modifications, whether by way of repeal or amendment, as both the Houses of the Parliament or the House or both Houses of the Legislature of the State may make during the session in which they are so laid.

(Part XIV, Article 320)

COMMENTS

The Public Service Commission cannot impose any extra qualification for maintaining efficiency in service. This is a policy matter which would be decided by the State Government. The action of the Commission in holding screening test and prescribing minimum qualifying marks was, therefore, unreasonable, arbitrary and discriminatory.[27]

The Supreme Court held that consultation is not mandatory. In the absence of consultation, the action of the government under Article 320(3) shall not be null and void.[28] However, Government cannot make arbitrary appointment of the Chairman, Public Service Commission. The High Court can involve its wide and extraordinary powers under Article 226 of the Constitution and quash the selection and appointment.[29]

This is high time that governments realize that they should fix high and requisite qualifications for the high posts like members of the Public Service Commission and should not pack Commission with men and women according to their whims and fancies, who will become subject of public ridicule and frustration.

321. Power to extend functions of Public Service Commissions: An Act made by the Parliament or, as the case may be, the Legislature of a State may provide for the exercise of additional functions by the Union Public Service Commission or the State Public Service Commission as respects the services of the Union or the State and also as respects the services of any local authority or other body corporate constituted by law or of any public institution.

322. Expenses of Public Service Commissions: The expenses of the Union or a State Public Service Commission, including any salaries, allowances and pensions payable to or in respect of the members or staff of the Commission, shall be charged on the Consolidated Fund of India or, as the case may be, the Consolidated Fund of the State.

323. Reports of Public Service Commissions: (1) It shall be the duty of the Union Commission to present annually to the President a report as to the work done by the Commission and on receipt of such report, the President shall cause a copy thereof together with a memorandum explaining, as respects the cases, if any, where the advice of the Commission was not accepted, the reason for such non-acceptance to be laid before each House of the Parliament.

(2) It shall be the duty of a State Commission to present annually to the Governor of the State a report as to the work done by the Commission, and it shall be the duty of a Joint Commission to present annually to the Governor of each of the States the needs of which are served by the Joint Commission a report as to the work done by the Commission in relation to that State, and in either case, the Governor, shall, on receipt of such report, cause a copy thereof together with a memorandum explaining, as respects the cases, if any, where the advice of the Commission was not accepted, the reasons for such non-acceptance to be laid before the Legislature of the State.

(Part XIV, Article 323)

COMMENTS

The annual reports are to be laid before the Parliament and the State Legislatures, respectively together with a memorandum as regards the cases where the advice of the Commission was not accepted and the reasons for such non-acceptance.

The Supreme Court has deprecated the practice adopted by the Government of making ad hoc appointment to bypass the Commission due to delay by the commission or to fill up posts as per their choice. The Supreme Court did not allow regularisation of ad hoc employees.[30]

Tribunals

323A. Administrative Tribunals: (1) The Parliament may, by law, provide for the adjudication or trial by administrative tribunals of disputes and complaints with respect to recruitment and conditions of service of persons appointed to public services and posts in connection with the affairs of the Union or of any State or of any local or other authority within the Territory of India or under the control of the Government of India or of any corporation owned or controlled by the Government.

(2) A law made under clause (1) may:

(a) Provide for the establishment of an administrative tribunal for the Union and a separate administrative tribunal for each State or for two or more States;

(b) Specify the jurisdiction, powers (including the power to punish for contempt) and authority which may be exercised by each of the said tribunals;

(c) Provide for the procedure (including provisions as to limitation and rules of evidence) to be followed by the said tribunals;

(d) Exclude the jurisdiction of all courts, except the jurisdiction of the Supreme Court under Article 136, with respect to the disputes or complaints referred to in clause (1);

(e) Provide for the transfer to each such administrative tribunal of any cases pending before any court or other authority.

(Part XIV-A, Article 323A)

COMMENTS

Administrative tribunals are agencies created by specific enactments to adjudicate upon controversies that may arise during numerous governmental activities. Their determinations affect the rights of parties. They, therefore, have been held to be quasi-judicial bodies. They are constituted to lessen the overburdened judiciary by persons who have intimate and specialised knowledge of the working of that Act. Their procedure is not so technical and costs are not prohibitive. Resultant will be speedy and cheap justice in the relevant field.

The Administrative Tribunals were created by the Administrative Tribunals Act, 1985 under new Part XIVA of the Constitution to adjudicate disputes relating to the recruitment and conditions of services of the public services of the Union and of the States. It took away the jurisdiction of the High Court while appeal lies to the Supreme Court under Article 136 only. However, this did not go well with the Supreme Court. The Supreme Court held that the High Courts and the Supreme Court shall continue to have jurisdiction over service matters. The only thing is that the High Court will not entertain the petition in first instance. An aggrieved party may go to the High Court by way of appeal.[31]

The Apex Court is of the view that the tribunals should have judicial person as Chairman. Induction of the Judges would ensure independence, efficiency and fair play and also confidence of people in them. But people are slowly losing faith in judges as they bring the judicial process with them in tribunals. The other members are meek and docile. As a result, tribunals, rather than becoming expert decision- making bodies, are becoming other judicial forums, symbolic of delays with lengthy decision-making and tardy procedure. Thus, the purpose of creation of tribunals is being defeated to remove hurdles in the laws providing for socio-economic reforms. It is high time that the co-operative societies are also brought under their umbrella.

The Tribunal would not ordinarily interfere with the decision of the competent authority unless it is malafide or arbitrary and is not in the public interest.

323B. Tribunals for other matters: (1) The appropriate Legislature may, by law, provide for the adjudication or trial by tribunals of any disputes, complaints, or offences with respect to all or any of the matters specified in clause (2) with respect to which such Legislature has power to make laws.

(2) The matters referred to in clause (1) are the following, namely—

(a) levy, assessment, collection and enforcement of any tax;

(b) foreign exchange, import and export across customs frontiers;

(c) industrial and labour disputes;

(d) land reforms by way of acquisition by the State of any estate as defined in Article 31A or of any rights therein or the extinguishment or modification of any such rights or by way of ceiling on agricultural land or in any other way;

(e) ceiling on urban property;

(f) elections to either House of the Parliament or the House or either House of the Legislature of a State, but excluding the matters referred to in Article 329 and Article 329A;

(g) production, procurement, supply and distribution of food-stuffs (including edible oilseeds and oils) and such other goods as the President may, by public notification, declare to be essential goods for the purpose of this Article and control of prices of such goods;

(h) rent, its regulation and control and tenancy issues including the right, title and interest of landlords and tenants;

(i) offences against laws with respect to any of the matters specified in sub-clauses (a) to (h) and fees in respect of any of those matters;

(j) any matter incidental to any of the matters specified in sub-clauses (a) to (i).

(3) A law made under clause (1) may—

(a) provide for the establishment of a hierarchy of tribunals;

(b) specify the jurisdiction, powers (including the power to punish for contempt) and authority which may be exercised by each of the said tribunals;

(c) provide for the procedure (including provisions as to limitation and rules of evidence) to be followed by the said tribunals;

(d) exclude the jurisdiction of all courts, except the jurisdiction of the Supreme Court under Article 136, with respect to all or any of the matters falling within the jurisdiction of the said tribunals;

(e) provide for the transfer to each such tribunal of any cases pending before any court or any other authority immediately before the establishment of such tribunal as would have been within the jurisdiction of such tribunal if the causes of action on which such suits or proceedings are based had arisen after such establishment;

(f) contain such supplemental, incidental and consequential provisions (including provisions as to fees) as the appropriate Legislature may deem necessary for the effective functioning of, and for the speedy disposal of cases by, and the enforcement of the orders of, such tribunals.

(4) The provisions of this Article shall have effect notwithstanding anything in any other provision of this Constitution or in any other law for the time being in force.

Explanation: In this Article, "appropriate Legislature", in relation to any matter, means the Parliament or, as the case may be, a State Legislature competent to make laws with respect to such matter in accordance with the provisions of Part XI.

(PART XIV-A, Article 32B)

COMMENTS

Service Tribunals have been set up under the Administrative Tribunals Act, 1985. Tribunals like taxation, customs, Excise and Gold Control, land reforms, rent and even to deal with offences under above tribunals can be constituted by the State which has the power to legislate on the subject concerned. The words 'all courts' in respect of both types of tribunals include the High Court and the jurisdiction of the High Court under Articles 226-227 except writ jurisdiction has been exclusively vested in the Administrative Tribunal set up under the Act.[32]

The State of West Bengal levied cess on the basis of the value of coal raised by mining companies. It was held invalid as the power to legislate relating to cess on coal or other minerals belonged to the Parliament and not the State Legislature.[33]

Similarly, it was held that the State Legislature has jurisdiction to set up a tribunal only in respect of the assessment, collection or enforcement of the particular tax in relation to which the Tribunal is sought.

The State Governments can set up other tribunals not covered by Article 323B, like for co-operative societies.[34]

REFERENCES

1. Sukh Dev Singh vs. Bhagatram Sardar Singh Raghuvanshi, (1975) 1 SCC 421.
2. Roshan Lal vs. Union of India, AIR 1967 SC 1889.
3. B.S. Vadera vs. Union of India, AIR 1969 SC 118.
4. Indian Ex. Service League vs. Union of India, (1991) 2 SCC 104.
5. State of West Bengal vs. Debdas, (1991) 1 SCC 138.
6. State of Haryana vs. Piara, (1992) 4 SCC 118.
7. Motiram vs. North Eastern Frontier Railway, AIR 1968 SC 600 (p. 609).
8. Sukhdev Singh vs. Bhagat Ram, AIR 1975 SC 1331.
9. Kendriya Vidyalaya Sangathan vs. Ram Ratan Yadav (2003) 3 SCC 437.
10. Rama Ekbal Sharma vs. State of Bihar, (1990) 3 SCC 504.
11. Union of India vs. E.G. Nambudri, (1991) 3 SCC 38.
12. Vinod Kumar vs. State of Haryana, AIR 2014 SC 33.
13. Union of India vs. Tulsiram Patel, (1985) 3 SCC 398.
14. Inspector General of Police vs. S. Samuthiram, (2013) 1 SCC 598.
15. Devendra Kumar vs. State of Uttranchal, (2013) 9 SCC 363.
16. Union of India vs. Sunil Kumar Sarkar (2001) 3 SCC 414.
17. S.R. Bommai vs. Union of India (1994) 3 SCC 1.
18. All India Judges' Association vs. Union of India, (1997) 8 SCC 520 & also of 1992, 1993 and of 1994.
19. Satya Narain Shukla vs. Union of India, (2006) 9 SCC 69.
20. Union of India vs. U.D. Dwivedi, AIR 1997 SC 1313.
21. Sanjay Kumar Manjul vs. Chairman, UPSC, (2006) 8 SCC 42.
22. State of Uttar Pradesh vs. Rafiquddin, AIR 1988 SC 162.
23. State of Mysore vs. R.V. Bidap, (1974) 3 SCC 337.
24. State of Punjab vs. Salil Sabhlok, (2013) 5 SCC 1 (33).
25. Sher Singh, re (1997) 3 SCC 216.
26. Ram Kumar Kashyap vs. Union of India, (2009) 9 SCC 378.

27. State of Punjab vs. Manjit, AIR 2003 SC 4580.
28. Ram Gupta Chaturvedi vs. State of M.P. (1969) 2 SCC 240.
29. State of Punjab vs. Salil Sabhlok, (2013) 5 SCC 1 (38).
30. P. Ravindran vs. Union Territory of Pondicherry (1997) 1 SCC 35.
31. Chandra Kumar vs. Union of India, (1997) 3 SCC 261.
32. Union of India vs. Deep (1992)4 SCC 432.
33. Kesoram Industries Ltd. (Textile Division) vs. Coal India Ltd., AIR 1993 Cal 78.
34. State of Karnataka vs. Viswabharathi House Building Co-operative Society, (2003) 2 SCC 412.

□

Chapter 16
ELECTIONS

324. Superintendence, direction and control of elections to be vested in an Election Commission: (1) The superintendence, direction and control of the preparation of the electoral rolls for, and the conduct of, all elections to the Parliament and to the Legislature of every State and of elections to the offices of President and Vice-President held under this Constitution shall be vested in a Commission (referred to in this Constitution as the Election Commission).

(2) The Election Commission shall consist of the Chief Election Commissioner and such number of other Election Commissioners, if any, as the President may from time to time fix and the appointment of the Chief Election Commissioner and other Election Commissioners shall, subject to the provisions of any law made in that behalf by the Parliament, be made by the President.

(3) When any other Election Commissioner is so appointed, the Chief Election Commissioner shall act as the Chairman of the Election Commission.

(4) Before each general election to the House of the People and to the Legislative Assembly of each State, and before the first general election and thereafter before each biennial election to the Legislative Council of each State having such Council, the President may also appoint after consultation with the Election Commission such Regional Commissioners as he may consider necessary to assist the Election Commission in the performance of the functions conferred on the Commission by clause (1).

(5) Subject to the provisions of any law made by the Parliament, the conditions of service and tenure of office of the

Election Commissioners and the Regional Commissioners shall be such as the President may by rule determine:

Provided that the Chief Election Commissioner shall not be removed from his office except in the like manner and on the like grounds as a Judge of the Supreme Court and the conditions of service of the Chief Election Commissioner shall not be varied to his disadvantage after his appointment:

Provided further that any other Election Commissioner or a Regional Commissioner shall not be removed from office except on the recommendation of the Chief Election Commissioner.

(6) The President, or the Governor of a State, shall, when so requested by the Election Commission, make available to the Election Commission or to a Regional Commissioner such staff as may be necessary for the discharge of the functions conferred on the Election Commission by clause (1).

COMMENTS

Election Commission is a permanent constitutional body. Initially, the Election Commission had only a Chief Election Commissioner. At present, it consists of Chief Election Commissioner and two Election Commissioners. For the first time, two additional Election Commissioners were appointed on 16th October, 1989 but they had a short tenure till 1st January, 1990. Later, on 1st October, 1993, two additional Election Commissioners were appointed. Since then, the multi-member Election Commission has been in operation.

Election Commission—a multi-member Body: The Supreme Court in the S.S. Dhanoa versus Union of India case[1] had observed: "When an institution like the Election Commission is entrusted with vital functions and candidates armed with criminal background will be given the party ticket, it is both necessary and desirable that the powers are not exercised by one individual, however wise he may be. It also conforms to the tenets of democratic rule."

On 1st October, 1993, the President of India, in exercise of powers conferred by clause (2) of Article 324 of the Constitution, fixed, until further orders, the number of Election Commissioners (other than the Chief Election Commissioner) at two. By a further notification of even date, the President was pleased to appoint Dr. M.S. Gill and Shri G.V.G. Krishnamurty as Election Commissioners with effect from 1st October, 1993. Simultaneously, the President also promulgated an Ordinance entitled the Chief Election Commissioner and other Election Commissioners (Conditions of Service) Amendment Ordinance, 1993 (32 of 1993) to amend the "Chief Election Commissioner and other Election Commissioners (Conditions of Service) Act, 1991." By this amending Ordinance, the Chief Election Commissioner and other Election Commissioners were, inter alia, placed at par in the matter of their salary and allowances (which were to be the same as admissible to a Judge of the Supreme Court of India), the term of the Chief Election Commissioner and other Election Commissioners was fixed as 6 years from the date of their appointment, subject to the maximum age limit of 65 years. The Ordinance further made provisions for transaction of business of the multi-member Election Commission and provided, inter alia, that the Chief Election Commissioner and other Election Commissioners shall have equal powers in the matter of decision making and in the case of any difference of opinion amongst them, the matter would be decided by the opinion of the majority. The Ordinance also renamed the principal Act of 1991Chief Election Commissioner and other Election Commissioners (Conditions of Service) Act, 1991 as the "Election Commission (Conditions of Service of Election Commissioners and Transaction of Business) Act, 1991." This Ordinance was later on replaced by a the Parliamentary Act (4 of 1994) on 4th January, 1994, without any change.

The aforesaid amendments made by the above mentioned Ordinance were challenged by Shri T.N. Seshan, the then Chief Election Commissioner, as being unconstitutional, before the Supreme Court, by way of the present writ petition. He also challenged the appointment of Dr. M.S. Gill and Shri G.V.G. Krishnamurty, alleging malafides against the Government. A Constitution Bench of the Supreme Court, by its landmark judgement dated 14th July, 1995, dismissed the writ petition of Shri T.N. Seshan, fully upholding the constitutional validity of the impugned Ordinance and the Act, and also upholding the appointment of Dr. M.S. Gill and Shri G.V.G. Krishnamurty as Election Commissioners.

With the 1993 Amendment Act, the Election Commission was made a multi-member body. The EC was made a multi-member body by the government in the wake of certain controversial decisions taken by the Chief Election Commissioner, T.N. Seshan. The Act provided that the decision of three members 'shall, as far as possible, be unanimous'. But in case of difference of opinion among three members, the matter 'shall be decided according to the opinion of the majority'. It was a significant step to remove a one-man show in such an important function as that of conducting elections. A single-member EC would have no longer 'unbridled' powers. The Supreme court clarified that irrespective of these differences, the Chief Election Commissioner is only one of the members of the multi-member Election Commission[2]. However, T.N. Seshan has done yeoman service to purge the election process in India.

The Chief Election Commissioner and Election Commissioners are appointed by the President of India. As per the Chief Election Commissioner and Other Election Commissioners (Conditions of Service) Act, 1991, they have tenure of six years, or up to the age of 65 years, whichever is earlier. They enjoy the same status and received salary and perks as are available to Judges of the Supreme Court of India. The Chief Election Commissioner can be removed from office only in the like manner and on the like grounds as a Judge of the Supreme Court.

The Election Commission has its independent Secretariat for the work relating to the smooth conduct of elections to the Parliament and State Legislatures.

In terms of the Allocation of Business Rules, the Union ministry of Law and Justice (Legislative Department) is entrusted with the functions as the nodal Department for providing Governmental sanctions to the Election Commission of India.

Legislative Department in the Ministry of Law and Justice is also administratively concerned with the Acts in connection with the conduct of elections to the Parliament, State Legislatures and to the offices of the President and the Vice-President. These Acts are:

(i) The Representation of the People Act, 1950,
(ii) The Representation of the People Act, 1951,
(iii) The Presidential and Vice-Presidential Elections Act, 1952,
(iv) The Delimitation Act, 2002,
(v) The Parliament (Prevention from Disqualification) Act, 1959.

Scope of Article 324: The power of superintendence, direction and control of the preparation of electoral rolls and the conduct of elections has been vested in the Election Commission under Article 324 of the Constitution of India. Where the enacted laws are silent or make insufficient provision to deal with a given situation in the conduct of elections, the Election Commission has the residuary powers to act in a given situation. If there is a valid law relating to or in connection with elections, the Commission is required to act in conformity with the said provisions. In case where law is silent, Article 324 is a reservoir of power to act for the avowed purpose of having free and fair election and to maintain purity of election.

In June 2002, the Election Commission of India on the direction of the Supreme Court in Union of India vs. Association for Democratic Reforms[3], issued an order under Article 324 that each candidate must submit an affidavit regarding the information of his/her criminal antecedents; assets (both movable and immovable) of self and those of spouses and dependents as well; and qualifications at the time of filing his/her nomination papers for election to the Lok Sabha, the Rajya Sabha and the State Legislative Assemblies. The decision of the Supreme Court in Association for Democratic Reforms case was sought to be nullified by inserting a new Section 33-B in the Representation of People Act, 1951, PUCL[4] challenged the validity of newly inserted Section 33-B and the Supreme Court gave its judgement on March 13, 2003, asserting its Association for Democratic Reforms June 2002 decision, which required full disclosure by all candidates. Earlier candidates were required to file two affidavits along with nomination paper. One as per the Election law and another as per the orders of Hon'ble Supreme Court of India. Now, information required under both affidavits has been merged in one consolidated form 26 appended to the Conduct of Election Rules, 1961.

Furnishing of wrong or incomplete information shall result in the rejection of nomination papers, apart from inviting penal consequences under the Indian Penal Code.

The legal and constitutional position on the scope of Article 324 is as follows:

(a) where there is an Act and express Rules made thereunder, it is not open to the Commission to override the Act or the Rules and pass orders in direct disobedience to the mandate contained in the Act or the Rules.

(b) when there is no the Parliamentary legislation or rule made under the said legislation, the Commission is free to pass any orders in respect of the conduct of elections.

325. No person to be ineligible for inclusion in, or to claim to be included in a special electoral roll on grounds of religion, race, caste or sex: There shall be one general electoral roll for every territorial constituency for election to either House of the Parliament or to the House or either House of the Legislature of a State and no person shall be ineligible for inclusion in any such roll or claim to be included in any special electoral roll for any such constituency on grounds only of religion, race, caste, sex or any of them.

COMMENTS

The Representation of the People Act, 1950 and rules made thereunder provide for the registration of a voter. The inclusion in an electoral roll is constituencywise, meaning thereby that each State of the union and other Territories are divided into assembly constituencies based on the criteria of the population. Every voter is eligible for enrolment and Article 325 of the

Constitution ensures that no such person shall be denied enrolment on grounds only of religion, race, caste, sex or any of them.

326. Elections to the House of the People and to the Legislative Assemblies of States to be on the basis of adult suffrage: The elections to the House of the People and to the Legislative Assembly of every State shall be on the basis of adult suffrage; that is to say, every person who is a citizen of India and who is not less than eighteen years of age on such date as may be fixed in that behalf by or under any law made by the appropriate Legislature and is not otherwise disqualified under this Constitution or any law made by the appropriate Legislature on the ground of non-residence, unsoundness of mind, crime or corrupt or illegal practice, shall be entitled to be registered as a voter at any such election.

COMMENTS

This Article is complementary to preceding Article 325. This Article confers on every person a right to be recognised as a voter and the qualifications provided in this Article are as to age, soundness of mind, presence in the constituency and a clean record as a citizen.

327. Power of the Parliament to make provision with respect to elections to Legislatures: Subject to the provisions of this Constitution, the Parliament may from time to time by law make provision with respect to all matters relating to, or in connection with, elections to either House of the Parliament or to the House or either House of the Legislature of a State including the preparation of electoral rolls, the delimitation of constituencies and all other matters necessary for securing the due constitution of such House or Houses.

COMMENTS

The Constituent Assembly as a provisional the Parliament enacted the Representation of People Act, 1950 and the Representation of People Act, 1951 respectively. These Acts were amended by the Parliament from time to time. Other Acts enacted under this Article include the Delimitation Act, 2002.

328. Power of Legislature of a State to make provision with respect to elections: Subject to the provisions of this Constitution and insofar as provision in that behalf is not made by the Parliament, the Legislature of a State may from time to time by law make provision with respect to all matters relating to, or in connection with, the elections to the House or either House of the Legislature of the State including the preparation of electoral rolls and all other matters necessary for securing the due constitution of such House or Houses.

COMMENTS

It seems that under this Article, the state legislatures have not enacted any law. The power under this Article may be invoked for the preparation of electoral rolls and all other matters necessary for securing the due constitution of such House or Houses where, in a State, there is both Legislative assembly and Legislative council. The only condition is that a law made by the state legislature must be in conformity with the provisions of the Constitution and the Acts of the Parliament.

The power of a State legislature under this Article is to be read with entry 37 of State List of the Seventh Schedule of the Constitution. The said entry reads as under:

'37. Elections to the Legislature of the State subject to the provisions of any law made by the Parliament'.

329. Bar to interference by courts in electoral matters: Notwithstanding anything in this Constitution—

(a) the validity of any law relating to the delimitation of constituencies or the allotment of seats to such constituencies, made or purporting to be made under Article 327 or Article 328, shall not be called in question in any court;

(b) no election to either House of the Parliament or to the House or either House of the Legislature of a State shall be called in question except by an election petition presented to such authority and in such manner as may be provided for by or under any law made by the appropriate Legislature.

COMMENTS

Article 329(b) came up for interpretation before the Constitution Bench of the Supreme Court in N.P.[3] Ponnuswamy vs. Returning Officer, Namakkal Constituency. In that case, the appellant was one of the persons who had filed nomination paper to Madras Legislative Assembly from Namakkal Constituency of Salem District. The Returning Officer rejected his nomination paper. The appellant moved the High Court by filing petition under Article 226 of the Constitution of India and prayed for quashing of the order of the Returning Officer and for issue of a mandamus for inclusion of his name in the list of valid nominations. The High Court dismissed the writ petition by observing that it did not have the jurisdiction to interfere with the order of the Retuning Officer. On appeal, the Supreme Court interpreted the word 'election' appearing in Part XV of the Constitution and held:

"the word 'election' has been used in Part XV of the Constitution in the right sense, that is to say, to connote the entire procedure to be gone through to return the candidate to the Legislature. The use of the expression 'conduct of elections' in Article 324 specifically points to the wide meaning and that meaning can also be read consistently into the other provisions which occur in Part XV including Article 329(b)."

The term 'election' in Article 329(b) connotes entire process culminating in a candidate being elected and it was held by the Supreme Court in The Election Commission of India vs. Shivaji and Others (5) that the High Court's jurisdiction under Article 226 to entertain petition challenging election has been taken away. In this case, the High Court issued notice and directed that the election fixed on 18th October, 1987 would have to be stayed till the High Court passed further order on 18th October, 1987. Aggrieved by the aforesaid orders of the High Court, first postponing the last date for withdrawal of candidatures and then staying the holding of poll, the Election Commission filed the present appeal before the Supreme Court. The Commission's appeal came up for hearing in the Supreme Court on 27th October, 1987 and the Supreme Court stayed the orders of the High Court and permitted the Election Commission to proceed with the election process. The appeal was finally heard on 30th October, 1987 and the Supreme Court set aside the High Court's both the orders, holding that the High Court had no jurisdiction, in view of Article 329(b) of the Constitution, to interfere in the electoral process, and that both the interim orders were without jurisdiction. The Supreme Court also expressed its anguish over the manner in which the High Court interfered in the electoral process twice.

In Mohinder Singh Gill vs. Chief Election Commissioner,[6] another Constitution Bench considered the scope of non-obstante clause contained in Article 329(b) and laid down the following propositions:

(1) Having regard to the important functions which the legislatures have to perform in democratic countries, it has always been recognised to be a matter of first importance that elections should be concluded as early as possible according to time schedule and all controversial matter and all disputes arising out of elections should be postponed till after the elections are over, so that the election proceedings may not be unduly retarded or protracted.

(2) In conformity with this principle, the scheme of the election law in this country as well as in England is that no significance should be attached to anything which does not affect the "election", and if any irregularities are committed while it is in progress and they belong to the category or class which, under the law by which elections are governed, would have the effect of vitiating the "election" and enable the person affected to call it in question, they should be brought up before a Special Tribunal by means of an election petition and not be made the subject of a dispute before any Court while the election is in progress.

329A. Special provision as to elections to the Parliament in the case of Prime Minister and Speaker. Rep. by the Constitution (Forty-fourth Amendment) Act, 1978, s. 36 (w.e.f. 20-6-1979).

REFERENCES

1. S.S. Dhanoa versus Union of India case Air 1991 SC 1745.
2. T.N. Sheshan vs. Union of India (1995) 4 SCC 611.
3. Union of India vs. Association for Democratic Reforms, (2002) 5. SCC 294.
4. PUCL vs. Union of India, (2003) 4 SCC 399.
5. The Election Commission of India vs. Shivaji and Others AIR 1988 SC 61.
6. Mohinder Singh Gili vs. Chief Election Commissioner AIR1978 SC 851.

□

Chapter 17
SPECIAL PROVISIONS RELATING TO CERTAIN CLASSES

330. Reservation of seats for Scheduled Castes and Scheduled Tribes in the House of the People: (1) Seats shall be reserved in the House of the People for—

(a) the Scheduled Castes;

(b) the Scheduled Tribes except the Scheduled Tribes in the autonomous districts of Assam; and

(c) the Scheduled Tribes in the autonomous districts of Assam.

(2) The number of seats reserved in any State or Union Territory for the Scheduled Castes or the Scheduled Tribes under clause (1) shall bear, as nearly as may be, the same proportion to the total number of seats allotted to that State or Union Territory in the House of the People as the population of the Scheduled Castes in the State or Union Territory or of the Scheduled Tribes in the State or Union Territory or part of the State or Union Territory, as the case may be, in respect of which seats are so reserved, bears to the total population of the State or Union Territory.

(3) Notwithstanding anything contained in clause (2), the number of seats reserved in the House of the People for the Scheduled Tribes in the autonomous districts of Assam shall bear to the total number of seats allotted to that State a proportion not less than the population of the Scheduled Tribes in the said autonomous districts bears to the total population of the State.

Explanation: In this Article and in Article 332, the expression "population" means the population as ascertained at the last preceding census of which the relevant figures have been published:

Provided that the reference in this Explanation to the last preceding census of which the relevant figures have been published shall, until the relevant figures for the first census taken after the year 2026 have been published, be construed as a reference to the 2001 census.

(Part XVI, Article 330)

COMMENTS

The principles of democratic equality can work only if the nation as a whole is brought on the same level as far as that is practicable to secure social and economic justice. The Constitution makes certain provisions to help the weaker sections of the society to come up to the level of the general body of citizens. Thus, the Scheduled Castes and Scheduled Tribes were provided special protection and seats in legislatures and positions in services were reserved for them perfectably in proportion to their population.

The President makes such order to reservation in consultation with the Governor of a State in relation to that State. At present, it is as per the 2001 census figures. Thus, reservation for SCs & STs is frozen till the year 2026. The reservation of seats is intended to guarantee a minimum number of seats to the Scheduled Castes (SCs) and Scheduled Tribes (STs). A person who makes to a general seat as well as to a reserved seat, he can elect to keep any one of the two.

331. Representation of the Anglo-Indian Community in the House of the People: Notwithstanding anything in Article 81, the President may, if he is of the opinion that the Anglo-Indian community is not adequately represented in the House of the People, nominate not more than two members of that community to the House of the People.

(Part XVI, Article 331)

332. Reservation of Seats for Scheduled Castes and Scheduled Tribes in the Legislative Assemblies of the States: (1) Seats shall be reserved for the Scheduled Castes and the Scheduled Tribes, except the Scheduled Tribes in the autonomous districts of Assam, in the Legislative Assembly of every State.

(2) Seats shall be reserved also for the autonomous districts in the Legislative Assembly of the State of Assam.

(3) The number of seats reserved for the Scheduled Castes or the Scheduled Tribes in the Legislative Assembly of any State under clause (1) shall bear, as nearly as may be, the same proportion to the total number of seats in the Assembly as the population of the Scheduled Castes in the State or of the Scheduled Tribes in the State or part of the State, as the case may be, in respect of which seats are so reserved, bears to the total population of the State.

(3A) Notwithstanding anything contained in clause (3), until the taking effect, under Article 170, of the re-adjustment, on the basis of the first census after the year 2026, of the number of seats in the Legislative Assemblies of the States of Arunachal Pradesh, Meghalaya, Mizoram and Nagaland, the seats which shall be reserved for the Scheduled Tribes in the Legislative Assembly of any such State shall be—

(a) if all the seats in the Legislative Assembly of such State in existence on the date of coming into force of the Constitution (Fifty-seventh Amendment) Act, 1987 (hereafter in this clause referred to as the existing Assembly) are held by members of the Scheduled Tribes, all the seats except one;

(b) in any other case, such number of seats as bears to the total number of seats, a proportion not less than the number (as on the said date) of members belonging to the Scheduled Tribes in the existing Assembly bears to the total number of seats in the existing Assembly.

(3B) Notwithstanding anything contained in clause (3), until the re-adjustment, under Article 170, takes effect on the basis of the first census after the year 22026, of the number of seats in the Legislative Assembly of the State of Tripura, the seats which shall be reserved for the Scheduled Tribes in the Legislative Assembly shall be, such number of seats as bears to the total number of seats, a proportion not less than the number, as on the date of coming into force of the Constitution (Seventy-second Amendment) Act, 1992, of members belonging to the Scheduled Tribes in the Legislative Assembly in existence on the said date bears to the total number of seats in that Assembly.

(4) The number of seats reserved for an autonomous district in the Legislative Assembly of the State of Assam shall bear to the total number of seats in that Assembly a proportion not less than the population of the district bears to the total population of the State.

(5) The constituencies for the seats reserved for any autonomous district of Assam shall not comprise any area outside that district.

(6) No person who is not a member of a Scheduled Tribe of any autonomous district of the State of Assam shall be eligible for election to the Legislative Assembly of the State from any constituency of that district: Provided that for elections to the Legislative Assembly of the State of Assam, the representation of the Scheduled Tribes and non-Scheduled Tribes in the constituencies included in the Bodoland Territorial Areas District, so notified, and existing prior to the constitution of Bodoland Territorial Areas District, shall be maintained.

(Part XVI, Article 332)

COMMENTS

It provides that the representation of Scheduled Tribes included in the Bodoland Territorial Areas District shall not affect the representation of Scheduled Tribes and non-Scheduled Tribes in the Legislative Assembly of the State of Assam.

333. Representation of the Anglo-Indian Community: Notwithstanding anything in Article 170, the Governor of a State may, if he is of opinion that the Anglo-Indian community needs representation in the Legislative Assembly of the State and is not adequately represented therein, nominate one member of that community to the Assembly.

(Part XVI, Article 333)

334. Reservation of seats and special representation to cease after seventy years: Notwithstanding anything in the foregoing provisions of this Part, the provisions of this Constitution relating to—

(a) the reservation of seats for the Scheduled Castes and the Scheduled Tribes in the House of the People and in the Legislative Assemblies of the States; and

(b) the representation of the Anglo-Indian community in the House of the People and in the Legislative Assemblies of the States by nomination, shall cease to have effect on the expiration of a period of seventy years from the commencement of this Constitution:

Provided that nothing in this Article shall affect any representation in the House of the People or in the Legislative Assembly of a State until the dissolution of the then existing House or Assembly, as the case may be.

(Part XVI, Article 334)

COMMENTS

It means that reservations of seats for SCs, STs and Anglo-Indian in the Lok Sabha and in the State Assemblies will continue upto 2020 unless extended.

335. Claims of Scheduled Castes & Scheduled Tribes to services and posts: The claims of the members of the Scheduled Castes and the Scheduled Tribes shall be taken into consideration, consistently with the maintenance of efficiency of administration, in the making of appointments to services and posts in connection with the affairs of the Union or of a State:

Provided that nothing in this Article shall prevent in making of any provision in favour of the members of the Scheduled Castes and the Scheduled Tribes for relaxation in qualifying marks in any examination or lowering the standards of evaluation, for reservation in matters of promotion to any class or classes of services or posts in connection with the affairs of the Union or of a State.

(Part XVI, Article 335)

COMMENTS

Constitution of India mandates to have a balance between the claims of members of the Scheduled Castes and the Scheduled Tribes and maintenance of efficiency of administration. This was held in the epoch-making judgement of the Supreme Court in Indra Sawhney case.[1] It was further held that whether a particular class is adequately represented in the services under the State is a matter within the subjective satisfaction of the appropriate Government based on the materials in the possession of the Government and the existing conditions in the society. The proviso was inserted to get over the decision of the court that relaxation in qualifications was not permissible for reservation in promotion to SCs and STs under Article 16(4).[2]

However, the Supreme Court still recognizes, "It is for the State concerned to decide in a given case, whether the overall efficiency of the system is affected by such relaxation. If the relaxation is so excessive that it ceases to be qualifying marks then certainly in a given cases, as in the past, the State is free not to relax such standards. In other cases, the State may evolve, a mechanism under which efficiency, equity and justice, all three variables could be accommodated.[3]

Sometimes, the States are pressurised by agitations and violent demonstrations to succumb for increasing reservation or provide reservation for fresh caste. This ruling of the Apex Court can help them to decide in favour of the system without being guided by short-term problems or interests.

336. Special Provision for Anglo-Indian Community in certain services: (1) During the first two years after the commencement of this Constitution, appointments of members of the Anglo-Indian community to posts in the railway, customs, postal and telegraph services of the Union shall be made on the same basis as immediately before the fifteenth day of August, 1947.

During every succeeding period of two years, the number of posts reserved for the members of the said community in the said services shall, as nearly as possible, be less by ten per cent than the numbers so reserved during the immediately preceding period of two years:

Provided that at the end of ten years from the commencement of this Constitution all such reservations shall cease.

(2) Nothing in clause (1) shall bar the appointment of members of the Anglo-Indian community to posts other than, or in addition to, those reserved for the community under that clause if such members are found qualified for appointment on merit as compared with the members of other communities.

(Part XVI, Article 336)

337. Special provision with respect to educational grants for the benefit of Anglo-Indian community: During the first three financial years after the commencement of this Constitution, the same grants, if any, shall be made by the Union and by each State for the benefit of the Anglo-Indian community in respect of education as were made in the financial year ending on the thirty-first day of March 1948.

During every succeeding period of three years, the grants may be less by ten per cent than those for the immediately preceding period of three years:

Provided that at the end of ten years from the commencement of this Constitution such grants, to the extent to which they are a special concession to the Anglo-Indian community, shall cease:

Provided further that no educational institution shall be entitled to receive any grant under this Article unless at least forty per cent of the annual admissions therein are made available to members of communities other than the Anglo-Indian community.

(Part. XVI, Article 337)

COMMENTS

The special grant to the Anglo-Indian Community ceased at the end of 10 years from the commencement of the Constitution. It was held that as per the second proviso to the Article 337, the order of the Government to prevent schools from admitting children of other communities would be violative of the Constitutional obligation.[4]

338. National Commission for Scheduled Castes: (1) There shall be a Commission for the Scheduled Castes to be known as the National Commission for the Scheduled Castes.

(2) Subject to the provisions of any law made in this behalf by the Parliament, the Commission shall consist of a Chairperson, Vice-Chairperson and three other Members and the conditions of service and tenure of office of the Chairperson, Vice-Chairperson and other Members so appointed shall be such as the President may by rule determine.

(3) The Chairperson, Vice-Chairperson and other Members of the Commission shall be appointed by the President by warrant under his hand and seal.

(4) The Commission shall have the power to regulate its own procedure.

(5) It shall be the duty of the Commission—

(a) to investigate and monitor all matters relating to the safeguards provided for the Scheduled Castes under this Constitution or under any other law for the time being in force or under any order of the Government and to evaluate the working of such safeguards;

(b) to inquire into specific complaints with respect to the deprivation of rights and safeguards of the Scheduled Castes;

(c) to participate and advise on the planning process of socio-economic development of the Scheduled Castes and to evaluate the progress of their development under the Union and any State;

(d) to present to the President, annually and at such other times as the Commission may deem fit, reports upon the working of those safeguards;

(e) to make in such reports recommendations as to the measures that should be taken by the Union or any State for the effective implementation of those safeguards and other measures for the protection, welfare and socio-economic development of the Scheduled Castes; and

(f) to discharge such other functions in relation to the protection, welfare and development and advancement of the Scheduled Castes as the President may, subject to the provisions of any law made by the Parliament, by rule specify.

(6) The President shall cause all such reports to be laid before each House of the Parliament along with a memorandum explaining the action taken or proposed to be taken on the recommendations relating to the Union and the reasons for the non-acceptance, if any, of any of such recommendations.

(7) Where any such report, or any part thereof, relates to any matter with which any State Government is concerned, a copy of such report shall be forwarded to the Governor of the State who shall cause it to be laid before the Legislature of the State along with a memorandum explaining the action taken or proposed to be taken on the recommendations relating to the State and the reasons for the non-acceptance, if any, of any of such recommendations.

(8) The Commission shall, while investigating any matter referred to in sub-clause (a) or inquiring into any complaint referred to in sub-clause (b) of clause (5), have all the powers of a civil court trying a suit and, in particular, in respect of the following matters, namely:

(a) summoning and enforcing the attendance of any person from any part of India and examining him on oath;

(b) requiring the discovery and production of any document;

(c) receiving evidence on affidavits;

(d) requisitioning any public record or copy thereof from any court or office;

(e) issuing commissions for the examination of witnesses and documents;

(f) any other matter which the President may, by rule, determine.

(9) The Union and every State Government shall consult the Commission on all major policy matters affecting Scheduled Castes.

(10) In this Article, references to the Scheduled Castes shall be construed as including references to such other backward classes as the President may, on receipt of the report of a Commission appointed under clause (1) of Article 340, by order specify and also to the Anglo-Indian community.

(Part XVI, Article 338)

COMMENTS

The National Commission for the Scheduled Castes is also conferred power to go into the affairs of the socially and educationally backward classes and also regarding the Anglo-Indian Community as per clause 10 of Article 338.

The Commission is not authorised to enquire or adjudicate in regard to the rights of the parties or their caste states. Such rights or status must be determined as provided by law.[5]

But like the National Human Rights Commission and other commissions, it can approach the appropriate court for injunction or mandamus to protect the interests of these sections of society.

338A. National Commission for Scheduled Tribes: (1) There shall be a Commission for the Scheduled Tribes to be known as the National Commission for the Scheduled Tribes.

(2) Subject to the provisions of any law made in this behalf by the Parliament, the Commission shall consist of a Chairperson, Vice-Chairperson and three other Members and the conditions of service and tenure of office of the Chairperson, Vice-Chairperson and other Members so appointed shall be such as the President by rule determine.

(3) The Chairperson, Vice-Chairperson and other Members of the Commission shall be appointed by the President by warrant under his hand and seal.

(4) The Commission shall have the power to regulate its own procedure.

(5) It shall be the duty of the Commission—

(a) to investigate and monitor all matters relating to the safeguards provided for the Scheduled Tribes under this Constitution or under any other law for the time being in force or under any order of the Government and to evaluate the working of such safeguards;

(b) to inquire into specific complaints with respect to the deprivation of rights and safeguards of the Scheduled Tribes;

(c) to participate and advise on the planning process of socio-economic development of the Scheduled Tribes and to evaluate the progress of their development under the Union and any State;

(d) to present to the President, annually and at such other times as the Commission may deem fit, reports upon the working of those safeguards;

(e) to make in such reports recommendations as to the measures that should be taken by the Union or any State for the effective implementation of those safeguards and other measures for the protection, welfare and socio-economic development of the Scheduled Tribes; and

(f) to discharge such other functions in relation to the protection, welfare and development and advancement of the Scheduled Tribes as the President may, subject to the provisions of any law made by the Parliament, by rule specify.

(6) The President shall cause all such reports to be laid before each House of the Parliament along with a memorandum explaining the action taken or proposed to be taken on the recommendations relating to the Union and the reasons for the non-acceptance, if any, of any of such recommendations.

(7) Where any such report, or any part thereof, relates to any matter with which any State Government is concerned, a copy of such report shall be forwarded to the Governor of the State who shall cause it to be laid before the Legislature of the State along with a memorandum explaining the action taken or proposed to be taken on the recommendations relating to the

State and the reasons for the non-acceptance, if any, of any of such recommendations.

(8) The Commission shall, while investigating any matter referred to in sub-clause (a) or inquiring into any complaint referred to in sub-clause (b) of clause (5), have all the powers of a civil court trying a suit and in particular in respect of the following matters, namely:

(a) summoning and enforcing the attendance of any person from any part of India and examining him on oath;

(b) requiring the discovery and production of any document;

(c) receiving evidence on affidavits;

(d) requisitioning any public record or copy thereof from any court or office;

(e) issuing commissions for the examination of witnesses and documents;

(f) any other matter which the President may, by rule, determine.

(9) The Union and every State Government shall consult the Commission on all major policy matters affecting Scheduled Tribes.

339. Control of the Union over the administration of Scheduled Areas and the welfare of Scheduled Tribes: (1) The President may at any time and shall, at the expiration of ten years from the commencement of this Constitution, by order appoint a Commission to report on the administration of the Scheduled Areas and the welfare of the Scheduled Tribes in the States.

The order may define the composition, powers and procedure of the Commission and may contain such incidental or ancillary provisions as the President may consider necessary or desirable.

(2) The executive power of the Union shall extend to the giving of directions to 1a State as to the drawing up and execution of schemes specified in the direction to be essential for the welfare of the Scheduled Tribes in the State.

(Part XVI, Article 339)

COMMENTS

As concerns of STs are different from SCs and one Commission is inadequate to look after the interests of both, the Commission for STs has been separated from the Commission for SCs.

340. Appointment of a Commission to investigate the conditions of background classes: (1) The President may by order appoint a Commission consisting of such persons as he thinks fit to investigate the conditions of socially and educationally backward classes within the Territory of India and the difficulties under which they labour and to make recommendations as to the steps that should be taken by the Union or any State to remove such difficulties and to improve their condition and as to the grants that should be made for the purpose by the Union or any State and the conditions subject to which such grants should be made, and the order appointing such Commission shall define the procedure to be followed by the Commission.

(2) A Commission so appointed shall investigate the matters referred to them and present to the President a report setting out the facts as found by them and making such recommendations as they think proper.

(3) The President shali cause a copy of the report so presented together with a memorandum explaining the action taken thereon to be laid before each House of the Parliament.

(Part XVI, Article 340)

COMMENTS

The Constitution does not define as to who are the persons who belong to the Backward Classes. It is for the Central and the State Governments to specify such classes of persons for the purposes of reservation or otherwise under Articles 15(4) and 16(4).

Two Commissions, one in 1953 under the chairmanship of Kaka Kalekar and the other in 1978 under the chairperson of B.P. Mandal, were appointed by the President under this provision.

There was a sharp division whether the caste or economic condition should be the criteria. The then Prime Minister V.P. Singh's Government issued notification predominantly on political consideration, on 13th August 1990 to reserve 27 percent jobs in Central services and public undertakings for the backward classes. However, there was much opposition. Many students burnt themselves. But politics, though transitory, leave a trail to be made up by the Society. Generally, such politicians leave, society to pay for their decisions. The Supreme Court upheld the notification but laid down that the creamy layers of the backward classes are not entitled.[6]

But the administration has failed miserably to find out creamy layers and take action as per mandates of the Supreme Court. All the malaise is due to inept and inefficient administration. Had it performed, there was no need of further reservation for any caste or tribe whatsoever and all would have been equal economically, educationally and socially.

For constituting a permanent statutory body, the National Commission for Backward Classes Act, 1993 has been passed which constitutes a National Commission for Backward Classes. In pursuance of the Supreme Court's directions, states have also constituted Commission for Backward classes.

341. Scheduled Caste: (1) The President may with respect to any State or Union Territory, and where it is a State, after consultation with the Governor thereof, by public notification, specify the castes, races or tribes, or parts of or groups within castes, races or tribes which shall for the purposes of this Constitution be deemed to be Scheduled Castes in relation to that State or Union Territory, as the case may be.

(2) The Parliament may by law include in or exclude from the list of Scheduled Castes specified in a notification issued under clause (1) any caste, race or tribe or part of or group within any caste, race or tribe, but save as aforesaid a notification issued under the said clause shall not be varied by any subsequent notification.

(Part XVI, Article 341)

COMMENTS

It is well recognised that only the castes or sub-castes notified by the President will be deemed as Scheduled the Castes. Any other caste or sub-caste recognised locally will not be entitled for benefit of reservation in job.[7]

A person described as 'mochi' in Punjabi does not fall within the castes of 'chamars' as included in the Order of 1950, issued by the President. If a person converts to Christianity and afterwards comes back to Hinduism, he will be treated as Scheduled Caste because his Social and Economical backwardness has not changed.[8]

342. Scheduled Tribes: (1) The President may with respect to any State or Union Territory, and where it is a State, after consultation with the Governor thereof, by public notification, specify the tribes or tribal communities or parts of or groups within tribes or tribal communities which shall for the purposes of this Constitution be deemed to be Scheduled Tribes in relation to that State or Union Territory, as the case may be.

(2) The Parliament may by law include in or exclude from the list of Scheduled Tribes specified in a notification issued under clause (1) any tribe or tribal community or part of or group within any tribe or tribal community, but save as aforesaid a notification issued under the said clause shall not be varied by any subsequent notification.

(Part XVI, Article 342)

COMMENTS

In respect of declaration as Scheduled Tribe, Presidential Order under Article 342 regarding Scheduled Tribes is final. Court cannot add or subtract any entry. Any amendment to the Presidential Order can only be by legislation.

Though one may acquire tribal status by marriage, for purposes of reservation only those belong to S.T. and not those who claim to acquire that status by marriage, shall be eligible. Under a circular of the Government of India dated 06.08.1984, a person who is a Scheduled Tribe in a State, according to the

President's Order, continues to be Scheduled Tribe in another State to which he has migrated.[9]

REFERENCES

1. Indra Sawhney vs. Union of India, AIR 1993 SC 477.
2. S. Vinod Kumar vs. Union of India (1996) SCC 580.
3. M. Nagaraj vs. Union of India (2006) 8 SCC 212, 267.
4. State of Bombay vs. Bombay Education Society, AIR 1954 SC 561.
5. Collector vs. Ajit Jogi (2011) 10 5CC 357.
6. Indra Sawhney vs. Union of India, AIR 1993 SC 427.
7. Bhaiyalal vs. Harikishan Singh, AIR 1965 SC 1557.
8. C.M. Arumugum V.S. Rajgopal (1976) 1 SCC 863.
9. State of Gujarat vs. V.R.L. Patel, AIR 1992 Guj. 42.

□

Chapter 18

OFFICIAL LANGUAGE

343. Official Language of the Union: (1) The official language of the Union shall be Hindi in Devanagari script.

The form of numerals to be used for the official purposes of the Union shall be the international form of Indian numerals.

(2) Notwithstanding anything in clause (1), for a period of fifteen years from the commencement of this Constitution, the English language shall continue to be used for all the official purposes of the Union for which it was being used immediately before such commencement:

Provided that the President may, during the said period, by order authorise the use of the Hindi language in addition to the English language and of the Devanagari form of numerals in addition to the international form of Indian numerals for any of the official purposes of the Union.

(3) Notwithstanding anything in this Article, the Parliament may by law provide for the use, after the said period of fifteen years, of—

(a) the English language, or

(b) the Devanagari form of numerals, for such purposes as may be specified in the law.

(Part XVII, Article 343)

COMMENTS

The Official Language of the Union shall be Hindi in Devanagari script but the form of numerals to be used for the official purposes of Union shall be the international form of Indian numerals. However, for a period of fifteen years from the commencement of the Constitution, the English language continued to be used for all the official purposes of the Union. Even after fifteen years, the Parliament may by law provide for the use of English language for specified purposes. Even during this period of fifteen years, the President may authorise the use of the Hindi Language in addition to the English Language, and of the Devanagari forms of numerals for any official purposes of the Union. However, States are free to have Hindi as official language for communication amongst them.

344. Commission and Committee of the Parliament on Official Language: (1) The President shall, at the expiration of five years from the commencement of this Constitution and thereafter at the expiration of ten years from such commencement, by order constitute a Commission which shall consist of a Chairman and such other members representing the different languages specified in the Eighth Schedule as the President may appoint, and the order shall define the procedure to be followed by the Commission.

(2) It shall be the duty of the Commission to make recommendations to the President as to—

(a) the progressive use of the Hindi language for the official purposes of the Union;

(b) restrictions on the use of the English language for all or any of the official purposes of the Union;

(c) the language to be used for all or any of the purposes mentioned in Article 348;

(d) the form of numerals to be used for any one or more specified purposes of the Union;

(e) any other matter referred to the Commission by the President as regards the official language of the Union and the language for communication between the Union and a State or between one State and another and their use.

(3) In making their recommendations under clause (2), the Commission shall have due regard to the industrial, cultural and scientific advancement of India, and the just claims and the

interests of persons belonging to the non-Hindi-speaking areas in regard to the public services.

(4) There shall be constituted a Committee consisting of thirty members, of whom twenty shall be members of the House of the People and ten shall be members of the Council of States to be elected respectively by the members of the House of the People and the members of the Council of States in accordance with the system of proportional representation by means of the single transferable vote.

(5) It shall be the duty of the Committee to examine the recommendations of the Commission constituted under clause (1) and to report to the President their opinion thereon.

(6) Notwithstanding anything in Article 343, the President may, after consideration of the report referred to in clause (5), issue directions in accordance with the whole or any part of that report.

(Part XVII, Article 344)

COMMENTS

After the expiry of initial 15 years, the Parliament by law provided in the form of the Official Language Act, 1963, amended later to empower the Central Government to make rules that those having proficiency either in Hindi or in English may not put to any disadvantage on the basis of language. Thus, this Act, sealed the process for the time being to declare Hindi as the National Language. The Constitution makers also avoided division on the basis of language and coined the terms Official Language. A nation is dumb without its national language. It is the language of masses which is entitled to be declared as National Language. Hindi is the language of more than 60 per cent of people and is being understood by about 90 per cent of population of India. It extends from North to South and from West to East. It unites the country. Therefore, all great men of India advocated to make Hindi as National Language.

Mahatma Gandhi, Father of the Nation, said that if he was the dictator of India for one day, he would declare Hindi as National Language. Articles 351 also envisages developing Hindi so that it may serve as a medium of expression for all the elements of the composite culture of India. We may fight for language to secure jobs but pure and simple declaration of Hindi as National Language will not harm anybody. It will be our national symbol apart from the National Flag and the National Anthem.

The Official Language Commission set up for this purpose under Article 344 has not discharged its functions in true spirit and with requisite vigour. The Official Language Department has not gone beyond popularising Hindi in the Central Government departments and made it obligatory on all its employees to learn Hindi. More has been done by the Government of U.P., the most populous State in India to adopt Hindi as its Official Language and has vigorously promoted it.

However, orders of the Central Government were challenged before the Supreme Court by Murasoli Maran from Tamil Nadu. The Supreme Court held that the President has wide power to issue directions or orders irrespective of the power of the Parliament in Article 343.

Therefore, the Central Government can issue orders to continue beyond 2016. This is an open-ended power which should be limited. The Supreme Court further held that there is power to adopt any language in use in State as Official language and such power can be exercised from time to time.[2]

345. Official Language or Languages for State: Subject to the provisions of Articles 346 and 347, the Legislature of a State may by law adopt any one or more of the languages in use in the State or Hindi as the language or languages to be used for all or any of the official purposes of that State:

Provided that, until the Legislature of the State otherwise provides by law, the English language shall continue to be used for those official purposes within the State for which it was being used immediately before the commencement of this Constitution.

(Part XII, Article 345)

COMMENTS

The States are left free to adopt any language to be used for official purposes. The State can use its power to adopt Hindi as the Official language of the State at any time.[3] The State of U.P. was allowed to declare Urdu as the Second Official Language. In case of supply of information, the public authority is under obligation to give information to citizen in the language, which he understands.[4]

346. Official Language for communication between one State and another or between a State and the Union: The Language for the time being authorised for use in the Union for official purposes shall be the official language for communication between one State and another State and between a State and the Union:

Provided that if two or more States agree that the Hindi language should be the official language for communication between such States, that language may be used for such communication.

(Part XVII, Article 346)

COMMENTS

Two or more States may agree that Hindi may be used as Official Language for communication between such States.

347. Special provision relating to language spoken by a section of the population of a State: On a demand being made in that behalf, the President may, if he is satisfied that a substantial proportion of the population of a State desires the use of any language spoken by them to be recognised throughout that State or any part thereof for such purpose as he may specify.

(Part XVII, Article 347)

COMMENTS

The President may respond to a demand for an additional official language. The States may also yield to such a demand.[5]

348. Language to be used in the Supreme Court and in the High Courts and for Acts, Bills, etc.: (1) Notwithstanding anything in the foregoing provisions of this Part. until the Parliament by law otherwise provides—

(a) all proceedings in the Supreme Court and in every High Court,

(b) the authoritative texts—

(i) of all Bills to be introduced or amendments thereto to be moved in either House of the Parliament or in the House or either House of the Legislature of a State,

(ii) of all Acts passed by the Parliament or the Legislature of a State and of all Ordinances promulgated by the President or the Governor of a State, and

(iii) of all orders, rules, regulations and bye-laws issued under this Constitution or under any law made by the Parliament or the Legislature of a State, shall be in the English language.

(2) Notwithstanding anything in sub-clause (a) of clause (1), the Governor of a State may, with the previous consent of the President, authorise the use of the Hindi language, or any other language used for any official purposes of the State, in proceedings in the High Court having its principal seat in that State:

Provided that nothing in this clause shall apply to any judgement, decree or order passed or made by such High Court.

(3) Notwithstanding anything in sub-clause (b) of clause (1), where the Legislature of a State has prescribed any language other than the English language for use in Bills introduced in, or Acts passed by, the Legislature of the State or in Ordinances promulgated by the Governor of the State or in any order, rule, regulation or bye-law referred to in paragraph (iii) of that sub-clause, a translation of the same in the English language published under the authority of the Governor of the State in the Official Gazette of that State shall be deemed to be the authoritative text thereof in the English language under this Article.

(Part XVII, Article 348)

COMMENTS

This Article represents as if the country cannot get rid of English. More surprising is the recognition of the fact that widely recognised Hindi as National language is not competent to be the language of the Supreme Court or High Courts (judgement, decree or order only).

However, 58th Amendment of the Constitution in 1987 has done some repair by providing in Article 394A that Hindi text of the Constitution will have the same meaning as the original text in the English Language.

It was expected that after expiration of the period of fifteen years, Hindi will take place of English. But that didn't happen. English continued to be used in addition to Hindi. However, Hindi is on its way to take place of English. All Central Acts or Ordinance orders, regulations, bye-laws, will have their authoritative texts in Hindi. Even Acts or Ordinances of States will be accompanied by their Hindi text. Now States may authorise Hindi with the consent of President, as their official language and judgement, decree or order passed by the concerned High Court may be in Hindi accompanied by the English translation. Many States like U.P., M.P., Rajasthan, Bihar have adopted Hindi as official language of the State. Even some judgements of High Courts have successfully been delivered in Hindi which can be easily understood by the affected parties even without the aid of their lawyers.

In inter-state communication, Hindi can be adopted as their official language. For the non-Hindi State, English version will be accompanied. State may adopt any other language as the official language to protect the interests of the linguistic minorities. In any case, the domination of English as official language should end.

For International communication and business, English is indispensable and a limited number of people may continue with expertise in English to exploit scope outside India especially in view of globalisation. India has done so. To that extent, the use of English in India so far has not gone waste. India has now become one of the leading nations in qualitative use of English language and India has got the advantage throughout the world in the field of service sector like I.T. services.

349. Special Procedure for enactment of certain laws relating to language: During the period of fifteen years from the commencement of this Constitution, no Bill or amendment making provision for the language to be used for any of the purposes mentioned in clause (1) of Article 348 shall be introduced or moved in either House of the Parliament without the previous sanction of the President, and the President shall not give his sanction to the introduction of any such Bill or the moving of any such amendment except after he has taken into consideration the recommendations of the Commission constituted under clause (1) of Article 344 and the report of the Committee constituted under clause (4) of that Article.

(Part XVI, Article 349)

COMMENTS

This Article does away the possibility of imposition of Hindi in foregoing matters under Article 348(1) as a populist measure by the Union. It can only be done on the recommendation of the Commission and Committee of the Parliament on official language with the consent of the President.

However, the Constitution has not guarded against the opposition of Hindi by few political parties or State to appease their voters in violation of the spirit of the Constitution in respect of the official language.

350. Language to be used in representations for redress of grievances: Every person shall be entitled to submit a representation for the redress of any grievance to any officer or authority of the Union or a State in any of the languages used in the Union or in the State, as the case may be.

(Part XVII, Article 350)

COMMENTS

There is full freedom to a person in India to submit a

representation to redress his grievance to any officer in any of the languages used in the Union or in the State.

350A. Facilities for instruction in mother-tongue at primary stage: It shall be the endeavour of every State and of every local authority within the State to provide adequate facilities for instruction in the mother-tongue at the primary stage of education to children belonging to linguistic minority groups; and the President may issue such directions to any State as he considers necessary or proper for securing the provision of such facilities.

(Part XVII, Article 350-A)

COMMENTS

It is a good policy that education at the primary level will be provided in the mother-tongue so that the students have not to waste their energy to learn foreign language unnecessarily. In this case, the student's creativity and originality will find expression more easily. The Supreme Court has held that state has no power under Article 350A of the constitution to compel the linguistic minorities to choose their mother-tongue only as a medium of instruction in primary schools.[6] The imposition of mother-tongue affects the fundamental rights under Articles 19, 29 and 30 of the Constitution. The term 'linguistic minority' groups have been interpreted to mean a group of people who are in numerical minority in a State as a whole and not in particular area for region.

350B. Special officer for linguistic minorities: (1) There shall be a Special Officer for linguistic minorities to be appointed by the President.

(2) It shall be the duty of the Special Officer to investigate all matters relating to the safeguards provided for linguistic minorities under this Constitution and report to the President upon those matters at such intervals as the President may direct, and the President shall cause all such reports to be laid before each House of the Parliament, and sent to the Governments of the States concerned.

(Part XVII, Article 350B)

COMMENTS

There shall be a Special officer for linguistic minorities to be appointed by the President.

It shall be the duty of the Special Officer to investigate all matters relating to the safeguards provided for linguistic minorities under this Constitution and report to the President upon those matters at such intervals as the President may direct, and the President shall cause all such reports to be laid before each House of the Parliament, and sent to the Governments of the States concerned.

(Part XVII, Article 350B)

351. Directive for Development of the Hindi Language: It shall be the duty of the Union to promote the spread of the Hindi language to develop it, so that it may serve as a medium of expression for all the elements of the composite culture of India and to secure its enrichment by assimilating without interfering with its genius the forms, style and expressions used in Hindustani and in the other languages of India specified in the Eighth Schedule, and by drawing, wherever necessary or desirable, for its vocabulary, primarily on Sanskrit and secondarily on other languages.

(Part XVII, Article 351)

COMMENTS

Constitution makers were most confused about provisions relating to language. Their ambiguity is reflected through various Articles in Part XVII. They wanted to make Hindi as National language but could not lay down in so many words. But the very scheme points out to the fact that it is Hindi and Hindi only which occupies the highest seat among languages in use in India. They hoped that by assimilating new words from Sanskrit into Hindi, Hindi will become closer to its sister languages in India because all Indian languages have their origin in Sanskrit. It also professed Hindustani as a symbol of composite culture of India which Gandhi ji had advised to adopt. The unlimited power beyond initial 15 years assumed by the Parliament under the Official Language Act to allow

English as official language is in violation of the spirit and basic features of the Constitution of India. By establishing language Academies by the Union and States, the ideal enshrined in the Constitution can be implemented.

The Supreme Court also disapproved any attempt by Tamil Nadu to overlook Hindi at least as the link language. In R.R. Dalavi vs. State of Tamil Nadu,[8] the Supreme Court refused to approve the Tamil Nadu scheme of payment of pension to anti-Hindi agitators because, firstly, the scheme contained the vice of disintegration and fomenting fissiparous tendencies and had to be nipped in the bud, because it was anti-national and anti-democratic, and secondly, there was no legislative support for it. It was a flagrant violation of the Constitution and the Indian polity. The scheme was, therefore, held to be violative of Article 357 which imposes a duty on the Union to promote the spread of Hindi.

REFERENCES

1. Union of India vs. Murasoli Maran (1997) 2 SCC 410.
2. U.P. Hindi Sahitya Sammelan vs. State of U.P., AIR 2015-SC 1154.
3. Ibid.
4. State Consumer Disputes Redressal Commission, Uttarakhand vs. Uttarakhand State Information Commission, AIR 2010 Uttra 55.
5. U.P. Hindi Sahitya Sammelan vs. State of Uttar Pradesh, AIR 2015 SC 1154.
6. State of Karnataka vs. Associated Management, Primary and Secondary Schools, (2014) 9 SCC 485.
7. In re Kerala Education Bill, AIR 1958 SC 956.
8. (1976) 3 SCC 748.

□

Chapter 19
EMERGENCY PROVISIONS

352. Proclamation of Emergency: (1) If the President is satisfied that a grave Emergency exists, whereby the security of India or of any part of the Territory thereof is threatened, whether by war or external aggression or armed rebellion, he may, by Proclamation, make a declaration to that effect in respect of the whole of India or of such part of the Territory thereof as may be specified in the Proclamation.

Explanation: A Proclamation of Emergency declaring that the security of India or any part of the Territory thereof is threatened by war or by external aggression or by armed rebellion may be made before the actual occurrence of war or of any such aggression or rebellion, if the President is satisfied that there is imminent danger thereof.

(2) A Proclamation issued under clause (1) may be varied or revoked by a subsequent Proclamation.

(3) The President shall not issue a Proclamation under clause (1) or a Proclamation varying such Proclamation unless the decision of the Union Cabinet, that is to say, the Council consisting of the Prime Minister and other Ministers of Cabinet rank appointed under Article 75 that such a Proclamation may be issued has been communicated to him in writing.

(4) Every Proclamation issued under this Article shall be laid before each House of the Parliament and shall, except where it is a Proclamation revoking a previous Proclamation, cease to operate at the expiration of one month unless before the expiration of that period it has been approved by resolutions of both the Houses of the Parliament:

Provided that if any such Proclamation not being a Proclamation revoking a previous Proclamation is issued at a time when the House of the People has been dissolved, or the dissolution of the House of the People takes place during the period of one month referred to in this clause, and if a resolution approving the Proclamation has been passed by the Council of States, but no resolution with respect to such Proclamation has been passed by the House of the People before the expiration of that period, the Proclamation shall cease to operate at the expiration of thirty days from the date on which the House of the People first sits after its reconstitution, unless before the expiration of the said period of thirty days a resolution approving the Proclamation has been also passed by the House of the People.

(5) A Proclamation so approved shall, unless revoked, cease to operate on the expiration of a period of six months from the date of the passing of the second of the resolutions approving the Proclamation under clause (4):

Provided that if and so often as a resolution approving the continuance in force of such a Proclamation is passed by both the Houses of the Parliament, the Proclamation shall, unless revoked, continue in force for a further period of six months from the date on which it would otherwise have ceased to operate under this clause:

Provided further that if the dissolution of the House of the People takes place during any such period of six months and a resolution approving the continuance in force of such Proclamation has been passed by the Council of States but no resolution with respect to the continuance in force of such Proclamation has been passed by the House of the People during the said period, the Proclamation shall cease to operate at the expiration of thirty days from the date on which the House of the People first sits after its reconstitution unless before the expiration of the said period of thirty days, a resolution approving the continuance in force of the Proclamation has been also passed by the House of the People.

(6) For the purposes of clauses (4) and (5), a resolution may be passed by either House of the Parliament only by a majority

of the total membership of that House and by a majority of not less than two-thirds of the Members of that House present and voting.

(7) Notwithstanding anything contained in the foregoing clauses, the President shall revoke a Proclamation issued under clause (1) or a Proclamation varying such Proclamation if the House of the People passes a resolution disapproving, or, as the case may be, disapproving the continuance in force of, such Proclamation.

(8) Where a notice in writing signed by not less than one-tenth of the total number of members of the House of the People has been given, of their intention to move a resolution for disapproving, or, as the case may be, for disapproving the continuance in force of, a Proclamation issued under clause (1) or a Proclamation varying such Proclamation—

(a) to the Speaker, if the House is in session; or

(b) to the President, if the House is not in session, a special sitting of the House shall be held within fourteen days from the date on which such notice is received by the Speaker, or, as the case may be, by the President, for the purpose of considering such resolution.

(9) The power conferred on the President by this Article shall include the power to issue different Proclamations on different grounds, being war or external aggression or armed rebellion or imminent danger of war or external aggression or armed rebellion, whether or not there is a Proclamation already issued by the President under clause (1) and such Proclamation is in operation.

(Part XVIII, Article 352)

COMMENTS

The Indian Constitution has the flexibility to be unitary in Emergency situation. The Constitution envisages three types of Emergency:

(1) National Emergency: Due to war, internal aggression or armed rebellion.

(2) President's Rule or Emergency in State: Due to failure of Constitutional machinery of State or States.

(3) Financial Emergency: Financial stability or credit of India or part is threatened.

During Emergency, executive is entrusted with wide powers to take unified action to tackle emergent situation by quick decision-making.

After the Emergency provisions were misused by Prime Minister Late Mrs. Indian Gandhi in 1975, Article 352 has lost its edge except for war or external aggression in which case, Emergency can even be declared if there is a threat of war or external aggression or armed rebellion. The word 'internal disturbance' have since been repealed and subjective satisfaction of President has been subjected to the decision by the Cabinet. It was necessitated because Late Mrs. India Gandhi had declared Emergency without consulting her Cabinet which was informed as fait accompli.

Other safeguards added are:

(i) The Proclamation is to be approved within one month.

(ii) Approval by majority of both Houses and 2/3rd members present and voting.

(iii) Even 1/10th of members can convene the House through President at a 14 days' notice.

Earlier, it was held by the Supreme Court that there is no scope of judicial control, whether Emergency is invalid.[1]

The fetters were removed in the Rajasthan case, Minerva Mills' case followed by Bommai case.[2] It was held that if the satisfaction of the President was based on extraneous or irrelevant consideration, it is no satisfaction at all and courts can interfere.

It was held that the judiciary could act if it was established that the Union Government acted mala fide not based on facts. The remedy otherwise could be only political. If the satisfaction of the President was absurd, perverse or mala fide, the exercise of power would be unconstitutional and courts could certainly act under their power of limited judicial review in such a case. The proclamation of Emergency will continue to be operative as long as the proclamation of Emergency is not revoked by another proclamation. An armed rebellion like some in the North-Eastern States poses a threat to security of the State as distinguished from internal disturbance, contemplated under Article 355.[3]

353. Effect of Proclamation of Emergency: While a Proclamation of Emergency is in operation, then:

(a) Notwithstanding anything in this Constitution, the executive power of the Union shall extend to the giving of directions to any State as to the manner in which the executive power thereof is to be exercised;

(b) The power of the Parliament to make laws with respect to any matter shall include power to make laws conferring powers and imposing duties, or authorising the conferring of powers and the imposition of duties, upon the Union or Officers and authorities of the Union as respects that matter, notwithstanding that it is one which is not enumerated in the Union List:

Provided that where a Proclamation of Emergency is in operation only in any part of the Territory of India:

(i) The executive power of the Union to give directions under clause (a), and

(ii) The power of the Parliament to make laws under clause (b) shall also extend to any State other than a State in which or in any part of which the Proclamation of Emergency is in operation if and insofar as the security of India or any part of the Territory thereof is threatened by activities in or in relation to the part of the Territory of India in which the Proclamation of Emergency is in operation.

(Part XVIII, Article 353)

COMMENTS

Extension of Centre's Executive Power: During the operation of Proclamation of Emergency, the executive power of the Union has complete control over the State Governments' administration. It is not only to give direction but to ensure that the executive power is exercised in a manner directed by the Central Government.

The Parliament is empowered to legislate on State Subjects: The distribution of legislative power is fundamentally changed during Emergency. The Union the Parliament can make laws on any matters in the State List. The State can make law but it is subject to the overriding power of the Union the Parliament.

It was initially held that the Presidential order during proclamation cannot be circumscribed by any limitation and their applicability was not made dependent upon the fulfilment of any condition precedent. In ADM Jabalpur vs. Shivkant Shukla,[4] the detention under MISA was challenged and writ of habeas corpus was prayed for. The Supreme Court legitimised the suspension of right to move the High Court or the Supreme Court during the period of Emergency on the basis of higher claims of national security. In other words, the detenue had no locus standi to file the writ petition and question the reasons or grounds of detention.

Similar power was assumed under Hitler Germany under the Republican Weimer Constitution of Germany. The President of the Reich could, in the interest of public security and order, abrogate either wholly or partially the fundamental rights secured under the Constitution.

The majority view in the Shukla case has been completely negatived by the 44th Amendment of the Constitution as well as judicial interpretation and, therefore, it is no longer the law. Now the enforcement of Articles 20 and 21 cannot be suspended in any situation and the Court has held that Article 21 binds not only the executive but also the Legislature and no person can be deprived of his life or liberty without the authority of law.

It was held way back that the detenue has the liberty to send his book outside the jail for publication since there was no nexus between the Government order preventing it and the purpose of the enforcement of Emergency rules.[5]

354. Application of provisions relating to distribution of revenues while a Proclamation of Emergency is in operation: (1) The President may, while a Proclamation of Emergency is in operation, by order direct that all or any of the provisions of Articles 268 to 279 shall for such period, not extending in any case beyond the expiration of the financial year in which such Proclamation ceases to operate, as may be specified in the order, have effect subject to such exceptions or modifications as he thinks fit.

(2) Every order made under clause (1) shall, as soon as may be after it is made, be laid before each House of the Parliament.

(Part XVIII, Article 354)

COMMENTS

During the operation of the Proclamation of Emergency, the President has the Constitutional power to modify the provisions of the Constitution relating to allocation of financial resources, between the Union and the States, by his own order. But no such orders shall have effect beyond the financial year in which the Proclamation itself ceases to operate, and further, such order of the President shall be subject to approval by the Parliament.

355. Duty of the Union to protect States against external aggression and internal disturbance: It shall be the duty of the Union to protect every State against external aggression and internal disturbance and to ensure that the Government of every State is carried on in accordance with the provisions of this Constitution.

(Part XVIII, Article 355)

COMMENTS

If it is found that the Government of a State is not being carried on in accordance with the provisions of the Constitution of India, the State should be reminded of its responsibility. The Centre is within its right to dispatch army or the Central Reserve Police to a State if it fails to give adequate protection to the Central Government agencies in the State so that these may function normally, or to protect the Central Government properties in the State against destruction by agitators or strikers. It need not be so grave as to threaten the security of India. What is the interest of national security is a matter of policy. So, it is to be decided by the Executive and not by Court.

Thus, it seems to be a very wide power vested in the Union to deploy central forces in the situation of internal disturbance even without request from the State concerned.

356. Provisions in case of failure of constitutional machinery in States: (1) If the President, on receipt of a report from the Governor of a State or otherwise, is satisfied that a situation has arisen in which the Government of the State cannot be carried on in accordance with the provisions of this Constitution, the President may by Proclamation—

(a) assume to himself all or any of the functions of the Government of the State and all or any of the powers vested in or exercisable by the Governor or any body or authority in the State other than the Legislature of the State;

(b) declare that the powers of the Legislature of the State shall be exercisable by or under the authority of the Parliament;

(c) make such incidental and consequential provisions as appear to the President to be necessary or desirable for giving effect to the objects of the Proclamation, including provisions for suspending in whole or in part the operation of any provisions of this Constitution relating to any body or authority in the State:

Provided that nothing in this clause shall authorise the President to assume to himself any of the powers vested in or exercisable by a High Court, or to suspend in whole or in part the operation of any provision of this Constitution relating to High Courts.

(2) Any such Proclamation may be revoked or varied by a subsequent Proclamation.

(3) Every Proclamation under this Article shall be laid before each House of the Parliament and shall, except where it is a Proclamation revoking a previous Proclamation, cease to operate at the expiration of two months unless before the expiration of that period, it has been approved by resolutions of both the Houses of the Parliament:

Provided that if any such Proclamation (not being a Proclamation revoking a previous Proclamation) is issued at a time when the House of the People is dissolved or the dissolution of the House of the People takes place during the period of two months referred to in this clause, and if a resolution approving the Proclamation has been passed by the Council of States, but no resolution with respect to such Proclamation has been passed by the House of the People before the expiration of that period, the Proclamation shall cease to operate at the expiration of thirty days from the date on which the House of the People first sits after its reconstitution unless before the expiration of the said period of thirty days a resolution approving the Proclamation has been also passed by the House of the People.

(4) A Proclamation so approved shall, unless revoked, cease to operate on the expiration of a period of six months from the date of issue of the Proclamation:

Provided that if and so often as a resolution approving the continuance in force of such a Proclamation is passed by both the Houses of the Parliament, the Proclamation shall, unless revoked, continue in force for a further period of six months from the date on which under this clause, it would otherwise have ceased to operate, but no such Proclamation shall in any case remain in force for more than three years:

Provided further that if the dissolution of the House of the People takes place during any such period of six months and a resolution approving the continuance in force of such Proclamation has been passed by the Council of States, but no resolution with respect to the continuance in force of such Proclamation has been passed by the House of the People during the said period, the Proclamation shall cease to operate at the expiration of thirty days from the date on which the House of the People first sits after its reconstitution unless before the expiration of the said period of thirty days, a resolution approving the continuance in force of the Proclamation has been also passed by the House of the People:

Provided also that in the case of the Proclamation issued under clause (1) on the 11th day of May, 1987 with respect to the

State of Punjab, the reference in the first proviso to this clause to "three years" shall be construed as a reference to five years.

(5) Notwithstanding anything contained in clause (4), a resolution with respect to the continuance in force of a Proclamation approved under clause (3) for any period beyond the expiration of one year from the date of issue of such Proclamation shall not be passed by either House of the Parliament unless—

(a) a Proclamation of Emergency is in operation, in the whole of India or, as the case may be, in the whole or any part of the State, at the time of the passing of such resolution, and (b) the Election Commission certifies that the continuance in force of the Proclamation approved under clause (3) during the period specified in such resolution is necessary on account of difficulties in holding general elections to the Legislative Assembly of the State concerned:

Provided that nothing in this clause shall apply to the Proclamation issued under clause (1) on the 11th day of May, 1987 with respect to the State of Punjab.

(Part XVIII, Article 356)

COMMENTS

The provisions regarding failure of Constitutional machinery are quite elaborate so that error is not committed to take over the administration and legislatures of the State. The grounds of proclamation under Article 356 regarding subjective satisfaction of the President of India are questionable if it is based on wholly extraneous or irrelevant purpose and there is no reasonable nexus between the reasons disclosed and the satisfaction of the President. The exercise of power cannot be mala fide because a statutory order which lacks bone fides has no existence in law.[7]

In the absence of mala fide, etc., Court cannot grant relief in law. But as a matter of propriety, ministry should not be unseated without giving to the Legislative Assembly an opportunity expressing its confidence or want (or confidence) in the ministry.[8] If the Court strikes down the proclamation, it has power to restore the dismissed State Government to office.

A State Government pursuing anti secular politics is liable to action under Article 356.

'Mere dissolution of the Assembly on the advice of the Chief Minister does not bring the case within Article 356 of the Constitution.[9] Proclamation under Section 356 is open to judicial review only when the power is exercised mala fide or is based on wholly extraneous or irrelevant grounds.[10]

The President's Rule in a State can be imposed even without the report of the Governor if the President is satisfied as was done in early 1991, when Karunanidhi Government in Tamil Nadu was removed without any report from the Governor.

Duration: The duration of a proclamation issued under Article 356 is two months unlike six months earlier. If after two months the proclamation is to be continued, it has to be ratified by the Parliament. However, for further extension beyond the expiration of one year, a resolution requires confirmation of the Election Commission that it is necessary for such a proclamation/declaration to continue in view of the difficulties in holding elections in the State. A maximum limit of three years is prescribed because it is the most misused Article by the party in power at the centre.

Various Instances: In July 1959, Communist Government in West Bengal was dismissed due to an atmosphere of hatred, regionalism, incitement, discrimination and violence prevailing in the State.

"In 1967, the majority Government in Haryana was dismissed and the President's Rule was imposed due to large-scale defection of members of the Legislative Assembly, their flexible loyalty and abuse of power by Ministers resulting in political corruption in the State. The High Court dismissed the petition saying that there is ample material in the report of the Governor that the administration of the State had been paralysed."[11]

'In 1977, an unprecedented situation arose in nine States after a total or almost total rejection of candidates put up by the ruling party in the Parliamentary elections. The Supreme Court refused to intervene as reasons were not disclosed.[12]

When Sunder Lal Patwa (BJP) Government in Madhya Pradesh was dissolved on the grounds of Ayodhya mayhem, there was not much aftereffect in Madhya Pradesh. Accordingly, M.P. High Court did not find adequate ground for the President's rule.[13]

However, the operation of the High Court order was, however, stayed by the Supreme Court, pending the disposal of the appeal against it. In this connection, much more relevant and leading judgement is of the Pakistan Supreme Court of June 1993, invalidating the dismissal of Nawaz Shariff Government and dissolution of the National Assembly.[14]

It was insisted that test of majority on the floor of the House is the last alternative. The Governor cannot refuse formation of the Government and override the majority claim because of his subjective assessment that the majority was cobbled by illegal and unethical means.[15]

In U.P., the Governor, in order to please his political masters acted with connivance of the Centre, the BSP and Samajwadi party leaders, installed Mr. Jagadambika Pal as Chief Minister, in spite of advice of restraint by President K.R. Narayanan. The action of the Governor was challenged in the Allahabad High Court. The High Court held that the Governor acted with mala fide intentions. The Court directed the Governor that if he had any doubt about majority of the then C.M. Kalyan Singh, he may ask Kalyan Singh to prove his majority on the floor of the House.

On an SLP, the Supreme Court declined to stay the decision of the Allahabad High Court. In the composite trial of strength, Mr. Kalyan Singh emerged victorious.

Later on the recommendations of Justice Sarkaria Commission are the determining factors to impose the President's Rule.

"However, any Act enacted by the President during the President's rule continues to remain in force in spite of revocation of proclamation.[16]

The Constitution Commission's recommendations are worth following:

Article 350 should be sparingly used.

The majority in the Assembly decided only on the floor of the Assembly and nowhere else.

The proclamation should be issued after it has been laid before the Parliament for consideration.

357. Exercise of legislative powers under Proclamation issued under Article: (1) Where by a Proclamation issued under clause (1) of Article 356, it has been declared that the powers of the Legislature of the State shall be exercisable by or under the authority of the Parliament, it shall be competent—

(a) for the Parliament to confer on the President the power of the Legislature of the State to make laws, and to authorise the President to delegate, subject to such conditions as he may think fit to impose, the power so conferred to any other authority to be specified by him in that behalf;

(b) for the Parliament, or for the President or other authority in whom such power to make laws is vested under sub-clause (a), to make laws conferring powers and imposing duties, or authorising the conferring of powers and the imposition of duties, upon the Union or officers and authorities thereof;

(c) for the President to authorise when the House of the People is not in session expenditures from the Consolidated Fund of the State pending the sanction of such expenditures by the Parliament.

(2) Any law made in exercise of the power of the Legislature of the State by the Parliament or the President or other authority referred to in sub-clause (a) of clause (1) which the Parliament or the President or such other authority would not, but for the issue of a Proclamation under Article 356, have been competent to make shall, after the Proclamation has ceased to operate, continue in force until altered or repealed or amended by a competent Legislature or other authority.

(Part XVIII, Article 357)

COMMENTS

'Any Act enacted by the President during the President's

rule shall continue to remain in force in spite of revocation of the proclamation.[16]

358. Suspension of provisions of Article 19 during emergencies: (1) While a Proclamation of Emergency declaring that the security of India or any part of the Territory thereof is threatened by war or by external aggression is in operation, nothing in Article 19 shall restrict the power of the State as defined in Part III to make any law or to take any executive action which the State would but for the provisions contained in that Part be competent to make or to take, but any law so made shall, to the extent of the incompetency, cease to have effect as soon as the Proclamation ceases to operate, except as respects things done or omitted to be done before the law so ceased to have effect.

Provided that where such Proclamation of Emergency is in operation only in any part of the Territory of India, any such law may be made, or any such executive action may be taken, under this Article in relation to or in any State or Union Territory in which or in any part of which the Proclamation of Emergency is not in operation, if and insofar as the security of India or any part of the Territory thereof is threatened by activities in or in relation to the part of the Territory of India in which the Proclamation of Emergency is in operation.

(2) Nothing in clause (1) shall apply—

(a) to any law which does not contain a recital to the effect that such law is in relation to the Proclamation of Emergency in operation when it is made; or

(b) to any executive action taken otherwise than under a law containing such a recital.

(Part XVIII, Article 358)

359. Suspension of the enforcement of the Rights conferred by Part III during emergencies: (1) Where a Proclamation of Emergency is in operation, the President may by order declare that the right to move any court for the enforcement of such of the rights conferred by Part III (except Articles 20 and 21) as may be mentioned in the order and all proceedings pending in any court for the enforcement of the rights so mentioned shall remain suspended for the period during which the Proclamation is in force or for such shorter period as may be specified in the order.

(1A) While an order made under clause (1) mentioning any of the rights conferred by Part III (except Articles 20 and 21) is in operation, nothing in that Part conferring those rights shall restrict the power of the State as defined in the said Part to make any law or to take any executive action which the State would but for the provisions contained in that Part be competent to make or to take, but any law so made shall, to the extent of the incompetency, cease to have effect as soon as the order aforesaid ceases to operate, except as respects things done or omitted to be done before the law so ceases to have effect:

Provided that where a Proclamation of Emergency is in operation only in any part of the Territory of India, any such law may be made, or any such executive action may be taken, under this Article in relation to or in any State or Union Territory in which or in any part of which the Proclamation of Emergency is not in operation, if and insofar as the security of India or any part of the Territory thereof is threatened by activities in or in relation to the part of the Territory of India in which the Proclamation of Emergency is in operation.

(1B) Nothing in clause (1A) shall apply—

(a) to any law which does not contain a recital to the effect that such law is in relation to the Proclamation of Emergency in operation when it is made; or

(b) to any executive action taken otherwise than under a law containing such a recital.

(2) An order made as aforesaid may extend to the whole or any part of the Territory of India:

Provided that where a Proclamation of Emergency is in operation only in a part of the Territory of India, any such order shall not extend to any other part of the Territory of India unless the President, being satisfied that the security of India or any part of the Territory thereof is threatened by activities in or in relation to the part of the Territory of India in which the Proclamation of Emergency is in operation, considers such extension to be necessary.

(3) Every order made under clause (1) shall, as soon as may be after it is made, be laid before each House of the Parliament.

359A. Application of this Part to the State of Punjab. Rep. by the Constitution (Sixty-third Amendment) Act, 1989, s. 3 (w.e.f. 6-1-1990).

360. Provisions as to financial Emergency: (1) If the President is satisfied that a situation has arisen, whereby the financial stability or credit of India or of any part of the Territory thereof is threatened, he may by a Proclamation make a declaration to that effect.

(2) A Proclamation issued under clause (1)—

(a) may be revoked or varied by a subsequent Proclamation;

(b) shall be laid before each House of the Parliament;

(c) shall cease to operate at the expiration of two months, unless before the expiration of that period, it has been approved by resolutions of both Houses of the Parliament:

Provided that if any such Proclamation is issued at a time when the House of the People has been dissolved or the dissolution of the House of the People takes place during the period of two months referred to in sub-clause (c), and if a resolution approving the Proclamation has been passed by the Council of States, but no resolution with respect to such Proclamation has been passed by the House of the People before the expiration of that period, the Proclamation shall cease to operate at the expiration of thirty days from the date on which the House of the People first sits after its reconstitution unless before the expiration of the said period of thirty days, a resolution approving the Proclamation has been also passed by the House of the People.

(3) During the period, any such Proclamation as is mentioned in clause (1) is in operation, the executive authority of the Union shall extend to the giving of directions to any State to observe such canons of financial propriety as may

be specified in the directions, and to the giving of such other directions as the President may deem necessary and adequate for the purpose.

(4) Notwithstanding anything in this Constitution—

(a) any such direction may include—

(i) a provision requiring the reduction of salaries and allowances of all or any class of persons serving in connection with the affairs of a State;

(ii) a provision requiring all Money Bills or other Bills to which the provisions of Article 207 apply to be reserved for the consideration of the President after they are passed by the Legislature of the State;

(b) it shall be competent for the President during the period any Proclamation issued under this Article is in operation to issue directions for the reduction of salaries and allowances of all or any class of persons serving in connection with the affairs of the Union including the Judges of the Supreme Court and the High Courts.

(Part XVIII, Articles 360)

COMMENTS

The President is authorised by Article 360 of the Constitution to declare by a proclamation of financial emergency if he is satisfied that the financial stability or credit of India or of any part is threatened. Such a proclamation may be revoked or varied by a subsequent proclamation. It has to be laid before both the Houses of the Parliament and ceases to operate at the expiration of two months unless approved by resolutions of the two Houses. Once approved by the Parliament, unlike proclamation under Article 352, it may continue indefinitely until revoked or varied.

During such financial Emergency, it shall be competent for the President to reserve State Bills for consideration and approval.

It shall be competent for the President to issue directions, for reduction of salaries and allowances of all or any class of persons serving the Union or State, including Judges of the Supreme Court and High Courts.

A financial Emergency had arisen during the tenure of Chandrashekhar as Prime Minister when India had mortgaged its plane loads tonnes of gold to Bank of England to stabilise her volatile currency in international market. Through liberalisation of economy, then Finance Minister Manmohan Singh brought back the health of the Indian economy on track.

But lessons have not yet been learnt specially by States. Many of them indulge in financial impropriety by undertaking populist schemes which aim to garner votes and do not create assets, like distribution of television sets, laptops, necklaces, free meal, or free food grains and even travel to holy places by senior citizens. Such schemes will bring down the financial health of the States' economy or the Union. The Constitution makers had well anticipated such eventuality in an irresponsible democracy like India and kept the provision of financial Emergency. There is a way out before situation worsens to this extent. The party-in-power should not be allowed to pass bills beyond 33% debt or loan as per norms on the States' income. Such a Bill is pending in the Parliament which is not yet passed as politicians irrespective of their party affiliation want no limitation on them. It is high time that this provision though not used during the last 66 years should be used in a limited way to infuse financial discipline in our polity.

Now-a-days independence will be more threatened by financial instability than military weakness of a nation in view of globalisation. India had her inglorious days whenever the Central power grew weak. The Constitution does well in guarding against the forces of disintegration.

"Events may take place threatening the very existence of the State, and if there are no safeguards, against such eventualities, the State, together with all that is deserved to remain basic and immutable will be swept away."[17]

Thus, the Constitution of India is unique, that it contains a complete scheme of Emergency provisions for speedy readjustment of the peace-time Government machinery in the moment of national peril.

REFERENCES

1. Bhut Nath vs. State of West Bengal, AIR 197, SC 806.
2. State of Rajasthan vs. Union of India AIR 1977 SC 1361, Minister Mills vs. Union of India AIR 1980 SC, S.R. Bommai vs. Union of India (1994) 3 SCC 1.
3. Naga People's Movement of Human Rights vs. Union of India (1998) 2 SCC 109.
4. (1976) 2 SCC 521.
5. State of Maharashtra vs. Prabhakar, AIR 1966 SC 424.
6. Ex-Armymen's Protection Services Pvt. Ltd. vs. Union of India, AIR 2014 SC 1376.
7. State of Rajasthan vs. Union of India (1977) 3 SCC 592.
8. S.R. Bommai vs. Union of India, AIR 1990, Kant.
9. Arun Kumar Rai Chaudhary vs. Union of India, AIR 1992 All 1.
10. Rameshwar Prasad vs. Union of India (2006) 2 SCC 1.
11. Rao Birender Singh vs. Union of India, AIR 1968, P & H 441.
12. State of Rajasthan vs. Union of India (1977) 3 SCC 592.
13. Sunder Lal Patwa vs. Union of India, 1993 Job. LJ 387.
14. Ahmad Tarif Rahim vs. Federation of Pakistan, PLD 1992 SC 646 and Federation of Pakistan vs. Aftab Ahmed Khan Sherpau, PLD 1992 SC 723.
15. Rameshwar Prasad (6) vs. Union of India (2006) 2 SCC1.
16. Nishi Kant Mandal vs. State of W.B. (1972) 2 SCC 486.
17. V.N. Shukla – The Constitution of India, Page 1053 (12th Edition).

□

Chapter 20
AMENDMENT OF THE CONSTITUTION

368. Power of the Parliament to amend the Constitution and procedure therefor: (1) Notwithstanding anything in this Constitution, the Parliament may in exercise of its constituent power amend by way of addition, variation or repeal any provision of this Constitution in accordance with the procedure laid down in this Article.

(2) An amendment of this Constitution may be initiated only by the introduction of a Bill for the purpose in either House of the Parliament, and when the Bill is passed in each House by a majority of the total membership of that House and by a majority of not less than two-thirds of the members of that House present and voting, it shall be presented to the President who shall give his assent to the Bill and thereupon the Constitution shall stand amended in accordance with the terms of the Bill:

Provided that if such amendment seeks to make any change in—

(a) Article 54, Article 55, Article 73, Article 162 or Article 241, or

(b) Chapter IV of Part V, Chapter V of Part VI, or Chapter I of Part XI, or

(c) any of the Lists in the Seventh Schedule, or (d) the representation of States in the Parliament, or (e) the provisions of this Article, the amendment shall also require to be ratified by the Legislatures of not less than one-half of the States by resolutions to that effect passed by those Legislatures before the Bill making provision for such amendment is presented to the President for assent.

(3) Nothing in Article 13 shall apply to any amendment made under this Article.

(4) No amendment of this Constitution (including the provisions of Part III) made or purporting to have been made under this article whether before or after the commencement of Section 55 of the Constitution (Forty-second Amendment) Act, 1976 shall be called in question in any court on any ground.

(5) For the removal of doubts, it is hereby declared that there shall be no limitation whatever on the constituent power of the Parliament to amend by way of addition, variation or repeal the provisions of this Constitution under this Article.

(Part XIX, Article 368)

COMMENTS

The amendment procedure has been provided in the Constitution because:

(i) No generation has monopoly of wisdom nor has the right to bind future generations;

(ii) Nation is a vital organic entity. If it is made rigid, it would invite revolutions for change;

(iii) Amendment is a safety valve. But it should not be so easy as it can be changed on the whims and caprice of party in power without necessary foresight.

In view of the above, the Constitution of India has provided power and procedure in three categories.

Amendment by Simple Majority: The amendments contemplated in Article 4, 169 and 239-A and paras 7 and 9 of the Fifth and Sixth Schedules, namely creation of new States or Constitution of existing States, creation or abolition of upper chambers (Legislative Councils) in the States and constitution of centrally administered areas, etc. fell within this category. These are specifically excluded from the purview of the procedure prescribed in Article 368.

Amendment by Special Majority: All Constitutional amendments except above can be effected by a majority of the total membership of each House of the Parliament as well as by a majority of not less than two-thirds of the members of that House present and voting.

By Special Majority and Ratification: The following provisions require such ratification by not less than one-half of the States:

(1) Election of the President
(2) Extent of the Executive powers of the Union and States
(3) Provisions dealing with the Supreme Court and High Courts,
(4) Distribution of legislative powers between the Union and the States.
(5) The representation of States in the Parliament
(6) Seventh schedule to the Constitution, and
(7) Article 368 itself.

In case of amendment of class (1), normal procedure of each House is followed. In other cases, the amending Bill can be introduced in either House of the Parliament where it must be passed by special majority of 2/3 rd present and voting and absolute majority. The Bill, after it has been passed by both Houses and, if the amendment is such as it requires ratification by not less than half of States, is sent to the President for assent after ratification of the required number of States. After the assent of the President to the Bill, the Constitution shall stand amended.

Amendment of Para 7 of the Tenth Schedule was invalidated because it did not follow the required procedure of ratification by States while making bar to the jurisdiction of the Supreme Court and High Courts in matters of disqualification of the Members of the Parliament and State Legislatures on ground of defection.

The power to amend the Constitution conferred on the Parliament includes power to amend Article and that logically would include the power to cede national Territory in favour of a foreign State.[2]

This farsightedness of the Supreme Court was confirmed when during 2014-15, the enclaves & population with Bangladesh were mutually exchanged between India and Bangladesh and people belonging to both the countries returned back to their homelands without any geographical barriers. The procedure to amend the Constitution is however, not so difficult as in America or Australia. However, the Constitution of India has been amended for more than one hundred times and more is in offing. As a good Constitutional practice, the procedure for amendment should be adopted as a last resort so that respect to the Constitution is maintained in minds of the Indian people.

Amendment of Fundamental Rights: The question of the amendability of fundamental rights came before the Supreme Court as soon as in 1951, when the power of State Government to acquire lands was challenged in the garb of the Constitutional amendment by erstwhile Raja Shakari Prasad Singh Deo.[3] It was held that law as defined in Article 13(2) does not include constitutional amendment and therefore, it will be valid even if it abridges or takes away any of the fundamental rights.

In Sajjan Singh case,[3] 17th Amendment to include several legislations to the Ninth Schedule of the Constitution was challenged as violative of fundamental rights of ex-zamindars or jagirdars. It was held that the Parliament has power to amend the same as in Shakari Prasad case.

However, in Golak Nath case,[5] the inclusion of the Punjab Security of Land Tenure Act, 1953 in the Ninth Schedule was challenged. The Supreme Court with 6:5 majority held that the fundamental rights were outside the amendatory process. It cannot abridge or take away the fundamental rights but gave prospective effect to the ruling saving earlier two judgements of the same court. The Court held:

"The Constitution incorporates an implied limitation that the fundamental rights are outside the power of the Parliament."

Article 368 does not contain the power to amend but merely provides the procedure for amendment. This created a jolt in the march of State Governments to vest excess ceiling land to distribute among the landless and for other public purposes to establish a socialistic and egalitarian rural India.

Therefore, it again came for consideration in 1973 in Kesavananda Bharati case[6] in which eminent jurist N.A.

Palkhivala argued the case for a month before the Constitution Bench of the Supreme Court in favour of landowners and right to property but he also elaborated the basic concept of the Constitution and the Indian polity. The Supreme Court with 7:6 majority, in the longest judgement of the court held that Article 368 does not enable the Parliament to alter the 'basic structure' or framework of the Constitution. The Court struck down the amendment which took away judicial review under Article 39(b) & (c) by the 24th Amendment and reiterated that right to property is not a part of the basic structure or framework of the Constitution. Sikri C.J. gave illustrations of basic structure as:

1. Supremacy of the Constitution
2. Republican and democratic form of Government
3. Secular character of the Constitution
4. Separation of powers between the legislative, the executive and the judiciary, and
5. Federal character of the Constitution
6. Later, the Supreme Court confirmed that the amending power under Article 368 is the constituent power.[7] This paved way for Barga Operation in West Bengal, which established the rights of about 15 lakh sharecroppers in West Bengal, who had no security of tenure before that.

The Supreme Court consistently defended judicial review as a basic feature. In Minerva Mills case[8] the Supreme court struck down the provision in Article 368 that no amendment shall be called in question in any court on any ground." (Cl. 4)

In Waman Rao[9] case, the Supreme Court re-examined and upheld the validity of original and amended Article 31-A and of Article 31-B and the Ninth Schedule by 1st Amendment with reference to the basic structure doctrine. The Court supporting the cause of rural land poor observed that the 1st Amendment instead of weakening the amendment strengthens the basic structure because it made the Constitutional ideal of equal justice a living truth. Unfortunately, the Apex Court opened the pandora box by saying that the Acts included in the Ninth Schedule after the judgement in Kesavananda Bharti case on 24th April, 1973 under the umbrella of the Ninth Schedule are open to challenge on the ground that they damage the basic structure of the Constitution. Now there is no blanket protection available to the laws inserted or after 24.04.1973 and it shall be a matter of constitutional adjudication by examining the nature and extent of infraction of fundamental rights by a statute sought to be Constitutionally protected.[10] It would have been fair if reasonable reliance on wisdom of the Parliament and State Legislatures is placed by the Supreme Court as it will not be possible for the Supreme Court to review validity of large number of statutes, or Acts placed in the Ninth Schedule or are to be placed in the Ninth Schedule by Constitutional amendments on or after 24.04.1973. However, Supreme Court is open to reconsider. The Supreme Court has invalidated the Constitution (Ninety-Ninth) Amendment Act, 2014 and the National Judicial Appointments Act, 2014 ratified by more than 50% of State Legislatures and given assent by the President of India, which came into force with effect from 13.04.2015.[11]

Thus, Supreme Court has preserved the sanctity of judicial review at all costs. It has also laid down that for amendment purpose, any deadlock cannot be solved by a joint session of the two Houses.

However, the Supreme Court has an extended list of 'basic features' to include rule of law, free and fair elections, effective access to justice, social and economic justice, etc.

It is hoped that there is finality of such a list so that there is certainty in law. The Parliament may have self-constraint on exercise of its power of amendment of the Constitutions and allow the healthy Constitutional practices develop in India.

REFERENCES

1. Kihoto Hollohan vs. Zachillhu, 1992 Supp. (2) SCC 651. Also see Prakash Singh Badal vs. Union of India, AIR, 1987 P & H 263.
2. Berubari Union and Exchange of Enclaves, re. AIR, 1960 SC845.
3. Shankari Prasad vs. Union of India, AIR 1951 SC 458.
4. Sajjan Singh vs. State of Rajasthan, AIR 1965, 845.
5. Golak Nath vs. State of Punjab, AIR 1967 SC 1643.
6. Kesavananda Bharati vs. State of Kerala (1973) 4 SCC 225, AIR 1973 SC 1461.

7. Sasanka vs. Union of India, AIR 1981 SC 522.
8. Minerva Mills vs. Union of India, AIR 1980 SC 1789.
9. Waman Rao vs. Union of India (1981) 2 SCC 362.
10. IR Coelho by LRs vs. State of T.N. (2007) 2 SCC 1.
11. M. Nagraj vs. Union of India, AIR 2007 SC 71.
12. Supreme Court Advocate on Record Association & Anr. vs. Union of India, W.P. (C) 2013 of 2015.

□

Chapter 21
MISCELLANEOUS PROVISIONS

361. Protection of President and Governors and Rajpramukhs: (1) The President or the Governor or Rajpramukh of a State, shall not be answerable to any court for the exercise and performance of the powers and duties of his office or for any act done or purporting to be done by him in the exercise and performance of those powers and duties:

Provided that the conduct of the President may be brought under review by any court, tribunal or body appointed or designated by either House of the Parliament for the investigation of a charge under Article 61:

Provided further that nothing in this clause shall be construed as restricting the right of any person to bring appropriate proceedings against the Government of India or the Government of a State.

(2) No criminal proceedings whatsoever shall be instituted or continued against the President, or the Governor of a State, in any court during his term of office.

(3) No process for the arrest or imprisonment of the President, or the Governor of a State, shall issue from any court during his term of office.

(4) No civil proceedings, in which relief is claimed against the President, or the Governor of a State, shall be instituted during his term of office in any court in respect of any act done or purporting to be done by him in his personal capacity, whether before or after he entered upon his office as President, or as Governor of such State, until the expiration of two months next after notice in writing has been delivered to the President

or the Governor, as the case may be, or left at his office stating the nature of the proceedings, the cause of action, therefore, the name, description and place of residence of the party by whom such proceedings are to be instituted and the relief which he claims.

(Part XIX, Article 361)

COMMENTS

Article 361 protects the head of the Union (the President) and the heads of States (the Governors) from personal answerability before courts of law for action in discharge of their duties, institution of any criminal proceeding or arrest, while in office[1] or institution of any civil proceedings without giving at least two months' notice in writing. The immunity available to the President or the Governors cannot be extended to the orders passed in their name by the Ministers in the respective governments.[2] However, no immunity can be claimed by the Governor in respect of the exercise or performance of the powers and duties of his office as the Chancellor.[3] "The immunity does not take away the power of the court to examine the validity of the action including on the ground of malafides."[4]

361A. Protection of publication of proceedings of the Parliament and State Legislature: (1) No person shall be liable to any proceedings, civil or criminal, in any court in respect of the publication in a newspaper of a substantially true report of any proceedings of either House of the Parliament or the Legislative Assembly, or, as the case may be, either House of the Legislature, of a State, unless the publication is proved to have been made with malice:

Provided that nothing in this clause shall apply to the publication of any report of the proceedings of a secret sitting of either House of the Parliament or the Legislative Assembly, or, as the case may be, either House of the Legislature, of a State.

(2) Clause (1) shall apply in relation to reports or matters broadcast by means of wireless telegraphy as part of any programme or service provided by means of a broadcasting

station as it applies in relation to reports or matters published in a newspaper.

Explanation: In this Article, "newspaper" includes a news agency report containing material for publication in a newspaper.

(Part XIX, Article 361A)

COMMENTS

No person shall be liable to any proceedings in any court in respect of the publication in good faith in a newspaper of a substantially true report of any Legislative proceeding other than that of a secret meeting.

The protection extends to radio broadcasts but does not cover any other publication, e.g. in the form of a book, brochure, etc.

Article 361B. Disqualification for appointment on remunerative political post: A member of a House belonging to any political party who is disqualified for being a member of the House under paragraph 2 of the Tenth Schedule shall also be disqualified to hold any remunerative political post for duration of the period commencing from the date of his disqualification till the date on which the term of his office as such member would expire or till the date on which he contests an election to a House and is declared elected, whichever is earlier.

Explanation: For the purposes of this Article—

(a) the expression "House" has the meaning assigned to it in clause (a) of paragraph 1 of the Tenth Schedule;

(b) the expression "remunerative political post" means any office—

(i) under the Government of India or the Government of a State, where the salary or remuneration for such office is paid out of the public revenue of the Government of India or the Government of the State, as the case may be; or

(ii) under a body, whether incorporated or not, which is wholly or partially owned by the Government of India or the Government of a State and the salary or remuneration for such office is paid by such body, except where such salary or remuneration paid is compensatory in nature.

(Part XIX, Article 361B)

COMMENTS

Article 361B inserted by the 91st Constitution Amendment Act, 2003 makes defectors disqualified from membership and ineligible to be Ministers or to hold any remunerative political post without re-election.

362. Rights and privileges of Rulers of Indian States: Repealed by the Constitution (Twenty-Sixth Amendment) Act, 1971.

(Part XIX, Article 362)

363. Bar to interference by courts in disputes arising out of certain treaties, agreements, etc.: (1) Notwithstanding anything in this Constitution but subject to the provisions of Article 143, neither the Supreme Court nor any other court shall have jurisdiction in any dispute arising out of any provision of a treaty, agreement, covenant, engagement, sanad or other similar instrument, which was entered into or executed before the commencement of this Constitution by any Ruler of an Indian State and to which the Government of the Dominion of India or any of its predecessor Governments was a party and which has or has been continued in operation after such commencement, or in any dispute in respect of any right accruing under or any liability or obligation arising out of any of the provisions of this Constitution relating to any such treaty, agreement, covenant, engagement, sanad or other similar instrument.

(2) In this Article—

(a) "Indian State" means any Territory recognised before the commencement of this Constitution by His Majesty or the Government of the Dominion of India as being such a State; and

(b) "Ruler" includes the Prince, Chief or other person recognised before such commencement by His Majesty or the Government of the Dominion of India as the Ruler of any Indian State.

(Part XIX, Article 363)

COMMENTS

The recognition of rulership is one of personal status. It is not a matter of inheritance or descent. No claim to recognition of rulership by virtue of a covenant is justiciable in a court of law. The Constitution, therefore, provides for the act of recognition of rulership by the President as a political power.[5]

'In respect of a matter arising under a major agreement with the Nizam of Hyderabad, executed before the commencement of the Constitution, the Court refused to interfere on account of this Article. An intervention application asking the Supreme Court to declare certain jewellery of the Nizam of Hyderabad as State property was held to be outside the jurisdiction of the Court.[6]

Dr. Karan Singh also failed to make a claim to certain property, which his father Maharaja Hari Singh had handed over to the Government of India in terms of instrument of accession.[7]

363A. Recognition granted to Rulers of Indian States to cease and privy purses to be abolished: Notwithstanding anything in this Constitution or in any law for the time being in force—

(a) the Prince, Chief or other person who, at any time before the commencement of the Constitution (Twenty-sixth Amendment) Act, 1971, was recognised by the President as the Ruler of an Indian State or any person who, at any time before such commencement, was recognised by the President as the successor of such ruler shall, on and from such commencement, cease to be recognised as such Ruler or the successor of such Ruler;

(b) on and from the commencement of the Constitution (Twenty-sixth Amendment) Act, 1971, privy purse is abolished and all rights, liabilities and obligations in respect of privy purse are extinguished and accordingly the Ruler or, as the case may be, the successor of such Ruler, referred to in clause (a) or any other person shall not be paid any sum as privy purse.

(Part XIX, Article 363A)

COMMENTS

The order of the President withdrawing recognition of the rulers was challenged in the Supreme Court. The Supreme Court by a majority accepted the writ petitions and held that the order of the President was ultra vires. It was held that the President has no competence to exercise the executive power in violation of the mandates, given by the Constitution, and hence a nullity.[8]

Consequently, the Constitution (26th Amendment) Act, 1971, was passed, which altogether omitted Articles 291 and 362. As a result, the privy purses and the personal rights, privileges and dignities of the Indian rulers were abolished. The 26th Amendment has been upheld by the Court in Raghunatha Rao vs. Union of India.[9]

364. Special Provisions as to major ports and aerodromes: (1) Notwithstanding anything in this Constitution, the President may by public notification direct that as from such date as may be specified in the notification—

(a) any law made by the Parliament or by the Legislature of a State shall not apply to any major port or aerodrome or shall apply thereto subject to such exceptions or modifications as may be specified in the notification, or

(b) any existing law shall cease to have effect in any major port or aerodrome except as respects things done or omitted to be done before the said date, or shall in its application to such port or aerodrome have effect subject to such exceptions or modifications as may be specified in the notification.

(2) In this Article—

(a) "Major port" means a port declared to be a major port by or under any law made by the Parliament or any existing law and includes all areas for the time being included within the limits of such port;

(b) "Aerodrome" means aerodrome as defined for the purposes of the enactments relating to airways, aircraft and air navigation.

(Part XIX, Article 364)

COMMENTS

Article 364 provides that the President may by notification exclude major ports and aerodromes from the application of any law. Such provisions are aimed to give push to economic development near the ports and aerodromes and also to give fillip to economic development around major ports and aerodromes.

365. Effect of failure to comply with, or to give effect to, directions given by the Union: Where any State has failed to comply with, or to give effect to, any directions given in the exercise of the executive power of the Union under any of the provisions of this Constitution, it shall be lawful for the President to hold that a situation has arisen in which the Government of the State cannot be carried on in accordance with the provisions of this Constitution.

(Part XIX, Article 365)

COMMENTS

According to Article 365, failure to comply with the directions of the Union may be enough justification for the President to hold that the Government of the State cannot be carried on in accordance with the Constitution, thereby inviting imposition of President's rule in the State. The Union will have to prove that such directions were given and these were not complied with. For example, Union has time and again asked all State governments to set up three-tier Panchayat system as per Part IX and setting up Committee for District Planning under Part IX A (Article 243 ZD) but some of State governments have not complied with this Constitutional mandate. In these cases, President's rule can be imposed in those States read with Article 356.

366. Definitions: In this Constitution, unless the context otherwise requires, the following expressions have the meanings hereby respectively assigned to them, that is to say—

(1) "Agricultural income" means agricultural income as defined for the purposes of the enactments relating to Indian income-tax;

(2) "An Anglo-Indian" means a person whose father or any of whose other male progenitors in the male line is or was of European descent but who is domiciled within the Territory of India and is or was born within such Territory of parents habitually resident therein and not established there for temporary purposes only;

(3) "Article" means an Article of this Constitution; (4) "Borrow" includes the raising of money by the grant of annuities, and "loan" shall be construed accordingly;

(5) "Clause" means a clause of the Article in which the expression occurs;

(6) "Corporation tax" means any tax on income, so far as that tax is payable by companies and is a tax in the case of which the following conditions are fulfilled—

(a) that it is not chargeable in respect of agricultural income;

(b) that no deduction in respect of the tax paid by companies is, by any enactments which may apply to the tax, authorised to be made from dividends payable by the companies to individuals;

(c) that no provision exists for taking the tax so paid into account in computing for the purposes of Indian income-tax the total income of individuals receiving such dividends, or in computing the Indian income-tax payable by, or refundable to, such individuals;

(7) "Corresponding Province", "corresponding Indian State" or "corresponding State" means in cases of doubt such Province, Indian State or State as may be determined by the President to be the corresponding Province, the corresponding

Indian State or the corresponding State, as the case may be, for the particular purpose in question;

(8) "Debt" includes any liability in respect of any obligation to repay capital sums by way of annuities and any liability under any guarantee, and "debt charges" shall be construed accordingly;

(9) "Estate duty" means a duty to be assessed on or by reference to the principal value, ascertained in accordance with such rules as may be prescribed by or under laws made by the Parliament or the Legislature of a State relating to the duty, of all property passing upon death or deemed, under the provisions of the said laws, so to pass;

(10) "Existing law" means any law, Ordinance, order, bye-law, rule or regulation passed or made before the commencement of this Constitution by any Legislature, authority or person having power to make such a law, Ordinance, order, bye-law, rule or regulation;

(11) "Federal Court" means the Federal Court constituted under the Government of India Act, 1935;

(12) "Goods" includes all materials, commodities, and Articles;

(13) "Guarantee" includes any obligation undertaken before the commencement of this Constitution to make payments in the event of the profits of an undertaking falling short of a specified amount;

(14) "High Court" means any Court which is deemed for the purposes of this Constitution to be a High Court for any State and includes—(a) any Court in the Territory of India constituted or reconstituted under this Constitution as a High Court, and (b) any other Court in the Territory of India which may be declared by the Parliament by law to be a High Court for all or any of the purposes of this Constitution;

(15) "Indian State" means any Territory which the Government of the Dominion of India recognised as such a State;

(16) "Part" means a Part of this Constitution;

(17) "Pension" means a pension, whether contributory or not, of any kind whatsoever payable to or in respect of any

person, and includes retired pay so payable; a gratuity so payable and any sum or sums so payable by way of the return, with or without interest thereon or any other addition thereto, of subscriptions to a provident fund;

(18) "Proclamation of Emergency" means a Proclamation issued under clause (1) of Article 352;

(19) "Public notification" means a notification in the Gazette of India, or, as the case may be, the Official Gazette of a State;

(20) "Railway" does not include—

(a) a tramway wholly within a municipal area, or

(b) any other line of communication wholly situated in one State and declared by the Parliament by law not to be a railway;

(22) "Ruler" means the Prince, Chief or other person who, at any time before the commencement of the Constitution (Twenty-sixth Amendment) Act, 1971, was recognised by the President as the Ruler of an Indian State or any person who, at any time before such commencement, was recognised by the President as the successor of such Ruler;

(23) "Schedule" means a Schedule to this Constitution;

(24) "Scheduled Castes" mean such castes, races or tribes or parts of or groups within such castes, races or tribes as are deemed under Article 341 to be Scheduled Castes for the purposes of this Constitution;

(25) "Scheduled Tribes" means such tribes or tribal communities or parts of or groups within such tribes or tribal communities as are deemed under Article 342 to be Scheduled Tribes for the purposes of this Constitution;

(26) "Securities" includes stock;

(27) "Sub-clause" means a sub-clause of the clause in which the expression occurs;

(28) "Taxation" includes the imposition of any tax or impost, whether general or local or special, and "tax" shall be construed accordingly;

(29) "Tax on income" includes a tax in the nature of an excess profits tax;

(29A) "Tax on the sale or purchase of goods" includes—

(a) a tax on the transfer, otherwise than in pursuance of a

contract, of property in any goods for cash, deferred payment or other valuable consideration;

(b) a tax on the transfer of property in goods (whether as goods or in some other form) involved in the execution of a works contract;

(c) a tax on the delivery of goods on hire-purchase or any system of payment by instalments;

(d) a tax on the transfer of the right to use any goods for any purpose (whether or not for a specified period) for cash, deferred payment or other valuable consideration;

(e) a tax on the supply of goods by any unincorporated association or body of persons to a member thereof for cash, deferred payment or other valuable consideration;

(f) A tax on the supply, by way of or as part of any service or in any other manner whatsoever, of goods, being food or any other Article for human consumption or any drink (whether or not intoxicating), where such supply or service, is for cash, deferred payment or other valuable consideration, and such transfer, delivery or supply of any goods shall be deemed to be a sale of those goods by the person making the transfer, delivery or supply and a purchase of those goods by the person to whom such transfer, delivery or supply is made.

(30) "Union Territory" means any Union Territory specified in the First Schedule and includes any other Territory comprised within the Territory of India but not specified in that Schedule.

(Part XIX, Article 366)

COMMENTS

Article 366 lays down some definitions. The definitions mentioned herein are applicable only for the purpose of interpreting the Constitution.

Secondly, there will be volume of legislations by the Union and States. For the sake of uniformity in meaning and interpretation of laws, these definitions are guiding factors in law-making in India after independence in 1947 and promulgation of the Constitution of India on 26th January, 1950.

If any word is not defined in the Constitution but it appears in three or any of the legislative lists as per the well recognised canons of construction, the word used in the three legislative lists should receive the widest interpretation.[10]

367. Interpretation: (1) Unless the context otherwise requires, the General Clauses Act, 1897, shall, subject to any adaptations and modifications that may be made therein under Article 372, apply for the interpretation of this Constitution as it applies for the interpretation of an Act of the Legislature of the Dominion of India.

(2) Any reference in this Constitution to Acts or laws of, or made by, the Parliament, or to Acts or laws of, or made by, the Legislature of a State, shall be construed as including a reference to an Ordinance made by the President or, to an Ordinance made by a Governor, as the case may be.

(3) For the purposes of this Constitution, "foreign state" means any State other than India:

Provided that, subject to the provisions of any law made by the Parliament, the President may by order declare any State not to be a foreign state for such purposes as may be specified in the order.

(Part XIX, Article 367)

COMMENTS

The rules made in the exercise of the power after the Constitution cannot be claimed to be "existing law." However, existing law does not include personal laws such as Hindu or Mohammedan laws. The important words are 'passed or made'. Personal laws have not been passed or made by any competent legislative authority where there is no provision of Legislature like in Andaman & Nicobar Islands, the Parliament has plenary powers to make laws for the Union Territories on all matters."[11]

Article 367 is the interpretation clause and says that generally the General Clauses Act shall apply to the interpretation of the provisions of the Constitution, reference to Acts or laws shall cover Ordinances, issued by the President or the Governor of the State concerned General guidelines on constitutional interpretation are enumerated below. This will be a help to interpret any Article, clause, or para or subpara of the Constitution.

Constitutional interpretation, or Constitutional construction, the term more often used by the Founders, is the process by which meanings are assigned to words in a Constitution, to enable legal decisions to be made that are justified by it. Some scholars distinguish between "interpretation"—assigning meanings based on the meanings in other usages of the terms by those the writers and their readers had probably read, and "construction"—inferring the meaning from a broader set of evidence, such as the structure of the complete document from which one can discern the function of various parts. Discussion by the drafters or ratifiers during debate leading to adoption ("legislative history"), the background of controversies in which the terms were used that indicate the concerns and expectations of the drafters and ratifiers, alternative wordings and their meanings accepted or rejected at different points in development, and indications of meanings that can be inferred from what is not said, among other methods of analysis.[12]

A Constitution differs fundamentally in its nature from ordinary legislation passed by the Parliament. Canons of construction applicable to ordinary statutes should not be applied rigidly to Constitutional instruments. The central concern should be with purposes, not meanings.[13]

No word or phrase including punctuation of the Constitution may be excluded while considering its effect. The principle of reading down may not be applied to give narrow meaning to the constitutional provisions which gives certain benefits to public individually or collectively. Liberal construction may be given within its ambit keeping in view future development in various fields of human activity.[14]

The Constitution is a living and organic thing and construed broadly and liberally.[15] While interpreting Article 39(d), importance must be given to two words, i.e. "equal pay" and "equal work". It means right is flowing from Article 39(d) relates to work done by employees and categorization may be done on the basis of equality of work and not the post. It means it is enough in case different category (source) of employees are posted together on same post and performing the same job/ work, then they seem to be entitled for the same pay band.

In GVK Industries vs. Union of India[16], before the Constitution bench of the Supreme Court, the issue was whether the Parliament's powers to legislate, pursuant to Article 245, include legislative competence with respect to aspects or causes that occur, arise or exist or may be expected to do so, outside the Territory of India.

Arguing for the Union of India, Attorney General made a submission that the Parliament has inherent powers to legislate "for" any Territory, including Territories beyond India, and that no court in India may question or invalidate such laws on the ground that they are extraterritorial laws. The argument was negatived by the court in these words—

"Is the Parliament empowered to enact laws in respect of extra-territorial aspects or causes that have no nexus with India, and furthermore could such laws be bereft of any benefit to India? The answer would have to be 'no.'

While interpreting Article 245(1), the Court held as under—

"The grant of the power to legislate, to the Parliament, in Clause (1) of Article 245 comes with a limitation that arises out of the very purpose for which it has been constituted. That purpose is to continuously, and forever be acting in the interests of the people of India...The Parliament may not enact laws with respect to extra-territorial aspects or causes, wherein such aspects or causes have no nexus whatsoever with India."

In Kesavananda Bharti Case[17] in the words of Justice Khanna: The word "amendment" postulates that the old Constitution survives without loss of its identity despite the change and continues even though it has been subjected to alterations. As a result of the amendment, the old Constitution cannot be destroyed and done away with; it is retained though in the amended form.

The nature and scope of Presidential assent under Article 254(2) of the Constitution was considered by the Constitution in Kaiser-I-Hind Pvt. Ltd. vs. National Textile Corporation (Maharashtra North) Ltd.[18] Speaking for the majority of the Court, Shah, J. observed:

"In view of the aforesaid requirements, before obtaining the assent of the President, the State Government has to point out that the law made by the State Legislature is in respect of one of the matters enumerated in the Concurrent List by mentioning entry/entries of the Concurrent List and that it contains provision or provisions repugnant to the law made by the Parliament or existing law. Further, the words "reserved for consideration" would definitely indicate that there should be active application of mind by the President to the repugnancy pointed out between the proposed State law and the earlier law made by the Parliament and the necessity of having such a law, in the facts and circumstances of the matter, which is repugnant to a law enacted by the Parliament prevailing in a State. The word "consideration" would manifest that after careful thinking over and due application of mind regarding the necessity of having State law which is repugnant to the law made by the Parliament, the President may grant assent. This aspect is further reaffirmed by use of the word "assent" in clause (2), which implies knowledge of the President to the repugnancy between the State law and the earlier law made by the Parliament on the same subject-matter and the reasons for grant of such assent. The word "assent" would mean in the context as an expressed agreement of mind to what is proposed by the State." (emphasis supplied)

Shah, J. then referred to various meanings of the word "assent" and observed:

"Applying the aforesaid meaning of the word "assent" and from the phraseology used in clause (2), the object of Article 254(2) appears that even though the law made by the Parliament would have supremacy, after considering the situation prevailing in the State and after considering the repugnancy between the State legislation and the earlier law made by the Parliament, the President may give his assent to the law made by the State Legislature. This would require application of mind to both the laws and the repugnancy as well as the peculiar requirement of the State to have such a law, which is repugnant to the law made by the Parliament. The word "assent" is used purposefully indicating affirmative action of the proposal made by the State for having law repugnant to the earlier law made by the Parliament. It would amount to accepting or conceding and concurring to the demand made by the State for such law. This cannot be done without consideration of relevant material. Hence, the phrase used is "reserved for consideration", which under the Constitution cannot be an idle formality but would require serious consideration on the material placed before the President. The "consideration" could only be to the proposal made by the State. It is true that the President's assent as notified in the Act nowhere mentions that assent was obtained qua repugnancy between the State legislation and specified certain law or laws of the Parliament. But from this, it also cannot be inferred that as the President has given assent, all earlier law/laws on the subject would not prevail in the State. As discussed above before grant of the assent, consideration of the reasons for having such law is necessary and the consideration would mean consideration of the proposal made by the State for the law enacted despite it being repugnant to the earlier law made by the Parliament on the same subject. If the proposal made by the State is limited qua repugnancy of the State law and law or laws specified in the said proposal, then it cannot be said that the assent was granted qua repugnancy between the State law and other laws for which no assent was sought for. Take for illustration—that a particular provision, namely, Section 3 of the State law is repugnant to enactment A made by the Parliament; other provision, namely Section 4 is repugnant to some provisions of enactment B made by the Parliament and Sections 5 and 6 are repugnant to some provisions of enactment C and the State submits proposal seeking "assent" mentioning repugnancy between the State law and provisions of enactments A and B without mentioning anything with regard to enactment C. In this set of circumstances, if the assent of the President is obtained, the State law with regard to enactments A and B would prevail but with regard to C, there is no proposal and hence, there is no "consideration" or "assent". Proposal by the State pointing out repugnancy between the State law and of the law enacted by the Parliament is a sine qua non for "consideration" and "assent". If there is no proposal, no question of "consideration" or "assent" arises. For finding out whether "assent" given by the President is restricted or unrestricted, the letter written or the proposal made by the State Government for obtaining "assent" is required to be looked into."

In his concurring judgement, Doraiswamy Raju, J. made the following observations:

"The assent of the President envisaged under Article 254(2) is neither an idle or empty formality, nor an automatic event, necessitated or to be given for the mere asking, in whatever form or manner and whether specific, vague, general or indefinite—in the terms sought. In a federal structure, peculiar to the one adopted by our Constitution, it would become necessary for the President to be apprised of the reason as to why and for what special reason or object and purpose, predominance for the State law over the Central law is sought, deviating from the law in force made by the Parliament for the entire country, including that part of the State." (emphasis supplied)

REFERENCES

1. Vijay Pratap vs. Ajit Prasad, AIR 1966, All 305.
2. Common Cause vs. Union of India, (1999) 6 SCC 667.
3. SC Bharat vs. Hari Vinayak Pataskar AIR 1062 M.P. 73.
4. Rameswar Prasad (6) vs. Union of India (2006) 2 SCC 1.
5. KSV Rajendra Singh vs. Union of India (1969) 3 SCC 150.
6. Union of India vs. Prince Muffakam Jah, AIR 1995 SC 227.
7. Karan Singh vs. State of J & K (2004) 5 SCC 698.
8. Madhav Rao Jivaji Rao Scindia vs. Union of India (1971) 1 SCC 85.
9. AIR 1993 SC 1267.
10. Association of Leasing and Financial Companies vs. Union of India (2011) 2 SCC 352 (370).
11. T.M. Kanniyan vs. I.T.O., AIR 1968 SC 637.
12. The Yale Journal of International Law Vol. 34: 207.
13. Cement Ltd. vs. Union of India (1990) 1 SCC 12(seven judges).
14. Union of India vs. Navin Jindal and another. 2004 (2) SCC 510.
15. Goodyear India Ltd vs. State of Haryana (vide AIR 1990 (SC) 781.
16. GVK Industries vs. Union of India 2011 (4) SCC 36.
17. Kesavananda Bharti vs. Union of India.
18. Kaiser-I-Hind Pvt. Ltd. vs. National Textile Corporation (Maharashtra North) Ltd.(2002)8 SCC 182.

□

Chapter 22
TEMPORARY, TRANSITIONAL AND SPECIAL PROVISIONS

369. Temporary power to the Parliament to make laws with respect to certain matters in the State List as if they were matters in the Concurrent List: Notwithstanding anything in this Constitution, the Parliament shall, during a period of five years from the commencement of this Constitution, have power to make laws with respect to the following matters as if they were enumerated in the Concurrent List, namely:

(a) trade and commerce within a State in, and the production, supply and distribution of, cotton and woollen textiles, raw cotton (including ginned cotton and unginned cotton or kapas), cotton seed, paper (including newsprint), food-stuffs (including edible oilseeds and oil), cattle fodder (including oil-cakes and other concentrates), coal (including coke and derivatives of coal), iron, steel and mica;

(b) offences against laws with respect to any of the matters mentioned in clause (a), jurisdiction and powers of all courts except the Supreme Court with respect to any of those matters, and fees in respect of any of those matters but not including fees taken in any court; but any law made by the Parliament, which the Parliament would not but for the provisions of this Article have been competent to make, shall, to the extent of the incompetency, cease to have effect on the expiration of the said period, except as respects things done or omitted to be done before the expiration thereof.

(Part XXI, Article 369)

371. Special provision with respect to the States of Maharashtra and Gujarat: (2) Notwithstanding anything in this Constitution, the President may by order made with respect to the State of Maharashtra or Gujarat, provide for any special responsibility of the Governor for—

(a) the establishment of separate development boards for Vidarbha, Marathwada, and the rest of Maharashtra or, as the case may be, Saurashtra, Kutch and the rest of Gujarat with the provision that a report on the working of each of these boards will be placed each year before the State Legislative Assembly;

(b) the equitable allocation of funds for developmental expenditures over the said areas, subject to the requirements of the State as a whole; and

(c) an equitable arrangement providing adequate facilities for technical education and vocational training, and adequate opportunities for employment in services under the control of the State Government, in respect of all the said areas, subject to the requirements of the State as a whole.

(Part XXI, Article 371)

COMMENTS

The spirit of the special provision is to constitute separate development boards for Vidarbha, Marathwada and Saurashtra in Maharashtra and Kutch in Gujarat for equitable allocation of funds and adequate facilities for technical and vocational training and adequate opportunities for employment in services.

If such a development board could reduce the number of suicides by farmers in 'Vidarbha in Maharashtra', it can be hailed as special achievement itself.

371A. Special provisions with respect to the State of Nagaland: (1) Notwithstanding anything in this Constitution—

(a) no Act of the Parliament in respect of—

(i) religious or social practices of the Nagas,

(ii) Naga customary law and procedure,

(iii) administration of civil and criminal justice involving decisions according to Naga customary law,

(iv) ownership and transfer of land and its resources,

shall apply to the State of Nagaland unless the Legislative Assembly of Nagaland by a resolution so decides;

(b) the Governor of Nagaland shall have special responsibility with respect to law and order in the State of Nagaland for so long as in his opinion internal disturbances occurring in the Naga Hills-Tuensang Area immediately before the formation of that State continue therein or in any part thereof and in the discharge of his functions in relation thereto the Governor shall, after consulting the Council of Ministers, exercise his individual judgement as to the action to be taken:

Provided that if any question arises whether any matter is or is not a matter as respects which the Governor is under this sub-clause required to act in the exercise of his individual judgement, the decision of the Governor in his discretion shall be final, and the validity of anything done by the Governor shall not be called in question on the ground that he ought or ought not to have acted in the exercise of his individual judgement:

Provided further that if the President on receipt of a report from the Governor or otherwise is satisfied that it is no longer necessary for the Governor to have special responsibility with respect to law and order in the State of Nagaland, he may by order direct that the Governor shall cease to have such responsibility with effect from such date as may be specified in the order;

(c) in making his recommendation with respect to any demand for a grant, the Governor of Nagaland shall ensure that any money provided by the Government of India out of the Consolidated Fund of India for any specific service or purpose is included in the demand for a grant relating to that service or purpose and not in any other demand;

(d) as from such date as the Governor of Nagaland may by public notification in this behalf specify, there shall be established a regional council for the Tuensang district consisting of thirty-five members and the Governor shall in his discretion make rules providing for—

(i) the composition of the regional council and the manner in which the members of the regional council shall be chosen:

Provided that the Deputy Commissioner of the Tuensang district shall be the Chairman ex officio of the regional council and the Vice-Chairman of the regional council shall be elected by the members thereof from amongst themselves;

(ii) the qualifications for being chosen as, and for being, members of the regional council;

(iii) the term of office of, and the salaries and allowances, if any, to be paid to members of the regional council;

(iv) the procedure and conduct of business of the regional council;

(v) the appointment of officers and staff of the regional council and their conditions of services; and

(vi) any other matter in respect of which it is necessary to make rules for the constitution and proper functioning of the regional council.

(2) Notwithstanding anything in this Constitution, for a period of ten years from the date of the formation of the State of Nagaland or for such further period as the Governor may, on the recommendation of the regional council, by public notification specify in this behalf—

(a) the administration of the Tuensang district shall be carried on by the Governor;

(b) where any money is provided by the Government of India to the Government of Nagaland to meet the requirements of the State of Nagaland as a whole, the Governor shall in his discretion arrange for an equitable allocation of that money between the Tuensang district and the rest of the State;

(c) no Act of the Legislature of Nagaland shall apply to Tuensang district unless the Governor, on the recommendation of the regional council, by public notification so directs and the Governor in giving such direction with respect to any such Act may direct that the Act shall in its application to the Tuensang district or any part thereof have effect subject to such exceptions or modifications as the Governor may specify on the recommendation of the regional council:

Provided that any direction given under this sub-clause may be given so as to have retrospective effect;

(d) the Governor may make regulations for the peace, progress and good Governance of the Tuensang district and any regulations so made may repeal or amend with retrospective effect, if necessary, any Act of the Parliament or any other law which is for the time being applicable to that district;

(e) (i) one of the members representing the Tuensang district in the Legislative Assembly of Nagaland shall be appointed Minister for Tuensang affairs by the Governor on the advice of the Chief Minister and the Chief Minister in tendering his advice shall act on the recommendation of the majority of the members as aforesaid; the Minister for Tuensang affairs shall deal with, and have direct access to the Governor on, all matters relating to the Tuensang district but he shall keep the Chief Minister informed about the same;

(f) notwithstanding anything in the foregoing provisions of this clause, the final decision on all matters relating to the Tuensang district shall be made by the Governor in his discretion;

(g) in Articles 54 and 55 and clause (4) of Article 80, references to the elected members of the Legislative Assembly of a State or to each such member shall include references to the members or member of the Legislative Assembly of Nagaland elected by the regional council established under this Article;

(h) in Article 170—

(i) clause (1) shall, in relation to the Legislative Assembly of Nagaland, have effect as if for the word "sixty", the word "forty-six" had been substituted;

(ii) in the said clause, the reference to direct election from territorial constituencies in the State shall include election by the members of the regional council established under this Article;

(iii) in clauses (2) and (3), references to territorial constituencies shall mean references to territorial constituencies in the Kohima and Mokokchung districts.

(3) If any difficulty arises in giving effect to any of the foregoing provisions of this Article, the President may by order do anything (including any adaptation or modification of any other Article) which appears to him to be necessary for the purpose of removing that difficulty:

Provided that no such order shall be made after the expiration of three years from the date of the formation of the State of Nagaland.

Explanation—In this Article, the Kohima, Mokokchung and Tuensang districts shall have the same meanings as in the State of Nagaland Act, 1962.

(Part XXI, Article 371-A)

COMMENTS

Special provisions are there to satisfy the regional, tribal or other local needs and sentiments and to protect the interests of local people especially in Tuensang district by establishing an autonomous regional Council for the Tuensang district. Acts of the Parliament, affecting religious or social practices, customary laws, ownership of land, etc. shall not apply to Nagaland, and the Governor of Nagaland shall have certain special responsibilities. The Limitation Act, 1963 does not involve customary law. Hence, it can apply to Nagaland.[1]

371B. Special provision with respect to the State of Assam: Not withstanding anything in this Constitution, the President may, by order made with respect to the State of Assam, provide for the constitution and functions of a committee of the

Legislative Assembly of the State consisting of members of that Assembly elected from the tribal areas specified in Part I of the table appended to paragraph 20 of the Sixth Schedule and such number of other members of that Assembly as may be specified in the order and for the modifications to be made in the rules of procedure of that Assembly for the constitution and proper functioning of such committee.

(Part XXI, Article 371B)

COMMENTS

The special provision is to take proper care of regional or tribal issues in the State.

371C. Special Provision with respect to the State of Manipur: (1) Notwithstanding anything in this Constitution, the President may, by order made with respect to the State of Manipur, provide for the constitution and functions of a committee of the Legislative Assembly of the State consisting of members of that Assembly elected from the Hilly Areas of that State, for the modifications to be made in the rules of business of the Government and in the rules of procedure of the Legislative Assembly of the State and for any special responsibility of the Governor in order to secure the proper functioning of such committee.

(2) The Governor shall annually, or whenever so required by the President, make a report to the President regarding the administration of the Hilly Areas in the State of Manipur and the executive power of the Union shall extend to the giving of directions to the State as to the administration of the said areas.

Explanation: In this Article, the expression "Hilly Areas" means such areas as the President may, by order, declare to be Hilly areas.

(Part XIX, Article 371C)

COMMENTS

Manipur is an extremists' affected State. Therefore, these special provisions require to be implemented with due sincerity and promptness specially with regard to Hilly Areas of the State of Manipur.

371D. Special provisions with respect to the State of Andhra Pradesh: (1) The President may by order made with respect to the State of Andhra Pradesh provide, having regard to the requirements of the State as a whole, for equitable opportunities and facilities for the people belonging to different parts of the State, in the matter of public employment and in the matter of education, and different provisions may be made for various parts of the State.

(2) An order made under clause (1) may, in particular—

(a) require the State Government to organise any class or classes of posts in a civil service of, or any class or classes of civil posts under, the State into different local cadres for different parts of the State and allot in accordance with such principles and procedure as may be specified in the order the persons holding such posts to the local cadres so organised;

(b) specify any part or parts of the State which shall be regarded as the local area—

(i) for direct recruitment to posts in any local cadre (whether organised in pursuance of an order under this Article or constituted otherwise) under the State Government;

(ii) for direct recruitment to posts in any cadre under any local authority within the State; and

(iii) for the purposes of admission to any University within the State or to any other educational institution which is subject to the control of the State Government;

(c) specify the extent to which, the manner in which and the conditions subject to which, preference or reservation shall be given or made—

(i) in the matter of direct recruitment to posts in any such cadre referred to in sub-clause (b) as may be specified in this behalf in the order;

(ii) in the matter of admission to any such University or other educational institution referred to in sub-clause (b) as may be specified in this behalf in the order, to or in favour of candidates who have resided or studied for any period specified in the order in the local area in respect of such cadre, University or other educational institution, as the case may be.

(3) The President may, by order, provide for the constitution of an Administrative Tribunal for the State of Andhra Pradesh to exercise such jurisdiction, powers and authority including any jurisdiction, power and authority which immediately before the commencement of the Constitution (Thirty-second Amendment) Act, 1973, was exercisable by any court (other than the Supreme Court) or by any tribunal or other authority as may be specified in the order with respect to the following matters, namely:

(a) appointment, allotment or promotion to such class or classes of posts in any civil service of the State, or to such class or classes of civil posts under the State, or to such class or classes of posts under the control of any local authority within the State, as may be specified in the order;

(b) seniority of persons appointed, allotted or promoted to such class or classes of posts in any civil service of the State, or to such class or classes of civil posts under the State, or to such class or classes of posts under the control of any local authority within the State, as may be specified in the order;

(c) such other conditions of service of persons appointed, allotted or promoted to such class or classes of posts in any civil service of the State or to such class or classes of civil posts under the State or to such class or classes of posts under the control of any local authority within the State, as may be specified in the order.

(4) An order made under clause (3) may—

(a) authorise the Administrative Tribunal to receive representations for the redress of grievances relating to any matter within its jurisdiction as the President may specify in the order and to make such orders thereon as the Administrative Tribunal deems fit;

(b) contain such provisions with respect to the powers and authorities and procedure of the Administrative Tribunal (including provisions with respect to the powers of the Administrative Tribunal to punish for contempt of itself) as the President may deem necessary;

(c) provide for the transfer to the Administrative Tribunal of such classes of proceedings, being proceedings relating to matters within its jurisdiction and pending before any court (other than the Supreme Court) or tribunal or other authority immediately before the commencement of such order, as may be specified in the order;

(d) contain such supplemental, incidental and consequential provisions (including provisions as to fees and as to limitation, evidence or for the application of any law for the time being in force subject to any exceptions or modifications) as the President may deem necessary.

(5) The Order of the Administrative Tribunal finally disposing of any case shall become effective upon its confirmation by the State Government or on the expiry of three months from the date on which the order is made, whichever is earlier:

Provided that the State Government may, by special order made in writing and for reasons to be specified therein, modify or annul any order of the Administrative Tribunal before it becomes effective and in such a case, the order of the Administrative Tribunal shall have effect only in such modified form or be of no effect, as the case may be.

(6) Every special order made by the State Government under the proviso to clause (5) shall be laid, as soon as may be after it is made, before both Houses of the State Legislature.

(7) The High Court for the State shall not have any powers of superintendence over the Administrative Tribunal and no court (other than the Supreme Court) or tribunal shall exercise

any jurisdiction, power or authority in respect of any matter subject to the jurisdiction, power or authority of, or in relation to, the Administrative Tribunal.

(8) If the President is satisfied that the continued existence of the Administrative Tribunal is not necessary, the President may by order abolish the Administrative Tribunal and make such provisions in such order as he may deem fit for the transfer and disposal of cases pending before the Tribunal immediately before such abolition.

(9) Notwithstanding any judgement, decree or order of any court, tribunal or other authority—

(a) no appointment, posting, promotion or transfer of any person—

(i) made before the 1st day of November, 1956, to any post under the Government of, or any local authority within, the State of Hyderabad as it existed before that date; or

(ii) made before the commencement of the Constitution (Thirty-second Amendment) Act, 1973, to any post under the Government of, or any local or other authority within, the State of Andhra Pradesh; and (b) no action taken or thing done by or before any person referred to in sub-clause (a), shall be deemed to be illegal or void or ever to have become illegal or void merely on the ground that the appointment, posting, promotion or transfer of such person was not made in accordance with any law, then in force, providing for any requirement as to residence within the State of Hyderabad or, as the case may be, within any part of the State of Andhra Pradesh, in respect of such appointment, posting, promotion or transfer.

(10) The provisions of this Article and of any order made by the President thereunder shall have effect notwithstanding anything in any other provision of this Constitution or in any other law for the time being in force.

(Part XXI, Article 371-D)

COMMENTS

Article 371D does not militate against the basic structure of the Constitution.[2] However, clause (5) along with the proviso of Article 371D was struck down by the Supreme Court as the clause was against the concept of justice and the principle of rule of law because it conferred powers on the Government to override the decision of the Administrative Tribunal.[3] Once the President makes an order under Articles 371(D)(1) and (2), the State Government loses its inherent power to deal with matters relating to services.[4]

371E. Establishment of Central University in Andhra Pradesh: The Parliament may by law provide for the establishment of a University in the State of Andhra Pradesh.

(Part XXI, Article 371)

371F. Special provisions with respect to the State of Sikkim: Notwithstanding anything in this Constitution—

(a) the Legislative Assembly of the State of Sikkim shall consist of not less than thirty members;

(b) as from the date of commencement of the Constitution (Thirty-sixth Amendment) Act, 1975 (hereafter in this Article referred to as the appointed day)—

(i) the Assembly for Sikkim formed as a result of the elections held in Sikkim in April, 1974 with thirty-two members elected in the said elections (hereinafter referred to as the sitting members) shall be deemed to be the Legislative Assembly of the State of Sikkim duly constituted under this Constitution;

(ii) the sitting members shall be deemed to be the members of the Legislative Assembly of the State of Sikkim duly elected under this Constitution; and

(iii) the said Legislative Assembly of the State of Sikkim shall exercise the powers and perform the functions of the Legislative Assembly of a State under this Constitution;

(c) in the case of the Assembly deemed to be the Legislative Assembly of the State of Sikkim under clause (*b*), the references to the period of five years, in clause (1) of Article 172 shall be construed as references to a period of four years and the said period of four years shall be deemed to commence from the appointed day;

(d) until other provisions are made by the Parliament by law, there shall be allotted to the State of Sikkim one seat in the House of the People and the State of Sikkim shall form one Parliamentary constituency to be called the Parliamentary constituency for Sikkim;

(e) the representative of the State of Sikkim in the House of the People in existence on the appointed day shall be elected by the members of the Legislative Assembly of the State of Sikkim;

(f) The Parliament may, for the purpose of protecting the rights and interests of the different sections of the population of Sikkim make provision for the number of seats in the Legislative Assembly of the State of Sikkim which may be filled by candidates belonging to such sections and for the delimitation of the assembly constituencies from which candidates belonging to such sections alone may stand for election to the Legislative Assembly of the State of Sikkim;

(g) the Governor of Sikkim shall have special responsibility for peace and for an equitable arrangement for ensuring the social and economic advancement of different sections of the population of Sikkim and in the discharge of his special responsibility under this clause, the Governor of Sikkim shall, subject to such directions as the President may, from time to time, deem fit to issue, act in his discretion;

(h) all property and assets (whether within or outside the Territories comprised in the State of Sikkim) which immediately before the appointed day were vested in the Government of Sikkim or in any other authority or in any person for the purposes of the Government of Sikkim shall, as from the appointed day, vest in the Government of the State of Sikkim;

(i) the High Court functioning as such immediately before the appointed day in the Territories comprised in the State of Sikkim shall, on and from the appointed day, be deemed to be the High Court for the State of Sikkim;

(j) all courts of civil, criminal and revenue jurisdiction, all authorities and all officers, judicial, executive and ministerial, throughout the Territory of the State of Sikkim shall continue on and from the appointed day to exercise their respective functions subject to the provisions of this Constitution;

(k) all laws in force immediately before the appointed day in the Territories comprised in the State of Sikkim or any part thereof shall continue to be in force therein until amended or repealed by a competent Legislature or other competent authority;

(l) for the purpose of facilitating the application of any such law as is referred to in clause (*k*) in relation to the administration of the State of Sikkim and for the purpose of bringing the provisions of any such law into accord with the provisions of this Constitution, the President may, within two years from the appointed day, by order, make such adaptations and modifications of the law, whether by way of repeal or amendment, as may be necessary or expedient, and thereupon, every such law shall have effect subject to the adaptations and modifications so made, and any such adaptation or modification shall not be questioned in any court of law;

(m) neither the Supreme Court nor any other court shall have jurisdiction in respect of any dispute or other matter arising out of any treaty, agreement, engagement or other similar instrument relating to Sikkim which was entered into or executed before the appointed day and to which the Government of India or any of its predecessor Governments was a party, but nothing in this clause shall be construed to derogate from the provisions of Article 143;

(n) the President may, by public notification, extend with such restrictions or modifications as he thinks fit to the State of Sikkim any enactment which is in force in a State in India at the date of the notification;

(o) if any difficulty arises in giving effect to any of the foregoing provisions of this Article, the President may, by order, do anything (including any adaptation or modification of any other Article) which appears to him to be necessary for the purpose of removing that difficulty:

Provided that no such order shall be made after the expiry of two years from the appointed day;

(p) all things done and all actions taken in or in relation to the State of Sikkim or the Territories comprised therein during the period commencing on the appointed day and ending immediately before the date on which the Constitution (Thirty-sixth Amendment) Act, 1975, receives the assent of the President shall, insofar as they are in conformity with the provisions of this Constitution as amended by the Constitution (Thirty-sixth Amendment) Act, 1975, be deemed for all purposes to have been validly done or taken under this Constitution as so amended.

(Part XXI, Article 371F)

COMMENTS

Sikkim, a small hill State became an integral part of India by the 35th Constitutional Amendment Act, 1974. It became the twenty-second State of India. Article 371-F was inserted to empower the Parliament to pass necessary legislation to ensure that this infant State is well administrated.

Article 2 which enables the Parliament to admit new States into the Union on such terms as it thinks fit, and the non obstante clause in Article 371-F have to be read harmoniously, consistently with the basic structure of the Constitution. Clause (f) cannot go beyond the permissible latitudes under the Constitution. Any law or provision made under it is subject to judicial review.

371G. Special Provision with respect to the State of Mizoram: Notwithstanding anything in this Constitution—

(a) no Act of the Parliament in respect of—

(i) religious or social practices of the Mizos,

(ii) Mizo customary law and procedure,

(iii) administration of civil and criminal justice involving decisions according to Mizo customary law,

(iv) ownership and transfer of land, shall apply to the State of Mizoram unless the Legislative Assembly of the State of Mizoram by a resolution so decides:

Provided that nothing in this clause shall apply to any Central Act in force in the Union Territory of Mizoram immediately before the commencement of the Constitution (Fifty-third Amendment) Act, 1986;

(b) the Legislative Assembly of the State of Mizoram shall consist of not less than forty members.

(Part XXI, Article 371G)

371H. Special provision with respect to the State of Arunachal Pradesh: Notwithstanding anything in this Constitution:

(a) the Governor of Arunachal Pradesh shall have special responsibility with respect to law and order in the State of Arunachal Pradesh and in the discharge of his functions in relation thereto, the Governor shall, after consulting the Council of Ministers, exercise his individual judgement as to the action to be taken:

Provided that if any question arises whether any matter is or is not a matter as respects which the Governor is under this clause required to act in the exercise of his individual judgement, the decision of the Governor in his discretion shall be final, and the validity of anything done by the Governor shall not be called in question on the ground that he ought or ought not to have acted in the exercise of his individual judgement:

Provided further that if the President on receipt of a report from the Governor or otherwise is satisfied that it is no longer necessary for the Governor to have special responsibility with respect to law and order in the State of Arunachal Pradesh, he may by order direct that the Governor shall cease to have such responsibility with effect from such date as may be specified in the order;

(b) the Legislative Assembly of the State of Arunachal Pradesh shall consist of not less than thirty members.

(Part XXI, Articles 371H)

COMMENTS

This was inserted by the Constitution (55th Amendment) Act, 1986.

371I: Special Provisions with respect to the State of Goa: Notwithstanding anything in this Constitution, the Legislative Assembly of the State of Goa shall consist of not less than thirty members.

(Part XXI, Article 371I)

COMMENTS

Parliament passed the Goa, Daman and Diu Administration Act, 1987. Goa has become the 25th State in the Union of India.

The Act provides for formation of the State of Goa as 25th State in the Union of India and for formation of a new Union Territory of Daman and Diu and all other matters connected therewith. The High Court of Bombay will have jurisdiction over the State of Goa and the Union Territory of Daman and Diu also.

371J. Special provisions with respect to State of Karnataka: (1) The President may, by order made with respect to the State of Karnataka provide for any special responsibility of the Governor for—

(a) establishment of a separate development board for Hyderabad-Karnataka region with the provision that a report on the working of the board will be placed each year before the State Legislative Assembly;

(b) equitable allocation of funds for developmental expenditures over the said region, subject to the requirements of the State as a whole; and

(c) equitable opportunities and facilities for the people belonging to the said region, in matters of public employment, education and vocational training, subject to the requirements of the State as a whole.

(2) An order made under sub-clause (c) of clause (1) may provide for—

(a) reservation of a proportion of seats in educational and vocational training institutions in the Hyderabad-Karnataka region for students who belong to that region by birth or by domicile; and

(b) identification of posts or classes of posts under the State Government and in any body or organisation under the control of the State Government in the Hyderabad-Karnataka region and reservation of a proportion of such posts for persons who belong to that region by birth or by domicile and for appointment thereto by direct recruitment or by promotion or in any other manner as may be specified in the order.

(Part XXI, Article 371J)

COMMENTS

It was inserted by the Constitution (98th Amendment Act, 2012). It provides for establishment of a separate development board for Hyderabad-Karnataka region and special responsibility to the Governor for the region.

372. Continuance in force of Existing laws and their adaptation: (1) Notwithstanding the repeal by this Constitution of the enactments referred to in Article 395 but subject to the other provisions of this Constitution, all the law in force in the Territory of India immediately before the commencement of this Constitution shall continue in force therein until altered or repealed or amended by a competent Legislature or other competent authority.

(2) For the purpose of brining the provisions of any law in force in the Territory of India into accord with the provisions of this Constitution, the President may by order make such adaptations and modifications of such law, whether by way of repeal or amendment, as may be necessary or expedient, and provide that the law shall, as from such date as may be specified in the order, have effect subject to the adaptations and modifications so made, and any such adaptation or modification shall not be questioned in any court of law.

(3) Nothing in clause (2) shall be deemed—

(a) to empower the President to make any adaptation or modification of any law after the expiration of three years from the commencement of this Constitution; or

(b) to prevent any competent Legislature or other competent authority from repealing or amending any law adapted or modified by the President under the said clause.

Explanation I: The expression "law in force" in this Article shall include a law passed or made by a Legislature or other competent authority in the Territory of India before the commencement of this Constitution and not previously repealed, notwithstanding that it or parts of it may not be then in operation either at all or in particular areas.

Explanation II: Any law passed or made by a Legislature or other competent authority in the Territory of India which immediately before the commencement of this Constitution had extra-territorial effect as well as effect in the Territory of India shall, subject to any such adaptations and modifications as aforesaid, continue to have such extra-territorial effect.

Explanation III: Nothing in this Article shall be construed as continuing any temporary law in force beyond the date fixed for its expiration or the date on which it would have expired if this Constitution had not come into force.

Explanation IV: An Ordinance promulgated by the Governor of a Province under Section 88 of the Government of India Act, 1935, and in force immediately before the commencement of this Constitution shall, unless withdrawn by the Governor of the corresponding State earlier, cease to operate at the expiration of six weeks from the first meeting after such commencement of the Legislative Assembly of that State functioning under clause (1) of Article 382, and nothing in this Article shall be construed as continuing any such Ordinance in force beyond the said period.

(Part XXI, Article 372)

COMMENTS

The Article provides that all laws in force in the Territory of India immediately before the commencement of the Constitution shall continue to be in force until altered, repealed or amended by a competent Legislature. But this shall be "subject to the other provisions of the Constitution" which means that if an existing law is repugnant to any provision of the Constitution, that law shall not be saved. Again where the whole basis for the applicability of an Act has disappeared because India has become a sovereign democratic republic, Article 372 cannot save the law. Similarly, pre-constitutional law cannot violate fundamental rights.[5] An executive order cannot come without the definition of law."[6]

"An order passed by the sovereign Ruler of an erstwhile State granting annual allowances to sons of the Ruler with retrospective effect from the date of their birth till the date of attaining majority is not "Law, but ex-gratia payment in the nature of gift."[7]

This expression includes not only statutory law, but also custom or usage having the force of law and as such, it must be interpreted as including the common law of England, which was adopted as the law of this country before the Constitution came into force.[8]

These laws also include the Hindu and Mohammedan laws, law of torts and the rules of interpretation of statutes.[9]

372A. Power of the President to adapt laws: (1) For the purposes of bringing the provisions of any law in force in India or in any part thereof, immediately before the commencement of the Constitution (Seventh Amendment) Act, 1956, into accord with the provisions of this Constitution as amended by that Act, the President may by order made before the first day of November, 1957, make such adaptations and modifications of the law, whether by way of repeal or amendment, as may be necessary or expedient, and provide that the law shall, as from such date as may be specified in the order, have effect subject to the adaptations and modifications so made, and any such adaptation or modification shall not be questioned in any court of law.

(2) Nothing in clause (1) shall be deemed to prevent a competent Legislature or other competent authority from repealing or amending any law adapted or modified by the President under the said clause.

(Part XXI, Article 372-A)

COMMENTS

The President of India can adapt any law in India by making such adaptations and modifications, whether by way of repeal an amendment. The adaptations and modifications so made shall not be questioned in courts. This was a fresh power analogous to Article 372(2).

'Therefore when the President adopted the General Clauses Act, 1897 by giving a new definition of 'State', the new definition appropriate to the purpose applied to the interpretation of the Constitution. The word 'State' in Entry 80 of the Union List, therefore, applied to Union Territories also.[10]

373. Power of President to make order in respect of persons under preventive detention in certain cases: Until provision is made by the Parliament under clause (7) of Article 22, or until the expiration of one year from the commencement of this Constitution, whichever is earlier, the said Article shall have effect as if for any reference to the Parliament in clauses (4) and (7) thereof there were substituted a reference to the President and for any reference to any law made by the Parliament in those clauses there were substituted a reference to an order made by the President.

(Part XXI, Article 373)

374. Provisions as to Judges of the Federal Court and proceedings pending in the Federal Court or before his Majesty in Council: (1) The Judges of the Federal Court holding office immediately before the commencement of this Constitution shall, unless they have elected otherwise, become on such commencement the Judges of the Supreme Court and shall thereupon be entitled to such salaries and allowances and to such rights in respect of leave of absence and pension as are provided for under Article 125 in respect of the Judges of the Supreme Court.

(2) All suits, appeals and proceedings, civil or criminal, pending in the Federal Court at the commencement of this Constitution shall stand removed to the Supreme Court, and the Supreme Court shall have jurisdiction to hear and

determine the same, and the judgements and orders of the Federal Court delivered or made before the commencement of this Constitution shall have the same force and effect as if they had been delivered or made by the Supreme Court.

(3) Nothing in this Constitution shall operate to invalidate the exercise of jurisdiction by His Majesty in Council to dispose of appeals and petitions from, or in respect of, any judgement, decree or order of any court within the Territory of India insofar as the exercise of such jurisdiction is authorised by law, and any order of His Majesty in Council made on any such appeal or petition after the commencement of this Constitution shall for all purposes have effect as if it were an order or decree made by the Supreme Court in the exercise of the jurisdiction conferred on such Court by this Constitution.

(4) On and from the commencement of this Constitution the jurisdiction of the authority functioning as the Privy Council in a State specified in Part B of the First Schedule to entertain and dispose of appeals and petitions from or in respect of any judgement, decree or order of any court within that State shall cease, and all appeals and other proceedings pending before the said authority at such commencement shall be transferred to, and disposed of by, the Supreme Court.

(5) Further provision may be made by the Parliament by law to give effect to the provisions of this Article.

(Part XXI, Article 374)

375. Courts, authorities and officers to continue to function subject to the provisions of the Constitution: All courts of civil, criminal and revenue jurisdiction, all authorities and all officers, judicial, executive and ministerial, throughout the Territory of India, shall continue to exercise their respective functions subject to the provisions of this Constitution.

(Part XXI, Article 375)

376. Provisions as to Judges of High Courts: (1) Notwithstanding anything in clause (2) of Article 217, the Judges of a High Court in any Province holding office immediately before the commencement of this Constitution shall, unless they have elected otherwise, become on such commencement the Judges of the High Court in the corresponding State, and shall thereupon be entitled to such salaries and allowances and to such rights in respect of leave of absence and pension as are provided for under Article 221 in respect of the Judges of such High Court. 1Any such Judge shall, notwithstanding that he is not a citizen of India, be eligible for appointment as Chief Justice of such High Court, or as Chief Justice or other Judge of any other High Court.

(2) The Judges of a High Court in any Indian State corresponding to any State specified in Part B of the First Schedule holding office immediately before the commencement of this Constitution shall, unless they have elected otherwise, become on such commencement the Judges of the High Court in the State so specified and shall, notwithstanding anything in clauses (1) and (2) of Article 217 but subject to the proviso to clause (1) of that Article, continue to hold office until the expiration of such period as the President may by order determine.

(3) In this Article, the expression "Judge" does not include an acting Judge or an additional Judge.

(Part XXI, Article 376)

COMMENTS

Article 217 lays down that a Judge of a High Court must be a citizens of India.

However, the Judges on transfer to other High Court or promoted as Chief Justice continued until their retirement or otherwise.

377. Provisions as to Comptroller and Auditor-General of India: The Auditor-General of India holding office immediately before the commencement of this Constitution shall, unless he has elected otherwise, become on such commencement the Comptroller and Auditor-General of India and shall thereupon be entitled to such salaries and to such rights in respect of leave of absence and pension as are provided for under clause (3) of Article 148 in respect of the Comptroller and Auditor-

General of India and be entitled to continue to hold office until the expiration of his term of office as determined under the provisions which were applicable to him immediately before such commencement.

(Part XXI, Article 377)

378. Provisions as to Public Service Commissions: (1) The members of the Public Service Commission for the Dominion of India holding office immediately before the commencement of this Constitution shall, unless they have elected otherwise, become on such commencement the members of the Public Service Commission for the Union and shall, notwithstanding anything in clauses (1) and (2) of Article 316 but subject to the proviso to clause (2) of that Article, continue to hold office until the expiration of their term of office as determined under the rules which were applicable immediately before such commencement to such members.

(2) The members of a Public Service Commission of a Province or of a Public Service Commission serving the needs of a group of Provinces holding office immediately before the commencement of this Constitution shall, unless they have elected otherwise, become on such commencement the members of the Public Service Commission for the corresponding State or the members of the Joint State Public Service Commission serving the needs of the corresponding States, as the case may be, and shall, notwithstanding anything in clauses (1) and (2) of Article 316 but subject to the proviso to clause (2) of that Article, continue to hold office until the expiration of their term of office as determined under the rules which were applicable immediately before such commencement to such members.

(Part XXI, Article 378)

378. A. Special provision as to duration of Andhra Pradesh Legislative Assembly: Notwithstanding anything contained in Article 172, the Legislative Assembly of the State of Andhra Pradesh as constituted under the provisions of Sections 28 and 29 of the States Reorganisation Act, 1956, shall, unless sooner dissolved, continue for a period of five years from the date referred to in the said Section 29 and no longer and the expiration of the said period shall operate as a dissolution of that Legislative Assembly.

379.-391. Rep. by the Constitution (Seventh Amendment) Act, 1956, s. 29 and Schedule.

(Part XXI, Articles 379-391)

COMMENTS

These Articles were repealed by the Constitution (7th Amendment) Act, 1956.

392. Power of the President to remove difficulties: (1) The President may, for the purpose of removing any difficulties, particularly in relation to the transition from the provisions of the Government of India Act, 1935, to the provisions of this Constitution, by order direct that this Constitution shall, during such period as may be specified in the order, have effect subject to such adaptations, whether by way of modification, addition or omission, as he may deem to be necessary or expedient:

Provided that no such order shall be made after the first meeting of the Parliament duly constituted under Chapter II of Part V.

(2) Every order made under clause (1) shall be laid before the Parliament.

(3) The powers conferred on the President by this Article, by Article 324, by clause (3) of Article 367 and by Article 391 shall, before the commencement of this Constitution, be exercisable by the Governor-General of the Dominion of India.

(Part XXI, Article 392)

COMMENTS

The power given to the President to adapt the provisions of the Constitution was very wide and he was not required to wait for the provisional the Parliament to exercise the power conferred by that Article.[11]

REFERENCES

1. Temjenkaba vs. Temjenwati, AIR 1992 Gau. 8.

2. Dr. C. Surekha vs. Union of India (1988) 4 SCC 526.
3. P. Sambamurthy vs. State of A.P. (1987) 1 SCC 124.
4. R.C. Pondyal vs. Union of India (1994) Supp. 1 SCC 324.
5. Delhi Air Tech Services (1987) 1 SCC 52; P. Ltd. vs. State of Uttar Pradesh (2011) 9 SCC 354.
6. Union of India vs. Gwalior Rayan Silk Mfg. (Wvg.) Co. Ltd, AIR 1964, SC 1903.
7. Himmat Singh Ji vs. State of Rajasthan (1987) 1 SCC 52.
8. Builders Supply Corpn. vs. Union of India, AIR 1965 SC 1061, 1068.
9. Amine (in re), AIR 1992 Bombay 214.
10. Advance Insurance Co. vs. Gurudasmal (1970) 1 SCC 633.
11. Shankari Prasad vs. Union of India, AIR 1951 SC 458.

□

Chapter 23

SHORT TITLE, COMMENCEMENT, AUTHORITATIVE TEXT IN HINDI AND REPEALS

393. Short Title: This Constitution may be called the Constitution of India.

(Part XXII, Article 393)

COMMENTS

The Constitution of India was unequivocally christened as "The Constitution of India".

394. Commencement: This Article and Articles 5, 6, 7, 8, 9, 60, 324, 366, 367, 379, 380, 388, 391, 392 and 393 shall come into force at once, and the remaining provisions of this Constitution shall come into force on the twenty-sixth day of January, 1950, which day is referred to in this Constitution as the commencement of this Constitution.

(Part XXII, Article 394)

COMMENTS

Article 394 provides for commencement of Article in two parts. The judicial reference of such Article is given in one leading case.[1]

394A. Authoritative text in the Hindi Language: (1) The President shall cause to be published under his authority—

(a) the translation of this Constitution in the Hindi language, signed by the members of the Constituent

Assembly, with such modifications as may be necessary to bring it in conformity with the language, style and terminology adopted in the authoritative texts of Central Acts in the Hindi language, and incorporating therein all the amendments of this Constitution made before such publication; and

(b) the translation in the Hindi language of every amendment of this Constitution made in the English language.

(2) The translation of this Constitution and of every amendment thereof published under clause (1) shall be construed to have the same meaning as the original thereof and if any difficulty arises in so construing any part of such translation, the President shall cause the same to be revised suitably.

(3) The translation of this Constitution and of every amendment thereof published under this Article shall be deemed to be, for all purposes, the authoritative text thereof in the Hindi language.

(Part XXI, Article 394 A)

COMMENTS

It was inserted by 58th Amendment of the Constitution in 1987. There was a Hindi translation of the Constitution signed by the members of the Constituent Assembly which was also published in 1950 under the authority of the President of the Constituent Assembly in accordance with a resolution adopted by the Constituent Assembly.

However, it was felt necessary to publish the Hindi version of the Constituent Assembly in conformity with the languages, style and terminology adopted in the authoritative texts of the Central Acts in Hindi because Hindi, is the Official Language of the country. It was very degrading that the Constitution of India was not available in original or as authoritative text in Hindi which is informally recognised as the National Language of India.

The President has since published the authoritative text of the Constitution of India in Hindi for all purposes and the translation of the Constitution and subsequent amendments in Hindi shall be deemed to be the authoritative text of the Constitution of India.

395. Repeals: The Indian Independence Act, 1947, and the Government of India Act, 1935, together with all enactments amending or supplementing the latter Act, but not including the Abolition of Privy Council Jurisdiction Act, 1949, are hereby repealed.

(Part XXII, Article 395)

COMMENTS

The Indian Independence Act, 1947 and the Government of India Act, 1935 which governed India, have since been repealed by the Constitution of India and have submerged in the glory and authority of the Constitution of India.

REFERENCES

1. S. Raghbir Singh Gill vs. S. Gurucharan Tohra, AIR 1980 SC 1362.

□

Chapter 24
CONSTITUTION OF JAMMU AND KASHMIR

370. Temporary provisions with respect to the State of Jammu and Kashmir: (1) Notwithstanding anything in this Constitution—

(a) the provisions of Article 238 shall not apply in relation to the State of Jammu and Kashmir;

(b) the power of the Parliament to make laws for the said State shall be limited to—

  (i) those matters in the Union List and the Concurrent List which, in consultation with the Government of the State, are declared by the President to correspond to matters specified in the Instrument of Accession governing the accession of the State to the Dominion of India as the matters with respect to which the Dominion Legislature may make laws for that State; and

  (ii) such other matters in the said Lists as, with the concurrence of the Government of the State, the President may by order specify.

Explanation: For the purposes of this Article, the Government of the State means the person for the time being recognised by the President as the Maharaja of Jammu and Kashmir acting on the advice of the Council of Ministers for the time being in office under the Maharaja's Proclamation dated the fifth day of March, 1948;

(c) the provisions of Article 1 and of this Article shall apply in relation to that State;

(d) such of the other provisions of this Constitution shall apply in relation to that State subject to such exceptions and modifications as the President may by order[1] specify:

Provided that no such order which relates to the matters specified in the Instrument of Accession of the State referred to in paragraph (i) of sub-clause (b) shall be issued except in consultation with the Government of the State:

Provided further that no such order which relates to matters other than those referred to in the last preceding proviso shall be issued except with the concurrence of that Government.

(2) If the concurrence of the Government of the State referred to in paragraph (ii) of sub-clause (b) of clause (1) or in the second proviso to sub-clause (d) of that clause be given before the Constituent Assembly for the purpose of framing the Constitution of the State is convened, it shall be placed before such Assembly for such decision as it may take thereon.

(3) Notwithstanding anything in the foregoing provisions of this Article, the President may, by public notification, declare that this Article shall cease to be operative or shall be operative only with such exceptions and modifications and from such date as he may specify:

Provided that the recommendation of the Constituent Assembly of the State referred to in clause (2) shall be necessary before the President issues such a notification.

COMMENTS

Article 370 came into force on 26th January, 1950 – the day on which the first Constitution (Application to Jammu and Kashmir) Order, 1950 was issued by the then President of India, in consultation with the Government of Jammu and Kashmir, in exercise of the powers conferred by clause (1) of Article 370.

Article 370 envisages a Constitution for the State of Jammu and Kashmir. The Constituent Assembly met on 31st October, 1951. It started its work on November 5, 1951 and the drafting committee on October 10, 1956 presented the draft Constitution which was adopted on 17th November, 1956 and came into force from January 26, 1957.

Before 26th January, 1957, the internal Government of the State was governed by the Jammu and Kashmir Constitution Act, 1939 read with the Constitution (Application to Jammu and Kashmir) Order, 1950.

Constitution of Jammu and Kashmir which was adopted on 17th November, 1956 and came into force on 26th January, 1957. It contains 158 sections and seven schedules.

(Part XXI, Article 370)

COMMENTS

The most controversial have been the "temporary provisions with respect to the State of Jammu and Kashmir" in Article 370. Under this Article, the power of the Parliament to make laws for the State of Jammu and Kashmir shall be limited to matters specified in the Instrument of Accession and may extend to any others only with the concurrence of the State. The Supreme Court laid down: "Article 370 does not bring about any alternation either in the framework or the fundamentals of the Constitution. The only change effected is the designation of the head of the Government and the mode of his appointment."[12]

The following are some of the important features.

1. The State has its own Constitution which came into force on January, 26, 1957. The High Court of Jammu and Kashmir enjoys practically all the powers enjoyed by the other High Courts in India, except that it cannot issue writ for any other purpose.
2. The power of the Parliament to legislate on entries in the Union List with respect to Jammu and Kashmir is restricted only to certain entries. the Parliament cannot legislate on entries 8, 9, 34, 60, 79 and 97. The same is true about entries in the Concurrent List. The Parliament may legislate only on certain entries.
3. A Proclamation of Emergency under Article 352 will have no effect on the State unless it is made with the concurrence of the State Government.
4. Jurisdiction of the Supreme Court extends to the State except for Articles 135 and 139.

5. Directive Principles of State Policy do not operate in the State.

The Supreme Court upheld the authority of the President to issue orders and extend only certain provisions of the Constitution to the State of Jammu and Kashmir.[2]

The main features of the Constitution of Jammu and Kashmir are as follows:

(a) Article 3 read as under:

3. **Relationship of the State with the Union of India:** The State of Jammu and Kashmir is and shall be an integral part of the Union of India.

(b) **Preamble:** WE, THE PEOPLE OF THE STATE OF JAMMU AND KASHMIR, having solemnly resolved, in pursuance of the accession of this State to India which took place on the twenty sixth day of October, 1947, to further define the existing relationship of the State with the Union of India as an integral part thereof, and to secure to ourselves-

JUSTICE, social, economic and political;

LIBERTY of thought, expression, belief, faith and' worship;

EQUALITY of status and of opportunity; and to promote among us all;

FRATERNITY assuring the dignity of the individual and the unity of the Nation;

IN OUR CONSTITUENT ASSEMBLY this seventeenth day of November, 1956, do HEREBY ADOPT, ENACT AND GIVE TO OURSELVES THIS CONSTITUTION.

(c) Part IV

Directive Principles of State Policy

11. Definition: In this Part. unless the context otherwise requires, the State includes the Government and the Legislature of the State and all local or other authorities within the Territory of the State, or under the control of the Government of the State.

12. Application of the principles contained in this Part: The provisions contained in this Part shall not be enforceable by any court, but the principles therein laid down are nevertheless fundamental in the governance of the State and it shall be the duty of the State to apply these principles in making laws.

13. State to establish a socialist order of society for the promotion of welfare of the people: The prime object of the State consistent with the ideals and objectives of the freedom movement envisaged in "New Kashmir" shall be the promotion of the welfare of the mass of the people by establishing and preserving a socialist order of society wherein all exploitation of man has been abolished and wherein justice—social, economic and political—shall inform all the institutions of national life.

14. Economy of the State to be developed in a planned manner: Consistently with the objectives outlined in the foregoing Section, the State shall develop in a planned manner the productive forces of the country with, a view to enriching the material and cultural life of the people and foster and protect:

(a) the public sector where the means of production are owned by the State;

(b) the co-operative sector where the means of production are co-operatively owned by individuals or groups of individuals; and

(c) the private sector where the means of production are owned by an individual or a corporation employing labour; provided that the operation of this sector is not allowed to result in the concentration of wealth or of the means of production to the common detriment.

15. State to ensure speedy improvement in standard of living of rural masses: The State shall endeavour to organise and develop agriculture and animal husbandry by bringing to the aid of the cultivator the benefits of modern and scientific research and techniques so as to ensure a speedy improvement in the standard of living as also the prosperity of the rural masses.

16. Organisation of village Panchayats: The State shall take steps to organise village Panchayats and endow them with such powers and authority as may be necessary to enable them to function as units of self-Government.

17. State to take certain steps for promoting crafts and cottage industries: The State shall in order to rehabilitate, guide and promote the renowned crafts and cottage industries of the State, initiate and execute well considered programmes for refining and modernising techniques and modes of production, including the employment of cheap power so that unnecessary drudgery and toil of the workers are eliminated and the artistic value of the products enhanced while the fullest scope is provided for the encouragement and development of individual talent and initiative.

18. Separation of judiciary from executive: The state shall take steps to separate the judiciary from the executive in the public services and shall seek to secure a judicial system which is humane, cheap, certain, objective and impartial, whereby justice shall be done and shall be seen to be done and shall further strive to ensure efficiency, impartiality and incorruptibility of its various organs of justice, administration and public utility.

19. Right to work and to public assistance in certain cases: The State shall within the limits of its economic capacity and development, make effective provision for securing:

(a) that all permanent residents, men and women equally, have the right to work, that is the right to receive guaranteed work with payment for labour in accordance with its quantity and quality subject to a basic minimum and maximum wage established by law;

(b) that the health and strength of workers, men and women and the tender-age of children are not abused and that permanent residents are not forced by economic necessity to enter avocations unsuited to their sex, age or strength;

(c) that all workers, agricultural, industrial or otherwise, have reasonable, just and humane conditions of work with full enjoyment of leisure and social and cultural opportunities;

(d) that all permanent residents have adequate maintenance in old age as well as in the event of sickness, disablement, unemployment and other cases of undeserved want by providing social insurance, medical aid, hospitals, sanatoria and health resorts at State expense.

20. Rights of free and compulsory education in certain cases: The Statesh hall endeavour:

(a) to secure to every permanent resident the right to free education up to the University standard;

(b) to provide, within a period of ten years from the commencement of this Constitution, compulsory education for all children until they complete the age of fourteen years; and

(c) to ensure to all workers and employees adequate facilities for adult education and part-time technical, professional and vocational courses.

21. Rights of children: The State shall strive to secure:

(a) to all children the right to happy childhood with adequate medical care and attention; and

(b) to all children and youth equal opportunities in education and employment, protection against exploitation and against moral or material abandonment.

22. Right of women: The State shall endeavour to secure to all women:

(a) the right to equal pay for equal work;

(b) the right to maternity benefits as well as adequate medical care in all employments;

(c) the right to reasonable maintenance, extending to cases of married women who have been divorced or abandoned;

(d) the right to full equality in all social, educational, political and legal matters;

(e) special protection against discourtesy, defamation, hooliganism and other forms of misconduct.

23. Protection of educational, material and cultural interests of socially and economically backward sections: The State shall guarantee to the socially and educationally backward sections of the people special care in the promotion of their educational, material and cultural interests and protection against social injustice.

24. Duty of the State to improve public health: The State shall make every effort to safeguard and promote the health of the people by advancing public hygiene and by prevention of disease through sanitation, pest and vermin control, propaganda and other measures, and by ensuring widespread, efficient and free medical services throughout the State and, with particular emphasis, in its remote and backward regions.

25. Duty of the State to foster equality and secularism: The State shall combat ignorance, superstition, fanaticism, communalism, racialism, cultural backwardness and shall seek to foster brotherhood and equality among all communities under the aegis of a Secular State.

(d) At present, the relation between the Union and the State of Jammu and Kashmir are governed by the Constitution (Application to Jammu and Kashmir) Order 1954. The said order has been amended from time to time.

Legislative Relations: The Constitution (Application to Jammu and Kashmir) Order, 1954 extended the jurisdiction of the Union the Parliament from original three subjects of 'Defence, Foreign Affairs and Communications' to almost all subjects on the Union List, subject to some exceptions and modifications

So far as legislative relations are concerned, the State List of the Seventh Schedule of the Constitution does not extend to the State of Jammu and Kashmir. Union list and Concurrent List of the Seventh Schedule of the Constitution apply to the State of Jammu and Kashmir in its modified form. In the Union list following entries do not apply to the State of Jammu and Kashmir, namely:

Union List entries not applicable to the State:

(2A) Deployment of any armed force of the Union or any other fore subject to the control of the Union or any contingent or unit thereof in any State in aid of the civil power; powers, jurisdiction, privileges and liabilities of the members of such forces while on such deployment. This entry was inserted in the Union List by the Constitution (Forty-second Amendment) Act,

(8) Central Bureau of Intelligence and Investigation. This entry 8 of the Union List which deals with the Central bureau of Intelligence and Investigation is not applicable to Jammu and Kashmir.

(9) Preventive detention for reasons connected with defence, foreign affairs, or the security of India; persons subjected to such detention.

(34) Courts of wards for the estates of Rulers of Indian States. Entry 34 is not extended to the State of Jammu and Kashmir.

(79) Extension of the jurisdiction of a High Court to, and exclusion of the jurisdiction of a High Court from, any Union Territory. Entry 79 is also not made applicable to the State of Jammu and Kashmir.

(92B) Taxes on the consignment of goods (whether the consignment is to the person making it or to any other person), where such consignment takes place in the course of inter-state trade or commerce. This entry was inserted in the Union List by the Constitution (Forty-sixth Amendment) Act, 1982, but it is not extended to the State of Jammu and Kashmir.

The present form in which Article 248 is applicable to Jammu and Kashmir is as follows:

the Parliament has exclusive power to make any law with respect to

Prevention of activities involving terrorist acts directed towards overawing the Government as by law established or striking terror in the people or any Section of the people or alienating any Section of the people or adversely affecting the harmony amongst different sections of the people;

(a) Prevention of other activities directed towards disclaiming, questioning or disrupting the sovereignty and territorial integrity of India or bringing about cession of a part of the Territory of India or secession of a part of the Territory of India from the Union or causing insult to the Indian National Flag, the Indian National Anthem and this Constitution; and

(b) Taxes on –

(i) Foreign travel by sea or air;

(ii) Inland air travel;

(iii) Postal Articles, including money orders, phonograms and telegrams.

Explanation: In this Article, 'terrorist act' means any act or thing by using bombs, dynamite or other explosive substances or inflammable substances or firearms or other lethal weapons or poisons or noxious gases or other chemicals or any other substances (whether biological or otherwise) of a hazardous nature.

The Union List has 97 entries and also entry 2A, entry 92A, entry 92B and entry 92C in aggregate 101 entries. Out of these ninety-one entries have been applied to Jammu and Kashmir in full, four entries have been applied in modified form and six entries do not apply to the State at all.

Other modifications: By the Order of 1954, a new proviso was added to Article 3 of the Constitution of India relating to formation of new States and alteration of areas, boundaries or names of existing States. Thus, no action for changing the area, name or boundary of the State of Jammu and Kashmir can be taken without the consent of the Legislature of the State of Jammu and Kashmir.

By the Constitution (Application to Jammu and Kashmir) Order, 1954 a new Article 35A was added, which is applicable to the State of Jammu and Kashmir. Article 35A confers special treatment to the 'permanent residents' of the State of Jammu and Kashmir.

By the Constitution (Application to Jammu and Kashmir) Amendment Order, 1960 (C.O. 60) the right of appeal by special leave under Article 136 of the Constitution of India has been extended to the State of Jammu and Kashmir with effect from 20th January, 1960.

By the Constitution (Application to Jammu and Kashmir) Second Amendment Order, 1958 (C.O. 56) the functions of the Comptroller and Auditor-General of India were extended to the State of Jammu and Kashmir.

REFERENCES

1. Mohd. Maqbool Damroo vs. State of J & K (1972) 1 SCC 536.
2. Sampat Prakash vs. State of J&K, AIR 1970 SC 1118; Puran Lal Lakhanpal vs. President of India, AIR 1961 SC 1519.

□

Chapter 25
SIXTH SCHEDULE

Fifth and Sixth Schedules were existing in the Constitution of India ever since it was adopted on 26 January, 1950. Article 244(1) of the Constitution of India which appears in Part X provides that the administration of the Scheduled Areas and Scheduled Tribes in States (other than Assam, Meghalaya and Tripura) shall be according to the provisions of the Fifth Schedule and Clause (2) states that Sixth Schedule applies to the tribal areas in Assam, Meghalaya, Tripura and Mizoram.

Clause (2) of Article 244 of the Constitution provides that the provisions of the Sixth Schedule shall apply to the administration of the tribal areas in the States of Assam, Meghalaya, Tripura and Mizoram.

Historical Background of Sixth Schedule

The Sixth Schedule to the Constitution provides for special status to certain areas in the states of Assam, Meghalaya, Mizoram and Tripura in the North Eastern Region of the country, in terms of administrative and functional autonomy.

Regulation X of 1822 was the first Regulation enforced by the British for administering the tribal areas of North East India. This regulation laid down a special plan for administration of justice adaptable to peculiar custom and prejudice of the region.

The Government of India Act, 1854 enacted by the British the Parliament to bring certain Territories in India, including Kamrup, Darrang, Nowgong, Sibsagar, Lakhimpur, Garo Hills, Khasi & Jaintia Hills, Naga Hills, Cachar & Goalpara of erstwhile Assam, under the immediate authority and management of the Governor-General-in-Council. In 1874, the Scheduled Districts Act was passed, under which, areas inhabited by such backward tribal people were comprised into Scheduled Districts. Around 1880, a need was felt to render again a separate treatment to certain frontier tracts of Assam, owing to the stage of backwardness prevailing in such tracts or areas. Accordingly the Assam Frontier Tracts Regulation, 1880 was promulgated to give the power to the Chief Commissioner of Assam, to remove any part of that area from the coverage or extent of the laws in force in such tract. It was extended to the frontier tracts including the erstwhile Lushai Hills District of Assam.

The Government of India Act, 1935 created three types of special areas. Under the Act of 1935, these backward areas were classified as excluded areas and partially excluded area. The newly created excluded areas, to the extent of about 18,600 square miles in Assam and 10,000 square miles in the provinces of Madras, Bengal, North-West Frontier, Punjab and Assam, were placed under the personal rule of the Governor's in their discretion. The newly created partially excluded areas were placed under the responsibility of a Minister specifically in charge of such areas while the Governor was assigned with certain special responsibility in the administration of these areas only in certain matters in respect of which he had the power to act in his individual judgement and to overrule the Minister's advice.

While replying to the debate on the discussion on 6th Schedule Dr. B.R. Ambedkar, Chairman of the Drafting Committee of the Constitution stated:

"...The tribal people in areas other than Assam are more or less Hinduised, more or less assimilated with the civilisation and culture of the majority of the people in whose midst they live. With regard to the tribals in Assam that is not the case. Their roots are still in their own civilisation and their own culture.... Their laws of inheritance, their laws of marriage, customs and so on are quite different from that of the Hindus. I think that is the main distinction which influenced us to have a different sort of scheme for Assam from the one we have provided for other

Territories. In other words, the position of the tribals of Assam, whatever may be the reason for it, is somewhat analogous to the position of the Red Indians in the United States, as against the white emigrants there. Now, what did the Untied States do with regard to the Red Indians? So far as I am aware, what they did was to create what are called Reservations of Boundaries within which the Red Indians lived. They are a republic by themselves. No doubt, by the law of the Untied States, they are citizens of the United States. But that is only a nominal allegiance to the Constitution of the United States. Factually they are a separate, independent people. It was felt by the United States that their laws and modes of living, their habits and manners of life were so distinct that it would be dangerous to bring them at one shot, so to say, within the range of the laws made by the white people for white persons and for the purpose of the white civilisation. I agree that we have been creating Regional and District Councils to some extent on the lines which were adopted by the United States for the purpose of the Red Indians."

Development During Post-independence Period

The Constitution of India in its initial years inter alia described in Part A of the First schedule the Territories of Assam. as follows:

"The Territory of the State of Assam shall comprise the Territories which immediately before the commencement of this Constitution were comprised in the Province of Assam, the Khasi States and the Assam Tribal Areas."

After the Constitution (7th Amendment) Act, 1956, the whole of the First Schedule was substituted by another Schedule. The reference to the Territories of Assam was also altered and it now reads:

"The Territories which immediately before the commencement of this Constitution were comprised in the Province of Assam, the Khasi States and the Assam Tribal Areas, but excluding the Territories specified in the Schedule to the Assam (Alteration of Boundaries) Act, 1951."

As per the provisions of the Constitution, the provisions of Sixth Schedule can be amended in three different ways:

(a) by Constitutional amendment by following procedure laid down in Article 368 of the Constitution;

(b) by an ordinary the Parliamentary legislation as provided in paragraph 21 of the Sixth Schedule; and

(c) by notification issued by the Governor under paragraph 1(3) of the Sixth Schedule resulting in amendment to the table appended to paragraph 20 of the said Schedule.

After independence, the Sixth Schedule has been amended on 10 occasions as per the following details of amendments made from time to time:

1. State of Nagaland Act, 1962
2. Assam Reorganisation (Meghalaya) Act, 1969
3. North-Eastern Areas (Reorganisation) Act, 1971
4. Government of Union Territories (Amendment) Act, 1971
5. Repealing and Amending Act, 1974
6. Constitution (49th Amendment) Act, 1984
7. The State of Mizoram Act, 1986
8. Sixth Schedule to the Constitution (Amendment) Act, 1988
9. Sixth Schedule to the Constitution (Amendment) Act, 1995
10. Sixth Schedule to the Constitution (Amendment) Act, 2003

□

Chapter 26

THE CONSTITUTIONAL AMENDMENT ACTS

S. No.	Act	Amendment made
1.	The First Amendment Act, 1951	Articles amended—15, 19, 85, 87, 174, 176, 341, 342, 376.
2.	The Second Amendment Act, 1952	Ratified by States.
3.	The Third Amendment Act, 1954	Articles inserted—31A, 31B Schedule added—Ninth Article amended—81 Scheduled amended-Seventh Schedule-List III, Entry 33.
4.	The Fourth Amendment Act, 1955	Articles amended—31, 31A, 305 Schedule amended—Ninth.
5.	The Fifth Amendment Act, 1955	Article amended—3
6.	The Sixth Amendment Act, 1956	Articles amended—269, 286 Schedules amended— Seventh Schedule List-II, Entry 54; List I, Entry 92A inserted.

7.	The Seventh Amendment Act, 1956	Articles amended—49, 80, 81, 82, 131, 153, 158, 168, 170, 171, 216, 217, 220, 222, 224, 230, 231, 232, 239, 240, 298, 371, Articles inserted—258, 290A, 350A, 350B, 372A, 378A. Schedules amended—First, Second, Fourth, Seventh-List I, Entries 32, 67; List II, Entries 12, 24; List III, Entry 40. Articles omitted—238, 242, 243, 259, 278, 306, 379-391. Schedule omitted—Second, Part-B, consequential amendments in numerous provisions.
8.	The Eighth Amendment Act, 1959	Article 334 amended-20 years substituted for 10 years.
9.	The Ninth Amendment Act, 1960	First Schedule amended—to transfer certain Territories from the States of Assam, Punjab, West Bengal and the Union Territory of Tripura to Pakistan, implementing the Indo-Pakistan agreements of different dates.
10.	The Tenth Amendment Act, 1961	Article 240 and First Schedule amended-to incorporate Dadra and Nagar Haveli as a Union Territory.

11.	The Eleventh Amendment Act, 1961	Articles 66(1) and 71(3) to narrow down grounds for challenging validity of election of President or Vice-President.
12.	The Twelfth Amendment Act, 1962	Article 240 and First Schedule amended—to incorporate Goa, Daman and Diu as a Union Territory.
13.	The Thirteenth Amendment Act, 1962	Article 371 inserted to make special provisions for the administration of the State of Nagaland.
14.	The Fourteenth Amendment Act, 1962	Provided that Pondicherry, Karaikal, Mahe and Yanam, the former French Territories, should be specified in the Constitution as the Union Territory of Pondicherry.
15.	The Fifteenth Amendment Act, 1963	Amends a number of Articles 124, 128, 217, 222, 224, 224A, 226, 297, 311, 316, Entry 78, List I. The more important of these changes are the raising of the age of retirement of a High Court Judge from 60 to 62; the extension of the jurisdiction of a High Court to issue writs under Article 226 to a Government or authority situated outside its territorial jurisdiction where the cause of action arises within such jurisdiction; modifying the procedure imposed by Article 311 upon the pleasure of the President or Governor to dismiss a civil servant.

16.	The Sixteenth Amendment Act, 1963	Amends Article 19 to enable the Parliament to make laws providing restrictions upon the freedom of expression questioning the sovereignty or integrity of the Union of India, with consequential changes in Articles 84, 173, Third Schedule.
17.	The Seventeenth Amendment Act, 1964	Amends Article 31A (definition of 'estate' amended with retrospective effect); Entries 21-64 added to the Ninth Schedule.
18.	The Eighteen Amendment Act, 1966	Adding Explanations to Article 3. Provision was made for the formation of two States, Punjab and Haryana, by reorganizing Punjab on linguistic basis. The explanation added to Article 3, was to clarify that the Parliament has the power to create a new State or Union Territory.
19.	The Nineteenth Amendment Act, 1966	Amending Article 324 to clarify the duties of the Election Commission.
20.	The Twentieth Amendment Act, 1966	Article 233A inserted to validate the appointment of District Judges.
21.	The Twenty-first Amendment Act, 1967	Includes 'Sindhi' in the List of Languages in the Eighth Schedule.

22.	The Twenty-second Amendment Act, 1969	Inserts Articles 244A, 371B and Cl. (1A) in Article 275, to constitute an autonomous State within the State of Assam (Meghalaya) comprising certain areas specified in Part A of the Sixth Schedule.
23.	The Twenty-third Amendment Act, 1970	Amending Articles 330, 332, 333, 334 to extend the period of reservation for Scheduled Castes and Tribes).
24.	The Twenty-fourth Amendment Act, 1970	Inserting Clause (4) in Article 13, amending Article 368 to nullified the effect of Golak Nath case.
25.	The Twenty-fifth Amendment Act, 1971	Clause (2) of Article 31 amended and clause (2A) inserted, Article 31 C inserted. The jurisdiction of the Courts to determine the adequacy of compensation on acquisition of property was taken away. A new clause was added to lay down that no law which declared that it was for giving effect to the principles specified in clauses (b) and (c) of Article 39 would be called in question on the ground that it is inconsistent with the fundamental rights.

26.	The Twenty-sixth Amendment Act, 1971	Omitting Articles 291, 362; inserting Article 363A; amending Article 366 (22). The recognition to the Rulers of Princely States was withdrawn and their privy purses were abolished.
27.	The Twenty-seventh Amendment Act 1971	Amending Articles 239A; inserting Articles 239B; amending Articles 240; inserting Articles 371C. Two new Union Territories viz. Mizoram and Aurnachal Pradesh were formed.
28.	The Twenty-eighth Amendment Act, 1972.	Inserted Articles 312 A; omitting Articles 314. The conditions of service and privileges of former Indian Civil Service officers were abolished.
29.	The Twenty-ninth Amendment Act, 1972	Adding items 65-66 to the Ninth Schedule.
30.	The Thirtyth Amendment Act, 1972	Amending Article 133 (1). Appeals to the Supreme Court were curtailed.
31.	The Thirty-first Amendment Act, 1973.	Amending Articles 81, 330, 332. Elected seats in Lok Sabha increased from 525 to 545.
32.	The Thirty-second Amendment Act, 1973	Amending Articles 371 (1) and inserting Articles 371D-371E amending Entry 63 of List I, Seventh Schedule. The object was to include six provisions in regard to Andhra Pradesh.

33.	The Thirty-third Amendment Act, 1974	Amending Articles 101, 190.
34.	The Thirty-fourth Amendment Act, 1974	Adding items of 67-86 to the Ninth Schedule.
35.	The Thirty-fifth Amendment Act, 1974.	Inserting Article 2A and amending Articles 80-81; adding Tenth Schedule. Sikkim was made an associate State.
36.	The Thirty-sixth Amendment Act, 1975	Omitting Articles 2A, Schedule X; adding item 22 to Schedule I; inserting Article 371 F; adding Entry 22 to Schedule IV. Sikkim was made a fully -fledged State.
37.	The Thirty-seventh Amendment Act, 1975	Amending Articles 239A-240; repealing tenth Schedule. Provision was made for a Legislative Assembly and Council of Ministers for the Union Territory of Arunachal Pradesh.
38.	The Thirty-eighth Amendment Act, 1975	Amending Articles 123, 213, 239B, 352, 356, 359, 360. Declaration of Emergency by the President and promulgation of Ordinances by the President or Governor made issues over which the judiciary would not be able to exercise its power of review.

39.	The Thirty-ninth Amendment Act, 1975	Amending Article 71; inserting Article 329A. Questions regarding elections of President, Vice-President, Prime Minister and Speaker of Lok Sabha taken out of the purview of the judiciary.
40.	The Fortieth Amendment Act, 1976	Substituting Article 297; adding Entries 125 to 188 to Schedule IX. It was provided that all lands, minerals etc. underlying the ocean within the territorial waters or the continental shelf or the exclusive economic zone of India shall vest in the Union. Power to determine the limits of territorial waters, continental shelf, etc. was vested in the Parliament.
41.	The Forty-first Amendment Act, 1976	Amending Article 316, Upper age for members of State Public Service Commission raised from 60 to 62.
42.	The Forty-second Amendment Act, 1976	Amending Preamble Articles 31 C, 39, 55, 74, 77, 81, 82, 83, 100, 102, 105, 118, 145, 166, 170, 172, 189, 191, 194, 208, 217, 225, 227, 228, 311, 312, 330, 352, 353, 356, 357, 358, 359, 366, 368, 371 F, Seventh Schedule; Substituting Articles 103,

		150, 192, 226; inserting Articles 31 D, 32A, 39A, 43A, 48A, 51A, 131A, 139, 144A, 226A, 228A, 257A, 323A, 323B. This amendment was almost a complete revision of the Constitution and many material changes were incorporated. It was enacted during an Emergency. The next Government that came into power in 1977 repealed most of the amendments.
43.	The Forty-third Amendment Act, 1977	Omitting Articles 31D, 32A, 131A, and 144A; amending Article 145.
44.	The Forty-fourth Amendment Act, 1978	Omitting Articles 19 (1) (f), 31, 77 (4), 123 (4), 166 (4), 213 (4), 239 B (4), 257A, 329 A. Inserting Articles 30 (1A), 134 A, 300A, 361A. Amending and substituting, Articles: 19 (1), 22, 31A, 31C, 38, 71, 74, 83, 103, 105, 123, 132-134, 139A, 172, 192, 194, 217, 225, 226, 227, 329, 352, 356, 358, 359, 360, 361, 371F. Cancelling the amendments made by the 42nd Amendment Act to – Articles 100, 102, 105, 118, 191, 194, 208.

		(6 clauses of the Bill were rejected by the Rajya Sabha). The changes made by the 42nd Amendment Act were repealed or altered and the Constitution was brought back in its original form. But the Right to Property was taken away from the Chapter of Fundamental Rights and put as a new Article 300A.
45.	The Forty-fifth Amendment Act, 1980	Extending reservation under Article 334 from 30 to 40 years.
46.	The Forty-sixth Amendment Act, 1982	Amending Articles 269, 286, 366, List I, relating to Sales Tax.
47.	The Forty-seventh Amendment Act, 1984	Adding Entries 189-202, to the Ninth Schedule.
48.	The Forty-eight Amendment Act, 1984	Inserting Proviso to Clause (5) of Article 356 to extend President's Rule in Punjab.
49.	The Forty-ninth Amendment Act, 1984	Amending Article 244, Fifth & Sixth Schedules. Sixth Schedule was made applicable to Tripura.
50.	The Fiftieth Amendment Act, 1984	Substituting Article 33. Its scope was enlarged and many other forces were included in its ambit.
51.	The Fifty-first Amendment Act, 1984	Amending Articles 330, 332.

52.	The Fifty-second Amendment Act, 1985	Amending Articles 101, 102, 190, 191; adding Tenth Schedule (anti-defection). It was declared that a member who defects from his party would become subject to disqualification.
53.	The Fifty-third Amendment Act, 1986	Adding Article 371 G Mizoram was made a State.
54.	The Fifty-fourth Amendment Act, 1986	Amending Articles 125, 221, Second Schedule. Appropriate provisions were made to increase the salary of the judges of the Supreme Court and High Courts.
55.	The Fifty-fifth Amendment Act, 1986	Inserting Article 371-H. State of Arunachal Pradesh was formed.
56.	The Fifty-sixth Amendment Act, 1987	Inserting Article 371-I. The Union Territory of Goa, Daman, and Diu was divided. Goa was made a state and provision for State assemblies were inserted. Daman and Diu to be a Union Territory.
57.	The Fifty-seventh Amendment Act, 1987	Clause (3A) inserted in Article 332, Articles 330 and 332 were amended to make provision for reservation of seats for Scheduled Tribes of Nagaland, Meghalaya, Mizoram and Arunachal Pradesh, in the Lok Sabha and in the legislative assemblies of Nagaland and Meghalaya.

58.	The Constitution (Fifty-eighth Amendment Act, 1987)	Inserting Article 394A. The People had been demanding that the authoritative text of the Constitution should be published in Hindi. This amendment authorised the President to publish the authoritative text of the Constitution in Hindi.
59.	The Fifty-ninth Amendment Act, 1988	Inserting Article 359-A; Amending Article 356. Article 356 was amended to provide that the declaration of Emergency may remain in operation upto 3 years. The amendment made in Article 352 provided that the Emergency with respect to Punjab shall operate only in that State.
60.	The Sixtieth Amendment Act, 1988	Amending Article 276, to increase the limit of profession tax from ₹ 250 to ₹ 2,500.
61.	The Sixty-first Amendment Act, 1989	Amending Article 326, to reduce the voting age from 21 to 18 years.
62.	The Sixty-second Amendment Act, 1989	Amending Article 334, to increase the period of reservation of seats for Scheduled castes and tribes for 10 years i.e. upto the year 2000.A.D.
63.	The Sixty-third Amendment Act, 1989	Amending Article 356 omitting Proviso to Cl. (5) and omitting Article 359 A

64.	The Sixty-fourth Amendment Act, 1990	Amending Article 356. As normalcy could not be restored in Punjab, Emergency was to be continued. For that necessary provision was made in Article 356.
65.	The Sixty-fifth amendment Act, 1990	Amending Article 338 to provide for a National Commission for Scheduled castes and Scheduled Tribes. The Commission has been given wide powers.
66.	The Sixty-sixth Amendment Act, 1990	Inserting Entries 203 to 257 in the Ninth Schedule.
67.	The Sixty-seventh Amendment Act, 1990	Amending Article 356, 3rd Proviso, clause (a), was extending the period to 5 years.
68.	The Sixty-eighth Amendment Act, 1991	Amending Article 356, 3rd Proviso, clause (a), is extending the period to 5 years.
69.	The Sixty-ninth Amendment Act, 1991	Inserting Articles 239AA and 239AB, to provide for a legislative Assembly and Council of Ministers for the Union Territory of Delhi.
70.	The Seventieth Amendment Act, 1992	Amending Articles 54 and 368 to include members of legislative Assemblies of Union Territories of Delhi and Pondicherry in the electoral college.

71.	The Seventy-first Amendment Act, 1992	Inserting entries 7, 9, 11 and reinserting some entries in 8th Sch.
72.	The Seventy-second Amendment Act, 1992	Inserting clause (3B) in Article 332.
73.	The Seventy-third Amendment Act, 1992	Part IX, Re-Panchayats from Articles 243 to 243O, Eleventh Schedule.
74.	The Seventy-fourth Amendment Act, 1992	Re. Nagarpalika (Municipalities) Inserting Part IXA, containing Articles 243 P to 243 ZG; Twelfth Sch.
75.	The Seventy-fifth Amendment Act, 1993	Inserting sub-clause. (h) in Article 323 B (2).
76.	The Seventy-sixth Amendment Act, 1994	Inserting entry 237A, in the 9th Schedule
77.	The Seventy-seventh Amendment Act, 1995	Inserting clause (4A) in Article 16.
78.	The Seventy-eighth Amendment Act, 1995	Further addition of 27 entries to the 9th Schedule to the Constitution.
79.	The Seventy-Ninth Amendment Act, 1999	Substituting "sixty years" for the words "fifty years" in Article 334.
80.	The Eightieth Amendment Act, 1999	Substituting new clauses for Cls. (1) and (2) of Article 269; new Article for Article 270 and omitting Article 272.
81.	The Eighty-first Amendment Act, 2000	Inserting clause (4B) in Article 16.
82.	The Eighty-Second Amendment Act, 2000	Inserting a Proviso to Article 335.

83.	The Eighty-third Amendment Act, 2001	Inserting clause (3A) in Article 243M
84.	The Eighty-fourth Amendment Act, 2001	Substitution of the figure "2026" relating to census in Articles 55, 81, 82, 170, 330 and 332 for the figure "2000"
85.	The Eighty-fifth Amendment Act, 2001	Substitution of certain words in Article 16 (4A) to protect consequential seniority of reserved category retrospectively.
86.	The Eighty-sixth Amendment Act, 2002	Insertion of Article 21A, substitution of Article 45 and insertion of Article 51A (k).
87.	The Eighty-seventh Amendment) Act, 2003	Substitution of the figure "2001" relating to census in Articles 81, 82, 170 and 330 for the figure "1991."
88.	The Eighty-eighth Amendment Act, 2003	Insertion of Article 268A, substitution of the words, figures and letter "Articles 268, 268A and 269" for the words and figures "Articles 268 and 269" in Article 270 and insertion of Entry "92C" in Union List.
89.	The Eighty-ninth Amendment Act, 2003	Amendment of Article 338 and insertion of Article 338A.
90.	The Ninetieth Amendment Act, 2003	Insertion of a proviso to Article 332 (6).
91.	The Ninety-first amendment Act, 2003	Amendment of Articles 75, 164 and Sch. X, insertion of Article 361B.

92.	The Ninety-second amendment Act, 2003	Addition of "Bodo" "Dogri", "Maithilli" and "Santhali" languages in schedule VIII.
93.	The Ninety-third amendment Act, 2005	Insertion of clause (5) in Article 15.
94.	The Ninety-fourth Amendment Act, 2006	Amendment of Article 164.
95.	The Ninety-fifth Amendment Act, 2009	Amendment of Article 334.
96.	The Ninety-Sixth Amendment Act, 2011	Amendment of Eight Schedules.
97.	The Ninety-seventh Amendment Act, 2011	Amendment of Article 19 insertion of Article 43B, insertion of Part IXB consisting of Articles 243ZH to 243ZT regarding Co-operative Societies.
98.	The Ninety-eighth Amendment Act, 2012	Insertion of New Article 371
99.	The Ninety-ninth Amendment Act, 2014	Insertion of Articles 124A, 124B, 124C Amendments of Articles 124, 127, 128, 217, 222, 224, 224A, 231
100.	The Hundredth Amendment Act, 2015	Amendment to Schedule 1 with regard to States of Assam, West Bengal, Meghalaya and Tripura.

BIBLIOGRAPHY

1. Agrawal, P.K.: Land Reforms in India, Constitutional and Legal Approach, M.D. Publications Pvt. Ltd., New Delhi, Year 1993, Total pages 272.
2. Basu, Durga Das: Introduction to the Constitution of India, Lexis Nexis, Gurgaon, India, Year 2015, Total pages 554.
3. Bakshi, P.M.: The Constitution of India, Universal Law Publishing Co., Delhi-110033, Year 2014, Total pages 484.
4. Black's Law Dictionary.
5. Constituent Assembly of India,Debates, Volume X. 12th October, 1949.
6. Kashyap, Subhash C.: Our Constitution, An Introduction to India's Constitution and Constitutional Law, National Book Trust, New Delhi.
7. Kumar, Virendra, 2007. "Basic Structure of the Indian Constitution: Doctrine of Constitutionally Controlled Governance." Journal of the Indian Law Institute, 49:3, pp. 365-98.
8. Lahoti, R.C. 2004. Preamble: The Spirit and Backbone of the Constitution of India, Eastern Book Company, Lucknow.
9. Law Commission of India: Report titled 'Proposal for Reconsideration of Judges cases I, II and III' – S.P. Gupta vs. UOI reported in AIR 1982 SC 149, Supreme Court Advocates-on-Record Association vs. UOI reported in 1993 (4) SCC 441 and Special Reference 1 of 1998 reported in 1998(7) SCC 739' dated 21st November, 2008.
10. Order XLVII, Rule 1(1) of the Code of Civil Procedure, 1908.
11. Pandey, Dr. J.N.: Constitutional Law of India, Central Law Agency, Moti Lal Nehru Road, Allahabad-2, Year 2015, Total pages 867.

12. Part VIII Order XL of the Supreme Court Rules, 1966.
13. 'Sahil', Anil Kumar: Bharat Ka Savindhan (in Hindi), Prabhat Paperbacks, New Delhi-2, Year 2016, Total pages 323.
14. Shukla, V.N.: Constitution of India, Eastern Book Company, Lucknow-1, Year 2013, Total pages 1236.
15. The Constitution (Ninety-Ninth Amendment) Act, 2014.
16. The National Judicial Appointment Commission Act, 2014.
17. The Provisional Collection of Tax Act, 1931. Finance Bill Sub-Committee (the FBSC) constituted in 2003 by the Select Committee of the Economic Affairs (House of Lords).
18. Tope, T.K.: Constitutional Law of India, Eastern Book Company, Lalbagh, Lucknow-226001, Year 2010, Total pages.

□

INDEX

D

E

F

G

N

O

P

S

T

U

V

W

Y

Z

□□□